THE
FORGOTTEN MAN
AND
OTHER ESSAYS

BY
WILLIAM GRAHAM SUMNER

EDITED BY
ALBERT GALLOWAY KELLER

NEW HAVEN
YALE UNIVERSITY PRESS
LONDON: HUMPHREY MILFORD
OXFORD UNIVERSITY PRESS
MDCCCCXVIII

PREFACE

WITH the present collection the publication of
Sumner's Essays comes to an end. The original
project of publishers and editor contemplated but a single
volume — "War and Other Essays" — and they accordingly equipped that volume with a bibliography which
was as complete as they then could make it. But when,
later on, other materials came to be known about, and
especially after the discovery of a number of unpublished manuscripts, the encouraging reception accorded to
the first venture led us to publish a second, and then a
third collection: "Earth Hunger and Other Essays" and
"The Challenge of Facts and Other Essays." It was
during the preparation of the latter of these, now some
five years ago, that the late Professor Callender deplored to
the editor the omission of certain of Sumner's essays in
political economy — in particular those dealing with free
trade and sound money. And the reviewers of preceding
collections had reminded us, rightly enough, that there
should be a fuller bibliography and also an index covering
all the essays.

In this last volume we have striven to meet these several
suggestions and criticisms. And it is now the purpose of
the publishers to form of these singly issued volumes a set
of four, numbered in the order of their issue. Since the
series could not have been planned as such at the outset,
this purpose is in the nature of an after-thought; and there
is therefore no general organization or systematic classi-

3

fication by volumes. In so far as classification is possible, under the circumstances, it is made by way of the index. This and the bibliography are the work of Dr. M. R. Davie; and are but a part of the service he has performed in the interest of an intellectual master whom he could know only through the printed word and the medium of another man.

Sumner's dominant interest in political economy, as revealed in his teaching and writing, issued in a doughty advocacy of "free trade and hard money," and involved the relentless exposure of protectionism and of schemes of currency-debasement. As conveying his estimate of protectionism, it is only fitting that his little book on "The -Ism which teaches that Waste makes Wealth" should be recalled from an obscurity that it does not deserve; it is typical of the author's most vigorous period and witnesses to the acerbity of a former issue that may recur. In default of a single, comprehensive companion-piece in the field of finance, and one making as interesting reading, it has been necessary to confine selection to several rather brief articles, most of them dating from the campaign of 1896. In the choice of all economic essays I have been guided by the advice of my colleague, Professor F. R. Fairchild, a fellow-student under Sumner and a fellow-admirer of his character and career. Professor S. L. Mims also has been generous in his aid. I do not need to thank either of these men, for what they did was a labor of gratitude and love.

The title essay will be found at the end of the volume. It is the once-famous lecture on "The Forgotten Man," and is here printed for the first time. When "War and Other Essays" was being prepared, we had no knowledge of the existence of this manuscript lecture; and, in order to bring into what we supposed was to be a one-volume collection this character-creation of Sumner's, one often alluded to in modern writings, we reprinted two

chapters from "What Social Classes Owe to Each Other."
It has been found impracticable in later reprintings of
Vol. I to replace those chapters with the more complete
essay; and we have therefore decided to reproduce the
latter, despite the certain degree of repetition involved,
rather than leave it out of the series. In view of the fact
that Sumner has been more widely known, perhaps, as
the creator and advocate of the "Forgotten Man," than
as the author of any other of his works, we entitle this
volume "The Forgotten Man and Other Essays."

Several essays not of an economic order have been included because they have come to my knowledge within
the last few years and have seemed to me to call for preservation. It is almost impossible to fix the dates of such
manuscript essays, for I have not been able in all cases to
secure information from persons who might be able to
identify times and occasions. And there remain a good
number of articles and manuscripts, published or unpublished, which can receive no more than mention, with a
word of characterization, in the bibliography.

Some mention ought to be made here of a large body of
hand-written manuscript left by Sumner and representing
the work of several years — 1899 to 1905 or thereabouts —
upon a systematic treatise on "The Science of Society."
Printed as it was left, partially and unevenly completed
and with many small and some wide hiatuses, this manuscript would make several substantial volumes. It is a
monument of industry, involving, as it did, the collection
over many years of thousands of notes and memoranda,
and the extraction from the same, by a sort of *tour de force*,
of generalizations intended to be set forth, with the support of copious evidence, in the form of a survey of the
evolution and life of human society. These manuscripts,
as left, represent no more than a preliminary survey of a
wide field, together with more elaborately worked out

chartings of sections of that field. The author planned to re-write the whole in the light of "Folkways." The continuation, modification, and completion of this enterprise, in something approaching the form contemplated by its author, must needs be, if at all possible, a long task.

As one surveys, through these volumes of essays, the various phases of scholarly and literary activity of their author, and then recalls the teaching, both extensive and intensive, done by him with such unremitting devotion to what he regarded as his first duty — and when one thinks, yet again, of his labors in connection with college and university administration, with the Connecticut State Board of Education, and in other lines — it is hard to understand where one man got the time, with all his ability and energy, to accomplish all this. In the presence of evidence of such incessant and unswerving industry, scarcely interrupted by the ill-health that overtook Sumner at about the age of fifty, an ordinary person feels a sense of oppression and of bewilderment, and is almost willing to subscribe to the old, hopeless tradition that "there were giants in those days."

In the preparation of this set of books the editor has been constantly sustained and encouraged by the interest and sympathy of the woman who stood by the author's side through life, and to whom anything that had to do with the preservation of his memory was thereby just, perfect, and altogether praiseworthy. The completion of this editorial task would be the more satisfying if she were still among us to receive the final offering.

A. G. KELLER.

WEST BOOTHBAY HARBOR, ME.,
September 1, 1918.

CONTENTS

PROTECTIONISM

THE –ISM WHICH TEACHES THAT WASTE MAKES WEALTH

[1885]

PREFACE

DURING the last fifteen years we have had two great
questions to discuss: the restoration of the currency
and civil-service reform. Neither of these questions has yet
reached a satisfactory solution, but both are on the way
toward such a result. The next great effort to strip off the
evils entailed on us by the Civil War will consist in the repeal of those taxes which one man was enabled to levy on
another, under cover of the taxes which the government
had to lay to carry on the war. I have taken my share in
the discussion of the first two questions, and I expect to
take my share in the discussion of the third.

I have written this book as a contribution to a popular
agitation. I have not troubled myself to keep or to throw
off scientific or professional dignity. I have tried to make
my point as directly and effectively as I could for the
readers whom I address, *viz.*, the intelligent voters of all
degrees of general culture, who need to have it explained
to them what protectionism is and how it works. I have
therefore pushed the controversy just as hard as I could,
and have used plain language, just as I have always done
before in what I have written on this subject. I must therefore forego the hope that I have given any more pleasure
now than formerly to the advocates of protectionism.

9

Protectionism seems to me to deserve only contempt and
scorn, satire and ridicule. It is such an arrant piece of
economic quackery, and it masquerades under such an affectation of learning and philosophy, that it ought to be
treated as other quackeries are treated. Still, out of deference to its strength in the traditions and lack of information of many people, I have here undertaken a patient and
serious exposition of it. Satire and derision remain reserved for the dogmatic protectionists and the sentimental
protectionists; the Philistine protectionists and those who
hold the key of all knowledge; the protectionists of stupid
good faith and those who know their dogma is a humbug
and are therefore irritated at the exposure of it; the protectionists by birth and those by adoption; the protectionists for hire and those by election; the protectionists
by party platform and those by pet newspaper; the protectionists by "invincible ignorance" and those by vows
and ordination; the protectionists who run colleges and
those who want to burn colleges down; the protectionists
by investment and those who sin against light; the hopeless ones who really believe in British gold and dread the
Cobden Club, and the dishonest ones who storm about
those things without believing in them; those who may not
be answered when they come into debate, because they are
"great" men, or because they are "old" men, or because
they have stock in certain newspapers, or are trustees of
certain colleges. All these have honored me personally, in
this controversy, with more or less of their particular attention. I confess that it has cost me something to leave
their cases out of account, but to deal with them would
have been a work of entertainment, not of utility.

Protectionism arouses my moral indignation. It is a
subtle, cruel, and unjust invasion of one man's rights by
another. It is done by force of law. It is at the same
time a social abuse, an economic blunder, and a political

evil. The moral indignation which it causes is the motive which draws me away from the scientific pursuits which form my real occupation, and forces me to take part in a popular agitation. The doctrine of a "call" applies in such a case, and every man is bound to take just so great a share as falls in his way. That is why I have given more time than I could afford to popular lectures on this subject, and it is why I have now put the substance of those lectures into this book.

W. G. S.

Chapter I

DEFINITIONS: STATEMENT OF THE QUESTION TO BE INVESTIGATED

(*A*) The System of which Protection is a Survival.

1. The statesmen of the eighteenth century supposed that their business was the art of national prosperity. Their procedure was to form ideals of political greatness and civil prosperity on the one hand, and to evolve out of their own consciousness grand dogmas of human happiness and social welfare on the other hand. Then they tried to devise specific means for connecting these two notions with each other. Their ideals of political greatness contained, as predominant elements, a brilliant court, a refined and elegant aristocracy, well-developed fine arts and *belles lettres*, a powerful army and navy, and a peaceful, obedient, and hard-working peasantry and artisan class to pay the taxes and support the other part of the political structure. In this ideal the lower ranks paid upward, and the upper ranks blessed downward, and all were happy together. The great political and social dogmas of the period were exotic and incongruous. They were borrowed or accepted from the classical authorities. Of course the dogmas were

chiefly held and taught by the philosophers, but, as the century ran its course, they penetrated the statesman class. The statesman who had had no purpose save to serve the "grandeur" of the king, or to perpetuate a dynasty, gave way to statesmen who had strong national feeling and national ideals, and who eagerly sought means to realize their ideals. Having as yet no definite notion, based on facts of observation and experience, of what a human society or a nation is, and no adequate knowledge of the nature and operation of social forces, they were driven to empirical processes which they could not test, or measure, or verify. They piled device upon device and failure upon failure. When one device failed of its intended purpose and produced an unforeseen evil, they invented a new device to prevent the new evil. The new device again failed to prevent, and became a cause of a new harm, and so on indefinitely.

2. Among their devices for industrial prosperity were (1) export taxes on raw materials, to make raw materials abundant and cheap at home; (2) bounties on the export of finished products, to make the exports large; (3) taxes on imported commodities to make the imports small, and thus, with No. 2, to make the "balance of trade" favorable, and to secure an importation of specie; (4) taxes or prohibition on the export of machinery, so as not to let foreigners have the advantage of domestic inventions; (5) prohibition on the emigration of skilled laborers, lest they should carry to foreign rivals knowledge of domestic arts; (6) monopolies to encourage enterprise; (7) navigation laws to foster ship-building or the carrying trade, and to provide sailors for the navy; (8) a colonial system to bring about by political force the very trade which the other devices had destroyed by economic interference; (9) laws for fixing wages and prices to repress the struggle of the non-capitalist class to save themselves in the social press; (10) poor-laws

to lessen the struggle by another outlet; (11) extravagant criminal laws to try to suppress another development of this struggle by terror; and so on, and so on.

(B) OLD AND NEW CONCEPTIONS OF THE STATE.

3. Here we have a complete illustration of one mode of looking at human society, or at a state. Such society is, on this view, an artificial or mechanical product. It is an object to be molded, made, produced by contrivance. Like every product which is brought out by working up to an ideal instead of working out from antecedent truth and fact, the product here is haphazard, grotesque, false. Like every other product which is brought out by working on lines fixed by *a priori* assumptions, it is a satire on human foresight and on what we call common sense. Such a state is like a house of cards, built up anxiously one upon another, ready to fall at a breath, to be credited at most with naïve hope and silly confidence; or, it is like the long and tedious contrivance of a mischievous schoolboy, for an end which has been entirely misappreciated and was thought desirable when it should have been thought a folly; or, it is like the museum of an alchemist, filled with specimens of his failures, monuments of mistaken industry and testimony of an erroneous method; or, it is like the clumsy product of an untrained inventor, who, instead of asking: "what means have I, and to what will they serve?" asks: "what do I wish that I could accomplish?" and seeks to win steps by putting in more levers and cogs, increasing friction and putting the solution ever farther off.

4. Of course such a notion of a state is at war with the conception of a state as a seat of original forces which must be reckoned with all the time; as an organism whose life will go on anyhow, perverted, distorted, diseased, vitiated as it may be by obstructions or coercions; as a

seat of life in which nothing is ever lost, but every antecedent combines with every other and has its share in the
immediate resultant, and again in the next resultant, and
so on indefinitely; as the domain of activities so great that
they should appall any one who dares to interfere with
them; of instincts so delicate and self-preservative that it
should be only infinite delight to the wisest man to see
them come into play, and his sufficient glory to give them
a little intelligent assistance. If a state well performed its
functions of providing peace, order, and security, as *conditions* under which the people could live and work, it
would be the proudest proof of its triumphant success that
it had nothing to do — that all went so smoothly that it
had only to look on and was never called to interfere; just
as it is the test of a good business man that his business
runs on smoothly and prosperously while he is not harassed
or hurried. The people who think that it is proof of enterprise to meddle and "fuss" may believe that a good
state will constantly interfere and regulate, and they may
regard the other type of state as "non-government." The
state can do a great deal more than to discharge police
functions. If it will *follow* custom, and the growth of social
structure to provide for new social needs, it can powerfully
aid the production of structure by laying down lines of
common action, where nothing is needed but *some* common
action on conventional lines; or, it can systematize a number of arrangements which are not at their maximum utility
for want of concord; or, it can give sanction to new rights
which are constantly created by new relations under new
social organizations, and so on.

5. The latter idea of the state has only begun to win
way. All history and sociology bear witness to its comparative truth, at least when compared with the former.
Under the new conception of the state, of course liberty
means breaking off the fetters and trammels which the

"wisdom" of the past has forged, and *laissez-faire,* or "let alone," becomes a cardinal maxim of statesmanship, because it means: "Cease the empirical process. Institute the scientific process. Let the state come back to normal health and activity, so that you can study it, learn something about it from an observation of its phenomena, and then regulate your action in regard to it by intelligent knowledge." Statesmen suited to this latter type of state have not yet come forward in any great number. The new radical statesmen show no disposition to let their neighbors alone. They think that they have come into power just because they know what their neighbors need to have done to them. Statesmen of the old type, who told people that they knew how to make everybody happy, and that they were going to do it, were always far better paid than any of the new type ever will be, and their failures never cost them public confidence either. We have got tired of kings, priests, nobles and soldiers, not because they failed to make us all happy, but because our *a priori* dogmas have changed fashion. We have put the administration of the state in the hands of lawyers, editors, *littérateurs,* and professional politicians, and they are by no means disposed to abdicate the functions of their predecessors, or to abandon the practice of the art of national prosperity. The chief difference is that, whereas the old statesmen used to temper the practice of their art with care for the interests of the kings and aristocracies which put them in power, the new statesmen feel bound to serve those sections of the population which have put them where they are.

6. Some of the old devices above enumerated (§ 2) are, however, out of date, or are becoming obsolete.[1] Number

[1] February 4, 1884, Mr. Robinson of New York proposed, in the House of Representatives, an amendment to the Constitution, so as to allow Congress to lay an export duty on cotton for the encouragement of home manufactures. (Record, 862.)

3, taxes on imports for other than fiscal purposes, is not among this number. Just now such taxes seem to be coming back into fashion, or to be enjoying a certain revival. It is a sign of the deficiency of our sociology as compared with our other sciences that such a phenomenon could be presented in the last quarter of the nineteenth century, as a certain revival of faith in the efficiency of taxes on imports as a device for producing national prosperity. There is not a single one of the eleven devices mentioned above, including taxes on the exportation of machinery and prohibitions on emigration, which is not quite as rational and sound as taxes on imports.

I now propose to analyze and criticize protectionism.

(C) Definition of Protectionism — Definition of "Theory."

7. By protection*ism* I mean the doctrine of protective taxes as a device to be employed in the art of national prosperity. The protectionists are fond of representing themselves as "practical" and the free traders as "theorists." "Theory" is indeed one of the most abused words in the language, and the scientists are partly to blame for it. They have allowed the word to come into use, even among themselves, for *a conjectural explanation*, or *a speculative conjecture*, or *a working hypothesis*, or *a project which has not yet been tested by experiment*, or *a plausible and harmless theorem about transcendental relations*, or *about the way in which men will act under certain motives*. The newspapers seem often to use the word "theoretical" as if they meant by it imaginary or fictitious. I use the word "theory," however, not in distinction from fact, but, in what I understand to be the correct scientific use of the word, to denote *a rational description of a group of coördinated facts in their sequence and relations*. A theory may, for a special purpose, describe only certain features of facts and disre-

gard others. Hence "in practice," where facts present themselves in all their complexity, he who has carelessly neglected the limits of his theory may be astonished at phenomena which present themselves; but his astonishment will be due to a blunder on his part, and will not be an imputation on the theory.

8. Now free trade is not a theory in any sense of the word. *It is only a mode of liberty;* one form of the assault (and therefore negative) which the expanding intelligence of the present is making on the trammels which it has inherited from the past. Inside the United States, absolute free trade exists over a continent. No one thinks of it or realizes it. No one "feels" it. We feel only constraint and oppression. If we get liberty we reflect on it only so long as the memory of constraint endures. I have again and again seen the astonishment with which people realized the fact when presented to them that they have been living under free trade all their lives and never thought of it. When the whole world shall obtain and enjoy free trade there will be nothing more to be said about it; it will disappear from discussion and reflection; it will disappear from the text-books on political economy as the chapters on slavery are disappearing; it will be as strange for men to think that they might *not* have free trade as it would be now for an American to think that he might not travel in this country without a passport, or that there ever was a chance that the soil of our western states might be slave soil and not free soil. It would be as reasonable to apply the word "theory" to the protestant reformation, or to law reform, or to anti-slavery, or to the separation of church and state, or to popular rights, or to any other campaign in the great struggle which we call liberty and progress, as to apply it to free trade. The pro-slavery men formerly did apply it to abolition, and with excellent reason, if the use of it which I have criticized ever was correct; for it re-

quired great power of realizing in imagination the results
of social change, and great power to follow and trust abstract reasoning, for any man bred under slavery to realize,
in advance of experiment, the social and economic gain to
be won — *most of all for the whites* — by emancipation.
It now requires great power of "theoretical conception"
for people who have no experience of the separation of
church and state to realize its benefits and justice. Similar observations would hold true of all similar reforms.
Free trade is a revolt, a conflict, a reform, a reaction and
recuperation of the body politic, just as free conscience,
free worship, free speech, free press, and free soil have been.
It is in no sense a theory.

9. Protectionism is not a theory in the correct sense of
the term, but it comes under some of the popular and incorrect uses of the word. It is purely dogmatic and *a
priori*. It is desired to attain a certain object — wealth
and national prosperity. Protective taxes are proposed as
a means. It must be assumed that there is some connection between protective taxes and national prosperity,
some relation of cause and effect, some sequence of expended energy and realized product, between protective
taxes and national wealth. If then by theory we mean a
speculative conjecture as to occult relations which have
not been and cannot be traced in experience, protection
would be a capital example. Another and parallel example was furnished by astrology, which assumed a causal
relation between the movements of the planets and the
fate of men, and built up quite an art of soothsaying on
this assumption. Another example, paralleling protectionism in another feature, was alchemy, which, accepting as
unquestionable the notion that we want to transmute lead
into gold if we can, assumed that there was a philosopher's
stone, and set to work to find it through centuries of repetition of the method of "trial and failure."

10. *Protectionism, then, is an* ism; that is, it is a doctrine or system of doctrine which offers no demonstration, and rests upon no facts, but appeals to faith on grounds of its *a priori* reasonableness, or the plausibility with which it can be set forth. Of course, if a man should say: "I am in favor of protective taxes because they bring gain to me. That is all I care to know about them, and I shall get them retained as long as I can" — there is no trouble in understanding him, and there is no use in arguing with him. So far as he is concerned, the only thing to do is to find his victims and explain the matter to them. The only thing which can be discussed is the doctrine of national wealth by protective taxes. This doctrine has the forms of an economic theory. It vies with the doctrine of labor and capital as a part of the science of production. Its avowed purpose is impersonal and disinterested — the same, in fact, as that of political economy. It is not, like free trade, a mere negative position against an inherited system, to which one is led by a study of political economy. It is a species of political economy, and aims at the throne of the science itself. If it is true, it is not a corollary, but a postulate, on which, and by which, all political economy must be constructed.

11. But then, lo! if the dogma which constitutes protectionism — *national wealth can be produced by protective taxes and cannot be produced without them* — is enunciated, instead of going on to a science of political economy based upon it, the science falls dead on the spot. What can be said about production, population, land, money, exchange, labor and all the rest? What can the economist learn or do? What function is there for the university or school? There is nothing to do but to go over to the art of legislation, and get the legislator to put on the taxes. The only questions which can arise are as to the number, variety, size, and proportion of the taxes. As to these questions the economist can offer no light. He has no method of investigating them. He can deduce no principles, lay down no laws in regard to them. The legislator must go on in the dark and experiment. If his taxes do not produce the required result, if there turn out to be "snakes" in the tariff which he has adopted, he has to change it. If the result still fails, change it again. Protectionism bars the science of political economy with a dogma, and the only process of the art of statesmanship to which it leads is eternal trial and failure — the process of the alchemist and of the inventor of perpetual motion.

(D) DEFINITION OF FREE TRADE AND OF A PROTECTIVE DUTY.

12. What then is a protective tax? In order to join issue as directly as possible, I will quote the definitions given by a leading protectionist journal,[1] of both free trade and protection. "The term 'free trade,' although much discussed, is seldom rightly defined. It does not mean the abolition of custom houses. Nor does it mean the substitution of direct for indirect taxation, as a few American disciples of the school have supposed. It means such an adjustment of taxes on imports as will cause no diversion of capital, from any channel into which it would otherwise flow, into any channel opened or favored by the legislation which enacts the customs. A country may collect its entire revenue by duties on imports, and yet be an entirely free trade country, so long as it does not lay those duties in such a way as to lead any one to undertake any employment, or make any investment he would avoid in the absence of such duties: thus, the customs duties levied by England — with a very few exceptions — are not inconsistent with her profession of being a country which be-

[1] Philadelphia *American*, August 7, 1884.

lieves in free trade. They either are duties on articles not produced in England, or they are exactly equivalent to the excise duties levied on the same articles if made at home. They do not lead any one to put his money into the home production of an article, because they do not discriminate in favor of the home producer."

13. "A protective duty, on the other hand, has for its object to effect the diversion of a part of the capital and labor of the people out of the channels in which it would run otherwise, into channels favored or created by law."

I know of no definitions of these two things which have ever been made by anybody which are more correct than these. I accept them and join issue on them.

(E) Protectionism Raises a Purely Domestic Controversy.

14. It will be noticed that this definition of a protective duty says nothing about foreigners or about imports. According to this definition, a protective duty is a device for effecting a transformation in our own industry. If a tax is levied at the port of entry on a foreign commodity which is actually imported, the tax is paid to the treasury and produces revenue. A protective tax is one which is laid to act as a bar to importation, in order to keep a foreign commodity out. It does not act protectively unless it does act as a bar, and is not a tax on imports but an obstruction to imports. Hence a protective duty is a wall to inclose the domestic producer and consumer, and to prevent the latter from having access to any other source of supply for his needs, in exchange for his products, than that one which the domestic producer controls. The purpose and plan of the device is to enable the domestic producer to levy on the domestic consumer the taxes which the government has set up as a barrier, but has not col-

lected at the port of entry. Under this device the government says: "I do not want the revenue, but I will lay the tax so that you, the selected and favored producer, may collect it." "I do not need to tax the consumer for myself, but I will hold him for you while you tax him."

(F) "A Protective Duty is not a Tax."

15. There are some who say that "a tariff is not a tax," or as one of them said before a Congressional Committee: "We do not like to call it so!" That certainly is the most humorous of all the funny things in the tariff controversy. If a tariff is not a tax, what is it? In what category does it belong? No protectionist has ever yet told. They seem to think of it as a thing by itself, a Power, a Force, a sort of Mumbo Jumbo whose special function it is to produce national prosperity. They do not appear to have analyzed it, or given themselves an account of it, sufficiently to know what kind of a thing it is or how it acts. Any one who says that it is not a tax must suppose that it costs nothing, that it produces an effect without an expenditure of energy. They do seem to think that if Congress will say: "Let a tax of —— per cent be laid on article A," and if none is imported, and therefore no tax is paid at the custom house, national industry will be benefited and wealth secured, and that there will be no cost or outgo. If that is so, then the tariff is magic. We have found the philosopher's stone. Our congressmen wave a magic wand over the country and say: "Not otherwise provided for, one hundred and fifty per cent," and, presto! there we have wealth. Again they say: "Fifty cents a yard and fifty per cent *ad valorem*"; and there we have prosperity! If we should build a wall along the coast to keep foreigners and their goods out, it would cost something. If we maintained a navy to blockade our own coast for the same

purpose, it would cost something. Yet it is imagined that if we do the same by a tax it costs nothing.

16. This is the fundamental fallacy of protection to which the analysis will bring us back again and again. Scientifically stated, it is that *protectionism sins against the conservation of energy.* More simply stated, it is that *the protectionist either never sees or does not tell the other side of the account, the cost, the outlay for the gains which he alleges from protection, and that when these are examined and weighed they are sure vastly to exceed the gains, if the gains were real,* even taking no account of the harm to national growth which is done by restriction and interference.

17. There are only three ways in which a man can part with his product, and different kinds of taxes fall under different modes of alienating one's goods. First, he may exchange his product for the product of others. Then he parts with his property voluntarily, and for an equivalent. Taxes which are paid for peace, order, and security, fall under this head. Secondly, he may give his product away. Then he parts with it voluntarily without an equivalent. Taxes which are voluntarily paid for schools, libraries, parks, etc., fall under this head. Thirdly, he may be robbed of it. Then he parts with it involuntarily and without an equivalent. Taxes which are protective fall under this head. The analysis is exhaustive, and there is no other place for them. Protective taxes are those which a man pays to his neighbor to hire him (the neighbor) to carry on his own business. The first man gets no equivalent (§ 108). Hence any one who says that a tariff is not a tax would have to put it in some such category as tribute, plunder, or robbery. In order, then, that we may not give any occasion for even an unjust charge of using hard words, let us go back and call it a tax.

18. In any case it is plain that *we have before us the case of two Americans.* The protectionists who try to discuss

the subject always go off to talk English politics and history, or Ireland, or India, or Turkey. I shall not follow them. I shall discuss the case between two Americans, which is the only case there is. Whether Englishmen like our tariff or not is of no consequence. As a matter of fact, Englishmen seem to have come to the opinion that if Americans will take their own home market as their share, and will keep out of the world's market, they (the Englishmen) will agree to the arrangement; but it is immaterial whether they agree, or are angry. The only question for us is: What kind of an arrangement is it for one American to tax another American? How does it work? Who gains by it? How does it affect our national prosperity? These and these only are the questions which I intend to discuss.

19. I shall adopt *two different lines of investigation.* First, I shall examine protectionism on its own claims and pretensions, taking its doctrines and claims for true, and following them out to see whether they will produce the promised results; and secondly, I shall attack protectionism adversely, and controversially. If any one proposes a device for the public good, he is entitled to candid and patient attention, but he is also under obligation to show how he expects his scheme to work, what forces it will bring into play, how it will use them, etc. The joint stock principle, credit institutions, coöperation, and all similar devices must be analyzed and the explanation of their advantage, if they offer any, must be sought in the principles which they embody, the forces they employ, the suitableness of their apparatus. We ought not to put faith in any device (*e.g.*, bi-metalism, socialism) unless the proposers offer an explanation of it which will bear rigid and pitiless examination; for, if it is a sound device, such examination will only produce more and more thorough conviction of its merits. I shall therefore first take up protectionism

just as it is offered, and test it, as any candid inquirer might do, to see whether, as it is presented by its advocates, it has any claims to confidence.

CHAPTER II

PROTECTIONISM EXAMINED ON ITS OWN GROUNDS

20. It is the peculiar irony in all empirical devices in social science that they not only fail of the effect expected of them, but that they produce the exact opposite. Paper money is expected to help the non-capitalist and the debtor and to make business brisk. It ruins the non-capitalists and the debtors, and reduces industry and commerce to a standstill. Socialistic devices are expected to bring about equality and universal happiness. They produce despotism, favoritism, inequality, and universal misery. The devices are, in their operation, true to themselves. They act just as an unprejudiced examination of them should have led any one to expect that they would act, or just as a limited experience has shown that they must act. If protectionism is only another case of the same kind, an examination of it on its own grounds must bring out the fact that it will issue in crippling industry, diminishing capital, and lowering the average of comfort. Let us see.

(A) ASSUMPTIONS IN PROTECTIONISM.

21. Obviously the doctrine includes two assumptions. The first is, that if we are left to ourselves, each to choose, under liberty, his line of industrial effort, and to use his labor and capital, under the circumstances of the country, as best he can, we shall fail of our highest prosperity. Secondly, that, if Congress will only tax us (properly) we can be led up to higher prosperity. Hence it is at once

evident that free trade and protection here are not on a level. No free trader will affirm that he has a device for making the country rich, or saving it from hard times, any more than a respectable physician will tell us that he can give us specifics and preventives to keep us well. On the contrary, so long as men live they will do foolish things, and they will have to bear the penalty; but if they are free, they will commit only the follies which are their own, and they will bear the penalties only of those. The protectionist begins with the premise that we shall make mistakes, and that is why he, who knows how to make us go right, proposes to take us in hand. He is like the doctor who can give us just the pill we need to "cleanse our blood" and "ward off chills." *Hence either prosperity in a free-trade country, or distress in a protectionist country, is fatal to protectionism,* while distress in a free-trade country, or prosperity in a protectionist country proves nothing against free trade. Hence the fallacy of all Mr. R. P. Porter's letters is obvious. (§§ 52, 92, 102, 154.)

22. The device by which we are to be made better than ourselves is to select some of ourselves, who certainly are not the best business men among ourselves, to go to Washington, and there turn around and tax ourselves blindly, or, if not blindly, craftily and selfishly. Surely this would be the triumph of stupidity and ignorance over intelligent knowledge, enterprise and energy. The motive which would control each of us, if we were free, would be the hope of the greatest gain. We should have to put industry, prudence, economy, and enterprise into our business. If we failed, it would be through error. How is the congressional interference to act? How is it to meet and correct our error? It can appeal to no other motive than desire for profit, and can only offer us a profit where there was none before, if we will turn out of the industry which we have selected, into one which we do not know. It offers a

greater profit there only by means of what it takes from somebody else and somewhere else. Or, is congressional interference to correct the errors of John, James and William, and to make the idle, industrious, and the extravagant prudent? Any one who believes it must believe that the welfare of mankind is not dependent on the reason and conscience of the interested persons themselves, but on the caprices of blundering ignorance, embodied in a selected few, or on the trickery of lobbyists, acting impersonally and at a distance.

(B) NECESSARY CONDITIONS OF SUCCESSFUL PROTECTIVE LEGISLATION.

23. Suppose, however, that it were true that Congress had the power (by some exercise of the taxing function) to influence favorably the industrial development of the country: is it not true that men of sense would demand to be satisfied on three points, as follows?

24. (a) If Congress can do this thing, and is going to try it, *ought it not, in order to succeed, to have a distinct idea of what it is aiming at and proposes to do?* Who would have confidence in any man who should set out on an enterprise and who did not satisfy this condition? Has Congress ever satisfied it? Never. They have never had any plan or purpose in their tariff legislation. Congress has simply laid itself open to be acted upon by the interested parties, and the product of its tariff legislation has been simply the resultant of the struggles of the interested cliques with each other, and of the log-rolling combinations which they have been forced to make among themselves. In 1882 Congress did pay some deference, real or pretended, to the plain fact that it was bound, if it exercised this mighty power and responsibility, to bring some intelligence to bear on it, and it appointed a Tariff Commission which

spent several months in collecting evidence. This Commission was composed, with one exception, of protectionists. It recommended a reduction of twenty-five per cent in the tariff, and said: "Early in its deliberations the Commission became convinced that a substantial reduction of tariff duties is demanded, not by a mere indiscriminate popular clamor, but by the best conservative opinion of the country." "Excessive duties are positively injurious to the interests which they are supposed to benefit. They encourage the investment of capital in manufacturing enterprises by rash and unskilled speculators, to be followed by disaster to the adventurers and their employees, and a plethora of commodities which deranges the operations of skilled and prudent enterprise." (§ 111.) This report was entirely thrown aside, and Congress, ignoring it entirely, began again in exactly the old way. The Act of 1883 was not even framed by or in Congress. It was carried out into the dark, into a conference committee,[1] where new and gross abuses were put into the bill under cover of a pretended revision and reduction. When a tariff bill is before Congress, the first draft starts with a certain rate on a certain article, say twenty per cent. It is raised by amendment to fifty, the article is taken into a combination and the rate put up to eighty per cent; the bill is sent to the other house, and the rate on this article cut down again to forty per cent; on conference between the two houses the rate is fixed at sixty per cent. He who believes in the protectionist doctrine must, if he looks on at that proceeding, believe that the prosperity of the country is being kicked around the floor of Congress, at the mercy of the chances which are at last to determine with what per cent of tax these articles will come out. And what is it that determines with what tax any given article will come out? Any intelligent knowledge of industry? Not a word of it. Nothing

[1] Taussig: "History of the Existing Tariff," 78 ff.

in the case of a given tax on a given article, but just this: "Who is behind it?" The history of tariff legislation by the Congress of the United States throws a light upon the protective doctrine which is partly grotesque and partly revolting.

25. (*b*) If Congress can exert the supposed beneficent influence on industry, *ought not Congress to understand the force which it proposes to use?* Ought it not to have some rules of protective legislation so as to know in what cases, within what limits, under what conditions, the device can be effectively used? Would that not be a reasonable demand to make of any man who should propose a device for any purpose? Congress has never had any knowledge of the way in which the taxes which it passed were to do this beneficent work. It has never had, and has never seemed to think that it needed to get, any knowledge of the mode of operation of protective taxes. It passes taxes, as big as the conflicting interests will allow, and goes home, satisfied that it has saved the country. What a pity that philosophers, economists, sages, and moralists should have spent so much time in elucidating the conditions and laws of human prosperity! Taxes can do it all.

26. (*c*) If Congress can do what is affirmed and is going to try it, is it not the part of common sense to demand that *some tests be applied to the experiment after a few years to see whether it is really doing as was expected?* In the campaign of 1880 it was said that if Hancock was elected we should have free trade, wages would fall, factories would be closed, etc. Hancock was not elected, we did not get any reform of the tariff, and yet in 1884 wages were falling, factories were closed, and all the other direful consequences which were threatened had come to pass. *Bradstreet's* made investigations in the winter of 1884–1885 which showed that 316,000 workmen, thirteen per cent of the number employed in manufacturing in 1880, were out of work, 17,550 on strike,

and that wages had fallen since 1882 from ten to forty per cent, especially in the leading lines of manufacturing which are protected. What did these calamities all prove then? If we had had any revision of the tariff, should we not have had these things alleged again and again as results of it? Did they not, then, in the actual case, prove the folly of protection? Oh, no! that would be attacking the sacred dogma, and the sacred dogma is a matter of faith, so that, as it never had any foundation in fact or evidence, it has just as much after the experiment has failed as before the experiment was made.

27. If, now, it were possible to devise a scheme of legislation which should, according to protectionist ideas, be just the right jacket of taxation to fit this country to-day, *how long would it fit?* Not a week. Here are certain millions of people on three and a half million square miles of land. Every day new lines of communication are opened, new discoveries made, new inventions produced, new processes applied, and the consequence is that the industrial system is in constant flux and change. How, if a correct system of protective taxes was a practicable thing at any given moment, could Congress keep up with the changes and readaptations which would be required? The notion is preposterous, and it is a monstrous thing, even on the protectionist hypothesis, that we are living under a protective system which was set up in 1864. The weekly tariff decisions by the treasury department may be regarded as the constant attempts that are required to fit that old system to present circumstances, and, as it is not possible that new fabrics, new compounds, and new processes should find a place in schedules which were made twenty years before they were invented, those decisions carry with them the fate of scores of new industries which figure in no census, and are taken into account by no congressman. Therefore, even if we believed that the protective doctrine was sound

and that some protective system was beneficial, and that
the one which we have was the right one when it was
made, we should be driven to the conclusion that one which
is twenty years old is sure to be injurious to-day.

28. There is nothing then in the legislative machinery
by which the tariff is to be made which is calculated to win
the confidence of a man of sense, but everything to the contrary; and the experiments of such legislation which have
been made have produced nothing but warnings against
the device. Instead of offering any reasonable ground for
belief that our errors will be corrected and our productive
powers increased, an examination of the tariff as a piece of
legislation offers to us nothing but a burden, which must
cripple any economic power which we have.

(C) EXAMINATION OF THE MEANS PROPOSED, viz., TAXES.

29. Every tax is a burden, and in the nature of the case
can be nothing else. In mathematical language, every tax
is a quantity affected by a minus sign. If it gets peace and
security, that is, if it represses crime and injustice and prevents discord, which would be economically destructive,
then it is a smaller minus quantity than the one which
would otherwise be there, and that is the gain by good
government. Hence, like every other outlay which we
make, taxes must be controlled by the law of economy —
to get the best and most possible for the least expenditure.
Instead of regarding public expenditure carelessly, we
should watch it jealously. Instead of looking at taxation
as conceivably a good, and certainly not an ill, we should
regard every tax as on the defensive, and every cent of tax
as needing justification. If the statesman exacts any
more than is necessary to pay for good government economically administered, he is incompetent, and fails in his

duty. I have been studying political economy almost exclusively for the last fifteen years, and when I look back over that period and ask myself what is the most marked effect which I can perceive on my own opinion, or on my standpoint, as to social questions, I find that it is this: I am convinced that nobody yet understands the multiplied and complicated effects which are produced by taxation. I am under the most profound impression of the mischief which is done by taxation, reaching, as it does, to every dinner-table and to every fireside. *The effects of taxation vary with every change in the industrial system and the industrial status,* and they are so complicated that it is impossible to follow, analyze, and systematize them; but out of the study of the subject there arises this firm conviction: taxation is crippling, shortening, reducing all the time, over and over again.

30. Suppose that a man has an income of one thousand dollars, of which he has been saving one hundred dollars per annum with no tax. Now a tax of ten dollars is demanded of him, no matter what kind of a tax or how laid. Is he to get the tax out of the nine hundred dollars expenditure or out of the one hundred dollars savings? If the former, then he must cut down his diet, or his clothing, or his house accommodation, that is, lower his standard of comfort. If the latter, then he must lessen his accumulation of capital, that is, his provision for the future. Either way his welfare is reduced and cannot be otherwise affected, and, through the general effect, the welfare of the community is reduced by the tax. Of course it is immaterial that he may not know the facts. The effects are the same. In this view of the matter it is plain what mischief is done by taxes which are laid to buy parks, libraries, and all sorts of grand things. The tax-layer is not providing public order. He is spending other people's earnings for them. He is deciding that his neighbor shall have less clothes and

more library or park. But when we come to protective taxes the abuse is monstrous. The legislator who has in his hands this power of taxation uses it to say that one citizen shall have less clothes in order that he may contribute to the profits of another citizen's private business.

31. Hence if we look at the nature of taxation, and if we are examining protectionism from its own standpoint, under the assumption that it is true, instead of finding any confirmation of its assumptions, in the nature of the means which it proposes to use, we find the contrary. Granting that people make mistakes and fail of the highest prosperity which they might win when they act freely, we see plainly that more taxes cannot help to lift them up or to correct their errors; on the contrary, *all taxation, beyond what is necessary for an economical administration of good government, is either luxurious or wasteful*, and if such taxation could tend to wealth, waste would make wealth.

(D) Examination of the Plan of Mutual Taxation.

32. Suppose then that the industries and sections all begin to tax each other as we see that they do under protection. Is it not plain that the taxing operation can do nothing but *transfer* products, never by any possibility create them? The object of the protective taxes is to "effect the diversion of a part of the capital and labor of the country from the channels in which it would run otherwise." To do this it must find a fulcrum or point of reaction, or it can exert no force for the effect it desires. The fulcrum is furnished by those who pay the tax. Take a case. Pennsylvania taxes New England on every ton of iron and coal used in its industries. Ohio taxes New England on all the wool obtained from that state for its

industries.[1]   New England taxes Ohio and Pennsylvania on
all the cottons and woolens which it sells to them.   What
is the net final result?   It is mathematically certain that
the only result can be that (1) New England gets back
just all she paid (in which case the system is nil, save for
the expense of the process and the limitation it imposes on
the industry of all), or, (2) that New England does not get
back as much as she paid (in which case she is tributary to
the others), or, (3) that she gets back more than she paid
(in which case she levies tribute on them).   Yet, on the
protectionist notion, this system extended to all sections,
and embracing all industries, is the means of producing
national prosperity.   When it is all done, what does it
amount to except that *all Americans must support all
Americans?*   How can they do it better than for each to
support himself to the best of his ability?   Then, however,
all the assumptions of protectionism must be abandoned
as false.

33.   In 1676 King Charles II granted to his natural son,
the Duke of Richmond, a tax of a shilling a chaldron on
all the coal which was exported from the Tyne.   We regard such a grant as a shocking abuse of the taxing power.
It is, however, a very interesting case because the mine
owner and the tax owner were two separate persons, and
the tax can be examined in all its separate iniquity.   If,
as I suppose was the case, the Tyne Valley possessed such
superior facilities for producing coal that it had a qualified
monopoly, the tax fell on the coal mine owner (landlord);
that is, the king transferred to his son part of the property
which belonged to the Tyne coal owners.   In that view the

[1] The wool growers held a convention at St. Louis May 28, 1885, at which they
estimated their loss by the reduction of the tax on wool in 1883, or the *difference*
between what they got by this tax before that date and after, at ninety million
dollars (New York *Times*, May 29).   If that sum is what they lost, it is what the
consumers gained.   They are very angry, and will not vote for any one who will
not help to re-subject the consumers to this tribute to them.

case may come home to some of our protectionists as it would not if the tax had fallen on the consumers. If Congress had pensioned General Grant by giving him seventy-five cents a ton on all the coal mined in the Lehigh Valley, what protests we should have heard from the owners of coal lands in that district! If the king's son, however, had owned the coal mines, and worked them himself, and if the king had said: "I will authorize you to raise the price of your coal a shilling a chaldron, and, to enable you to do it, I will myself tax all coal but yours a shilling a chaldron," then the device would have been modern and enlightened and American. We have done just that on emery, copper, and nickel. Then the tax comes out of the consumer. Then it is not, according to the protectionist, harmful, but the key to national prosperity, the thing which corrects the errors of our incompetent self-will, and leads us up to better organization of our industry than we, in our unguided stupidity, could have made.

(E) EXAMINATION OF THE PROPOSAL TO "CREATE AN INDUSTRY."

34. The protectionist says, however, that he is going to create an industry. Let us examine this notion also from his standpoint, assuming the truth of his doctrine, and see if we can find anything to deserve confidence. A protective tax, according to the protectionist's definition (§ 13), "has for its object to effect the diversion of a part of the labor and capital of the people . . . into channels favored or created by law." If we follow out this proposal, we shall see what those channels are, and shall see whether they are such as to make us believe that protective taxes can increase wealth.

35. *What is an industry?* Some people will answer: It is an enterprise which gives employment. Protectionists

seem to hold this view, and they claim that they "give work" to laborers when they make an industry. On that notion we live to work; we do not work to live. But we do not want work. We have too much work. We want a living; and work is the inevitable but disagreeable price we must pay. Hence we want as much living at as little price as possible. We shall see that the protectionist does "make work" in the sense of lessening the living and increasing the price. But if we want a living we want capital. If an industry is to pay wages, it must be backed up by capital. Therefore protective taxes, if they were to increase the means of living, would need to increase capital. How can taxes increase capital? Protective taxes only take from A to give to B. Therefore, if B by this arrangement can extend his industry and "give more employment," A's power to do the same is diminished in at least an equal degree. Therefore, even on that erroneous definition of an industry, there is no hope for the protectionist.

36. *An industry is an organization of labor and capital for satisfying some need of the community.* It is not an end in itself. It is not a good thing to have in itself. It is not a toy or an ornament. If we could satisfy our needs without it we should be better off, not worse off. How, then, can we create industries?

37. If any one will find, in the soil of a district, some new power to supply human needs, he can endow that district with a new industry. If he will invent a mode of treating some natural deposit, ore or clay, for instance, so as to provide a tool or utensil which is cheaper and more convenient than what is in use, he can create an industry. If he will find out some new and better way to raise cattle or vegetables, which is, perhaps, favored by the climate, he can do the same. If he invents some new treatment of wool, or cotton, or silk, or leather, or makes a new combination which produces a more convenient or attractive

fabric, he may do the same. The telephone is a new industry. What measures the gain of it? Is it the "employment" of certain persons in and about telephone offices? The gain is in the satisfaction of the need of communication between people at less cost of time and labor. It is useless to multiply instances. It can be seen what it is to "create an industry." It takes brains and energy to do it. How can taxes do it?

38. Suppose that we create an industry even in this sense — *What is the gain of it?* The people of Connecticut are now earning their living by employing their labor and capital in certain parts of the industrial organization. They have changed their "industries" a great many times. If it should be found that they had a new and better chance hitherto undeveloped, they might all go into it. To do that they must abandon what they are now doing. They would not change unless gains to be made in the new industry were greater. Hence the gain is the *difference* only between the profits of the old and the profits of the new. The protectionists, however, when they talk about "creating an industry," seem to suppose that the total profit of the industry (and some of them seem to think that the total expenditure of capital) measures their good work. In any case, then, even of a true and legitimate increase of industrial power and opportunity, the only gain would be a margin. But, by our definition, "a protective duty has for its object to effect the diversion of a part of the capital and labor of the people out of the channels in which it would otherwise run." Plainly this device involves coercion. People would need no coercion to go into a new industry which had a natural origin in new industrial power or opportunity. No coercion is necessary to make men buy dollars at ninety-eight cents apiece. The case for coercion is when it is desired to make them buy dollars at one hundred and one cents apiece. Here the statesman with his

taxing power is needed, and can do something. What? He can say: "If you will buy a dollar at one hundred and one cents, I can and will tax John over there two cents for your benefit; one to make up your loss and the other to give you a profit." Hence, *on the protectionist's own doctrine*, his device is not needed, and cannot come into use, when a new industry is created in the true and only reasonable sense of the words, but *only when and because he is determined to drive the labor and capital of the country into a disadvantageous and wasteful employment.*

39. Still further, it is obvious that the protectionist, instead of "creating a new industry," has *simply taken one industry and set it as a parasite to live upon another*. Industry is its own reward. A man is not to be paid a premium by his neighbors for earning his own living. A factory, an insane asylum, a school, a church, a poorhouse, and a prison cannot be put in the same economic category. We know that the community must be taxed to support insane asylums, poorhouses, and jails. When we come upon such institutions we see them with regret. They are wasting capital. We know that the industrious people all about, who are laboring and producing, must part with a portion of their earnings to supply the waste and loss of these institutions. Hence *the bigger they are the sadder they are.*

40. As for the schools and churches, we know that society must pay for and keep up its own conservative institutions. They cost capital and do not pay back capital directly, although they do indirectly, and in the course of time, in ways which we could trace out and verify if that were our subject. Here, then, we have a second class of institutions.

41. But the factories and farms and foundries are the productive institutions which must provide the support of these consuming institutions. If the factories, etc., put

themselves on a line with the poorhouses, or even with the schools, what is to support them and all the rest too? They have nothing behind them. If in any measure or way they turn into burdens and objects of care and protection, they can plainly do it only by part of them turning upon the other part, and this latter part will have to bear the burden of all the consuming institutions, *including the consuming industries.* For a protected factory is not a producing industry. *It is a consuming industry!* If a factory is (as the protectionist alleges) a triumph of the tariff, that is, if it would not be but for the tariff (and otherwise he has nothing to do with it), then it is not producing; it is consuming. It is a burden to be borne. *The bigger it is the sadder it is.*

42. If a protectionist shows me a woolen mill and challenges me to deny that it is a great and valuable industry, I ask him whether it is due to the tariff. If he says "no," then I will assume that it is an independent and profitable establishment, but in that case it is out of this discussion as much as a farm or a doctor's practice. If he says "yes," then I answer that the mill is not an industry at all. We pay sixty per cent tax on cloth *simply in order that that mill may be.* It is not an institution for getting us cloth, for if we went into the market with the same products which we take there now and if there were no woolen mill, we should get all the cloth we want. The mill is simply *an institution for making cloth cost per yard sixty per cent more of our products than it otherwise would.* That is the one and only function which the mill has added, by its existence, to the situation. I have called such a factory a "nuisance." The word has been objected to. The word is of no consequence. He who, when he goes into a debate, begins to whine and cry as soon as the blows get sharp, should learn to keep out. What I meant was this: A nuisance is something which by its existence and presence in society works

loss and damage to the society — works against the general interest, not for it. A factory which gets in the way and hinders us from attaining the comforts which we are all trying to get — which makes harder the terms of acquisition when we are all the time struggling by our arts and sciences to make those terms easier — is a harmful thing, and noxious to the common interest.

43. Hence, once more, starting from the protectionist's hypothesis, and assuming his own doctrine, we find that he cannot create an industry. He only fixes one industry as a parasite upon another, and just as certainly as he has intervened in the matter at all, just so certainly has he forced labor and capital into less favorable employment than they would have sought if he had let them alone. When we ask which "channels" those are which are to be "favored or created by law," we find that they are, by the hypothesis, and by the whole logic of the protectionist system, *the industries which do not pay*. The protectionists propose to make the country rich by laws which shall favor or create these industries, but these industries can only waste capital, so that if they are the source of wealth, *waste is the source of wealth*. Hence the protectionist's assumption that by his system he could correct our errors and lead us to greater prosperity than we would have obtained under liberty, has failed again, and we find that he wastes what power we do possess.

(F) EXAMINATION OF THE PROPOSAL TO DEVELOP OUR NATURAL RESOURCES.

44. "But," says the protectionist, "do you mean to say that, if we have an iron deposit in our soil, it is not wise for us to open and work it?" "You mean, no doubt," I reply, "open and work it *under protective help and stimulus;* for, if there is an iron deposit, the United States does not

own it. Some man owns it. If he wants to open and
work it, we have nothing to do but wish him God-speed."
"Very well," he says, "understand it that he needs protection." Let us examine this case, then, and still we will
do it assuming the truth of the protectionist doctrine.
Let us see where we shall come out.

The man who has discovered iron (on the protectionist
doctrine), when there is no tax, does not collect tools and
laborers and go to work. He goes to Washington. He
visits the statesman, and a dialogue takes place.

Iron man. — "Mr. Statesman, I have found an iron deposit on my farm."

Statesman. — "Have you, indeed? That is good news.
Our country is richer by one new natural resource than we
have supposed."

Iron man. — "Yes, and I now want to begin mining
iron."

Statesman. — "Very well, go on. We shall be glad to
hear that you are prospering and getting rich."

Iron man. — "Yes, of course. But I am now earning
my living by tilling the surface of the ground, and I am
afraid that I cannot make as much at mining as at farming."

Statesman. — "That is indeed another matter. Look
into that carefully and do not leave a better industry for a
worse."

Iron man. — "But I want to mine that iron. It does
not seem right to leave it in the ground when we are importing iron all the time, but I cannot see as good profits
in it at the present price for imported iron as I am making
out of what I raise on the surface. I thought that perhaps you would put a tax on all the imported iron so that
I could get more for mine. Then I could see my way to
give up farming and go to mining."

Statesman. — "You do not think what you ask. That
would be authorizing you to tax your neighbors, and would

be throwing on them the risk of working your mine, which you are afraid to take yourself."

Iron man (aside). — "I have not talked the right dialect to this man. I must begin all over again. (Aloud.) Mr. Statesman, the natural resources of this continent ought to be developed. American industry must be protected. The American laborer must not be forced to compete with the pauper labor of Europe."

Statesman. — "Now I understand you. Now you talk business. Why did you not say so before? How much tax do you want?"

The next time that a buyer of pig iron goes to market to get some, he finds that it costs thirty bushels of wheat per ton instead of twenty.

"What has happened to pig iron?" says he.

"Oh! haven't you heard?" is the reply. "A new mine has been found down in Pennsylvania. We have got a new 'natural resource.'"

"I haven't got a new 'natural resource,'" says he. "It is as bad for me as if the grasshoppers had eaten up one-third of my crop."

45. That is just exactly the significance of a new resource on the protectionist doctrine. We had the misfortune to find emery here. At once a tax was put on it which made it cost more wheat, cotton, tobacco, petroleum, or personal services per pound than ever before. A new calamity befell us when we found the richest copper mines in the world in our territory. From that time on it cost us five (now four) cents a pound more than before. By another catastrophe we found a nickel mine — thirty cents (now fifteen) a pound tax! Up to this time we have had all the tin that we wanted above ground, because beneficent nature has refrained from putting any underground in our territory. In the metal schedule, where the metals which we unfortunately possess are taxed from

forty to sixty per cent, tin alone is free. Every little while
a report is started that tin has been found. Hitherto these
reports have happily all proved false. It is now said that
tin has been found in West Virginia and Dakotah. We
have reason devoutly to hope that this may prove false,
for, if it should prove true, no doubt the next thing will
be forty per cent tax on tin. The mine-owners say that
they want to exploit the mine. They do not. They want
to make the mine an excuse to exploit the taxpayers.

46. Therefore, when the protectionist asks whether we
ought not by protective taxes to force the development of
our own iron mines, the answer is that, on his own doctrine,
he has developed a new philosophy, hitherto unknown, by
which "natural resources" become national calamities, and
the more a country is endowed by nature the worse off it
is. Of course, if the wise philosophy is not simply to use,
with energy and prudence, all the natural opportunities
which we possess, but to seek "channels favored or created
by law," then this view of natural resources is perfectly
consistent with that philosophy, for it is simply saying
over again that *waste is the key of wealth.*

(G) Examination of the Proposal to Raise Wages.

47. "But," he says again, "we want to raise wages and
favor the poor working man." "Do you mean to say,"
I reply, "that protective taxes raise wages — that that is
their regular and constant effect?" "Yes," he replies,
"that is just what they do, and that is why we favor them.
We are the poor man's friends. You free-traders want to
reduce him to the level of the pauper laborers of Europe."
"But here, in the evidence offered at the last tariff discussion in Congress, the employers all said that they wanted
the taxes to protect them *because* they had to pay such
high wages." "Well, so they do." "Well then, if they

get the taxes raised to help them out when they have high wages to pay, how are the taxes going to help them any unless the taxes *lower* wages? But you just said that taxes raise wages. Therefore, if the employer gets the taxes raised, he will no sooner get home from Washington than he will find that the very taxes which he has just secured have raised wages. Then he must go back to Washington to get the taxes raised to offset that advance, and when he gets home again he will find that he has only raised wages more, and so on forever. You are trying to teach the man to raise himself by his boot straps. Two of your propositions brought together eat each other."

48. We will, however, pursue the protectionist doctrine of wages a little further. It is totally false that protective taxes raise wages. As I will show further on (§ 91 and following), protective taxes lower wages. Now, however, I am assuming the protectionist's own premises and doctrines all the time. He says that his system raises wages. Let us go to see some of the wages class and get some evidence on this point. We will take three wage-workers, a boot man, a hat man, and a cloth man. First we ask the boot man, "Do you win anything by this tariff?" "Yes," he says, "I understand that I do." "How?" "Well, the way they explain it to me is that when anybody wants boots he goes to my boss, pays him more on account of the tax, and my boss gives me part of it." "All right! Then your comrades here, the hat man and the cloth man, pay this tax in which you share?" "Yes, I suppose so. I never thought of that before. I supposed that rich people paid the taxes, but I suppose that when they buy boots they must do it too." "And when you want a hat you go and pay the tax on hats, part of which (as you explain the system) goes to your friend the hat man; and when you want cloth you pay the tax which goes to benefit your friend the cloth man?" "I suppose that it must

be so." We go, then, to see the hat man and have the same conversation with him, and we go to see the cloth man and have the same conversation with him. Each of them then gets two taxes and pays two taxes. Three men illustrate the whole case. If we should take a thousand men in a thousand industries we should find that each paid nine hundred and ninety-nine taxes, and each got nine hundred and ninety-nine taxes, if the system worked as it is said to work. What is the upshot of the whole? Either they all come out even on their taxes paid and received, or *some of the wage receivers are winning something out of other wage receivers to the net detriment of the whole class.* If each man is creditor for nine hundred and ninety-nine taxes, and each debtor for nine hundred and ninety-nine taxes, and if the system is "universal and equal," we can save trouble by each drawing nine hundred and ninety-nine orders on the creditors to pay to themselves their own taxes, and we can set up a clearing house to wipe off all the accounts. Then we come down to this as the net result of the system when it is "universal and equal," that *each man as a consumer pays taxes to himself as a producer.* That is what is to make us all rich. We can accomplish it just as well and far more easily, when we get up in the morning, by transferring our cash from one pocket to the other.

49. One point, however, and the most important of all, remains to be noticed. How about the thousandth tax? How is it when the boot man wants boots, and the hat man hats, and the cloth man cloth? He has to go to the store on the street and buy of his own boss, at the market price (tax on), the very things which he made himself in the shop. He then pays the tax to his own employer, and the employer, according to the doctrine, "shares" it with him. Where is the offset to that part which the employer keeps? There is none. The wages class, even on the protectionist explanation, may give or take from each other,

but to their own employers they give and take not. At election time the boss calls them in and tells them that they must vote for protection or he must shut up the shop, and that they ought to vote for protection, because it makes their wages high. If, then, they believe in the system, just as it is taught to them, they must believe that it causes him to pay them big wages, out of which they pay back to him big taxes, out of which he pays them a fraction back again, and that, but for this arrangement, the business could not go on at all. A little reflection shows that this just brings up the question for a wage-earner: *How much can I afford to pay my boss for hiring me?* or, again, which is just the same thing in other words: *What is the net reduction of my wages, below the market rate under freedom, which results from this system?* (See § 65.)

50. Let it not be forgotten that this result is reached by accepting protectionism and reasoning forward from its doctrines and according to its principles. In truth, the employees get no share in any taxes which the boss gets out of them and others (see § 91 ff. for the truth about wages). Of course, when this or any other subject is thoroughly analyzed, it makes no difference where we begin or what line we follow, we shall always reach the same result if the result is correct. If we accept the protectionist's own explanation of the way in which protection raises wages we find that it proves that protection lowers wages.

(*H*) Examination of the Proposal to Prevent Competition by Foreign Pauper Labor.

51. The protectionist says that he does not want the American laborer to compete with the foreign "pauper laborer" (see § 99). He assumes that if the foreign laborer is a woolen operative, the only American who may have to compete with him is a woolen operative here. His device

for saving our operatives from the assumed competition is
to tax the American cotton or wheat grower on the cloth
he wears, to make up and offset to the woolen operative
the disadvantage under which he labors. If then, the case
were true as the protectionist states it, and if his remedy
were correct, he would, when he had finished his operation,
simply have allowed the American woolen operative to
escape, by transferring to the American cotton or wheat
grower the evil results of competition with "foreign pauper
labor."

(I) EXAMINATION OF THE PROPOSAL TO RAISE THE STANDARD OF PUBLIC COMFORT.

52. But the protectionist reiterates that he wants to
make our people well off, and to diffuse general prosperity,
and he says that his system does this. He says that the
country has prospered under protection and on account of
it. He brings from the census the figures for increased
wealth of the country, and, to speak of no minor errors,
draws an inference that we have prospered *more than we
should have done under free trade*, which is what he has to
prove, without noticing that the second term of the comparison is absent and unattainable. In the same manner
I once heard a man argue from statistics, who showed by
the *small* loss of a city by fire that its fire department cost
too much. I asked him if he had any statistics of the fires
which we should have had but for the fire department
(see § 102).

53. The people of the United States have inherited an
untouched continent. The now living generation is practicing bonanza farming on prairie soil which has never
borne a crop. The population is only fifteen to the square
mile. The population of England and Wales is four hundred and forty-six to the square mile; that of the British

Islands two hundred and ninety; that of Belgium four hundred and eighty-one; of France one hundred and eighty; of Germany two hundred and sixteen. Bateman [1] estimates that in the better part of England or Wales a peasant proprietor would need from four and a half to six acres, and, in the worse part, from nine to forty-five acres on which to support "a healthy family." The soil of England and Wales, equally divided between the families there, would give only seven acres apiece. The land of the United States, equally divided between the families there, would give two hundred and fifteen acres apiece. These old nations give us the other term of the comparison by which we measure our prosperity. They have a dense population on a soil which has been used for thousands of years; we have an extremely sparse population on a virgin soil. We have an excellent climate, mountains full of coal and ore, natural highways on the rivers and lakes, and a coast indented with sounds, bays, and some of the best harbors in the world. We have also a population of good national character, especially as regards the economic and industrial virtues. The sciences and arts are highly culti- vated among us, and our institutions are the best for the development of economic strength. As compared with old nations we are prosperous. Now comes the protectionist statesman and says: "The things which you have enu- merated are not the causes of our comparative prosperity. Those things are all vain. Our prosperity is not due to them. I made it with my taxes."

54. (a) In the first place the fact is that we surpass most in prosperity those nations which are most like us in their tax systems, and those compared with whom our prosperity is least remarkable are those which have by free trade offset as much as possible the disadvantage of age and dense population. Since, then, we find greatest difference in

[1] Broderick, "English Land and English Landlords," p. 194.

prosperity with least difference in tax, and least difference in prosperity with greatest difference in tax, we cannot regard tax as a cause of prosperity, but as an obstacle to prosperity which must have been overcome by some stronger cause. That such is the case lies plainly on the face of the facts. The prosperity which we enjoy is the prosperity which God and nature have given us *minus what the legislator has taken from it.*

55. (*b*) We prospered with slavery just as we have prospered with protection. The argument that the former was a cause would be just as strong as the argument that the latter is a cause.

56. (*c*) The protectionists take to themselves as a credit all the advance in the arts of the last twenty-five years, because they have not entirely offset it and destroyed it.

57. (*d*) The protectionists claim that they have increased our wealth. All the wealth that is produced must be produced by labor and capital applied to land. The people have wrought and produced. The tax gatherer has only subtracted something. Whether he used what he took well or ill, he subtracted. He could not do anything else. Therefore, whatever wealth we see about us, and whatever wealth appears in the census is what the people have produced, *less* what the tax gatherer has taken out of it.

58. (*e*) If the members of Congress can establish for themselves some ideal of the grade of comfort which the average American citizen ought to enjoy, and then just get it for him, they have used their power hitherto in a very beggarly manner. For, although the average status of our people is high when compared with that of other people on the globe, nevertheless, when compared with any standard of ideal comfort, it leaves much to be desired. If Congress has the power supposed, they surely ought not to measure the exercise of it by only making us better off than Europeans.

59. (*f*) During the late presidential campaign the pro-

tectionist orators assured the people that they meant to make everybody well off, that they wished our people to be prosperous, contented, etc. I wish so too. I wish that all my readers may be millionaires. I freely and sincerely confer on them all the bounty of my good wishes. They will not find a cent more in their pockets on that account. The congressmen have no power to bless my readers which I have not, save one; that is, the power to tax them.

60. (*g*) If the congressmen are determined to elevate the comfort of the population by taxing the population, then every new ship load of immigrants must be regarded as a new body of persons whom we must "elevate" by the taxes we have to pay. It is said that an Irishman affirmed that a dollar in America would not buy more than a shilling in Ireland. He was asked why then he did not stay in Ireland. He replied that it was because he could not get the shilling there. That is a good story, only it stops just where it ought to begin. The next question is: How does he get the dollar when he comes to America? The protectionist wants us to suppose that he gets it by grace of the tariff. If so he gets it out of those who were here before he came. But plainly no such thing is true. He gets it by earning it, and he adds two dollars to the wealth of the country while earning it. The only thing the tariff does in regard to it is to lower the purchasing power of the dollar, if it is spent for products of manufacture, to seventy cents.

61. Here, again, then, we find that protective taxes, if they do just what the protectionist says that they will do, produce the very opposite effects from those which he says they will produce. They lessen wealth, reduce prosperity, diminish average comfort, and lower the standard of living. (See § 30.)

Chapter III

PROTECTIONISM EXAMINED ADVERSELY

62. I have so far examined protectionism as a philosophy of national wealth, assuming and accepting its own doctrines, and following them out, to see if they will issue as is claimed. We have found that they do not, but that protectionism, on its own doctrines, issues in the impoverishment of the nation and in failure to do anything which it claims to do. On the contrary, an examination in detail of its means, methods, purposes, and plans shows that it must produce waste and loss, so that *if it were true, we should have to believe that waste and loss are means of wealth.* Now I turn about to attack it in face, on an open issue, for if any project which is advocated proves, upon free and fair examination, to be based on errors of fact and doctrine, it becomes a danger and an evil to be exposed and combated, and truth of fact and doctrine must be set against it.

1. *PROTECTIONISM INCLUDES AND NECESSARILY CARRIES WITH IT HOSTILITY TO TRADE OR, AT LEAST, SUSPICION AGAINST TRADE*

(*A*) Rules for Knowing when it is Safe to Trade.

63. Every protectionist is forced to regard trade as a mischievous or at least doubtful thing. Protectionists have even tried to formulate rules for determining when trade is beneficial and when harmful.

64. It has been said that we ought to trade only on meridians of longitude, not on parallels of latitude.

65. It has been affirmed that we cannot safely trade unless we have taxes to exactly offset the lower wages of foreign countries. But it is plain that if the case stands

so that an American employer says: "I am at a disadvantage compared with my foreign competitor, because he pays less wages than I" — then, by the same token, the American laborer will say: "I am at an advantage, compared with my foreign comrade, for I get better wages than he." If the law interferes with the state of things so that the employer is enabled to say: "I am now at less disadvantage in competition with my foreign rival, because I do not now have to pay as much more wages than he as formerly" — then, by the same token, the American laborer must say: "I am not now as much better off than my foreign comrade as formerly, for I do not now gain as much more than he as I did — there is not now as much advantage in emigrating to this country as formerly." Therefore, whenever the taxes just offset the difference in wages, *they just take away from the American laborer all his superiority over the foreigner,* and take away all reason for caring to come to this country. So much for the laborer. But the employer, if he has arrested immigration, has cut off one source of the supply of labor, tending to raise wages, and is at war with himself again (§ 47).

66. It has been said that two nations cannot trade *if the rate of interest in the two differs by two per cent.* The rate of interest in the Atlantic States and in the Mississippi Valley has always differed by two per cent, yet they have traded together under absolute free trade, and the Mississippi Valley has had to begin a wilderness and grow up to the highest standard of civilization in spite of that state of things.

67. It has been said that we ought to *trade only with inferior nations.* The United States does not trade with any other nation, save when it buys territory. A in the United States trades with B in some foreign country. If I want caoutchouc I want to trade with a savage in the forests of South America. If I want mahogany I want to

trade with a man in Honduras. If I want sugar I want to trade with a man in Cuba. If I want tea I want to trade with a man in China. If I want silk or champagne I want to trade with a man in France. If I want a razor I want to trade with a man in England. I want to trade with the man who has the thing which I want of the best quality and at the lowest rate of exchange for my products. What is the definition or test of an "inferior nation," and what has that got to do with trade any more than the race, language, color, or religion of the man who has the goods?

68. If trade was an object of suspicion and dread, then indeed we ought to have *rules for distinguishing safe and beneficial trade* from mischievous trade, but these attempts to define and discriminate only expose the folly of the suspicion. We find that the primitive men who dwelt in caves in the glacial epoch carried on trade. The earliest savages made footpaths through the forests by which to traffic and trade, winning thereby mutual advantages. They found that they could supply more wants with less effort by trade, which gave them a share in the natural advantages and acquired skill of others. They trained beasts of burden, improved roads, invented wagons and boats, all in order to extend and facilitate trade. They were foolish enough to think that they were gaining by it, *and did not know that they needed a protective tariff to keep them from ruining themselves.* Or, why does not some protectionist sociologist tell us at what stage of civilization trade ceases to be advantageous and begins to need restraint and regulation?

(B) Economic Units not National Units.

69. The protectionists say that their system advances civilization inside a state and makes it great, but the facts are all against them (see § 136 ff). It was by trade that civi-

lization was extended over the earth. It was through the contact of trade that the more civilized nations transmitted to others the alphabet, weights and measures, knowledge of astronomy, divisions of time, tools and weapons, coined money, systems of numeration, treatment of metals, skins, and wool, and all the other achievements of knowledge and invention which constitute the bases of our civilization. On the other hand, the nations which shut themselves up and developed an independent and self-contained civilization (China and Japan) present us the types of arrested civilization and stereotyped social status. It is the penalty of isolation and of withdrawal from the giving and taking which properly bind the whole human race together, that even such intelligent and highly endowed people as the Chinese should find their high activity arrested at narrow limitations on every side. They invent coin, but never get beyond a cast copper coin. They invent gunpowder, but cannot make a gun. They invent movable types, but only the most rudimentary book. They discover the mariner's compass, but never pass the infancy of ship-building.

70. The fact is, then, that *trade has been the handmaid of civilization.* It has traversed national boundaries, and has gradually, with improvement in the arts of transportation, drawn the human race into closer relations and more harmonious interests. The contact of trade slowly saps old national prejudice and religious or race hatreds. The jealousies which were perpetuated by distance and ignorance cannot stand before contact and knowledge. To stop trade is to arrest this beneficent work, to separate mankind into sections and factions, and to favor discord, jealousy, and war.

71. Such is the action of protectionism. The protectionists make much of their pretended "nationalism," and they try to reason out some kind of relationship be-

tween the scope of economic forces and the boundaries of existing nations. The argumentation is fatally broken at its first step. They do not show what they might show, *viz.*, that the scope of economic forces on any given stage of the arts does form economic units. An English county was such a unit a century ago. I doubt if anything less than the whole earth could be considered so to-day, when the wool of Australia, the hides of South America, the cotton of Alabama, the wheat of Manitoba, and the meat of Texas meet the laborers in Manchester and Sheffield, and would meet the laborers in Lowell and Paterson, if the barriers were out of the way. But what the national protectionist would need to show would be that the economic unit coincides with the political unit. He would have to affirm that Maine and Texas are in one economic unit, but that Maine and New Brunswick are not; or that Massachusetts and Minnesota are in one economic unit, but that Massachusetts and Manitoba are not. Every existing state is a product of historic accidents. Mr. Jefferson set out to buy the city of New Orleans. He awoke one morning to find that he had bought the western half of the Mississippi Valley. Since that turned out so, the protectionists think that Missouri and Illinois prosper by trading in perfect freedom.[1] If it had not turned out so, it would have been very mischievous for them to trade

[1] Since the above was in type, I have, for the first time, seen an argument from a protectionist, that a tariff between our states is, or may become, desirable. It is from the Chicago *Inter-Ocean*, and marks the extreme limit reached, up to this time, by protectionist fanaticism and folly, although it is thoroughly consistent, and fairly lays bare the spirit and essence of protectionism:

"In the United States the present ominous and overshadowing strike in the iron trade, by which from 75,000 to 100,000 men have been thrown out of work, is an incisive example of the tendency of this country, also, to a condition of trade which will compel individual states and certain sections of the country to ask for legislation, in order to protect them against the cheaper labor and superior natural advantage of others." The remedy for the harm done by taxes on our foreign trade is to lay some on our domestic trade. (See §§ 26, 95.)

in perfect freedom. Nova Scotia did not join the revolt of our thirteen colonies. Hence it is thought ruinous to let coal and potatoes come in freely from Nova Scotia. If she had revolted with us, it would have been for the benefit of everybody in this union to trade with her as freely as we now trade with Maine. We tried to conquer Canada in 1812–1813 and failed. Consequently the Canadians now put taxes on our coal and petroleum and wheat, and we put taxes on their lumber, which our coal and petroleum industries need. We did annex Texas, at the cost of war, in 1845. Consequently we trade with Texas now under absolute freedom, but, if we trade with Mexico, it must be only very carefully and under stringent limitations. Is this wisdom, or is it all pure folly and wrongheadedness, by which men who boast of their intelligence throw away their own chances? [1]

72. *Trade is a beneficent thing.* It does not need any regulation or restraint. There is no point at which it begins to be dangerous. It is mutually beneficent. If it ceases to be so, it ceases entirely, because he who no longer gains by it will no longer carry it on. (See § 125.)

II. *PROTECTIONISM IS AT WAR WITH IMPROVEMENT*

73. The cities of Japan are built of very combustible material, and when a fire begins it is rarely arrested until the city is destroyed. It was suggested that a steam fire-engine would there reach its maximum of utility. One was imported and proved very useful on several occasions.

---

[1] Since the above was in type, a treasury order has subjected all goods from Canada to the same taxes as imported goods, although they may be going from Minnesota to England. Nature has made man too well off. The inhabitants of North America will not simply use their chances, but they divide into two artificial bodies so as to try to harm each other. Millions are spent to cut an isthmus where nature has left one, and millions more to set up a tax-barrier where nature has made a highway.

Thereupon the carpenters got up a petition to the government to send the fire-engine away, because it ruined their business.

74. The instance is grotesque and exaggerated, but it is strictly true to the principle of protectionism. The southern counties of England, a century ago, protested against the opening of the great northern turnpike, because that would bring the products of the northern counties to the London market, of which the southern counties had had a monopoly. After the St. Gothard tunnel was opened the people of southern Germany petitioned the Government to lay higher taxes on Italian products to offset the cheapness which the tunnel had produced. In 1837 the first two steamers which ever made commercial voyages across the Atlantic arrived at the same time. A grand celebration was held in New York. The foolish people rejoiced as if a new blessing had been won. Man had won a new triumph over nature. What was the gain of it? It was that he could satisfy his needs with less labor than before; or, in plain language, get things cheaper. But in 1842 a Home Industry Convention was held in New York, at which it was alleged as the prime reason why more taxes were needed, that this steam transportation had made things cheap here.[1] Taxes were needed to neutralize the improvement.

(A) TAXES TO OFFSET CHEAPENED TRANSPORTATION.

75. For the last twenty-five years, to go no farther back, we have multiplied inventions to facilitate transportation. Ocean cables, improved marine engines, and screw steamers, have been only improved means of supplying the wants of people on two continents more abundantly with the products each of the other. The

---

[1] 62, Niles's "Register," 132.

scientific journals and the daily papers boast of every step in this development as a thing to be proud of and rejoice in, but in the meantime the legislators on both sides of the water are hard at work to neutralize it by taxation. We, in the United States, have multiplied monstrous taxes on all the things which others make and which we want, to prevent them from being brought to us. The statesmen of the European continent are laying taxes on our meat and wheat, lest they be brought to their people. The arts are bringing us together; the taxes are needed to keep us apart. In France, for instance, the agriculturist complains of American competition — not "pauper labor," but gratuitous soil and sunlight. He does not want the French artisan to have the benefit of our prairie soil. The government yields to him and lays a tax on our meat and wheat. This raises the price of bread in Paris, where the reconstruction of the city has collected a large artisan population. The government then finds itself driven to fix the price of bread in Paris, to keep it down. But the reconstruction of the city was accomplished by contracting a great debt, which means heavy taxes. These taxes drive the population out into the suburbs. At least one voice has been raised by an owner of city property that a tax ought to be laid on suburban residents to drive them back to the city,[1] and not let them escape the efforts of the city landlord to throw his taxes on them. Then, again, France has been subsidizing ships, and when the question of renewing the subsidy came up, it was argued that the ships subsidized at the expense of the French taxpayer had lowered freight on wheat and made wheat cheap; that is, as somebody justly replied, had wrought the very mischief against which the increased tax had just been demanded on wheat. Therefore the taxpayer had been taxed first to make wheat cheap, and then again to make it dear.

[1] *Journal des Economistes*, March, 1885, page 496.

76. Tax A to favor B. If A complains, tax C to make it up to A. If C complains, tax B to favor C. If any of them still complain, begin all over again. Tax them as long as anybody complains, or anybody wants anything. This is the statesmanship of the last quarter of the nineteenth century.

77. Bismarck, too, is going into the business. He has to rule a people who live on a poor soil and have to bear a crushing military system. The consequence is that the population is declining. Emigration exceeds the natural increase. Bismarck's cure for it is to lay protective taxes against American pork and wheat and rye. This will protect the German agriculturist. If it lowers still more the comfort of the buyers of food, and drives more of them out of the country, then he will go and buy or fight for colonies at the expense of the German agriculturists whom he has just "protected," although the surplus population of Germany has been taking itself away for thirty years without asking help or giving trouble. What can Germany gain by diverting her emigrants to her own colony unless she means to bring the able-bodied men back to fight her battles? If she means that, the emigrants will not go to her colony.

78. France is also reviving the old colonial policy with discriminating favors and compensatory restraints. She already owns a possession in Algeria, which is the best example of a colony for the sake of a colony. It has been asserted in the French Chambers that each French family now in Algeria has cost the Government (*i.e.*, the French taxpayer) 25,000 francs.[1] The longing of these countries for "colonies" is like the longing of a negro dandy for a cane or a tall hat so as to be like the white gentlemen.

[1] Paris correspondent of the New York *Evening Post*, February 9, 1884.

(B) Sugar Bounties.

79. The worst case of all, however, is sugar. The protectionists long boasted of beet-root sugar as a triumph of their system. It is now an industry in which an immense amount of capital is invested on the Continent, but cheap transportation for cane sugar, and improvements in the treatment of the latter, are constantly threatening it. Mention is made in *Bradstreet's* for June 28, 1885, of a very important improvement in the treatment of cane which has just been invented at Berlin. Germany has an excise tax on beet-root sugar, but allows a drawback on it when exported which is greater than the tax. This acts as a bounty paid by the German taxpayer on the exportation. Consequently, beet-root sugar has appeared even in our market. The chief market for it, however, is England. The consequence is that the sugar, which is nine cents a pound in Germany, and seven cents a pound here, is five cents a pound in England, and that the annual consumption of sugar per head in the three countries [1] is as follows: England, sixty-seven and a half pounds; United States, fifty-one pounds; Germany, twelve pounds. I sometimes find it difficult to make people understand the difference between wanting an "industry" and wanting goods, but this case ought to make that distinction clear. Obviously *the Germans have the industry and the Englishmen have the sugar.*

80. No sooner, however, does Germany get her export bounty in good working order than the Austrian sugar refiners besiege their government to know whether Germany is to have the monopoly of giving sugar to the Englishmen.[2]

---

[1] *Economist*, Commercial Review, 1884, p. 15.

[2] The Vienna correspondent of the *Economist* writes, June 15, 1885, "The representatives of the sugar trade addressed a petition to the Finance Minister, asking, above all things, that the premium on export should be retained, without which, they say, they cannot continue to exist, and which is granted in all countries where beet-root sugar is manufactured."

They get a bounty and compete for that privilege. Then the French refiners say that they cannot compete, and must be enabled to compete in giving sugar to the Englishmen. I believe that their case is under favorable consideration.

80 a. I have found it harder (as is usually the case) to get recorded information about the trade and industry of our own country than about those of foreign nations. However, we too, although we do not raise beet-sugar, have our share in this bounty folly, as may be seen by the following statement, which comes to hand just in time to serve my purpose.[1] "The export of refined sugar [from the United States] is entirely confined to hard sugars, or, to be more explicit, loaf, crushed, and granulated. This is because the drawback upon this class of sugar is so large that refiners are enabled to sell them at less than cost. The highest collectable duty upon sugar testing as high as 99° is but 2.36, but the drawback upon granulated test- ing the same, and in the case of crushed and loaf less, is 2.82 less 1 per cent. This is exactly 43 cents per one hundred pounds more than the government receives in duty. But it rarely happens that raw sugar is imported testing 99°, and never for refining purposes. The following table gives the rates of duty upon the average grades used in refining:

	Degrees	Duty
Fair refining testing	89	1.96
Fair refining testing	90	2.00
Centrifugal testing	96	2.28
Beet-sugar testing	88	1.92

It will be clearly seen from the above figures that with a net drawback upon hard sugar of 2.79 our refiners are able to sell to foreigners, through the assistance of our Treasury, sugar at less than cost. Taking, for instance, the net price of centrifugal testing only 97° and the net price less drawback of granulated:

[1] *Bradstreet's*, July 25, 1885.

Centrifugal raw sugar testing 97°......................	6.00	
Less duty...	2.28	
Net...		3.72
Granulated refined testing 99°........................	6.37½	
Less drawback......................................	2.71	
Net...		3.66½
		6½

Nothing could demonstrate the absurdity of the present rate of drawback more clearly than the above. A refiner pays 6½ cents per hundred more for raw sugar testing 2° less saccharine than he sells refined for. Not, however, to the American consumers, but to foreigners. After paying the expenses necessary to refining by the assistance of a drawback, which clearly amounts to a subsidy of about 50 cents a hundred pounds, our large sugar monopolists are assisted by the government to increase the cost of sugar to American consumers. One firm controls almost the entire trade of the east; at all events it is safe to say that the trade of the entire country is controlled by three firms, and the Treasury assists this monopoly in sustaining prices against the interest of the country at large. Up to date the exports of refined sugar have amounted to 83,340 tons, which, taken at 50 cents a hundred, has cost the treasury over $830,000. All this may not have gone into the pockets of the refiners, as the ship owners have obtained a share, but the fact remains that the Treasury is the loser by this amount. Besides this bounty presses hard upon the consumers. They not only have to pay the tax, but during the late rise they were compelled to pay more for their sugar than they otherwise would have done had not the export demand caused by selling sugar to foreigners at less than cost, the Treasury paying the difference, increased prices. While an American consumer is charged 6½ cents for granulated, foreign buyers, through the liberality of our government, can buy it under 3¾ cents. Certainly it is time that the Secretary of the Treasury asked the sugar commission to commence a comprehensive and impartial inquiry."

81. Of course the story would not be complete if the English refiners did not besiege their government for a tax to keep out this maleficent gift of foreign taxpayers. This, say they, is not free trade. This is protection turned the other way around. We might hold our own on an equal footing, but we cannot contend against a subsidized industry. A superficial thinker might say that this protest was conclusive. The English government set on foot an investigation, not of the sugar refining, but of *those other interests which were in danger of being forgotten*. There was a tariff investigation which was worth something and was worthy of an enlightened government. It was found that the consumers of sugar had gained more than all the wages paid in sugar refining. But, on the side of the producers, it was found that 6,000 persons are employed and 45,000 tons of sugar are used annually in the neighborhood of London in manufacturing jam and confectionery. In Scotland there are eighty establishments, employing over 4,000 people and using 35,000 tons of sugar per annum in similar industries. In the whole United Kingdom, in those industries, 100,000 tons of sugar are used and 12,000 people are employed, three times as many as in sugar refining. Within twenty years the confectionery trade of Scotland has quadrupled and the preserving trade — jam and marmalade — has practically been originated. In addition, refined sugar is a raw material in biscuit making and the manufacture of mineral waters, and 50,000 tons are used in brewing and distilling. Hence the *Economist* argues (and this view seems to have controlled the decision): "It may be that the gain which we at present realize from the bounties may not be enduring, as it is impossible to believe that foreign nations will go on taxing themselves to the ex-

tent of several millions a year in order to supply us and others with sugar at less than its fair price, but that is no reason for refusing to avail ourselves of their liberality so long as it does last." [1]   (See § 83, note.)

82. One point in this case ought not to be lost sight of. If the English government had yielded to the sugar refiners without looking further, all these little industries which are mentioned, and which in their aggregate are so important, would have been crushed out. Ten years later they would have been forgotten. It is from such an example that one must learn to form a judgment as to *the effect of our tariff in crushing out industries* which are now lost and gone, and cannot even be recalled for purposes of controversy, but which would spring into existence again if the repeal of the taxes should give them a chance.

83. On our side the water efforts have been made to get us into the sugar struggle by the proposed commercial treaties with Spain and England, which would in effect have extended our protective tariff around Cuban and English West Indian sugar.[2] The sugar consumers of the United States were to pay to the Cuban planters the twenty-five million dollars revenue which they now pay to the treasury on Cuban sugar, on condition that the Cubans should bring back part of it and spend it among our manufacturers. It was a new extension of the plan of taxing some of us for the benefit of others of us. Let it be noticed, too, that when it suited their purpose, the protectionists were ready to sacrifice the sugar industry of Louisiana without the least concern. We have been trying for twenty-five years to secure the home market and keep

---

[1] *Economist*, 1884, p. 1052.

[2] A friend has sent me a report (Barbados *Agricultural Report*, April 24, 1885) of an indignation meeting at Bridgetown to protest because the English Government refused to ratify the commercial treaty with the United States. The islanders feel the competition of the "bounty-fed" sugar in the English market; a new complication, a new mischief.

everybody else out of it. *As soon as we get it firmly shut, so that nobody else can get in, we find that it is a question of life and death with us to get out ourselves.* The next device is to tax Americans in order to go and buy a piece of the foreign market. At the last session of Congress Senator Cameron proposed to allow a drawback on raw materials used in exported products. On that plan the American manufacturer would have two costs of production, one when he was working for the home market, and another much lower one when working for the foreign market. As it is now, the exports of manufactured products, of which so much boasting is heard, are for the most part articles sold abroad lower than here so as not to break down the home monopoly market. The proposed plan would raise that to a system, and we should be giving more presents to foreigners.

84. To return to sugar, our treaty with the Sandwich Islands has produced anomalous and mischievous results on the Pacific coast. In the southern Pacific New Zealand is just going into the plan of bounties and protection on sugar.[1] It would not, therefore, be very bold to predict a worldwide catastrophe in the sugar industry within five years.

85. Now what is it all for? What is it all about? Napoleon Bonaparte began it in a despotic whim, when he determined to force the production of beet-root sugar to show that he did not care for the supremacy of England at sea which cut him off from the sugar islands. In order not to lose the capital engaged in the industry, protection was continued. But this led to putting more capital into it and further need of protection. The problem has tormented financiers for seventy-five years. There are two natural products, of which the cane is far richer in sugar. But the processes of the beet-sugar industry have been

---

[1] *Economist*, Commercial Supplement, February 14, 1885, p. 7.

improved, until recently, far more rapidly than those of the cane industry. Then the refining is a separate interest. If, then, a country has cane-sugar colonies which it wants to protect against other colonies, and a beet-sugar industry which it wants to protect against neighbors who produce beet-sugar, and refiners to be protected against foreign refiners, and if the relations of its own colonial cane-sugar producers to its own domestic beet-sugar producers must be kept satisfactorily adjusted, in spite of changes in processes, transportation, and taxation, and if it wants to get a revenue from sugar, and to use the colonial trade to develop its shipping, and if it has two or three commercial treaties in which sugar is an important item, the statesman of that country has a task like that of a juggler riding several horses and keeping several balls in motion. Sugar is the commodity on which the effects of a world-embracing commerce, produced by modern inventions, are most apparent, and it is the commodity through which all the old protectionist anti-commercial doctrines will be brought to the most decisive test.

(C) Forced Foreign Relations to Regulate Improvement which can no Longer be Defeated.

86. If we turn back once more to our own case, we note the rise in 1883–1884 of the policy of commercial treaties and of a "vigorous foreign policy." For years a "national policy" for us has meant "securing the home market." The perfection of this policy has led to isolation and ostentatious withdrawal from cosmopolitan interests. I may say that I do not write out of any sympathy with vague humanitarianism or cosmopolitan sentiments. It seems to me that local groupings have great natural strength and obvious utility so long as they are subdivisions of a higher organization of the human race, or so long as they are

formed freely and their relations to each other are developed naturally. But now suddenly rises a clap-trap demand for a "national policy," which means that we shall force our way out of our tax-created isolation by diplomacy or war. The effort, however, is to be restrained carefully and arbitrarily to the western hemisphere, and we have anxiously disavowed any part or lot in the regulation of the Congo, although we shall certainly some day desire to take our share in the trade of that district. Our statesmen, however, if they are going to let us have any foreign trade, cannot bear to let us go and take it where we shall make most by it. They must draw *a priori* lines for it. They have taxed us in order to shut us up at home. This has killed the carrying trade, for, if we decided not to trade, what could the shippers find to do? Next ship-building perished, for if there was no carrying trade why build ships, especially when the taxes to protect manufactures were crushing ships and commerce? (§ 101.) Next the navy declined, for with no commerce to protect at sea, we need no navy. Next we lost the interest which we took thirty years ago in a canal across the isthmus, because we have now, under the no-trade policy, no use for it. Next diplomacy became a sinecure, for we have no foreign relations.

87. Now comes the "national policy," not because it is needed, but as an artificial and inflated piece of political bombast. We are to galvanize our diplomacy by contracting commercial treaties and meddling in foreign quarrels. No doubt this will speedily make a navy necessary. In fact our proposed "American policy" is only an old, cast-off, eighteenth-century, John Bull policy, which has forced England to keep up a big army, a big navy, heavy debt, heavy taxes, and a constant succession of little wars. Hence we shall be taxed some more to pay for a navy. Then it is proposed to tax us some more to pay for canals through

which the navy can go. Then we are to be taxed some
more to subsidize merchant ships to go through the canal.
Then we are to be taxed some more to subsidize voyages,
i.e., the carrying trade. Then we are to be taxed some
more to provide the ships with cargoes (§ 83).

88. All this time, the whole West Indian, Mexican, and
Central and South American trade is ours if we will only
stand out of the way and let it come. It is ours by all
geographical and commercial advantage, and would have
been ours since 1825 if we had but taken down the barriers.
Instead of that we propose to tax ourselves some more to
lift it over the barriers. Take the taxes off goods, let exchange go on, and the carrying trade comes as a consequence. If we have goods to carry, we shall build or buy
ships in which to carry them. If we have merchant ships,
we shall need and shall keep up a suitable navy. If we
need canals, we shall build them, as, in fact, private capital
is now building one and taking the risk of it. If we need
diplomacy we shall learn and practice diplomacy of the
democratic, peaceful, and commercial type.

89. Thus, under the philosophy of protectionism, the
very same thing, if it comes to us freely by the extension
of commérce and the march of improvement, is regarded
with terror, while, if we can first bar it out, and then only
let a little of it in at great cost and pains, it is a thing worth
fighting for. Such is the fallacy of all commercial treaties.
The crucial criticism on all the debates at Washington in
1884–1885 was: *Have these debaters made up their minds to*
any standard by which to measure what you get and what you
give under a commercial treaty? It was plain that they
had not. A generation of protectionism has taken away
the knowledge of what trade is (§§ 125, 139), and whence
its benefits arise, and has created a suspicion of trade
(§§ 63 ff.). Hence when our public men came to compare
what we should get and what we should give, they set

about measuring this by things which were entirely foreign
to it.   Scarcely two of them agreed as to the standards by
which to measure it.   Some thought that it was the number
of people in one country compared with the number in the
other.   Others thought that it was the amount sold to as
compared with the amount bought from the country in
question.   Others thought that it was the amount of
revenue to be sacrificed by us as compared with the amount
which would be sacrificed by the other party.   If any one
will try to establish a standard by which to measure the
gain by such a treaty to one party or the other, he will be
led to see the fallacy of the whole procedure.   The greatest gain to both would be if the trade were perfectly free.
If it is obstructed more or less, that is a harm to be corrected as far and as soon as possible.   If then either party
lowers its own taxes, that is a gain and a movement toward
the desirable state of things.   No state needs anybody's
permission to lower its own taxes, and entanglements
which would impair its fiscal independence would be a new
harm.[1]

[1] Since the above was in type, a report from the "South American Commission"
has been received and published. This Commission submitted certain propositions to the President of Chili on behalf of the United States. The report says:
"The second proposition involved the idea of a reciprocal commercial treaty
between the two countries under which special products of each should be admitted free of duty into the other when carried under the flag of either nation.
This did not meet with any greater favor with President Santa Maria, who was
not disposed to make reciprocity treaties. His people were at liberty to sell where
they could get the best prices and buy where goods were the cheapest. In his
opinion commerce was not aided by commercial treaties, and Chili neither asked
from nor gave to other nations especial favors. Trade would regulate itself, and
there was no advantage in trying to divert it in one direction or the other. So
far as the United States was concerned, there could be very little trade with Chili,
owing to the fact that the products of the two countries were almost identical.
Chili produced very little that we wanted, and although there were many industrial
products of the United States that were used in Chili, the merchants of the latter
country must be allowed to buy where they sold and where they could trade to
the greatest advantage. With reference to the provision that reduced duties

90. Protectionism, therefore, is at war with improvement. It is only useful to annul and offset the effects of those very improvements of which we boast. In time, the improvements win power so great that protectionism cannot withstand them. *Then it turns about and tries to control and regulate them at great expense by diplomacy or war.* The greater and more worldwide these improvements are, the more numerous are the efforts in different parts of the world to revive or extend protection. No doubt there is loss and inconvenience in the changes which improvement brings about. A notable case is the loss and inconvenience of a laborer where a machine is first introduced to supplant him. Patient endurance and hope, in the confidence that he will in the end be better off, has long been preached to him. It is true that he will be better off; but why not apply the same doctrine in connection with the other inconveniences of improvement, where it is equally true?

3. *PROTECTION LOWERS WAGES*

91. On a pure wages system, that is, where there is a class who have no capital and no land, wages are determined by supply and demand of labor. The demand for labor is measured by the capital in hand to pay for it just as the demand for anything else is measured by the supply of goods offered in exchange for it. In Cobden's language: "When two men are after one boss, wages are low; when two bosses are after one man, wages are high."

should be allowed only upon goods carried in Chilian or American vessels, he said that Chili did not want any such means to encourage her commerce: her ports were open to all the vessels of the world upon an equality, and none should have especial privileges." — (N. Y. *Times*, July 3, 1885.)

If this is a fair specimen of the political and economic enlightenment which prevails at the other end of the American Continent, it is a great pity that the "Commission" is not a great deal larger. They are like the illiterate missionaries who found themselves unawares in a theological seminary. We would do well to send our whole Congress out there.

(*A*) No True Wages Class in the United States.

92. The United States, however, have never yet been on a pure wages system because there is no class which has no land or cannot get any. In fact, the cheapening of transportation which is going on is making the land of this continent, Australia, and Africa available for the laborers of Europe, and is breaking down the wages system there. This is the real reason for the rise of the proletariat and the expansion of democracy which are generally attributed to metaphysical, sentimental, or political causes. A man who has no capital and no land cannot live from day to day except by getting a share in the capital of others in return for services rendered. In an old society or dense population, such a class comes into existence. It has no reserves; no other chances; no other resource. In a new country no such class exists. The land is to be had for going to it. On the stage of agriculture which is there existing very little capital and very little division of labor are necessary. Hence he who has only unskilled manual strength can get at and use the land, and he can get out of it an abundant supply of the rude primary comforts of existence for himself and his family. If it is made so cheap and easy to get from the old centers of population to the new land that the lowest class of laborers can save enough to pay the passage, then the effect will reach the labor market of the old countries also. Such is now the fact.

93. The weakness of a true wages class is in the fact that they have no other chance. Obviously, however, *a man is well off in this world in proportion to the chances which he can command.* The advantage of education is that it multiplies a man's chances. *Our* noncapitalists have another chance on the land, and the chance is near and easy to grasp and use. It is not necessary that all or any number should use it. Every one who uses it leaves more room behind,

lessens the supply and competition of labor, and helps his class as a class. The other chance which the laborer possesses is also a *good* one, and consequently sets the minimum of unskilled wages high. Here we have the reason for high wages in a new country.

94. The relation of things was distinctly visible in the early colonial days. Winthrop tells how the General Court in Massachusetts Bay tried to fix the wages of artisans by law. It is obvious that artisans were in great demand to build houses, and that they would not work at their trades unless the wages would buy as good or better living than the farmers could get out of the ground, for these artisans could go and take up land and be farmers too. The only effect of the law was that the artisans "went West" to the valley of the Connecticut, and the law became a dead letter. The same equilibration between the gains from the new land and the wages of artisans and laborers has been kept up ever since.

95. In 1884 an attempt was made to unite the Eastern and Western Iron Associations for common effort in behalf of higher wages. The union could not be formed because the Eastern and Western Associations *never had had the same rate of wages*. The latter, being farther west, where the supply of labor is smaller and the land nearer, have obtained higher wages. It may be well to anticipate a little right here in order to point out that this difference in wages has not prevented the growth of the industry in the West, and has not made competition in a common market impossible.[1] The fact is of the first importance to controvert the current assumption of the protectionists. They say that an industry cannot be carried on in one place if the wages there are higher than must be paid by somebody in the same industry in another place. This

[1] This is the case for which the *Inter-Ocean* proposed the remedy described in § 71 note.

proposition has no foundation in fact at all. Farm laborers in Iowa get three times the wages of farm laborers in England. The products of the former pay 5,000 miles transportation, and then drive out the products of the latter. Wages are only one element, and often they are far from being the most important element, in the economy of production. *The wages which are paid to the men who make an article have nothing to do with the price or value of that article.* This proposition, I know, has a startling effect on the people who hold to the monkish notions of political economy, but it is only a special case of the theorem that *"Labor which is past has no effect on value,"* which is the true cornerstone of any sound political economy. Wages are determined by the supply and demand of labor. Value is determined by the supply and demand of the commodity. These two things have no connection. Wages are one element in the capitalist's outlay for production. If the total outlay in one line of production, when compared with the return obtained in that line, is not as advantageous as the total outlay in another line when compared with the return available in the second line, then the capital is withdrawn from the first line and put into the second; but the rate of wages in either case or any case is the market rate, determined by the supply and demand of labor, for that is what the employers must pay if they want the men, whether they are making any profits or not.

96. The facts and economic principles just stated above show plainly why wages are high, and put in strong light the assertion of the protectionists that their device makes wages high (§ 47), that is, higher than they would be otherwise, or higher here than they are in Europe. Wages are not arbitrary. They cannot be shifted up and down at anybody's whim. They are controlled by ultimate causes. If not, then what has made them fall during the last eighteen months, ten to forty per cent, most in the most pro-

tected industries (§ 26)?   Why are they highest in the least
protected and the unprotected industries, *e.g.*, the building trades?   Hod-carriers recently struck in New York for
three dollars for nine hours' work.   Where did the tariff
touch their case?   *Why does not the tariff prevent the fall in
wages?*   It is all there, and now is the time for it to come
into operation, if it can keep wages up.   Now it is needed.
When wages were high in the market, and it was not
needed, it claimed the credit.   Now when they fall and it is
needed, it is powerless.

97. Wages are capital.   If I promise to pay wages I
must find capital somewhere with which to fulfill my contract.   If the tariff makes me pay more than I otherwise
would, where does the surplus come from?   Disregarding
money as only an intermediate term, a man's wages are his
means of subsistence — food, clothing, house rent, fuel,
lights, furniture, etc.   If the tariff system makes him get
more of these for ten hours' work in a shop than he would
get without tariff, *where does the "more" come from?*   Nothing but labor and capital can produce food, clothing, etc.
Either the tax must make these out of nothing, or it can
only get them by taking them from those who have made
them, that is by subtracting them from the wages of somebody else.   Taking all the wages class into account, then
the tax cannot possibly increase, but is sure by waste and
loss to decrease wages.

(B) How Taxes Do Act on Wages.

98. If taxes are to raise wages they must be laid not on
goods but on men.   Let the goods be abundant and the
men scarce.   Then the average wages will be high, for the
supply of labor will be small and the demand great.   If
we tax goods and not men, the supply of labor will be great,
the demand will be limited, and the wages will be low.

Here we see why employers of labor want a tariff. For it is an obvious inconsistency and a most grotesque satire that the same men should tell the workmen at home that the tariff makes wages high, and should go to Washington and tell Congress that they want a tariff because the wages are too high. We have found that the high wages of American laborers have independent causes and guarantees, outside of legislation. They are provided and maintained by the economic circumstances of the country. This is against the interest of those who want to hire the laborers. No device can serve their interest unless it lowers wages. From the standpoint of an employer the fortunate circumstances of the laborer become an obstacle to be overcome (§ 65). The laborer is too well off. Nothing can do any good which does not make him less well off. The competition which troubles the employer is not the "pauper labor" of Europe.

99. "Pauper labor" had a meaning in the first half of this century, in England, when the overseers of the poor turned over the younger portion of the occupants of the poorhouses to the owners of the new cotton factories, under contracts to teach them the trade and pay them a pittance. Of course the arrangement had shocking evils connected with it, but it was a transition arrangement. The "pauper laborers'" children, after a generation, became independent laborers; the system expired of itself, and "pauper laborer" is now a senseless jingle.

100. The competition which the employers fear *is the competition of those industries in America which can pay the high wages and which keep the wages high because they do pay them.* These draw the laborer away. These offer him another chance. If he had no other way of earning more than he is earning, it would be idle for him to demand more. The reason why he demands more and gets it is because he knows where he can get it, if he cannot get it

where he is. If, then, he is to be brought down, the only way to do it is *to destroy, or lessen the value of, his other chance.* This is just what the tariff does.

101. The taxes which are laid for protection must come out of somebody. As I have shown (§§ 32 ff.) the protected interests give and take from each other, but, if they as a group win anything, they must win from another group, and that other group must be the industries which are not and cannot be protected. In England these were formerly manufactures and they were taxed, under the corn laws, for the benefit of agriculture. In the United States, of course, the case must be complementary and opposite. We tax agriculture and commerce to benefit manufactures. Commerce, *i.e.*, the ship-building and carrying trade, has been crushed out of existence by the burden (§ 86). But the burden thus thrown on agriculture and commerce lowers the gains of those industries, lessens the attractiveness of them to the laborer, lessens the value of the laborer's other chance, lessens the competition of other American industries with manufacturing, and so, by taking away from the blessing which God and nature have given to the American laborer, enable the man who wants to hire his services to get them at a lower rate. The effect of taxes is just the same as such a percentage taken from the fertility of the soil, the excellence of the climate, the power of tools, or the industrious habits of the people. Hence it reduces the average comfort and welfare of the population, and with that average comfort it carries down the wages of such persons as work for wages.

(*C*) Perils of Statistics, Especially of Wages.

102. Any student of statistics will be sure to have far less trust in statistics than the uninitiated entertain. The bookkeepers have taught us that figures will not lie, but

that they will tell very queer stories. Statistics will not lie, but they will play wonderful tricks with a man who does not understand their dialect. The unsophisticated reader finds it difficult, when a column of statistics is offered to him, to resist the impression that they must prove *something*. The fact is that a column of statistics hardly ever proves anything. It is a popular opinion that anybody can use or understand statistics. The fact is that a special and high grade of skill is required to appreciate the effect of the collateral circumstances under which the statistics were obtained, to appreciate the limits of their application, and to interpret their significance. The statistics which are used to prove national prosperity are an illustration of this, for they are used as absolute measures when it is plain that they have no use except for a comparison. Sometimes the other term of the comparison is not to be found and it is always ignored (§ 52).

103. A congressional committee in the winter of 1883–1884, dealing with the tariff, took up the census and proceeded to reckon up the wages in steel production by adding all the wages from the iron mine up. Then they took bar iron and added all the wages from the bottom up again, in order to find the importance of the wages element in that, and so on with every stage of iron industry. They were going to add in the same wages six or eight times over.

104. The statistics of comparative wages which are published are of no value at all.[1] It is not known how, or by whom, or from what selected cases, they were collected. It is not known how wide, or how long, or how thorough was the record from which they were taken. The facts about various classifications of labor in the division of labor, and about the rate at which machinery is run, or about the allowances of one kind and another which vary from mill

---

[1] I except those of Mr. Carroll Wright. He has sufficiently stated of how slight value his are.

to mill and town to town are rarely specified at all. Protected employers are eager to tell the wages they pay per day or week, which are of no importance. The only statistics which would be of any use for the comparison which is attempted would be such as show the proportion of wages to total cost per unit. Even this comparison would not have the force which is attributed to the other. Hence the statistics offered are worthless or positively misleading. In the nature of the case such statistics are extremely hard to get. If application is made to the employers, the inquiry concerns their private business. They have no interest in answering. They cannot answer without either spending great labor on their books (if the inquiry covers a period), or surrendering their books to some one else, if they allow him to do the labor. If inquiry is made of the men, it becomes long and tedious and full of uncertainties. Do United States Consuls take the trouble involved in such an inquiry? Have they the training necessary to conduct it successfully?

105. The fact is generally established and is not disputed that wages are higher here than in Europe. The difference is greatest on the lowest grade of labor — manual labor, unskilled labor. The difference is less on higher grades of labor. For what the English call "engineers," men who possess personal dexterity and creative power, the difference is the other way, if we compare the United States and England. The returns of immigration reflect these differences exactly (§ 122, note). The great body of the immigrants consists of farmers and laborers. The "skilled laborers" are comparatively a small class, and, if the claims of the individuals to be what they call themselves were tested by English or German trade standards, the number would be very small indeed. Engineers emigrate from Germany to England. Men of that class rarely come to this country, or, if they come, they come under special con-

tracts, or soon return. Each country, spite of all taxes and other devices, gets the class of men for which its industrial condition offers the best chances. The only thing the tariff does in the matter is to take from those who have an advantage here a part of that advantage.

4. *PROTECTIONISM IS SOCIALISM*

106. Simply to give protectionism a bad name would be to accomplish very little. When I say that protectionism is socialism I mean to classify it and bring it not only under the proper heading but into relation with its true affinities. *Socialism is any device or doctrine whose aim is to save individuals from any of the difficulties or hardships of the struggle for existence and the competition of life by the intervention of "the State."* Inasmuch as "the State" never is or can be anything but some other people, socialism is a device for making some people fight the struggle for existence for others. The devices always have a doctrine behind them which aims to show why this *ought* to be done.

107. The protected interests demand that they be saved from the trouble and annoyance of business competition, and that they be assured profits in their undertakings, by "the State," that is, at the expense of their fellow-citizens. If this is not socialism, then there is no such thing. If employers may demand that "the State" shall guarantee them profits, why may not the employees demand that "the State" shall guarantee them wages? If we are taxed to provide profits, why should we not be taxed for public workshops, for insurance to laborers, or for any other devices which will give wages and save the laborer from the annoyances of life and the risks and hardships of the struggle for existence? The "we" who are to pay changes all the time, and the turn of the protected employer to pay will surely come before long. The plan of all living on each

other is capable of great expansion. It is, as yet, far from being perfected or carried out completely. The protectionists are only educating those who are as yet on the "paying" side of it, but who will certainly use political power to put themselves also on the "receiving" side of it. The argument that "the State" must do something for me because my business does not pay, is a very far-reaching argument. If it is good for pig iron and woolens, it is good for all the things to which the socialists apply it.

Chapter IV

SUNDRY FALLACIES OF PROTECTIONISM

108. I can now dispose rapidly of a series of current fallacies put forward by the protectionists. They generally are fanciful or far-fetched attempts to show some equivalent which the taxpayer gets for his taxes.

(A) That Infant Industries can be Nourished up to Independence and that they then Become Productive.

109. I know of no case where this hope has been realized, although we have been trying the experiment for nearly a century. The weakest infants to-day are those whom Alexander Hamilton set out to protect in 1791. As soon as the infants begin to get any strength (if they ever do get any) the protective system forces them to bear the burden of other infants, and so on forever. The system superinduces hydrocephalus on the infants, and instead of ever growing to maturity, the longer they live, the bigger babies they are. It is the system which makes them so, and on its own plan it can never rationally be expected to have any other effect. (See further, under the next fallacy, §§ 111 ff.)

110. Mill [1] makes a statement of a case, as within the bounds of conceivability, where there might be an advantage for a young country to protect an infant industry. He is often quoted without regard to the limitation of his statement, as if he had affirmed the general expediency of protection in new countries and for infant industries. It amounts to a misquotation to quote him without regard to the limitations which he specified. The statement which he did make is mathematically demonstrable.[2] The doctrine so developed is very familiar in private enterprise. A business enterprise may be started which for some years will return no profits or will occasion losses, but which is expected later to recoup all these. *What are the limits within which such an enterprise can succeed?* It must either call for sinking capital only for a short period (like building a railroad or planting an orange grove), or it must promise enormous gains after it is started (like a patented novelty). The higher the rate of interest, as in any new country, the more stringent and narrow these conditions are. Mill said that it was conceivable that a case of an industry might occur in which this same calculation might be applied to a protective tax. If, then, anybody says that he can offer an industry which meets the conditions, let it be examined to see if it does so. If protection is never applied until such a case is offered, it will never be applied at all. A thing which is mathematically conceivable is one which is not absurd; but a thing which is practically possible is quite another thing. For myself, I strenuously dissent from Mill's doctrine even as he limits it. In the first place the state cannot by taxes work out an industrial enterprise of a character such that it, as any one can see, *demands the most intense and careful oversight by persons whose capital is*

---

[1] Bk. V, ch. 10, § 1.

[2] It has been developed mathematically by a French mathematician (*Journal des Economistes*, August and September, 1873, pp. 285 and 464).

at stake in it, and, in the second place, the state would bear
the loss, while it lasted, but private interests would take
the gain after it began.

(B) THAT PROTECTIVE TAXES DO NOT RAISE PRICES BUT LOWER PRICES.

111. To this it is obvious to reply: what good can they
then do toward the end proposed? Still it is true that,
under circumstances, protective taxes do lower prices. The
protectionist takes an infant industry in hand and proposes
to rear it by putting on taxes to ward off competition, and
by giving it more profits than the world's market price
would give. This raises the price. But the consumer then
raises a complaint. The protectionist turns to him and
promises that by and by there will be "overproduction,"
and prices will fall. This arrives in due time, for every
protected industry is organized as a more or less limited
monopoly, and a monopoly which has overproduced its
market, *at the price which it wants*, is the weakest industry
possible (§ 24). The consumer now wins, but a wail from
the cradle calls the protectionist back to the infant industry, which is in convulsions from "overproduction." Some
of the infants die. This gives a new chance to the others.
They combine for more effective monopoly, put the prices
up again by limiting production, and go on until "overproduction" produces a new collapse. This is another
reason why infants never win vitality. The net result is
that the market is in constant alternations of stringency
and laxity, and nothing at all is gained.

112. Whenever we talk of prices *it should be noticed that
our statements involve money* — the rate at which goods
exchange for money. If then we want to raise prices, we
must *restrict the supply* of goods, so that on the doctrine of
money also we shall come to the same result as before, that
protective taxes lessen production and diminish wealth.

113. The problem of managing any monopoly is to dose the market with just the quantity which it will take at the price which the monopolist wants to get. In a qualified monopoly, that is, one which is shared by a number of persons, the difficulty is to get agreement about the management. They may not have any communication with each other and may compete. If so they will overdose the market and the price will fall. Then they meet, to establish communication; form an "association," to get harmonious action, and agree to divide the production among them and limit and regulate it, to prevent the former mistake and restore prices (§ 24).

(C) That we should be a Purely Agricultural Nation under Free Trade.

114. A purely agricultural nation covering a territory as large as that of the United States is inconceivable. The distribution of industries now *inside* the United States is a complete proof that no such thing would come to pass, for we have absolute free trade inside, and manufactures are growing up in the agricultural states just as fast as circumstances favor, and just as fast as they can be profitably carried on. Under free trade there would be a subdivision of cotton, woolen, iron and other industries, and we should both export and import different varieties and qualities of these goods. The southern states are now manufacturing coarse cottons in competition with New England. The western states manufacture coarse woolens, certain grades of leather and iron goods, etc., in competition with the East. Here we see the exact kind of differentiation which would take place under free trade, and we can see the mischief of the tariff, whether on the one hand it strikes a whole category with the same brutal ignorance, or tries, by cunning sub-classification, to head off every effort to

save itself which the trade makes.[1] If, however, it was conceivable that we should become a purely agricultural nation, the only legitimate inference would be that our whole population could be better supported in that way than in any other. If there was a greater profit in something else some of them would go into it.

(D) That Communities which Manufacture are More Prosperous than those which are Agricultural.

115. This is as true as if it should be said that all tall men are healthy. It would be answered that some are and some are not; that tallness and health have no connection. Some manufacturing communities are prosperous and some not. The self-contradiction of protectionism appears in one of its boldest forms in this fallacy. We are told that manufactures are a special blessing. The protectionist says that he is going to give us some. Instead of that he makes new demands on us, lays a new burden on us, gives us nothing but more taxes. He promises us an income and increases our expenditure; promises an asset and gives a liability; promises a gift and creates a debt; promises a blessing and gives a burden. The very thing which he boasts of as a great and beneficial advantage gives us nothing, but takes from us more. Prosperity is no more connected with one form of industry than another. If it were so, some of mankind would have, by nature, a permanently better chance than others, and no one could emigrate to a new, that is agricultural country, without injuring his interests. The world is not made so.

[1] See a fallacy under this head: Cunningham, "Growth of English Industry," 410, note.

(*E*) THAT IT IS AN OBJECT TO DIVERSIFY INDUSTRY, AND THAT NATIONS WHICH HAVE VARIOUS INDUSTRIES ARE STRONGER THAN OTHERS WHICH HAVE NOT VARIOUS INDUSTRIES.

116. It is not an object to diversify industry, but to multiply and diversify our satisfactions, comforts, and enjoyments. If we can do this by unifying our industry, in greater measure than by diversifying it, then we should do, and we will do, the former. It is not a question to be decided *a priori*, but depends upon economic circumstances. If a country has a supremacy in some one industry it will have only one. California and Australia had only one industry until the gold mines declined in productiveness, that is, until their supreme advantage over other countries was diminished: they began to diversify when they began to be less well off. The oil region of Pennsylvania has a chance of three industries, the old farming industry, coal, and oil. It will have only one industry so long as oil gives chances superior to those enjoyed by any other similar district. When it loses its unique advantage by nature it will diversify. The "strongest" nation is the one which brings products into the world's market which are of high demand, but which cost it little toil and sacrifice to get; for it will then have command of all the good things which men can get on earth at little effort to itself. Whether the products which it offers are one or numerous is immaterial. All the tariff has to do with it is that when the American comes into the world's market with wheat, cotton, tobacco, and petroleum, all objects of high demand by mankind and little cost to him, it forces him to forego a part of his due advantage (§§ 125, 134).

(F) That Manufactures Give Value to Land.

117. This doctrine issued from the Agricultural Bureau. It has been thought a grand development of the protectionist argument. It is a simple logical fallacy based on some misconstrued statistics. The value of land depends on supply and demand. The demand for land is population. Hence where the population is dense the value of land is great. Manufactures can be carried on only where there is a supply of labor, that is, where the population is dense. Hence high value of land and manufacturing industry are common results of dense population. The statistician of the Agricultural Bureau connected them with each other as cause and effect, and the New York *Tribune* said that it was the grandest contribution to political economy since "the fingers of Horace Greeley stiffened in death"; which was true.

118. If manufactures spring up spontaneously out of original strength, and by independent development, of course they "add value to land," that is to say, the district has new industrial power and every interest in it is benefited; but if the manufactures have to be protected, paid for, and supported, they do not do any good as manufactures but only as a device for drawing capital from elsewhere, as tribute. In this way, protective taxes do alter the comparative value of land in different districts. This effect can be seen under some astonishing phases in Connecticut and other manufacturing states. The farmers are taxed to hire some people to go and live in manufacturing villages and carry on manufacturing there. This displacement of population, brought about at the expense of the rural population, diminishes the value of agricultural land and raises that of city land right here within the same state. The hillside population is being impoverished, and the hillside farms are being abandoned on account of the

tribute levied on them to swell the value of mill sites and adjoining land in the manufacturing towns (§§ 120, 137).

(G) That the Farmer, if he Pays Taxes to Bring into Existence a Factory, which would not otherwise Exist, will Win more than the Taxes by Selling Farm Produce to the Artisans.

119. This is an arithmetical fallacy. It proposes to get three pints out of a quart. The farmer is out for the tax and the farm produce and he can not get back more than the tax because, if the factory owes its existence to the protective taxes, it cannot make any profit outside of the taxes. The proposition to the farmer is that he shall pay taxes to another man who will bring part of the tax back to buy produce with it. This is to make the farmer rich. The man who owned stock in a railroad and who rode on it, paying his fare, in the hope of swelling his own dividends, was wise compared with a farmer who believes that protection can be a source of gain to him.

120. Since, as I have shown (§ 101), protective taxes act like a reduction in the fertility of the soil, they lower the "margin of cultivation," and raise rent. They do not, however, raise it in favor of the agricultural land owner, for, by the displacement just described, they take away from him to give to the town land owner. Of course, I do not believe that the protective taxes have really lowered the margin of cultivation in this country, for they have not been able to offset the greater richness of the newest land, and the advance in the arts. What protection costs us comes out of the exuberant bounty of nature to us. Still I know of very few who could not stand it to be a great deal better off than they are, and the New England farmer is the one who has the least chance, and the fewest advantages, with which to endure protection.

(*H*) That Farmers Gain by Protection, because it Draws so many Laborers out of Competition with them.

121. Since the farmers pay the taxes by which this operation is supposed to be produced, a simple question is raised, *viz.*, how much can one afford to pay to buy off competition in his business? He cannot afford to pay anything unless he has a monopoly which he wants to consolidate. Our farmers are completely open to competition on every side. The immigration of farmers every three or four years exceeds all the workers in all the protected trades. Hence the farmers, if they take the view which is recommended to them, instead of gaining any ground, are face to face with a task which gets bigger and bigger the longer they work at it. If one man should support another in order to get rid of the latter's competition as a producer, that would be the case where the taxpayer supports soldiers, idle pensioners, paupers, etc. A protected manufacturer, however, by the hypothesis, is not simply supported in idleness, but he is carrying on a business the losses of which must be paid by those who buy off his competition in their own production. On the other hand, when farmers come to market, they are in free competition with several other sources of supply. Hence, if they did any good to agricultural industry by hiring the artisans to go out of competition with them, they would have to share the gain with all their competitors the world over while paying all the expense of it themselves.

122. The movement of men over the earth and the movement of goods over the earth are complementary operations. Passports to stop the men and taxes to stop the goods would be equally legitimate. Since it is, once for all, a fact that some parts of the earth have advantages for one thing and other parts for other things, men avail

themselves of the local advantages either by moving themselves to the places, or by trading what they produce where they are for what others produce in the other places. The passenger trains and the freight trains are set in motion by the same ultimate economic fact. Our exports are all bulky and require more tonnage than our imports. On the westward trip, consequently, bunks are erected and men are brought in space where cotton, wheat, etc., were taken out. The tariff, by so much as it lessens the import of goods, leaves room which the ship owners are eager to fill with immigrants. To do this they lower the rates. Hence the tariff is a premium on immigration. The protectionists have claimed that the tariff does favor immigration. But nine-tenths of the immigrants are laborers, domestic servants, and farmers.[1] Probably more than one-third of the total number, including women, find their way to the land. As we have seen, the tariff also lowers the profits of agriculture, which discourages immigration and the movement to the land. Therefore, if the farmer believes what the protectionist tells him, he must understand that the taxes he pays bring in more people, and raise the value of land by settling it, and that they also bring more competition, which the farmer must buy off by lowering the profits of his own (the farming) industry. Then, too, so far as the immigrants are artisans, the premium on immigration is a tax paid to increase the supply of labor, that is,

[1] IMMIGRATION IN 1884

	Males	Females	Total
Professional occupations	2,184	100	2,284
Skilled occupations	50,905	4,156	55,061
Occupations not stated	19,778	11,887	31,665
No occupation	75,483	169,904	245,387
Miscellaneous occupations	160,159	24,036	184,195
Total	308,509	210,083	518,592

Under miscellaneous were 106,478 laborers and 42,050 farmers.

to lower wages, although the protectionists say that the tariff raises wages. Hence we see that when a tax is laid, in our modern complicated society, instead of being a simple and easy means or method to be employed for a specific purpose, its action and reaction on transportation, land, wages, etc., will produce erratic, contradictory, and confused effects, which cannot be predicted or analyzed thoroughly, and the protectionist, when he pleads three or four arguments for his system, is alleging three or four features of it which, if properly analyzed and brought together, are found to be mutually destructive, and cumulative only as to the mischief they do (see §§ 29, 101).

(I) THAT OUR INDUSTRIES WOULD PERISH WITHOUT PROTECTION.

123. Those who say this think only of manufacturing establishments as "industries." They also talk of "our" industries. They mean those we support by the taxes we pay; not those from which we get dividends. No industry will ever be given up except in order to take up a better one, and if, under free trade, any of our industries should perish, it would only be because the removal of restrictions enabled some other industry to offer so much better rewards that labor and capital would seek the latter. It is plain that, if a man does not know of any better way to earn his living than the one in which he is, he must remain in that, or move to some other place. If any one can suppose that the population of the United States could be forced, by free trade, to move away, he must suppose that this country cannot support its population, and that we made a mistake in coming here. This argument is especially full of force if the articles to be produced are coal, iron, wool, copper, timber, or any other primary products of the soil. For, if it is said that we cannot raise these products of the

soil in competition with some other part of the earth's surface, all it proves is that we have come to the wrong spot
to seek them. If, however, the soil can support the population under an arrangement by which certain industries
support themselves, and those which do not pay besides,
then it is plain that the former are really supporting the
whole population — part directly and part indirectly,
through a circuitous and wasteful organization. Hence
the same strong and independent industries could certainly still better support the whole population, if they
supported it directly.

124. I have been asked whether we should have had
any steel works in this country, if we had had no protection.
I reply that I do not know; neither does anybody else, but
it is certain that we should have had a great deal more steel,
if we had had no protection.

125. "But," it is said, "we should import everything."
Should we import everything and give nothing? If so,
foreigners would make us presents and support us. Should
we give equal value in exchange? If so, there would be just
as much "industry" and a great deal less "work" in that
way of getting things than in making them ourselves. The
moment that ceased to be true we should make and not
buy. Suppose that a district, A, has two million inhabitants, one million of whom produce a million bushels of
wheat, and one million produce a million hundredweight
of iron; and suppose that a bushel of wheat exchanges for
a hundredweight of iron. Now, by improved transportation and emigration, suppose that a new wheat country, B,
is opened, and that its people bring wheat to the first district, offering two bushels for a hundredweight of iron.
Plainly they must offer more than one bushel for one hundredweight, or it is useless for them to come. Now the
people of A, by putting all their labor and capital in iron
production, produce two million hundredweight. They

keep one million hundredweight, and exchange one million hundredweight of iron for two million bushels of wheat. The destruction of their wheat industry is a sign of a change in industry (unifying and not diversifying) by which they have gained a million bushels of wheat. Such is the gain of all trade. If the gain did not exist, trade would not be a feature of civilization.

(*J*) THAT IT WOULD BE WISE TO CALL INTO EXISTENCE VARIOUS INDUSTRIES, EVEN AT AN EXPENSE, IF WE COULD THUS OFFER EMPLOYMENT TO ALL KINDS OF ARTISANS, ETC., WHO MIGHT COME TO US.

126. This would be only maintaining public workshops at the expense of the taxpayers, and would be open to all the objections which are conclusive against public workshops. The expense would be prodigious, and the return little or nothing. This argument shows less sense of comparative cost and gain than any other which is ever proposed.

(*K*) THAT WE WANT TO BE COMPLETE IN OURSELVES AND SUFFICIENT TO OURSELVES, AND INDEPENDENT, AS A NATION, WHICH STATE OF THINGS WILL BE PRODUCED BY PROTECTION.

127. I will only refer to what I have already said about China and Japan (§ 69) as types of what this plan produces. If a number of families from among us should be shipwrecked on an island, their greatest woe would be that they could not trade with the rest of the world. They might live there "self-contained" and "independent," fulfilling the ideal of happiness which this proposition offers, but they would look about them to see a surfeit of things which, as they know, their friends at home would like to

have, and they would think of all the old comforts which
they used to have, and which they could not produce on
their island. They might be contented to live on there
and make it their home, if they could exchange the former
things for the latter. If now a ship should chance that
way and discover them and should open communication
and trade between them and their old home, a protectionist
philosopher would say to them: "You are making a great
mistake. You ought to make everything for yourselves.
The wise thing to do would be to isolate yourselves again
by taxes as soon as possible." We sent some sages to the
Japanese to induct them into the ways of civilization, who,
as a matter of fact, did tell them that the first step in civilization was to adopt a protective tariff and shut up again
by taxes the very ports which they had just opened.

(L) That Protective Taxes are Necessary to Prevent a Foreign Monopoly from Getting Control of
our Market.

128. It is said that English manufacturers once combined to lower prices in order to kill out American manufactures, and that they then put up their prices to monopoly
rates. If they did this, why did not their other customers
send to the United States and buy the goods here in the
first instance, and why did not the Americans go and buy
the goods of the Englishmen's other customers in the second
instance? If the Englishmen put down their prices for their
whole market in the first instance, why did they not incur
a great loss? and, if they raised it for their whole market
in the second instance, why did they not yield the entire
market to their competitors? The Englishmen are said
to be wonderfully shrewd, and are here credited with the
most stupid and incredible folly.

129. The protective system puts us certainly in the

hands of a home monopoly for fear of the impossible chance
that we may fall into the hands of a foreign monopoly.
Before the war we made no first quality thread. We got
it at four cents a spool (retail) of an English monopoly.
Under the tariff we were saved from this by being put into
the hands of a home monopoly which charged five cents
a spool. In the meantime the foreign monopoly lowered
thread to three cents a spool (retail) for the Canadians,
who were at its mercy. Lest we should have to buy nickel
of a foreign monopolist, Congress forced us to buy it of the
owner of the only mine in the United States, and added
thirty cents a pound to any price the foreigner might ask.

(*M*) That Free Trade is Good in Theory but Impossible in Practice; that it would be a Good Thing if
All Nations would have it.

130. That a thing can be true in theory and false in practice is the most utter absurdity that human language can
express. For, if a thing is true in practice (protectionism,
for instance) the theory of its truth can be found, and that
theory will be true. But it was admitted that free trade
is true in theory. Hence two things which are contradictory would both be true at the same time about the same
thing. The fact is, that *protectionism is totally impracticable*. It does not work as it is expected to work; it does not
produce any of the results which were promised from it;
it is never properly and finally established to the satisfaction of its own votaries. They cannot let it alone. They
always want to "correct inequalities," or revise it one way
or another. It was they who got up the Tariff Commission
of 1882. Their system is not capable of construction so
as to furnish a normal and regular status for industry. One
of them said that the tariff would be all right if it could only
be made stable; another said that it ought to be revised

every two years. One said that it ought to include everything; another said that it would be good "if it was only
laid on the right things."

131. If all nations had free trade, no one of them would
have any special gain from it, just as, if all men were honest,
honesty would have no commercial value. Some say that
a man cannot afford to be honest unless everybody is honest. The truth is that, if there was one honest man among
a lot of cheats, his character and reputation would reach
their maximum value. So the nation which has free trade
when the others do not have it gains the most by comparison with them. It gains while they impoverish themselves.
If all had free trade all would be better off, but then no one
would profit from it more than others. If this were not
true, if the man who first sees the truth and first acts wisely
did not get a special premium for it, the whole moral order
of the universe would have to be altered, for no reform or
improvement could be tried until unanimous consent was
obtained. If a man or a nation does right, the rewards of
doing right are obtained. They are not as great as could
be obtained if all did right, but they are greater than those
enjoy who still do wrong.

(N) That Trade is WAR, so that Free Trade Methods
    are Unfit for it, and that Protective Taxes are
    Suited to it.

132. It is evidently meant by this that trade involves a
struggle or contest of competition. It might, however, as
well be said that practicing law is war, because it is con-
tentious; or that practicing medicine is war, because doctors are jealous rivals of each other. The protectionists do,
however, always seem to think of trade as commercial war.
One of them was reported to have said in a speech, in the
late campaign, that nations would not fight any more with

guns but with taxes. The nations are to boycott each
other. One would think that the experience our Southerners made of that notion in the Civil War, upon which they
entered in the faith that "cotton is king," would have
sufficed to banish forever that antique piece of imbecility,
a commercial war. If trade is war, all the tariff can do
about it is to make A fight B's battles, although A has his
own battles to fight besides.

(O) That Protection Brings into Employment Labor
and Capital which would otherwise be Idle.

133. If there is any labor or capital which is idle, that
fact is a symptom of industrial disease; especially is this
true in the United States. If a laborer is idle he is in danger
of starving to death. If capital is idle it is producing nothing to its owner, who depends on it, and is suffering loss.
Therefore, if labor or capital is idle, some antecedent error
or folly must have produced a stoppage in the industrial
organization. The cure is, not to lay some more taxes, but
to find the error and correct it. If then things are in their
normal and healthy condition, the labor and capital of the
country are employed as far as possible under the existing
organization. We are constantly trying to improve our
exchange and credit systems so as to keep all our capital
all the time employed. Such improvements are important
and valuable, but to make them cost more thought and
skillful labor than to invent machines. Hence Congress
cannot do that work by discharging a volley of taxes at
selected articles, and leaving those taxes to find out the
proper points to affect, and to exert the proper influence.
It takes intelligent and hard-working men to do it. The
faith that anything else can do it is superstition.

(P) That a Young Nation Needs Protection and will Suffer some Disadvantage in Free Exchange with an Old One.

134. The younger a nation is the more important trade is to it (cf. §§ 127 ff.). The younger a nation is the more it wins by trade, for it offers food and raw materials which are objects of greatest necessity to old nations. The things England buys of us are far more essential to her than what she buys of France or Germany. The strong party in an exchange is not the rich party, or the old party, but the one who is favored by supply and demand — the one who brings to the exchange the thing which is more rare and more eagerly wanted.[1] If a poor woman went into Stewart's store to buy a yard of calico, she did not have to pay more because Stewart was rich. She paid less because he used his capital to serve her better and at less price than anybody else could. England takes 60 per cent of all our exports. We sell, first, wheat and provisions, prime articles of food; second, cotton, the most important raw material now used by mankind; third, tobacco, the most universal luxury and the one for which there is the intensest demand; fourth, petroleum, the lighting material in most universal use. These are things which are rare and of high demand. We are, therefore, strong in the market. Protection only robs us of part of our advantage (§ 116).

(Q) That we Need Protection to Get Ready for War.

135. We have no army, or navy, or fortifications worth mentioning. We are wasting more by protective taxes in a year than would be necessary to build a first-class navy

[1] See a fallacy under this point: Cunningham, "Growth of English Industry," 410 note.

and fortify our whole seacoast. It is said that, in some way, the taxes get us ready for war, and yet in fact we are not ready for war. It is plain that this argument is only a pretense put forward to try to cover the real motives of protection. If we prefer to go without army, navy, and fortifications, as we now do, then the best way to get ready for war, consistently with that policy, is *to get as rich as we can*. Then we can count on buying anything in the world which anybody else has got and which we need. Protection, then, which lessens our wealth, is only diminishing our power for war.

(R) That Protectionism Produces some Great Moral Advantages.

136. It is a very suspicious thing when a man who sets out to discuss an economic question shifts over on the "moral" ground. Not because economics and morals have nothing to do with each other. On the contrary, they meet at a common boundary line, and, when both are sound, straight and consistent lines run from one into the other. Capital is the first requisite of all human effort for goods of any kind, and the increase of capital is therefore the expansion of *chances* that intellectual, moral, and spiritual good may be won. The moral question is: How will the chances be used? If, then, the economic analysis shows that protective taxes lessen capital, it follows that those taxes lessen the regular chances for all higher good.

137. It is argued that hardship disciplines a man and is good for him; hence, that the free traders, who want people to do what is easiest, would corrupt them, and that protectionists, by "making work," bring in salutary discipline for the people. This is the effect upon those who pay the taxes. The counter-operation on the beneficiaries of the system I have never seen developed. Bastiat said

that the model at which the protectionist was aiming was Sisyphus, who was condemned in Hades to roll a stone to the top of a hill, from which, as soon as he got it there, it rolled down again to the bottom. Then he rolled it up again, and so on to all eternity. Here then was infinity of effort, zero of result; the ultimate type to which the protectionist system would come. Somebody pitied Sisyphus, to whom he replied: "Thou fool! I enjoy everlasting hope!" If Sisyphus could extract moral consolation from his case, I am not prepared to deny but that a New England farmer, ground between the upper millstone of free competition, in his production, with the Mississippi Valley, and the nether millstone of protective taxes on all his consumption, may derive some moral consolation from his case. There are a great many people who are apparently ready to inflict salutary chastisement on the American citizen for his welfare — and their own advantage.

138. The protectionist doctrine is that *if my earnings are taken from me and given to my neighbor, and he spends them on himself, there will be important moral gains to the community which will be lost if I keep my own earnings, and spend them on myself.* The facts of experience are all to the contrary. When a man keeps his own earnings he is frugal, temperate, prudent, and honest. When he gets and lives on another man's earnings, he is extravagant, wasteful, luxurious, idle, and covetous. The effects on the community in either case correspond.

139. The truth is that protectionism demoralizes and miseducates a people (§§ 89, 153, 155). It deprives them of individual self-reliance and energy, and teaches them to seek crafty and unjust advantages. It breaks down the skill of great merchants and captains of industry, and develops the skill of lobbyists. It gives faith in monopoly, combinations, jobbery, and restriction, instead of giving faith in energy, free enterprise, public purity, and freedom.

Illustrations of this occur all the time. Objection has been made to the introduction of machines to stop the smoke nuisance because they would interfere in the competition of anthracite and bituminous coal. People have resisted the execution of ordinances against gambling houses because said houses "make trade" for their neighbors. The theater men recently made an attempt to get regulations adopted against skating rinks — purely on moral grounds. The industries of the country all run to the form of combinations.[1] Our wisdom is developed, not in the great art of production, but in the tactics of managing a combination, and while we sustain all the causes and all the great principles of this system of business we denounce "monopoly" and "corporations."

(S) THAT A "WORKER MAY GAIN MORE BY HAVING HIS INDUSTRY PROTECTED THAN HE WILL LOSE BY HAVING TO PAY DEARLY FOR WHAT HE CONSUMES. A SYSTEM WHICH RAISES PRICES ALL ROUND — LIKE THAT IN THE UNITED STATES AT PRESENT — IS OPPRESSIVE TO CONSUMERS, BUT IS MOST DISADVANTAGEOUS TO THOSE WHO CONSUME WITHOUT PRODUCING ANYTHING, AND DOES LITTLE, IF ANY, INJURY TO THOSE WHO PRODUCE MORE THAN THEY CONSUME."

140. This is an English contribution to the subject dropped in passing by a writer on economic history.[2] It is a noteworthy fact that the "historical economists" and others who deride political economy as a science do not desist from it, but at once set to work to make very bad political economy of the "abstract" or "deductive" sort.

[1] See an interesting collection of illustrations in an article on "Lords of Industry" in the *North American Review* for June, 1884. The futile criticisms at the end of the article do not affect the value of the facts collected.

[2] Cunningham, "Growth of English Industry and Commerce," 316, note 2. (See also §§ 114, 134.)

The passage quoted involves three or four fallacies already noticed, and an assumption of the truth of protectionism as a philosophy.   As we have abundantly established, "workers" gain nothing by protection in their production (§ 48).   Also, "a system which raises prices all around" must either lessen the demand and requirement for money, *i.e.*, restrict business and the supply of goods (§ 112), or it must increase the amount of money.   In the former case it could not but injure "workers"; in the latter case we should find ourselves dealing with a greenback fallacy. But passing by that, who are they who consume more than they produce?   I can think only of (1) princes, pensioners, sinecurists, protected persons, and paupers, who draw support from taxes, and (2) swindlers, confidence men, and others who live by their wits on the produce of others. Those under (1), if they receive fixed money grants or subsidies, find an advance in price most disadvantageous.   So the protected, of course, as consumers of others' products, when they spend what they have received by protection, suffer.   Who are they who produce more than they consume?   I can think only of (1) taxpayers, and (2) victims of fraud and of those economic errors which give one man's earnings to another's use.   Rise in price is just as advantageous to this class as it was disadvantageous to the other, on the same hypothesis, *viz.*, if they pay fixed money taxes to the parasites, and can sell their products for more money. Evidently the writer did not understand correctly what his two classes consisted of, and he put the protected "workers" in the wrong one.   If in industry a person should produce more than he consumes, he could give it away, or it would decay on his hands.   If he should consume more than he produced, he would run in debt and become bankrupt.[1] Protection has nothing to do with that.

[1] Mill, "Political Economy," Bk. I, ch. 5, § 5. Cairnes, "Leading Principles," ch. I, § 5.

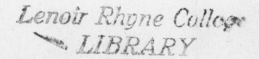

(*T*) That "A Duty may at once Protect the Native Manufacturer Adequately, and Recoup the Country for the Expense of Protecting him."

141. This is Professor Sidgwick's doctrine.[1] It has given great comfort to our protectionists because it is put forward by an Englishman and a Cambridge professor. It is offered under the "art" of political economy. It is a new thing; an *a priori* art. The "may" in it deprives it of the character of a doctrine or dogma such as our less cultivated protectionists give us — "Protective taxes come out of the foreigner" — but it is not a maxim of art. It has the air of a very astute contrivance (see § 3), and is therefore very captivating to many people, and it is very difficult to dissect and to expose in a simple and popular way. It has therefore given great trouble and done great mischief. It is, however, a complete error. It is not possible in any way or in any degree to use duties so as to make the foreigner pay for protection.

142. Professor Sidgwick states the hypothetical instance which he sets up to prove by illustration that there "may" be such a case, as follows: "Suppose that a five per cent duty is imposed on foreign silks, and that, in consequence, after a certain interval, half the silks consumed are the product of native industry, and that the price of the whole has risen $2\frac{1}{2}$ per cent. It is obvious that, under these circumstances, the other half, which comes from abroad, yields the state five per cent, while the tax levied from the consumers on the whole is only $2\frac{1}{2}$ per cent; so that the nation, in the aggregate, is at this time losing nothing by protection, except the cost of collecting the tax, while a loss equivalent to the whole tax falls on the foreign producer."

143. It is necessary, in the first place, to complete the hypothesis which is included in this case. Let us assume

[1] "Political Economy," 491–492.

that the consumption of silk, when all was imported, was 100 yards and that the price was $1 per yard. Then the following points are taken for granted, although not stated in the case as it is put: (1) That the state needs $5 revenue; (2) that it has determined to get this out of *the consumers of silk;* (3) that the advance in price does not diminish the consumption; (4) that the tax forces a reduction of price for the silk in the whole outside market; (5) that the *"silk"* in question is the same thing after the tax is laid as before. Of these assumptions, 3, 4, and 5 are totally inadmissible, but, if they be admitted in the first instance, and if the doctrine of the case which is put be deduced, it is this: If the part imported multiplied by the tax is equal to the total consumption multiplied by the advance in price, the consumers can pay the latter in protection, for it is equal to the former, and the former, which is paid to the government by the foreigner, is what the consumers of silk must otherwise have paid.

144. Obviously this deduction is arithmetically incorrect, even on the hypothesis. In the first place, the government has not obtained $5 revenue which it needed, but $2.50 (5 cents on 50 yards). In the second place, the foreigner sells at 1.02\frac{1}{2}$ (net 97$\frac{1}{2}$) the silk which he used to sell for $1. He therefore gets back from the consumers 2$\frac{1}{2}$ cents per yard on 50 yards, or $1.25 out of the $2.50 which he has paid to the government. Also, the domestic silk to compete must be equal to the dollar imported silk which now sells for 1.02\frac{1}{2}$. Hence, the consumers really pay in protection only 2$\frac{1}{2}$ cents on 50 yards, *.i.e* $1.25. This case, then, is, that the foreigner pays $1.25 revenue, and the consumers pay $1.25 revenue and $1.25 protection. Hence the result is not at all what is asserted, and there is no such operation of the contrivance as was expected. But the government needs $2.50 more revenue, the operation of its tax having been interfered with by

protection. As there is no equivalence or compensation in the case as it already stands, it is evident that the effect of any further tax, instead of bringing about equivalence or compensation, will be to depart from such a result still further.

145. It is, however, impossible to admit assumptions 3, 4, and 5 above, or to deal with any economic problem by any arithmetical process. The result above reached is totally incorrect and only serves to clear the ground for a correct analysis. The producer may have to bear part of a tax, if he is under the tax jurisdiction, or if he has a monopoly. If he has no monopoly, and is not under the tax jurisdiction, and works for the world's market, he cannot lower his price in order to assume part of the tax. What he does is that he differentiates his commodity. This is the fact in the art of production which is established by abundant experience. It is the explanation of the constant complaint, under the protective system, of "fraud" and of the constant demand for subclassification in the tariff schedules. The protected product never is, at least at first, as good in quality as the imported article which it aims to supersede. Hence the foreigner, if he desires to retain the protected market, can prepare a special quality for that market. The "silk" after the tax is laid is not the same silk as before. It nets to the foreign producer $97\frac{1}{2}$ cents, and pays him business profits at that price. Therefore when he sells it at $1.02\frac{1}{2}$ he gets back the whole tax from the consumers. The domestic silk sold at $1.02\frac{1}{2}$ is no better than might have been obtained for $97\frac{1}{2}$ cents. Hence the consumers are paying a tax for protection which is full and equal to the revenue rate. The fact that the price has fallen to $1.02\frac{1}{2}$, and is not $1.05, evidently proves that instead of disproving it, as many believe.

146. Thus this case falls to pieces. It gains a momentary plausibility from the erroneous assumptions which

are implicit in it. The foreign producer may suffer a narrowing of his market and a reduction of his aggregate profits, but there is no way to make him tributary (unless he has a monopoly) either to the treasury or the protected interests of the taxing country.[1] If it was true in general, or in any limited number of cases, that a country which lays protective taxes can make foreigners pay those taxes, then England, which has had no protective taxes since (say) 1850, and has been surrounded by countries which have had more or less protective taxes, must have been paying tribute to them all this time and must have been steadily impoverished accordingly.

CHAPTER V

SUMMARY AND CONCLUSION

147. I have now examined protectionism impartially on its own grounds, assuming them to be true, and adversely from ground taken against it, and have reviewed a series of the commonest arguments put forward in its favor. If now we return, with all the light we have obtained, to test the assumptions which we found in protectionism, that the people would not organize their industry wisely under liberty, and that protective taxes are the correct device for bringing about a better organization, we find that those two assumptions are totally false and have no semblance of claim upon our confidence. At every step the dogmas of protectionism, its claims, its apparatus, have proved fallacious, absurd, and impracticable. We can now group together some general criticisms of protectionism which our investigation suggests.

[1] I published a criticism of this case in the London *Economist*, December 1, 1883.

148. We have taken the protectionist's own definition of a protective duty, and have found that such a duty, instead of increasing national wealth, must, at every step, and by every incident of its operation, waste labor and capital, lower the efficiency of the national industry, weaken the country in trade, and consequently lower the standard of comfort of the whole population. We have found that protected industries, according to the statement of the protectionists, do not produce, but consume. If then these industries are *the* ones which make us rich, *consumption is production and destruction produces*. The object of a protective duty is "to effect the diversion of a part of the capital and labor of the people out of the channels in which it would run otherwise, into channels favored or created by law" (§ 13). We have seen that the channels *into* which the labor and capital of the people are to be diverted are offered by *the industries which do not pay*. Hence protectionism is found to mean that national prosperity is to be produced by forcing labor and capital into employments where the capital cannot be reproduced with the same increase which could be won by it elsewhere. If that is so, then capital in those employments will be wasted, and the final outcome of our investigation, which must be made the primary maxim of the art of national prosperity under protectionism, is that *Waste makes Wealth*. Such is its outcome when regarded as an economic philosophy.

149. As regards the social and jural relations which are established between citizen and citizen, protectionism is proved by a half-dozen independent analyses of it to be simply a device for forcing us to levy tribute on each other. If the law brings a cent to A it must have taken it from B, or else it must have produced it out of nothing, that is, it must be magic. Every soul pays protective taxes. If, then, anybody gets anything from them, he needs to remember what they cost him, and *he should insist on casting*

up both sides of the account.   If anybody gets nothing from them, then *he pays the taxes and gets no equivalent.*

150. During the anti-corn-law campaign in England, a writer in the *Westminster Review* illustrated protectionism by the story of the monkeys in a cage, each of whom received for his dinner a piece of bread. Each monkey dropped his own piece of bread and grabbed his neighbor's. The consequence was that soon the floor of the cage was strewn with fragments, and each monkey had to make the best dinner he could from these. It is a good and fair illustration. I saw a story recently in a protectionist newspaper about the peasants in the Soudan. Each owns pigeons, and at evening, when the pigeons come home, each tries to entice as many of his neighbors' pigeons as he can into his own pigeon house. "All of them do the same thing, and therefore each gets caught in his turn. They know this perfectly well, but no Egyptian fellah could resist the temptation of cheating his neighbor." They ought to *tax* each other's pigeons all around. Then they would put themselves at once on the level of free and enlightened Americans. The protectionist assures me that it is for the good of the community and for my good that he should tax me. I reply that, in his language, "these are fine theories," but that whether it is good for the community or not, and whether it is good for me or not, that he should tax me, I can see that it is for his good that he should tax me. Then he says: "Now you are abusive."

151. *If protectionism is anything else than mutual tribute, then it is magic.* The whole philosophy of it comes down to questions like this: How much can I afford to pay a man for hiring me? How much can I afford to pay a man for trading with me? How much can I afford to pay a man to cease to compete with me in my production? How much can I afford to pay a man to go and compete with those who supply me my consumption? It is only *an expensive way to*

get what we could get for nothing if it was worth having (§ 89). It is admitted that one man cannot lift himself by his boot straps. Suppose that a thousand men stand in a ring and each takes hold of the other's boot straps reciprocally and they all lift, can the whole group lift itself as a group? That is what protection comes to just as soon as we have drawn out into light the other side, the *cost side* of it. Whatever we win on one side, we must pay for by at least equal cost on another. The losses will all be distributed as net pure injury to the community. The harm of protection lies here. It is not measured by the tax. *It is measured by the total crippling of the national industry.* We might as well say that it would be a good thing to put snags in the rivers, to fell trees across the roads, to dull all our tools, as to say that unnecessary taxation could work a blessing. Men have argued that to destroy machines was to do a beneficial thing, and I have recently read an article in a Boston paper, quoting a Massachusetts man who thinks that what we need is another war in the United States. Such men may believe that protective taxes work a blessing, but to those who will see the truth, it is plain that, when the whole effect of the protective system is distributed, it benefits nobody. It is a dead weight and loss upon everybody, and those who think that they win by it would be far better off in a community where no such system existed, but where each man earned what he could and kept what he earned.

152. There is a school of political science in this country in whose deed of foundation it is provided that the professors shall teach how "by suitable tariff legislation, a nation may keep its productive industry alive, cheapen the cost of commodities, and oblige foreigners to sell to it at low prices, while contributing largely toward defraying the expenses of the government." [1] Is not that a fine thing? Those professors ought to likewise provide us a panacea,

---

[1] Quoted by Taussig: "History of the Existing Tariff," 73.

the philosopher's stone, a formula for squaring the circle, and all the other desiderata of universal happiness. It would be only a trifle for them. The only fear is that they may write the secret which they are to teach in books, and that other nations to whom we are "foreigners," may learn it. Then while Englishmen, Frenchmen, and Germans work for us at low prices and pay our taxes, we shall be forced to work for them at low prices and pay their taxes, and the old somber misery will settle down upon the world again the same as ever.

153. Some years ago we were told that protection was necessary because we had a big debt to pay. Well, we have paid the debt until we have reduced it from $78.25 per head to $28.41 per head. We, the people, have also raised our credit until the annual debt charge has been reduced from $4.29 per head to 95 cents per head. Now it is necessary to keep up the debt in order to keep up the taxes, and protectionism is now most efficient in forcing wasteful and corrupting expenditures to get rid of revenue, lest a surplus should furnish an argument for reducing taxation. This is right on the doctrine that waste makes wealth.

154. They tell us that protection has produced prosperity, and when we ask them to account for hard times in spite of the tariff, they say that hard times are caused by the free traders who will not keep still. Therefore *the prosperity produced by protection is so precarious that it can be overthrown by only talking about free trade.* They denounce *laissez-faire*, or "let alone," but the only question is *when* to let alone, *when* to keep still. They do not let the tariff alone if they want to revise it to suit them, or want to make it "equitable." When they get it "equitable" they will let it alone, but that insures agitation, and makes sure that they will cause it, for an indefinite time to come. On the other hand the victims of the tariff will not keep still. Their time to "let alone" is when it is repealed. If the

tariff did not hurt somebody somewhere it would not do any good to anybody anywhere, and the victims will resist.[1] Mr. Lincoln used to tell a story about hearing a noise in the next room. He looked in and found Bob and Tad scuffling. "What is the matter, boys?" said he. "It is Tad," replied Bob, "who is trying to get my knife." "Oh, let him have it, Bob," said Mr. Lincoln, "just to keep him quiet." "No!" said Bob, "it is my knife and I need it to keep me quiet." Mr. Lincoln used the story to prove that there is no foundation for peace save truth and justice. Now, in this case, *the man whose earnings are being taken from him needs them to keep him quiet.* Our fathers fought for free soil, and if we are worthy to be their sons we shall fight for free trade, which is the necessary complement of free soil. If a man goes to Kansas to-day and raises corn on "free soil," how does he get the good of it, unless he can exchange that corn for any product of the earth that he chooses on the best terms that the arts and commerce of to-day can give him?

155. The history of civil liberty is made up of campaigns against abuses of taxation. Protectionism is the great modern abuse of taxation; the abuse of taxation which is adapted to a republican form of government. *Protectionism is now corrupting our political institutions just as slavery used to do, viz.,* it allies itself with every other abuse which comes up. Most recently it has allied itself

---

[1] Illustrations of this are presented without number. Here is the most recent one: "The [silk] masters [of Lyons, France] look to the government for relief by a reduction of the duty on cotton yarn, or the right to import all numbers duty free for export after manufacture. With the present tariffs, they maintained, which is no doubt true, that they cannot compete with the Swiss and German makers. But the Rouen cotton spinners oppose the demand of the Lyons silk manufacturers, and protest that they will be ruined if the latter are allowed to procure their material from abroad. The Lyons weavers assert that they are being ruined because they cannot." — (*Economist*, 1885, p. 815.) The cotton men won in the Chamber of Deputies, July 23, 1885.

with the silver coinage, and it is now responsible, in a great measure, for that calamity. The silver coinage law would have been repealed three years ago if the silver mining interest had not served notice on the protectionists that that was their share of protection, and the price of their coöperation. The silver coinage is the chief cause of the "hard times" of the last two or three years. In a well-ordered state it is the function of government to repress every selfish interest which arises and endeavors to encroach upon the rights of others. The state thus maintains justice. Under protectionism *the government gives a license to certain interests to go out and encroach on others.* It is an iniquity as to the victims of it, a delusion as to its supposed beneficiaries, and a waste of the public wealth. There is only one reasonable question now to be raised about it, and that is: How can we most easily get rid of it?

TARIFF REFORM .

TARIFF REFORM[1]

A YEAR and a half ago a gentleman who had just been reëlected, by Republicans, to the Senate of the United States, made a five-minute speech acknowledging the honor. In respect to public affairs he uttered but one opinion: that the people of the United States were confronted by a most serious problem, *viz.*, how to reduce taxation. On the face of it, this was a most extraordinary statement, and the chronicler or historian might well take note of it as a new event in the life of the human race. Statesmen and historians are familiar enough with the difficulty of raising more revenue, and laying more taxes, but the solemn and calamitous position of a nation which is forced to reduce its taxes, and finds itself confronted by industrial disaster if it does it, is something new. Students of political economy are familiar with the question: What harm to industry may be done by levying taxes on it? But the problem of how to avert the economic disaster which may follow taking them off is new. Of course the state of mind revealed by the formulation of the above problem is the result of a long habit of regarding taxation as an industrial force, or, at least, as an effective condition of industrial success.

There is, however, a problem; in regard to that fact all concur. It is also a rare problem, one for which the only precedent is to be found in our own history, and when the case occurred before, it proved to be fraught with calamity. We are confronted by the dangers of a surplus revenue, and no proposal to do away with the surplus in extravagant

[1] *Independent,* August 16, 1888.

expenditures can stand before the common sense of the people.

If the taxes are collecting more than the public necessities require, then the simple and obvious, and, in fact, the only solution, is not to collect the taxes; let the people keep their own products and do what they please with them. If we do not make a problem there will not be any; if we simply do in the most straightforward manner what the common sense of the situation demands, there will be no difficulty; the consequences will all take care of themselves, and all the imaginary calamities will fail to appear. If, however, we must have a grand scheme of national prosperity established in advance, then the case is different.

During the war a notion grew up here that, through some new dispensation of fate, it was possible for the American people to make war and prosper by it. After the war the notion grew up that the paper money was a condition of success and that we should be ruined if we resumed specie payments. Now we are met by the doctrine that we cannot repeal the taxes which were laid during the war, partly in order to carry it on, because our national prosperity is bound up in them. These notions, in fact, are all consistent, and all hang together; they all belong to a philosophy that men prosper by discord and war, not by peace and harmony. According to that philosophy we touched unawares the springs of prosperity when we engaged in a civil war, incurred an immense debt, and laid crushing taxes. Now, therefore, when we ask that the taxes which are no longer necessary may be taken off, the men who have fallen under the dominion of these fallacies tell us that it cannot be done; that our prosperity would be undermined by it. They have been assuring us for years past that the protective system was sure to produce a solid and stable prosperity; now, by their own statement, it has produced a state of things so weak and unstable that it must be maintained by heavy taxes. The industrial prosperity of the United States proves to be as burdensome to it as the armaments of the European nations are to them.

The notion seems to be that protective taxes, laid on imports, are the particular kind of taxes which make national prosperity, and which therefore ought not to be touched. It is proposed that internal taxes shall be reduced. If local taxes on real estate, etc., are reduced, every one rejoices; that is supposed to be a clear and simple gain. I have known the same man to exert himself very actively to scrutinize local expenditures, and reduce local taxes, and to boil with rage against free traders who want to reduce protective taxes. However, there is probably no tax of any kind whatsoever which does not interfere with the conditions of supply and demand, or industrial competition, in such a way as to give "protection" to somebody at the expense of somebody else. There are persons who are now enjoying great advantages in their business from the whisky and tobacco taxes which they would lose if those taxes were repealed. This is one of the incidental mischiefs of all taxation and one of the reasons for insisting that taxation shall be as slight as possible, and, to that end, that government functions shall be limited as much as possible.

We are, therefore, face to face with the question whether we are able to reduce our own taxes, and whether we are free to do so. We may fairly ask: if not, why not? It is plain that this is a question of domestic policy and of our own interest altogether. All the attempts to prejudice it by talking about "England" are impertinent, and all allegations that those of us who want to reduce our own taxes are trying "to give away our market," etc., belong to the worst abuses of political discussion. What is true is that we have built up a vast combination of vested interests, which in a few cases have, and in nearly all cases think they have, an interest in maintaining the taxes. These are among ourselves; what they gain, they gain from us; it is with them that we have to contend. They have thus far carried on the fight by all the methods dear to vested interests; they have put forth plausible fallacies, sought alliances, procured delays, appealed to prejudices.

Behind these selfish and sordid interests, however, there is the strong and sincere prejudice which still prevails among the civilized nations of to-day, and which is dividing them into hostile parties, carrying on tariff wars with each other. I call it "protectionism," because it is not a policy, but a philosophy of national welfare. In the United States it takes the form of various fallacies about the home markets, diversification of industry, wages, etc. As these are all questions of political economy, and as all who talk on the subject at all are talking political economy of some sort or other, it seems that a great work of education is to be done here on the field of economic doctrine. Hitherto the attempt of the politicians has been not to perform this work of education but to thrust it aside.

As soon as the issue is formed, however, and the protectionists are forced to formulate their doctrine, as a doctrine, its absurdity becomes apparent. It is not capable of statement. If we are to have temporary protection, in order to start infant industries, then it will become imperatively necessary, so soon as public attention is occupied by the subject, to say how, and how far, and how long, the system is to be kept up, and the public will demand to know how it is getting on, and at what rate it is approaching its goal. For this reason those who have any logical directness of thinking, have already advanced to a more intense position; they advocate protectionism as a permanent and universal economic philosophy. In that form it flies in the face of common sense and civilization; in some of the latest forms which it has taken on in the hands of some professors of political economy, it is a kind of economic mysticism.

If, however, the United States could be cut off from all the rest of the world as regards trade and industry, then at least it should be plain that whatever material prosperity they could gain would be just what they, with their energy, enterprise, and capital, are able to extract from such soil and climate as nature has given to us here. What would be the difference if, then, there were no tax barriers? Certainly none whatever. The wealth which the American people get they must produce by applying their labor and capital to the natural advantages which they possess. With foreign trade open to them, they will not make use of it unless they find an advantage in it; that is, unless American labor and capital can attain more wealth through exchange than without it. The task of American producers will still be to attain the greatest possible wealth by expending their labor and capital on American soil, either directly, or with an intermediate step of exchange. Wages are only a part of the product of the country; if then, trade increased the amount of commodities at the disposition of the people, it would increase the amount of each share in the distribution. This is the simplest common sense of the matter, stripped of all technicalities, and to this the whole discussion must again and again return.

If now we begin to reduce and abolish the taxes which were laid during the war, we shall simply begin to free the American people from a clog on their energies and a waste of their industrial strength. Every step in this direction is an emancipation under which we may be sure that the national energy which is set free will spring up with the quickest response. The guarantee of this is in the character of the people, and in the natural advantages which they possess. Whatever chances we have, we have in the nature of the case; the tariff could not give us any; it could only divert in one way or another those which nature has given us. This diversion or perversion has now entered into the experience and education of our generation. We have no idea of the welfare we should enjoy if we were only free to use the chances which are within our reach, and a great many of us have spun out a kind of political economy to prove that the cords which bind us are the tools by which we work.

WHAT IS FREE TRADE?

WHAT IS FREE TRADE?[1]

THERE never would have been any such thing to fight for as free speech, free press, free worship, or free soil, if nobody had ever put restraints on men in those matters. We never should have heard of free trade, if no restrictions had ever been put on trade. If there had been any restrictions on the intercourse between the states of this Union, we should have heard of ceaseless agitation to get those restrictions removed. Since there are no restrictions allowed under the Constitution, we do not realize the fact that we are enjoying the blessings of complete liberty, where, if wise counsels had not prevailed at a critical moment, we should now have had a great mass of traditional and deep-rooted interferences to encounter.

Our intercourse with foreign nations, however, has been interfered with, because it is a fact that, by such interference, some of us can win advantages over others. The power of Congress to levy taxes is employed to lay duties on imports, not in order to secure a revenue from imports, but to prevent imports — in which case, of course, no revenue will be obtained. The effect which is aimed at, and which is attained by this device, is that the American consumer, when he wants to satisfy his needs, has to go to an American producer of the thing he wants, and has to give to him a price for the product which is greater than that which some foreigner would have charged. The object of this device, as stated on the best protectionist authority, is: "To effect the diversion of a part of the labor and capital of the people out of the channels in which it would run otherwise, into

<hr />

[1] In *Good Cheer* for April, 1886, p. 7.

channels favored or created by law." This description is strictly correct, and from it the reader will see that protection has nothing to do with any foreigner whatever. It is purely a question of domestic policy. It is only a question whether we shall, by taxing each other, drive the industry of this country into an arbitrary and artificial development, or whether we shall allow one another to employ each his capital and labor in his own way. Note that there is for us all the same labor, capital, soil, national character, climate, etc., — that is, that all the conditions of production remain unaltered. The only change which is operated is a wrenching of labor and capital out of the lines on which they would act under the impulse of individual enterprise, energy, and interest, and their impulsion in another direction selected by the legislator. Plainly, all the import duty can do is to close the door, shutting the foreigner out and the Americans in. Then, when an American needs iron, coal, copper, woolens, cottons, or anything else in the shape of manufactured commodities, the operation begins. He has to buy in a market which is either wholly or partially monopolized. The whole object of shutting him in is to take advantage of this situation to make him give more of his products for a given amount of the protected articles, than he need have given for the same things in the world's market. Under this system a part of our product is diverted from the satisfaction of our needs, and is spent to hire some of our fellow-citizens to go out of an employment which would pay under the world's competition, into one which will not pay under the world's competition. We, therefore, do with less clothes, furniture, tools, crockery, glassware, bed and table linen, books, etc., and the satisfaction we have for this sacrifice is knowing that some of our neighbors are carrying on business which according to their statement does not pay, and that we are paying their losses and hiring them to keep on.

Free trade is a revolt against this device. It is not a revolt against import duties or indirect taxes as a means of raising revenue. It has nothing to say about that, one way or the other. It begins to protest and agitate just as soon as any tax begins to act protectively, and it denounces any tax which one citizen levies on another. The protectionists have a long string of notions and doctrines which they put forward to try to prove that their device is not a contrivance by which they can make their fellow-citizens contribute to their support, but is a device for increasing the national wealth and power. These allegations must be examined by economists, or other persons who are properly trained to test their correctness, in fact and logic. It is enough here to say, over a responsible signature, that no such allegation has ever been made which would bear examination. On the contrary, all such assertions have the character of apologies or special pleas to divert attention from the one plain fact that the advocates of a protective tariff have a direct pecuniary interest in it, and that they have secured it, and now maintain it, for that reason and no other. The rest is all afterthought and excuse. If any gain could possibly come to the country through the gains of the beneficiaries of the tariff, obviously the country must incur at least an equal loss through the losses of that part of the people who pay what the protected win. If a country could win anything that way, it would be like a man lifting himself by his boot straps.

The protectionists, in advocating their system, always spend a great deal of effort and eloquence on appeals to patriotism, and to international jealousies. These are all entirely aside from the point. The protective system is a domestic system, for domestic purposes, and it is sought by domestic means. The one who pays, and the one who gets, are both Americans. The victim and the beneficiary are amongst ourselves. It is just as unpatriotic to oppress one American as it is patriotic to favor another. If we make one American pay taxes to another American, it will neither vex nor please any foreign nation.

The protectionists speak of trade with the contempt of feudal nobles, but on examination it appears that they have something to sell, and that they mean to denounce trade with their rivals. They denounce cheapness, and it appears that they do so because they want to sell dear. When they buy, they buy as cheaply as they can. They say that they want to raise wages, but they never pay anything but the lowest market rate. They denounce selfishness, while pursuing a scheme for their own selfish aggrandizement, and they bewail the dominion of self-interest over men who want to enjoy their own earnings, and object to surrendering the same to them. They attribute to government, or to "the state," the power and right to decide what industrial enterprises each of us shall subscribe to support.

Free trade means antagonism to this whole policy and theory at every point. The free trader regards it as all false, meretricious, and delusive. He considers it an invasion of private rights. In the best case, if all that the protectionist claims were true, he would be taking it upon himself to decide how his neighbor should spend his earnings, and — more than that — that his neighbor shall spend his earnings for the advantage of the men who make the decision. This is plainly immoral and corrupting; nothing could be more so. The free trader also denies that the government either can, or ought to regulate the way in which a man shall employ his earnings. He sees that the government is nothing but a clique of the parties in interest. It is a few men who have control of the civic organization. If they were called upon to regulate business, they would need a wisdom which they have not. They do not do this. They only turn the "channels" to the advantage of themselves and their friends. This corrupts the institutions of government and continues under our system all the old abuses by which the men who could get control of the governmental machinery have used it to aggrandize themselves at the expense of others. The free trader holds that the people will employ their labor and capital to the best advantage when each man employs his own in his own way, according to the maxim that "A fool is wiser in his own house than a sage in another man's house"; — how much more, then, shall he be wiser than a politician? And he holds, further, that by the nature of the case, if any governmental coercion is necessary to drive industry in a direction in which it would not otherwise go, such coercion must be mischievous.

The free trader further holds that protection is all a mistake and delusion to those who think that they win by it, in that it lessens their self-reliance and energy and exposes their business to vicissitudes which, not being incident to a natural order of things, cannot be foreseen and guarded against by business skill; also that it throws the business into a condition in which it is exposed to a series of heats and chills, and finally, unless a new stimulus is applied, reduced to a state of dull decay. They therefore hold that even the protected would be far better off without it.

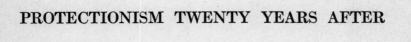

PROTECTIONISM TWENTY YEARS AFTER

PROTECTIONISM TWENTY YEARS AFTER [1]

I THINK it must be now nearly twenty years since I
have made a free-trade speech or been able to take
share in a free-trade dinner.

When I was invited here this evening I thought I would
try to come for the pleasure of hearing the gentlemen,
especially the members of Congress, who were announced
to speak here. I have been so out of health that it has been
impossible for me to sit up evenings or to attempt public
speaking in the evenings, but things are going a little better
and I will make an attempt to say a little — not very
much, as the hour is now late.

Thirty-five or forty years ago I became a free trader for
two great reasons, as far as I can now remember.

One was because, as a student of political economy, my
whole mind revolted against the notion of magic that is
involved in the notion of a protective tariff. That is, there
are facts that are accounted for by protectionism through
assertions that are either plainly untrue or are entirely
irrational. The other reason was because it seemed to
me that the protective tariff system nourished erroneous
ideas of success in business and produced immoral results
in the minds and hopes of the people.

I cannot say that I have got any more light on the matter within the last twenty years; it looks to me still as
if the great objections to protectionism were these two. No
man who enjoys the benefit of a protective tariff, as he
believes, can ever tell whether he gets back anything for

[1] Address at a dinner of the committee on Tariff Reform of the Reform Club
in the city of New York, June 2, 1906.

131

the taxes which he pays or not. He never has any analysis of the operation and never knows whether or not he really recovers from the action of the tariff what he pays in.

I say now the taxes which he pays, because — let us not make any mistake about this — the matter we are talking about is one entirely of Americans and between Americans. If the protective tariff operates so as to perform what is attributed to it, it prevents things from being imported into this country. That may be a disadvantage to the foreigner, it may disappoint him in his hopes, but we may leave him out of account. Then the increase of the cost of these commodities for the American consumer at home is the source from which the American protected manufacturer must obtain his benefit, if he ever obtains any. Therefore he has to pay also taxes to the other protected industries on account of the operation of the system. Therefore he is both paying and receiving, but whether or not he gets back the part that he hoped to receive is a question which he never can sift and never can know.

I should myself suppose that possibly the Pennsylvanian on his coal and iron might stand a good chance of winning something. The operation is direct and simple in that case, and coal and iron are to-day the very first conditions of industry. They must be obtained as raw material, because they enter into everything, and it is possible that under those circumstances the game might be sufficiently direct so that its effect could be felt and perceived. But the Connecticut manufacturer has to pay taxes on coal and iron and copper and the other metals, and he has to pay also the taxes on wool and the other raw materials, and then comes the question whether he ever gets it back again or not. He never knows; he cannot know; he cannot feel it and he cannot possibly know whether the operation of the system is to bring him back a return for his outlay or not.

We hear a great deal about a rightly adjusted tariff. It is a constant ideal that is presented, whenever the tariff subject comes up again for discussion in Congress, that it ought to be rightly adjusted, and when it is, it is going to perform its beneficial operation.

How can a tariff ever be rightly adjusted unless the industry will stand still? The taxes stand still for years without change. The industries never stand still. There are new inventions in machinery, there are new raw materials brought into use, there are new processes developed, and all that changes the character of the industry. These inventions and improvements and processes are all ignored by the protective system. It contains no allowance for them at all. But our people are full of enterprise, they are fond of improvements, they like novelties, and they adopt changes. The consequence is that the industry changes, and then again the decisions that are made by somebody or other as to the doubtful questions in the interpretation of the law are also constantly changing, and then by and by we find a lot of people who want the tariff changed. They say it needs to be adapted to the time, it is out of date, it has fallen behind, it does not fit the requirements of the moment, and they would like to have a tariff revision; but they are told then that they ought to keep still and not make a disturbance which will bring up a discussion of the entire tariff system, and that they ought to allow it to go on for the sake of the "system."

What is the system then? The system means that the import duties that we have in this country have raised the prices of all commodities in our market, I may say thirty or forty per cent on a very low calculation. Is not that a very extraordinary thing when you stand off and try to realize it for a minute — that we have raised the prices in the United States thirty or forty per cent — perhaps more nearly fifty per cent — above the level of the prices for the same commodities in the other civilized countries of our grade; and that we believe that we have done a grand and noble thing by raising these prices, putting the whole level of life in this country on an artificial plane that much above the level of the world's market? In fact, if you should listen to a protectionist he would make you believe that this continent would not be habitable if it was not for the protective tariff that is here working this operation all the time on the American market.

I am of the opinion — I am not very confident about it — but it looks to me as if it were true that a protective tariff wears out in a little while — I mean, so far as its expected beneficial effect is concerned. Its effects are distributed, they are taken up and they are allowed for all around the market until the expected benefit to the protected people is lost and there remains nothing but the dead weight of the system itself as an interference with the industries. There is then a call for a new tariff in order to get another impulse or another fillip, as I have heard it called, to give things a new impulse, to start them on again.

That has been the history of our tariff now for one hundred years, that it has been restarted, reinvigorated from time to time in order to give a new impulse. Then in the very nature of the case, therefore, it seems to me that a new impulse is constantly required.

As I said at the outset, the tariff system seems to me to teach us to believe that a man needs a "pull" of some kind or other to make any industry a success. It is an idea that there must always be a provision of easy profit in connection with the industry that shall demand no labor or no expediture of capital to get it. That is the pure doctrine of graft. The tariff teaches us to look for a fee or a gratuity or a rake-off which will be a pure and net profit. People are told that tariff taxes are a rightful gift to the beneficiary. Those who do not get that gain seek another one of the same kind somewhere, and when they do that they have recourse to graft.

It is a shameful fact that this notion of graft, and this word, should have come to us, as it has within the last four or five years, and should have extended so far and become so familiar to us in connection with a great many of the operations of business. It is customary, as we have known for a long time, in some nations, for instance in Russia, China, and Turkey; and with us it has seemed to spread and win acceptance and currency in a most astonishing manner. I cannot believe but what the tariff system has educated us in this direction and prepared us to tolerate and accept the development of this idea. It also seems to me that now, after one hundred years of this system, the tariff is no longer properly an economic question. It is a practical political question. The politics and the business are interwoven in it inextricably. There is no economic discussion possible of the propositions that are made, economic in form, in connection with the tariff system. There is only a war of partial views and of superficial inferences.

Our American protectionism has grown out of the peculiar circumstances of this country. It is an old idea that has come down to us from Europe, and, indeed, from the Middle Ages in Europe, and here it found a chance for a new and very remarkable development. There were new conditions here, and the chances were so big and grand that, as a matter of fact, the protective system has never done more than exact a certain tribute from us on these chances. It has never really touched us in an acute and sensible way, and in spite of it we have enjoyed marvelous prosperity which is due really to the circumstances of advantage and favor which we have enjoyed here.

In the year 1892 we got an issue on this matter and went to the electorate with it, with the result that we all know. But the mandate of the people was neglected and disobeyed by the government and the purpose that the people showed at that time was defied.

We have also had opportunity to notice the great power of the protected interests in Congress. The fact is that we are being governed at the present time by a combination of these protected interests which have got control of the machinery of government, and have control of the personnel of the government to such an extent that it is almost impossible, practically, to make any breach in this system at all. That is because the political combinations have been so thoroughly wrought out and so ingeniously developed that they look at present as if they were impregnable.

I look around to see if I can find some encouragement. I thought that it was something of an encouragement when Mr. Dalzell made this speech in Congress that Mr. Williams has referred to, in which he poured such scorn on the idea of "incidental protection." I have never said anything so severe about any protectionist idea as that which he said about incidental protection. But suppose that the people of 1850, the middle of the nineteenth century, could come to life again, the old protectionists of that time. What would they think to hear a man speak with scorn of incidental protection? It was what they believed in; it was the whole business to them. When an old protectionist like Mr. Dalzell can turn around and pour scorn upon incidental protection I feel as if we never could tell what they might throw overboard next time, in some paroxysm of some kind or other, of fear or hope or something else, and we might get a chance that we have not been able to get in the past.

Then, as has been well said by other gentlemen to-night, there has been within the last year or two a very great revolt in the public mind against graft and political and business corruption. How far will this go? We do not know, but it is, at any rate, an opening in the public mind that is full of chances. It may go very far; it may have very great effects; it is certainly something to be noticed and taken advantage of.

Then, again, there are new conflicts of interests arising. We have become very great people in the world's commerce, with a billion dollars' worth of exports and imports in a year, and we are so interwoven with the whole world that it will not be possible for us to go on with our old policy of discouraging commerce and rejecting it, and trying to stop it, and paying no attention at all to the remonstrances of our neighbors. In future we shall be obliged to pay some attention to these remonstrances. They are just, they are reasonable, and they will command our attention; and then we shall have to make concessions to them. In other words, we cannot any longer afford to reject and neglect these remonstrances.

It may be, therefore, that in the time that is now before us we shall have better chances for a practical war upon this system than we have had hitherto. As long, however, as I can remember, and as long as I have had any share in it, we have got along without any encouragement in it at all. We have done what we could without that. We got so we did not expect it. We knew that we should be neglected and treated as persons whose opinions in these matters were not of any importance or worthy of any attention, and so we went on and kept up our arguments, as we considered them, to the best of our ability and without very much result.

Now, it may be that we are on the eve of a different time, when the circumstances will be more favorable, more hopeful, more full of opportunities, and I certainly, for my part, most profoundly hope that that is so.

I have noticed with some discouragement the efforts that Mr. Williams has made on the floor of Congress to get some modifications of the tariff made, or some argument even opened up there that might give the matter activity and life in the legislative domain. They did not seem any more encouraging than what we used to see in the old times. But it is certainly in the nature of things that the difficulties and absurdities of this system must come out in practice more and more distinctly as we go on, and the need for reform will therefore force itself in the shape of a play of interests that will bring new and counteracting forces into operation to which we may look for help in the overthrow of the system.

PROSPERITY STRANGLED BY GOLD

PROSPERITY STRANGLED BY GOLD [1]

SOME of the silver fallacies were stated by Mr. St. John, in his address before the silver convention, with such precision that his speech offers a favorable opportunity for dealing with them.

He says that "it is amongst the first principles in finance that the value of each dollar, expressed in prices, depends upon the total number of dollars in circulation." There is no such principle of finance as the one here formulated. The "quantity doctrine" of currency is gravely abused by all bimetallists, from the least to the greatest, and it is at best open to great doubt. When the dollars in question are dollars of some money of account which can circulate beyond the territory of the State in which it is issued, the quantity doctrine cannot be true within that territory. It may be noted, in passing, that this is the reason why no scheme of the silver people for manipulating prices in the United States can possibly succeed. Silver and gold will be exported and imported until their values conform throughout the world, and prices fixed in one or the other of them will conform to the world's prices, after all the trouble and waste and loss of translating them two or three times over have been endured.

The quantity doctrine, however, means that the value of the currency is a question of supply and demand, and everybody knows that to double or halve the supply does not halve or double the value, or have any other effect which is simple and direct. If it did have such effect speculation would not be what it is.

[1] *Leslie's Weekly*, August 20, 1896.

141

Mr. St. John goes on to argue that our population increases two millions every year, on account of which we need more dollars; that the production of gold does not furnish enough to meet this need, and that, therefore, prices fall. This argumentation is very simple and very glib. Prosperity and adversity are put into a syllogism of three lines. But, if we can avert the fall in prices and adversity by coining silver, it must be by adding the silver to the gold which we now have. "High" and "low" prices are only relative terms. They mean higher and lower than at another time or place; higher and lower than we have been used to. If misery depends on ten-cent corn we are advised to cut the cents in two and we shall get twenty-cent corn and prosperity. Corn will not be altered in value in gold, or outside of the United States, and, as all other things will be marked up at the same time and in the same way, its value in other things will not be altered by this operation. When we get used to twenty-cent corn it will seem just as low and just as "hard for the debtor" as ten-cent corn is now. Then we can divide by ten and get two-dollar corn, by adding free coinage of copper. When we get used to that we shall be no better satisfied with it. We can then make paper dollars and coin them without limit. Million-dollar corn will then become as bitter a subject for complaint as ten-cent corn is now. The fact that people are discontented is no argument for anything.

The fact that prices are low is made the subject of social complaint and of political agitation in the United States. Prices have undergone a wave since 1850. They arose until about 1872. They have fallen again. They are lower than they were at the top of the wave all the world over. This fact, the explanation of which would furnish a very complicated task for trained statisticians and economists, is made a topic of easy interpretation and solution in political conventions and popular harangues, and it is proposed to

adopt violent and portentous measures upon the basis of
the flippant notions which are current about it. But what
difference does it make whether the "plane" of prices is
high or low? If corn is at forty cents a bushel and calico
at twenty cents a yard, a bushel buys two yards. If corn
is at ten cents a bushel and calico at five cents a yard, a
bushel will buy two yards. So of everything else. If, then,
there has been a *general* fall, and that is the alleged grievance, neither farmers nor any other one class has suffered
by it.

It is undoubtedly true that a period of advancing prices
stimulates energy and enterprise. It does so even when, if
all the facts were well known, it might be found that capital was really being consumed in successive periods of production. Falling prices discourage enterprise, although, if
all facts were known to the bottom, it might be found
that capital was being accumulated in successive periods
of production.

It is also true that a depreciation of the money of account, *while it is going on,* stimulates exports and restrains
imports.

But who can tell how we are to make prices always go
up, unless by constant and unlimited inflation? Who can
tell how we are to avoid fluctuations in prices or eliminate
the element of contingency, risk, foresight, and speculation?

It is also true that, although high prices and low prices
are immaterial at any one time, the change from one to the
other, from one period of time to another, affects the burden
of outstanding time contracts. Men make contracts for
dollars, not for dollar's-worths. Selling long or short is one
thing; lending is another. Borrowers and lenders never
guarantee each other the purchasing power of dollars at a
future time. If the contracts were thus complicated they
would become impossible. Between 1850 and 1872 the
debtors made no complaint and the creditors never thought

of getting up an agitation to have debts scaled up. The debtors now are demanding that they be allowed to play heads I win, tails you lose, and Mr. St. John and others tell us that they have the votes to carry it; as if that made any difference in the forum of discussion.

Increase in population does not prove an increased need of money. It may prove the contrary. If the population becomes more dense over a given area, a higher organization may make less money necessary. If railroads and other means of communication are extended, money is economized. If banks and other credit institutions are multiplied, and if credit operations are facilitated by public security, good administration of law, etc., less money is needed. If these changes are going on at the same time that population is increasing (and such is undoubtedly the case in the United States), who can tell whether the net result is to make more or less currency necessary? Nobody; and all assertions about the matter are wild and irresponsible.

If it was true that an increase of two millions in the population called for more dollars, how does anybody know whether the current gold production is adequate to meet the new requirement or not? The assertion is arithmetical. It says that two quantities are not equal to each other. The first quantity is the increase in the currency called for by two million more people. How much more is needed? Nobody knows, and there is no way to find out. The silver men have put figures for it from time to time, but the figures rested on nothing and were mere bald assertions. The second quantity is the amount of new gold annually available for coinage in the United States. How much is this? Nobody knows, because if an attempt is made to define what is meant it is found that there is no idea in the words. The people of the United States buy and coin just as much gold as they want at any time. Hence

two things are said to be unequal to each other, when nobody knows how big either one of them is. It may be
added that it makes no difference how big either one of
them is. How much additional tin is needed annually for
the increase of our population? Do the mines produce it?
Nobody knows or asks. The mines produce, and the people
buy, what they want. The case is the same as to gold.

We find, then, that Mr. St. John begins with a doctrine
which is untenable; then he asserts a relation between
population and the need of money which does not exist;
then he assumes that this need is greater than the amount
of new gold produced, although neither he nor anybody else
knows how big either one of these quantities is. This is
the argumentation by which he aims to show that prices
are reduced and misery produced by the single gold standard. It is the argumentation which is current among the
silver people. Not a step of it will bear examination. The
inference that we must restore the free coinage of silver, to
escape this strangulation of prosperity, falls to the ground.

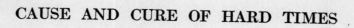

CAUSE AND CURE OF HARD TIMES

CAUSE AND CURE OF HARD TIMES [1]

IT is an essential part of the case of the silver men that the country is having "hard times." The bolters from the Republican convention say, in their manifesto: "Discontent and distress prevail to an extent never before known in the history of the country." This is an historical assertion. It is distinctly untrue. There is no such discontent and distress as there was in 1819, or in 1840, or in 1875, to say nothing of other periods. The writers did not know the facts of the history, and they made use of what is nowadays a mere figure of speech. People who want to say that a social phenomenon is big, and who do not know what has been before, say that it is unparalleled in history.

There has been an advancing paralysis of enterprise and arrest of credit ever since the Sherman act of 1890 was passed. The bolters say that "No reason can be found for such an unhappy condition of things save in a vicious monetary system." The reason for it has been that the cumulative effect of the silver legislation was steadily advancing to a crisis. The efforts by which the effects of that legislation had been put off were no longer effective, and it was evident that the country was on the verge of a cataclysm in which the standard of value would be changed. What man can fail to see the effect of such a fear on credit and enterprise? And with such a fear in the market, how idle it is to try to represent the trouble as caused by the fact that the existing standard was of gold, or of silver, or of anything else! Men will make contracts and go on with business by the use of any medium, the terms of which can be defined, understood, and maintained until the contract

[1] *Leslie's Weekly*, September 3, 1896.

is solved, but uncertainty as to the terms, or danger of change in them, makes credit and enterprise impossible. In the whole history of finance no crisis can be found which was so utterly unnecessary, and so distinctly caused by the measures of policy which had gone before it, as that of 1893.

So much being admitted as to "hard times," it remains true, however, that by far the greatest part of the current declamation about hard times is false. Prosperity and adversity of society are not capable of exact verification. At all times some people, classes, industries, are less prosperous than others. The fashion has grown up among politicians and stump orators of using assertions about prosperity and distress as arguments for their purpose, and parties come before the public with prosperity policies. They have programs for "making the country prosperous." If this country, with its population, its resources, and its chances, is not prosperous by the intelligence, industry, and thrift of its population, does any sane man suppose that politicians and stump orators have any devices at their control for making it so? The orators of the present day see prosperity where they need to see it for the purposes of their argument. They say that all gold-standard countries in Europe are in distress. Mr. St. John says that Mexico is prosperous. As to Canada, we have seen no statement. According to some discussions which are current, the bicycle rivals the gold standard as a calamity-producer. As the bicycle has certainly gravely affected the distribution of expenditure and the accumulation of capital, its efficiency as a crisis-maker, in its degree, whatever that may be, can be rationally discerned, but nobody has ever been able to show any rational grounds of belief that the gold standard is a crisis-maker.

A crisis will also be produced whenever capital has been invested on a large scale in any unproductive investment, whereby it is not reproduced, but is lost. The enterprises are always made the basis of engagements and contracts. When the enterprises fail, the engagements cannot be met; other engagements based on these also fail, and so on through the whole industrial organization. Such crises are inevitable in a new country. Enterprises run in fashions. At any one time great groups of producers tend to one line of industry. That industry is sure to be overdone and to come to a crisis. In a free country, where every man is at liberty to direct his enterprise as he sees fit, what is the sense, when it turns out that he has made a mistake, of trying to throw the losses on other people? No one would propose it as to an individual or a number, but when there is a great interest it makes itself a political power and produces a platform for the same purpose, generally with inflated principles of humanity, justice, democracy, and Americanism as wind-attachments to make it float.

Mr. St. John says that the farmers are spending ten dollars an acre to get eight or nine dollars an acre. What farmer in the United States can tell how many dollars he spends on an acre? What is the sense of these pretendedly accurate figures? But, if they had sense, what would be the gain of cutting the dollars in two? If the farmer spent twenty silver dollars on an acre and got back sixteen or eighteen, how would he be benefited? The dollars of outlay are of the same kind as the dollars of return in any case. If it is true that the return does not equal the outlay, it must be on account of some facts of production, and it requires but a moment's reflection to see that changing the currency in which outlay and income are reckoned cannot change the relation between the two.

A dispassionate view of facts will go to prove that the world is reasonably and ordinarily prosperous at the present time, except where particular classes and industries are affected by special circumstances, as some classes and industries are being affected at all times. The land-owners of western Europe are in distress on account of the competition of new land, with cheapened means of transportation, but now we are told that the holders of the other side of the competition, the land-owners of the new soil, are victims of distress. It must be, then, that too much labor and capital are being expended on the soil the world over, and that, too, in spite of all the protective tariffs drawing people to the textile and metal industries. Our silver men say that this is not the correct inference. They say that the people on the new land suffer because the prices are set in coins of gold and the debits and credits are kept in terms of those coins. The prices are fixed in the world's market in gold. They will be so fixed, whatever we may do with our coinage laws. If the proceeds, in being brought home, are converted into silver value, a new opportunity for brokerage and exchange gambling will be given to the hated bankers and brokers of Wall Street. That is the only difference which will be produced. It would be far more sensible to say that distress is produced by doing the business on the English system of weights and measures, in bushels and pecks, and that prosperity would be produced by doing it on the metric system, in litres and hectolitres, for that charge would at least be harmless. Our distress could all be dispelled in a week by an act of Congress making all contracts, beyond political peradventure, that which they are in law and fact, gold contracts.

There is, however, another cause of hard times for some people which is far more important in our present case than any other. That is the case of the boom which has collapsed. We hear a great deal about "Wall Street gambling." The gambling in Wall Street is insignificant compared with the gambling in land, buildings, town sites, and crops which goes on all over the country, and which is participated in chiefly by the men who declaim about Wall Street. For three hundred years our history has been marked by the alternations of "prosperity" and "distress" which are produced by the booms and their collapses. When the collapse comes the people who are left long of goods and land always make a great outcry and start a political agitation. Their favorite device always is to try to inflate the currency and raise prices again until they can unload.

It is a very popular thing to tell men that they have a grievance. That most of them find it hard to earn as much money as they need to spend goes without saying. Now comes the wily orator and tells them that this is somebody's fault. In old times, if a man was sick, it was always assumed that somebody had bewitched him. The witch was to be sought. The medicine-man had to name somebody, and then woe to the one who was named. Our medicine-men say that it is the gold-bugs, Wall Street, England, who are to blame for hard times. Whether there is any rational proof of connection is as immaterial as it always was in witchcraft. It is a case of pain and passion. The "gold standard" has done it! There is something to hate and denounce. All would be well if silver could be coined at four hundred and twelve and a half grains to the dollar. But the assumption is that while the farmers would sell their products for twice as many "dollars" as now, in silver, all the prices of things which they want to buy would remain at the same number of dollars and cents as now, in gold; that is, it is believed that wheat would be at, say, one dollar and fifty cents per bushel in silver, instead of seventy-five cents in gold, but that cloth would remain at fifty cents a yard in silver, if it is now fifty cents a yard in gold. When this assumption is brought out into clear words, every one knows that such can never be the result. The proposed cure is like a witch cure. It lacks rational basis, and cannot command the confidence of men of sense. If the times were ever so bad, such a cure could only make them worse.

THE FREE–COINAGE · SCHEME IS IMPRAC-
TICABLE AT EVERY POINT

THE FREE–COINAGE SCHEME IS IMPRAC-
TICABLE AT EVERY POINT [1]

The Program.

IN two former articles I have discussed some points
which are presented by the advocates of the free coinage of silver, on the assumption that their project was
feasible and their conception of its operation correct.
They have laid out a program; free coinage, silver standard,
great demand for silver, rise of prices, rise in the value of
silver, cancellation of debts, prosperity. They now admit that this program would involve a panic, but it would
come out, they say, at the desired result in two or three
years. They denounce the gold standard as having caused
hard times, but they plan a program with a panic as an
incident on the way to a silver standard as if it was a trifle.
*There is not a step in this program which could or would
be carried out as planned.*

Free Silver Means Fiat Paper Money.

The amount of circulating cash of all kinds in the hands
of the people at the present time is about nine hundred
millions. If the dollar was reduced to half its present
value, and if allowance was made for reserves, two thousand million silver dollars would be the specie requirement
of the country. We already have nearly five hundred
millions of such dollars. Hence the country could not use
at the utmost, if the new silver dollar was worth not more
than half the present gold dollar, and if the total circula-

[1] *Leslie's Weekly*, September 10, 1896.

tion consisted of silver without any paper, but three times
as many more silver dollars as we have now.   But every
one knows that such a state of the currency never would
exist.   We should have paper "based on silver"; that is
to say, the silver inflation never will be carried out.   It
will turn to paper inflation at the first step.   Who can believe that, if the silver standard was adopted, silver would
be bought and piled up dollar for dollar against the paper,
and that the paper would be issued only as fast as the silver
could be coined?   In fact, silver would no doubt be dropped
and forgotten, and we should have plain and straightforward fiat money of paper.   Such ought to be faced as the
only real sense and probable outcome of the present agitation for the free coinage of silver.

Limit of the Amount of Silver which could be Absorbed.

Let us, however, proceed upon the assumption that the
plan proposed is sincere, and that the attempt would be
made to carry it out in good faith.   The circulation in the
hands of the people would be paper, for they would become sick of silver and revolt against it.   There would
then be two thousand million dollars in paper afloat, each
"dollar" being of silver and worth half a present gold one.
We have now five hundred million silver dollars.   At the
utmost not more than another five hundred millions of
silver could be absorbed into the system.   That would give
reserves of fifty per cent of the total currency, and that is
the maximum of the demand for silver which could be
created if the United States went over to the silver standard.   The supply would come from all over the earth.   Mr.
St. John is sure that none would come from Europe, because legal tender silver there is at a higher ratio than sixteen to one.   Not a nation in Europe which is now under

the yoke of silver would hesitate a moment to demonetize it and send it here if we opened our mints to it at sixteen to one. He also assures us that none would come here from the East because the course of silver has always been from West to East. The course of silver has turned from East to West more than once when there was a profit on bringing it back, and that is the only condition necessary to bring it back again. Japan would adopt a gold currency the moment that the United States adopted a silver one.

It is Impossible Indefinitely to Increase the Circulation.

The power of our currency to absorb silver is not unlimited. People seem to believe that they can go on and increase the monetary circulation indefinitely. This is possible with paper, which has no commodity value and cannot be exported, always understanding that the paper will depreciate as issued, but it is not possible with any money which has commodity value. When silver has been put into circulation here to such an amount that all the fictitious value given to it by the coinage law has been eliminated — that is to say, when so many silver dollars, or paper bearing the obligation of silver dollars, have been issued as will equal in value the present circulation — then there will be no profit in sending silver here from elsewhere, and no more profit in minting silver here than in sending it elsewhere. As we have seen, there is no reason to estimate the amount of silver which would be absorbed in this operation at more than five hundred millions. The miners are making all this agitation for the sake of that share which they could get in furnishing this sum. That share would really not exceed the silver they had on hand when the law was put in force.

ANTAGONISTIC INTERESTS OF MINERS AND POPULISTS.

What share, then, would the silver-miners get in the results of the enterprise? They could get none unless the new silver was bought only of them, and only bought gradually as they produced it, and bought at a rising price as the demand of debtors acted upon it. Not one of these conditions would be fulfilled. The debtors and the silver-miners really have antagonistic interests at every point. It has been proposed that only American silver should be accepted at the mint. That plan is impracticable in any case, but, when the Populists had their victory in hand, does anybody suppose that they would wait eight or ten years for the realization of their hopes while the mines were producing new silver, being certain that that delay would cause all they hoped for to slip through their fingers? I repeat: The interests of the two factions are all antagonistic to each other, and one of them is destined inevitably to be the dupe of the other. That destiny is reserved for the miners who, besides, are paying all the expenses.

Already, so far as the campaign has proceeded, this antagonism has begun to manifest itself. Mr. Bryan says that his plan will make silver worth one dollar and twenty-nine cents per ounce fine. He thus takes his position with the miners' faction. Thereupon the organs of the repudiators' faction have begun to remonstrate. That is not at all what they are fighting for. They do not want their scheme to raise silver at all. But if it does not, the miners gain nothing. If it does, then again the repudiators take to paper money and the miners win nothing.

The mechanical difficulty of recoining the silver with the necessary rapidity could probably be overcome. There are machine-shops enough to do it if there was a party in power which had that reckless determination to execute its will which these people show. We may, therefore, go on to consider the rise of prices.

The Rise of Prices.

The rise in prices would regularly occur only as the new silver or paper was put out, but as the consequences would all be discounted it would be sudden and rapid. It would not, however, affect all things at the same time or to an equal degree. It is here that one of the first disappointments would occur. It is not possible to put up prices when and as one would like to do it, even when the rise is due to inflation. The effect cannot all be distributed at once. An advance in price reacts on business relations, that is, on the industrial organization. Many people and many interests find that they cannot push against others until long after they have been pushed against themselves. The wages class and the farmers are the ones who are most clearly in this position, at least as far as the latter do not produce articles for export. It must be plain that in such a convulsion of the market everybody will try to save himself at the expense of others. Who will succeed? Those certainly who spend their lives in the market and already possess the control of its machinery; not those whose time is occupied in the details of production.

Where the Expected Gains would Go.

It is said that the farmer would sell his grain and cotton, as now, for gold; that he would exchange the gold for silver; would get the silver coined and would pay his debts with it. Would any individual farmer do this? Would any one man go through the steps of this operation? — see the buyer of his products, handle the gold and silver, go to the mint? Certainly not. All these operations would go on through the commercial and financial machinery. They would be executed by different individuals, in the way of business, through the organization, and every one of them would be lost to view. Every operation would have to be paid for. Every operation would give a new chance for more middlemen and more charges. Would, then, the gains of this grand scheme go to the farmer? Not at all. They would go to the "brokers and speculators of Wall Street." They would be lost in commissions and charges. The type of operator whom the Populist seems to think of when he talks about "Wall Street sharks," exists, although his importance in Wall Street is not as great as that of the political farmer in agriculture; but this type of man does not care what the currency legislation is, except that he would like to have a great deal of it, and to have it very mixed. Whatever it is, when it is made and he sees what it is, he will proceed to operate upon it.

PLAYING INTO THE HANDS OF THE MONEY SHARKS.

We hear fierce denunciations of what is called the "money power." It is spoken of as mighty, demoniacal, dangerous, and schemes are proposed for mastering it which are futile and ridiculous, if it is what it is said to be. Every one of these schemes only opens chances for money-jobbers and financial wreckers to operate upon brokerages and differences while making legitimate finance hazardous and expensive, thereby adding to the cost of commercial operations. The parasites on the industrial system flourish whenever the system is complicated. Confusion, disorder, irregularity, uncertainty are the conditions of their growth. The surest means to kill them is to make the currency absolutely simple and absolutely sound. Is it not childish for simple, honest people to set up a currency system which is full of subtleties and mysteries, and then to suppose that they, and not the men of craft and guile, will get the profits of it?

THE DELUSION OF THE DEBTORS

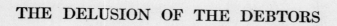

THE DELUSION OF THE DEBTORS [1]

FIFTY years ago a political agitation was started for the annexation of Texas. As the enterprise appeared like a barefaced piece of land-grabbing, it was necessary to invent some historical, political, and moral theories which would give it another color. One such theory was that Texas had properly belonged to us, but that it was given away by Monroe and Adams in 1819. Therefore the project was presented as one for the *re*-annexation of Texas.

THE RE-MONETIZATION OF SILVER.

An attempt is now made to impugn the coinage act of 1873 under various points of view, in order to lay a foundation for the claim that it is only sought now to *re*-monetize silver. Not a single imputation on the act of 1873 has ever been presented which will stand examination, but, if that were not so, that act was like any other act of Congress which has become the law of the land, and under which we have all been obliged to live for twenty-five years. We cannot go back and undo the law and live the twenty-five years over again. All the mistakes and follies of the past are gone into the past for all classes and all persons amongst us. The men of the past must be assumed to have acted according to their light, and we who inherit the consequences of what they did must make the best of both the good and ill of it, as the case may be, or as we think it is. If now we make a new coinage law it must stand on its own merits, and on the responsibility of the men who make it, now and for the future. All references back to 1873 are idle and irrelevant.

[1] *Leslie's Weekly*, September 17, 1896.

The plain fact, therefore, to be faced without any disguise, is that we are invited to debase the coinage and lower the standard of value, *now* and for the future, as a free act of political choice, to be deliberately adopted in a time of profound peace, and that this is to be done with the intention and hope that it will perpetrate a bankruptcy at fifty cents on the dollar for all existing debtors. Can this project be executed? It cannot. The scheme and plan of it for a nation of seventy million people is silly and wicked at the same time, and is both, beyond the power of words to express. The projectors of it deal with the economic phenomena of a great nation as if they were talking about a game at cards, and they plan to do this with prices and that with debts, this with exports and that with banks, as if they were planning a program for building a barn. If we try to realize the operation proposed we shall see how childish and absurd it is.

We must distinguish between three classes of debtors: great financial institutions, small mortgagors, and partners in collapsed booms.

Financial Institutions as Debtors.

The great financial institutions are intermediaries between debtors and creditors. They have received capital from some people and lent it to others. They have to recover it and pay it back. If they only recover it at fifty cents on the dollar, they can only repay it in the same way. What this would mean is that the creditors of those institutions would be paid "dollars," but that when they tried to re-invest them they would find that prices had risen to a greater or less degree in those dollars for the things which they wanted to buy. To this the Populists answer, triumphantly, that now the debtors find that the prices of their products have fallen, so that when they try to sell them they cannot get enough to pay their debts; but the debtors are those who made contracts and undertook enterprises five, ten, fifteen, or twenty years ago, expecting to make gains which they certainly would have kept. As things have turned out they have not made the gains, and their plan is to escape the loss by throwing it on some one else. The institutions in question, however, are bound to protect the interests of either body of their clients, borrowers or depositors, when either is unjustly threatened, and they are by no means destitute of means to do it. A law to forbid specific coin contracts is but one step in the desperate policy of prostituting law and corrupting the administration of justice, which would be necessary in the attempt to force through the plan under discussion. It would fail at last, because the advocates of it would find that, as the popular saying is, it would "fly up and hit them in the face." It is not possible to throw society and all its most important institutions into confusion without ruining all the interests of everybody, and at last everybody but the tramp or pauper has to ask himself whether it will pay. As for the institutions, many of them would be ruined in the operation. It is not possible for them simply to collect and repay in the debased dollars. The operation would produce snarls and knots at every turn. Lawsuits would multiply on all sides, and would so entangle the affairs of the institution as to ruin it. The proof of this is presented by the difficulties of liquidation in any case, even when there is no question of currency revolution, and when general affairs are in a normal condition, unless there is time and security for all the operations. In this case the demands on the institution would be precipitated at once, so far as the form of contract would allow.

SMALL MORTGAGORS.

The small mortgagors are either wages-men or farmers. As to the wages-men, their wages would undoubtedly go up in time as prices went up, but in the paralysis of industry which would be the first distinct effect of the plan, as soon as it was known that the experiment was to be made, immense numbers of wages-men would be thrown out of employment, and all wages would fall on account of this condition of the labor market. Later, when things began to adjust themselves to the new basis, wages would be low with prices high, both in silver. Advance of wages would come, but it would have to be won through strikes and a prolonged industrial war. In the state of things supposed it would be every man for himself. The wages class would be weakest of all under the circumstances, as they are in every case of "hard times." How would mortgagors of this class traverse such a time and keep up their interest? As to the principal, which is to be halved, it cannot be halved unless it is paid, and the mortgagor has nothing to pay it with except the *surplus* which he can save from his wages over the cost of living. The project promises woe and ruin to the wages class, with industrial war and class hatred as moral consequences of the most far-reaching importance.

FARMER-MORTGAGORS.

The farmers expect to double the price of their products, and so get silver to pay off their mortgages. It has been shown elsewhere [1] how illusory this expectation is as regards prices. Prices would rise, indeed, in silver, but irregularly and unequally. They would rise for all things which a farmer buys as well as for all that he sells. If, as the silver theorists generally say, all prices were to rise

[1] Pp. 161–162.

uniformly, the farmer would gain but little. For the only means he would win toward paying off his mortgage would be the *surplus* of his income over his outgo, and this he could only apply year by year as he won it. If, then, the whole scheme could be made to work smoothly provided the victims of it would submit to it without resistance, does this afford any probability of realizing the great hopes which are built upon the scheme?

Social War the Consequence.

But victims would not submit without resistance, and once more we come to the result that no effect can be expected from this undertaking but social war, and a convulsion of the entire social system, whose consequences defy analysis or prediction. If a man says that he "does not see" what great difference going over to the silver standard will make, it must be that he is little trained to understand the workings of the industrial system in which he lives and on which he depends. It is a monstrous thing that a free, self-governing people should join a political battle, in this year of grace 1896, over the question whether to debase their coinage or not.

The Exploded Booms.

The third class of debtors is by far the most important in this matter — those who are caught in exploded booms. The peaceful and honest mortgagors of farms and homesteads are not the ones who have gotten up this political agitation. The jobbers, speculators, and boom-promoters have been one of the curses of this country from the earliest colonial days. They are men of the "hustling" type, jobbing in politics with one hand and in land or town lots with the other. It is they who, at the worst periods of financial trouble in our history, have always appeared in the lobby, eager for "relief," declaiming about the "people," the "money power," the "banks," "England," etc. They have always favored schemes for fraudulent banks, or paper money, or state subsidies, or other plans by which they could unload on the state or on their creditors. Just now it is silver, because silver has fallen within twenty-five years so much that it is what is called "cheap money." This type of men have always used a dialect, part of which is quoted above, which is so well marked that it suffices to identify them. The history of financial distress in this country is full of it. No scheme which has ever been devised by them has ever made a collapsed boom go up again. With very few exceptions, they have, on account of such expedients, only floundered deeper in the mire. The exceptions have been those who have succeeded in making the state provide them with capital, although by no means all of these have been hard-headed enough to use it to "get out." Generally they believe in themselves and their schemes, and use new capital only to plunge in again still deeper.

It is men of this class and the silver-miners who have brought the present trouble upon us, who have invented and preached the notions about the crime of '73, the hard times, the magical influence of silver, and all the rest. It is they who have filled and engineered conventions. They will gain no more now than in any former crisis, but they insist on involving us all in turmoil, risk, and ruin by their schemes to save themselves.

THE CRIME OF 1873

THE CRIME OF 1873 [1]

LEGISLATIVE HISTORY OF THE ACT OF 1873.

IT is alleged that the law of 1873 was enacted surreptitiously. Mr. Bryan is quoted as having said that the free-coinage men only ask for a restoration of "that system that we had until it was stricken down in the dark without discussion." Within the last ten years the facts of the legislative history of that law have been published over and over again. They are to be found in the report of the Comptroller of the Currency for 1876, page 170; in "Macpherson's Political Manual" for 1890, page 157, and in "Sound Currency," Vol. III, No. 13. The bill was before Congress three years, was explained and debated again and again. The fact that the silver dollar was dropped was expressly pointed out. It is not now justifiable for any man who claims to be honest and responsible to assert that it was passed "in the dark and without discussion." The fact is that nobody cared about it. It is noteworthy that the act is not in "Macpherson's Manual" for 1874. It was not thought to be of any importance. It was not until after the panic of 1873 that attention began to be given to the currency. To that, I who write can testify, since I tried in vain, before that time, to excite any interest in the subject. I was once in the gallery of the House of Representatives when a question of coinage was before the House. I counted those members who, as far as I could judge, were paying any attention. There were six. What is it necessary to do in such a case in order to prevent the claim, twenty-five years later, when countless interests have vested

[1] *Leslie's Weekly*, September 24, 1896.

under the law, that the law is open to "reversal" because it was passed "in the dark"?

Was it Passed Surreptitiously?

How can a law be passed through Congress surreptitiously? We have indeed heard of bills being "smuggled through" in the confusion attending the last hours of the session, or as an amendment, or under a misleading title. There are the rules of order, however, by which all legislation is enacted. All laws which get through the mill are equally valid. There never has been and never can be any distinction drawn between them according to their legislative history. In the present case there was not the slightest manœuvre or trick, nor is there even room to trump up an allegation of the kind.

That the People Did Not Know of It.

It is said that "the people" did not know what was being done. How do they ever know what is being done? There is all the machinery of publicity, and it is all at work. If people do not heed (and of course in nearly all cases they do not), whose fault is it? Who is responsible to go to the ten million voters individually and make sure that they heed, lest twenty-five years later somebody may say that the fact that they did not heed lays down a justification for a new project which certainly is "a crime" in the new sense which is given to that word here?

Motive of the Law.

The act of 1873 did not affect any rights or interests. It took away an option which had existed since 1834, but had never been used, and, for ten years before this act was passed, had sunk entirely out of sight under paper-money inflation. Secretary Boutwell, when he first brought the matter to the attention of Congress in 1870, explained the proposed legislation as a codification of existing coinage laws. Later it took the shape of a complete simplification of existing law, history, and fact, in order to put the coinage on the simplest and best system as a basis for resumption. As we had then no coin, we had a free hand to put the system on the best basis, there being no vested rights or interests to be disturbed. That this was a wise and sound course to pursue under the circumstances is unquestionable. Three years later, by the rise in greenbacks and the fall in silver, it came about that four hundred twelve and one-half grains of silver, nine-tenths fine, was worth a little less than a greenback dollar. The old option would, therefore, if still existent, have been an advantage to debtors. Complaint and clamor for the restoration of the option then began, but to give such an option, after the market had changed, would be playing with loaded dice. The European countries which still retained the option abolished it as soon as silver began to fall, and we, if we had retained it open until that time, ought to have done the same.

Alternate Ruin to Debtors and Creditors.

The inflation of the Civil War had a direful effect upon all creditors on contracts outstanding in 1862. The resumption of specie payments had a similar effect on debtors under contracts made between 1868 and 1878. Greenbackism and silver debasement were produced by resistance to this operation. The debtors of to-day are not those of that period. The debts of that period are paid off. The pain and strain have been borne. The credit of the United States has been established, the currency restored, and the whole business of the country for seventeen years has been completely established on the gold dollar as the dollar of account for all transactions whatsoever. The population of the country is now two and a half times what it was in the war time, and its wealth is probably a much greater multiple. The debts now outstanding have, with unimportant exceptions, been contracted since the resumption of specie payments. What is now proposed is to enter upon a new period of these alternations of wrong and injustice, first to creditors, then to debtors, and so on, and to do this in a time of peace, not from any political necessity, but on the ground of some economic interpretations of the facts of the market, which are incapable of verification and proof, when they are not obviously erroneous and partisan. The effect of the various compromises with silver is that the currency is once more intricate and complicated, excessive and confused, so that few can understand it, and it offers all sorts of chances for perverse and mischievous interpretations.

Demonetization Removed No Money from Use.

The law of 1873 never threw a dollar of silver or other currency out of circulation. We hear it asserted that "demonetization" destroyed half the people's money. People say this who know nothing of the facts, but infer that demonetization must mean that some silver dollars which were money had that character taken from them. No one of the other demonetizations, which took place in Europe at about the same time, diminished the money in use. The result of changes in 1873–1874 was that the amount of silver coin in use in Europe was greatly increased, and has remained so since.

The resumption of specie payments after 1873 by a number of nations which had issued paper money in the previous period, and the alternate expenditure and re-collection of war-hoards of gold, had far greater importance than the demonetizations.

There has been no diminution of the world's coined money within fifty years, but a steady and rapid increase of it. There have been fluctuations in the production of gold and silver such as belong to the production of all metals and are inevitable.

THE ALLEGED SCRAMBLE FOR GOLD.

There has been no "scramble for gold." Those who do not put any obstacle in the way of gold get more of it than they want. The Bank of England has had lately the largest stock of gold that it ever had, and complaints have begun to be heard of a glut. The gold-production in the last five years is the greatest ever known and there is no fear of any lack of it, whatever may be the sense in which any one chooses to speak of a "lack." There is not and has not been any "scarcity of gold." There is no such thing conceivable, except where paper has been issued in excess, so that it is hard to keep enough gold to redeem it with.

PROOF THAT THERE HAS BEEN NO SCARCITY OF GOLD.

There is one proof that there has been no scarcity of money for twenty-five years past which has not indeed passed unnoticed, but which has not received the attention which it deserves; that is the rate of interest. The rate of interest is normally due to the supply and demand of loanable capital, and has nothing to do with money. The value of money is registered by prices, not by the rate of interest. But whenever there is a special demand for money of account — that is, for the solvent of debts — the rate of interest on capital passes over into a rate for the solvent of debts. Banks lend capital in its most universal form, i.e., the currency or money of account, or bank credits. If credit fails, as in a time of crisis and panic, actual cash in the money of account is wanted. This now is loaned, under a rate, by the same persons and institutions who formerly loaned capital, and the one phenomenon passes into the other without any line of demarcation. The transition, however, never takes place except in time of crisis, and therefore at a *high* rate. From this it follows certainly that never when the market rate is *low* can it be a rate for the solvent of debts. Now, ever since 1873, with the exception of periods of special stringency in 1884, 1890, and 1893, we have had very low rates of interest; the rate for call loans (which in this connection are the most important) has been about two per cent. This is a demonstration that the country has not been suffering from a crisis on account of a lack of currency for the normal needs of business. Proofs could be presented, on the other hand, that the currency for the last six years has been constantly in excess, excepting in 1893, when the credit of the currency failed for a time.

How to Get Poor and Rich at the Same Time.

Mr. St. John tries his hand at the relation between prices and interest in connection with our subject. He says: "If the dollar can be cheapened by increasing the number of dollars, so that each dollar will buy less wheat, the increasing price of wheat will increase the demand for dollars to invest in its production." Evidently he fails to distinguish between the rise in price of wheat from one gold dollar to two gold dollars per bushel, and the rise in wheat from one gold dollar to two fifty-cent silver dollars per bushel. The former would undoubtedly stimulate production. The latter would do so also, among farmers who shared Mr. St. John's confusion on this matter. There would be many of them. They would imagine that they were getting rich by raising wheat to sell at two silver dollars, or five, ten, fifteen, or twenty paper dollars, as depreciation went on. Hence, as he says, they would pay a banker eight, ten, twelve, or fifteen per cent, in the depreciated dollars, in order to get "money," as he calls it, with which to raise wheat. Mr. St. John thinks that this would mean that farmer and banker were both magnificently prosperous. It would mean that the real value which came in was steadily growing less than that which went out, so that the capital was being consumed. Hence the high rates of inflation times, and the disaster which follows when the truth is realized. They told a story in Revolutionary times of a man who invested his capital in a hogshead of rum which he sold out at an enormous advance — in Continental paper; but when he went to buy a new supply, all his "money" would only buy a barrel. This he retailed out at another enormous advance — in Continental — but when he went to buy more he had only enough money to buy a gallon. If he had borrowed his first capital he might have paid twenty per cent for it — in Continental — but the banker would hardly have made a good affair.

Monopoly of the Money.

We hear it asserted that the gold standard gives the owners of gold power to appropriate the money and make it scarce, and that they have used this power. Why, then, under silver or paper, may not the holders of silver or paper do the same? That the holders of gold have not done it has been shown above. But nobody can do it with any kind of value money. There are no "holders of gold." He who holds gold wins no gains on it. The bankers who are supposed to hold it, if peace and security reign, put it all out at loan in order to get gain on it. When peace and security do not reign it is not safe to put it out, and borrowers, fearing to engage in new enterprises, do not present a demand for it.   Furthermore, the greatest gains can then be won by holding money ready to buy property when the crash comes.   That is what those who own surpluses are doing now.   Hence there are no "holders of gold" until monetary threats and dangers call them into existence. Silver legislation has made a great many.   The law of 1873 never made any.

There is not, therefore, a fact or deduction about the law of 1873, or the history of the market since, which the silver men have put forward, which will stand examination.

A CONCURRENT CIRCULATION OF GOLD
AND SILVER

A CONCURRENT CIRCULATION OF GOLD AND SILVER

[1878]

IT seems as if the United States were destined to be the arena for testing experimentally every fallacy in regard to money which has ever been propounded. A few years ago only a very few people here had ever heard of the "double standard" or knew what it meant. In 1873 we became simply and distinctly a "gold country" in law, as we had been for forty years in fact. Immediately after that date silver began to fall in value relatively to gold, so that, if we had been on the "double standard," and had not been deterred by considerations of honor, morality, and public credit, which considerations kept the double-standard countries from taking that course, we could have paid our debts in silver at an advantage. Forthwith all those persons who had before been racking their brains to devise some scheme for resumption without pain or sacrifice, turned their attention to silver, and began to devise plans for getting back to the position which, as they thought, we had unwisely abandoned. The consequence has been that, for the last year, the country has produced numberless editorials, essays, lectures, and speeches, full of the most crude sophistry, and the most astonishing errors as to all the elementary doctrines of coinage and money. The favorite object of all these schemes is to find some means of increasing the amount of money at the disposal of the world, or of this nation, so as to raise prices and make it easier to pay debts. These schemes have taken their point of departure in the speculations of some European economists. In Europe the propositions of the economists in question have never passed beyond the realm of speculation and theoretical discussion amongst professional economists. They have been regarded by some as probably sound, and capable of being made the basis of advantageous legislation. By others, superior in number and authority, they have been regarded as unsound. Inasmuch as they involve an international coinage union between all civilized countries and could be put to the experiment only on a scale involving immeasurable risks, the overwhelming judgment has been that they were out of the question. Here, however, our amateurs and empirics are in hot haste to make the experiments, without any coinage convention, or with the coöperation of only a few and the less important nations, that is to say under circumstances which even the most extreme bimetallists condemn as ruinous.

It must be observed then that there lies back of all this popular discussion a scientific and technical question of great delicacy. I might even say that it is a speculative question, or a question in speculative economics, for we have no experience of an international coinage union, or of a concurrent circulation, of the metals. We have to imagine the state of things proposed and reason *a priori* as to what must be the result. There is a postulate to all these schemes which has never been expressed and never been discussed, but which is assumed to be true. It has two different forms: (1) A concurrent circulation of gold and silver may be established in any country: (2) A concurrent circulation of gold and silver may be established by a coinage union of all civilized nations. These postulates, or we may say this postulate, for the latter includes the former, I have now to bring in question. If the science of money teaches that there cannot be a concurrent circulation of the metals, then the schemes which I have referred to are all condemned. The question, moreover, has won such an immediate and practical significance in the country that it is no longer a subject for academical discussion amongst economists, about whom opinions may differ without importance.

The Senate of the United States has just passed a bill containing the following provision:

"Sec. 2. That immediately after the passage of this act the President shall invite the governments of the countries composing the Latin Union, so called, and of such other European nations as he may deem advisable, to join the United States in a conference to adopt a common ratio between gold and silver for the purpose of establishing internationally the use of bimetallic money and securing a fixity of the relative value between those metals; such conference to be held at such a place in Europe or in the United States at such a time within six months as may be mutually agreed upon by the executives of the governments joining in the same. Whenever the governments so invited, or any three of them, shall have signified their willingness to unite in the same, the President shall, by and with the advice and consent of the Senate, appoint three commissioners who shall attend such conference on behalf of the United States, and shall report the doings thereof to the President, who shall transmit the same to Congress."

The conception which governed this legislation is plain enough. It proposes to secure a concurrent circulation of the two metals at a fixed ratio by an international agreement. The proposition is to put the experiment at work when only three nations besides ourselves consent and in the meantime to remonetize silver here at sixteen to one when the market ratio is seventeen and one-half to one. This adds to the absurdity of the bill, but has no bearing on my present controversy. I challenge the postulate which is assumed, which has never been discussed, much less proved, that a concurrent circulation is possible if an international union can be made. Anybody who concedes this concedes, as I view it, the fundamental and controlling error in the silver craze. If this premise is conceded, there can be no further controversy on the arena of science. It remains only to try to overcome practical difficulties. Such is the issue I raise with those who, under any reservations whatsoever, concede that a concurrent circulation is possible. In a body of scientific gentlemen I need only refer to the mischief done in science by assuming the truth of postulates without examination, and I need make no apology for bringing forward with all possible force and vigor a controversy on a point so essential. It is my duty to say that I may be in error, and I have the misfortune to differ here with gentlemen from whom I dissent seldom and unwillingly, but it will not be denied that, while there is controversy on a point so essential, and at a moment when practical measures of high importance to every person in this country are proposed, based on certain views of the matter, I am right in promoting discussion. I wish to be understood as paying full respect to everybody, but I address myself, without compliments, to the question in hand. I shall be satisfied if I make it appear that I have some strong grounds for the position I take in a long, careful, and mature study of this question in all its bearings.

It will economize time and space, if, before entering on my subject, I try to clear up two points: (1) what is an economic force or an economic law, and how ought we to go about the study of economic phenomena? (2) What is a legal tender?

(1) What should be our conception of an economic force or an economic law, and how ought we to study economic phenomena? Some people seem to think that economic phenomena constitute a domain of arbitrary and

artificial action. They think that social phenomena of every kind are subject to chance or to control. They see no sequence between incidents of this kind. They have no conception of social forces. They think economic laws are only formulae established by grouping a certain number of facts together, like a rule in grammar, and they are prepared for a list of exceptions to follow. This conception, in its grosser forms, is now banished from the science, but it still has strong hold on popular opinion. It also still colors a great many scientific discussions, those, namely, who seek to carry forward the science by following out the complicated cases produced by the combined action of economic forces in our modern industrial life, and describing them in detail. In my opinion such efforts are all mistaken.

I regard economic forces as simply parallel to physical forces, arising just as spontaneously and naturally, following a sequence of cause and effect just as inevitably as physical forces — neither more nor less. The perturbations and complications which present themselves in social phenomena are strictly analogous to those which appear in physical phenomena. The social order is, to my mind, the product of social forces tending always towards an equilibrium at some ideal point, which point is continually changing under the ever-changing amount or velocity of the forces or under their new combinations. Consequently, I do not believe that the advance of economic science depends upon fuller and more minute description of complicated social phenomena as they present themselves in experience, but on a stricter analysis of them in order to get a closer and clearer knowledge of the laws by which the forces producing them operate. If this can be attained, all the complications which arise from their combined action will be easily solved. Of course we have peculiar difficulties to contend with, inasmuch as we cannot constitute experi-

ments, and it is necessary to rely largely upon historical
cases which present now one and now another force or set
of forces in peculiar prominence. The facts which show
the difficulty of the task, however, have nothing to do
with its nature.

According to this view of the matter there is no more
reason to be satisfied with generalities in economics than
in physics. Some writers on economic subjects, who
pride themselves upon scientific reluctance, remind me of
Mr. Brooks, in "Middlemarch." They believe in things
up to a certain point, and are always afraid of going too
far. They would be careful about the multiplication table,
and not bear down too hard on the rule of three. They
do not discriminate between care in the application of rules,
and confidence in scientific results; or between harshness
in personal relations and firm convictions in science. The
more we come to understand economic science the more
clear it is that we are dealing with only another presentation
of matter and force, that is to say, with quantity and law,
so that we have mathematical relations, and have every
encouragement to severity and exactitude in our methods.
When, therefore, it is said that the economists do not pay
sufficient heed to the power of legislation, that is no stop-
ping place for the argument any more than it would be in
physics to say that sufficient heed was not paid to friction.
The question would then arise: What is the force of legislation? Let us study it, just as we would go on to study
friction in mechanics. When it is loosely said (as if that
dismissed the subject) that men have passions and emotions and do not act by rule, the objection is not pertinent
at all. It is connected with another wide and common,
but very erroneous notion, that economic laws involve
some stress of obligation on men to do or abstain from
doing certain things. I suppose this notion arises from the
classification of political economy amongst the moral

sciences. Economic laws only declare relations of cause and effect which will follow, if set in motion. Whether a man sets the sequence in motion at all or not, and if he does so, whether he does it from passion or habit or upon reflection, is immaterial. Such is the case, as I understand it, with all sciences. They simply instruct men as to the laws of this world in which we live that they may know what to expect if they take one course or another, or they instruct men so that they may understand the relations of phenomena of forces beyond our control so that we may foresee and guard ourselves against harm. It follows from all this that I demand and aim at just as close thinking in political economy as in any other science. I think we must try to get as firm hold of principles and fundamental laws as we can, and that, especially in the face of speculative propositions, we ought to cling to and trust the firmly established laws of the science.

(2) As to legal tender, it seems to me that the public mind has been sadly confused under the régime of paper money. Money is any commodity which is set apart by common consent to serve as a medium of exchange. If it is a commodity, it will exchange by the laws of value, and will therefore serve to measure value. It must therefore be a commodity, an object of desire requiring onerous exertion to get it. In theory, it may be any commodity. The question as to what commodity is a question of convenience — that one which will answer the purpose best. Through a long period of experiments we have come to use gold or silver, simply because we found them the best. Convenience here gave rise to custom, and money of gold or silver owes its existence to custom entirely, and not to law at all. Law has only in very few instances even selected that one of the two metals which should be used. Even that has come about through custom. Law, therefore, here as elsewhere where it has been beneficent and

not arbitrary, has followed custom, recognized it, ratified it, and given it sanctions. (1) A legal tender law, therefore, where customary money is used, simply declares that the parties to a contract shall not vex each other by arbitrarily departing from the custom. The creditor shall not demand, and the debtor shall not offer, out of spite or malice, anything but the customary money of the nation. Such a legal tender law has no significance whatever. No one thinks of it or speaks of it or takes it into account, unless he be one of those whose idle malice it prevents.

(2) A legal tender law is used where a subsidiary token currency is employed as a part of the system, to prevent debtors from using it in payment, and to prevent the system from bringing about a depreciation of the money. In this case it is part of the device for using a token currency, and is open to no objection. It would check the debtor when he meant to perpetrate a wrong. It would not enable him to do one.

(3) A legal tender law has been used very often, however, to give forced circulation to a depreciated currency of little or no value as a commodity. In that case the legal tender act enables the debtor to discharge his obligations with less commodities than he and the creditor understood and expected when the contract was made. If the creditor appeals to the courts, they are obliged to rule that the debtor has discharged his obligation, when he has not, and they give the creditor no relief. Hence it appears that a legal tender act giving forced circulation to depreciated currency amounts simply to this: it withdraws the protection of the courts from one party to a contract, and leaves him at the mercy of the other party to the extent of the depreciation of the currency. Obviously no other act of legislation more completely reverses the whole proper object of legislation, or more thoroughly subverts civil order. The English passed two or three acts of this

nature, although they were not specifically acts for making banknotes legal tender, during the bank suspension at the beginning of this century. It would have been interesting to see what English courts would have made of an act which reversed the whole spirit of English law by diminishing the rights of one party under a contract, and which made the courts an instrument for his oppression instead of an institution to provide a remedy, but no case came up. The twelve judges on appeal overturned the sentence of a man convicted of buying and selling gold at a premium. Some few persons demanded and obtained gold payments throughout the suspension but the paper circulation was really sustained by public opinion and consent, it being believed that the bank suspension was necessary. This form of legal tender, therefore, is totally different from that first described. I call it, for the sake of discrimination, a forced circulation. When a legal tender act giving forced circulation to a depreciated currency is first passed, if it applies to existing contracts it transfers a percentage of all capital engaged in credit operations from the creditor to the debtor. In its subsequent action it subjects either party to the fluctuations which may occur in the forced circulation, robbing first one and then another. Hence the debtor interest is that the depreciation once begun shall go on steadily, because any recovery would rob debtors as creditors were robbed in the first place.

Having disposed of these two points I now take up the question I proposed at the outset: Is a concurrent circulation of gold and silver possible under an international coinage union?

Here we have to make a radical distinction between two different propositions for an international coinage union. The first is that of M. Wolowski. He pointed to the comparatively small fluctuations of the precious metals and to the effect which France had exerted by the double standard, and inferred that if all civilized nations would join France in her system they might arrest the fall of either metal before it became important. If the coinage union fixed upon a ratio of one to fifteen and one-half, then, if silver fell all would use silver, which would arrest its fall. If gold should fall, all would use gold. As the metal in use would always be the one which was cheaper than the legal ratio, the other would be above it, if I may so express it. Hence neither would be permanently demonetized, because neither could fall so low as to go out of use. Only one would be used at a time but the other would be within reach, and if either should rise relatively to commodities, debtors would not suffer but might even be benefited by being enabled to turn to the falling metal. This system would require of the law nothing except to prescribe that the mint should coin either metal indifferently which people might bring, silver coins being made fifteen and one-half times as heavy as gold coins of the same denomination, both being of the same fineness. This is Wolowski's plan, and these are the advantages he expected from it. He thought that it would hold the alternative open between the two metals. He feared that silver, if universally demonetized, would fall so low as to go out of use entirely for money. He thought that France and, later, the Latin Union ought not to bear alone the cost of keeping up the value of silver. He thought the debtor ought not to be oppressed by being forced to rely on one metal alone which might rise relatively to commodities. He did not propose to give the debtor the use of the whole mass of both metals at the same time. Indeed that arrangement would defeat Wolowski's purpose, for if the whole mass of both metals could be brought into use at once prices would rise. Those who are indebted now would win, but when prices and credit had adjusted themselves to the bimetallic money the effect would be exhausted. Debts contracted after that would be relatively just as heavy to pay as they are now, and if the precious metals taken together rose relatively to commodities, debtors would have no recourse to anything else. Now this chance of recourse, when the standard of value rose, was just what Wolowski wanted. His language is very guarded and scientific. He never went further than to say that his scheme would restrain and limit the fluctuations of the metals — how far he did not know and did not pretend to say. He thought the fluctuations would be so narrow that the transition from one metal to the other would be a relief to debtors without any appreciable injustice to creditors. All this is very clear and very sensible. On theory it is open to no radical objection. The discussion of it turns upon considerations of practicability and expediency. It is much to be wished that this plan should be called by its proper name: the alternative standard, or, better still, the alternate standard. It counts among its adherents a number of strong men, and many others have signified assent to it on theoretical grounds.

The term "bimetallism" ought to be restricted to another theory of which Cernuschi is the advocate, which has for its purpose to unite the two metals at once in the circulation and give debtors the whole mass of both metals as a means of payment. Cernuschi believes that the international coinage union could arrest the fluctuations of the metals entirely; or that there is some narrow limit of fluctuation within which both would remain in use, and that the coinage union could hold the value-fluctuations of the metals within these limits. The American schemes are numerous and so crude that it is difficult to analyze or classify them. They are also of many different grades. They all, however, seem to have this in common, that they want to secure to the debtor the use of both metals at once, and that they aim at a concurrent circulation. They must, therefore, be classed under bimetallism. These schemes all involve not simply what Wolowski said — that legislation and union could limit the fluctuations — but the proposers know how much it would limit them, and they can control the results. This view has very few adherents in Europe. It has not been discussed there save by one or two writers. It is passed by in silence for reasons which I shall soon show.

The opinion has been expressed that these two propositions differ only in degree. From this opinion I must express my earnest dissent. It is the very cardinal point of my present argument. Wolowski's alternate standard seems to me to rest upon the belief that legislation of the kind proposed would restrict the fluctuations in value of the metals. It affirms that legislation would have a certain tendency. Any plan for a concurrent circulation giving debtors the use of the whole mass of both metals pretends to say how far the tendency would go and what its results would be. To my mind the difference between those two propositions is that between a scientific and an unscientific proposition. We have a parallel case before us. Some say re-monetization would cause an advance in silver. Others say re-monetization would make a four hundred and twelve and one-half grain silver dollar equal in value to a gold one. Are those two propositions the same save in degree? It seems to me that only a very superficial consideration of them could so declare. Obviously they differ in quality more than in degree. The former of these propositions is not false in principle; the question in regard to it must be decided by circumstances. The second is false and erroneous from beginning to end, and would be false even if temporarily and by force of circumstances the silver dollar should become equal to the gold dollar, because it rests, like the old doctrine that nature abhors a vacuum, upon false views of all the forces involved. Just so with regard to a concurrent circulation or bimetallism as compared with the alternate standard. The latter predicts tendencies to arise from the play of certain forces. Those tendencies are the true effect of those forces. The question may be raised whether the means proposed would bring those forces into action, whether they would be as great as is expected, whether they would be counteracted by others, but there is no error as to the nature and operation of economic forces. Bimetallism predicts results, not tendencies. It assumes to measure the consequences and say what will result as a permanent state of things. It therefore involves the doctrine that legislation can control natural forces for definite results. If legislation cannot so control natural forces, then we cannot secure a concurrent circulation, giving the debtor the use of the whole mass of both metals with which to pay his debts. At a time like this, when the silver craze seems to be asserting itself as a mania, by sweeping away some who ought to be most staunch in their adherence to economic laws and most clear in their perception of economic truths, I may be pardoned for insisting most strenuously upon this distinction and upon its importance. Many of the American writers have been betrayed into error by not having examined these two plans and discriminated between them with sufficient care. It is very common to see arguments based upon the alternate standard and inferences drawn as to bimetallism which are entirely fallacious because they cross the gulf between the two theories without recognizing it. Bimetallism is so plainly opposed to fundamental doctrines of political economy that few European economists have felt called upon to discuss it. Here the case is different, and the more ground it wins, and the more danger there is that it will affect legislation, the more urgent is the necessity to resist every form of it.

Now my proposition is that a concurrent circulation,

that is a permanent union of the two metals in the coinage, so that the debtor can use both or either, is impossible. Permanent stability of the metals in the coinage, whether with or without an international coinage union, is just as impossible in economics as perpetual motion is in physics. Against perpetual motion the physicist sets a broad and complete negation, because action and reaction are equal. He does not care what the principle may be on which any one may try to construct perpetual motion. If any one brings to him a perpetual motion perhaps he will spend time to examine and analyze it and show how it contravenes the great law of motion. I claim that a concurrent circulation is impossible on any scheme or under any circumstances because it contravenes the law of value. Value fluctuates under supply and demand at a limit fixed by what Cairnes calls cost of production, or Jevons calls the final increment of utility, or Walras calls scarcity, all of which on analysis will be found to be the same thing. Bimetallism affirms that, under legislation, although supply and demand may vary, value shall not. In order to test this let us next examine the influence of legislation on value.

The cases in which legislation acts on value are all cases of monopoly. Such is the case with token money; such is the case with irredeemable paper. As with every other monopoly, the successful manipulation of these monopolies consists in controlling supply, to fit the supply to the demand at the price which the monopolist wants to get. The history of every monopoly shows the great difficulty, I might say, in the long run, the impossibility, of doing this. The bimetallists propose not to act on the supply, and so create a monopoly, but to act upon the demand. This is a new exercise of legislation, different from any yet tried, and not guaranteed by any experience. Now to act upon the demand is, in the phrase of the stock brokers, to make a corner, that is to buy all that is offered at a price. Stock gamblers do this so as to sell out again at an advance to those who are forced to buy. If there are none who are forced to buy, then those who bought above the market have lost their capital. The propositions of the advocates of the alternate standard and of bimetallism are alike in proposing that all civilized nations shall combine to make a corner on the falling metal. Whether that is a worthy undertaking or not I will not stop to inquire. It is evident that the nations of the coinage union would have no one on whom to unload after they had bought, and that there would be an inevitable loss and waste of capital in the transaction. This, however, is not all. A corner is effective or not according to its scope. It must embrace the whole object to be raised in price, and above all it must act upon a limited amount which is not fed from any new source of supply. A corner on the precious metals is not to be made effective even by a combination of all civilized nations. In my opinion there is a grand fallacy in the notion that a coinage union would do what France did, only on a larger scale. Wolowski saw France, lying between Germany, a silver nation, and England, a gold nation, carry out the compensatory operation, and he inferred that all nations could agree to do the same, more widely, more easily, and with wider distribution of the loss. It seems to me that there was an action and reaction here between members of the group of nations which one can easily understand, but that if all nations joined in the system, the alternation would not work at all for want of a point of reaction. If all nations agreed to join the corner on the falling metal, they could not all bring their new demand to bear on the new supply at the same time. As the mines are limited and local, a new supply would touch the market only at one point. Hence the coinage union implies no aggregation of force at all. Make the union embrace the whole world,

and the effect is just the same as if there were none at
all, the matter standing simply on the natural laws for
the distribution of the precious metals. Control of demand
by a corner or of supply by a monopoly acts more efficiently
the smaller and closer the market is, and, conversely, the
larger and wider the transaction, the less the efficiency.
Furthermore, a corner to succeed must make sure that
there is no source of supply, and that it has to deal only
with an amount which can be computed. The gold corner
on Black Friday, 1869, was ruined when the Secretary of
the Treasury ordered sales of gold. A monopoly in like
manner, must be able to count on steady and uniform demand. The coal combination failed when the hard times
suddenly contracted the demand for coal. Hence the
movement towards a wider market, embracing a larger
quantity, is always a movement towards less, and not
towards greater control by artificial expedients.

Applying these observations to the matter before us, I
have to say (1) that I consider the inference that a coinage
union would do what France did under the double standard,
only more surely and efficiently, quite mistaken; (2) as to
the alternate standard, I do not believe that the alternation would work on a worldwide scale at all. I regard its
operation in France as fully accounted for by the relations
of the three countries, England, France, and Germany;
(3) as to bimetallism, the coinage union, instead of gaining
more stringent control to counteract and nullify the effect
of changes in supply of either metal, would have less effect
in that direction the larger it was.

Having thus examined the nature of artificial interferences with value, and their limitations, I return to my
proposition that to establish a concurrent circulation is
just as impossible as to square the circle or to invent perpetual motion. No doubt it is difficult, perhaps impossible,
to make a demonstration of a negative proposition like

this. The burden of proof lies upon those who bring forward attempts to solve the problem, and I can justly be held only to examine and refute such attempts. No proof has ever been offered by any of the persons in question. No one of them has attempted as much of an analysis of the effect of artificial expedients on value as the one I have just offered. No one of them has attempted to analyze the operation of the proposed coinage union, to show how or why they expect it to act as they say. They pass over this assumption as lightly as our popular advocates of silver assume that re-monetization would put an end to the hard times. They content themselves with analogies, or with loose and general guesses that such and such things would result from a coinage union. We all know what dangers lurk in the argument from analogy. The further you follow it the further you are from the point. An analogy has no proper use save to set in clearer light an opinion or a proposition which must rest for its merits on an appropriate demonstration. Thus the attempt has been made to illustrate the power of governments to control the fluctuations of the metals by the analogy of a man driving two horses. It is said that this is "controlling natural forces for definite results," and it is asked, "if one man in his sphere can do this, why may not the collective might of the nation do this in its sphere?" My answer is that it is in the sphere of man to tame horses, but it is not in the sphere of nations to control value, and therefore the analogy is radically false. I cannot be held to argue both sides of the question. I am not bound to put all the cases of the adversaries into proper shape for discussion and then to refute them. I plant myself squarely upon the fundamental principles of the science of which I am a student and deny that any concurrent circulation is possible except under temporary and accidental circumstances, because it involves the proposition that legislation can control value to bring about desired results. A concurrent circulation must mean one which is concurrent, and if it is to offer debtors the whole mass of both metals to pay their debts with, it must be permanent. If both metals should be used for a time until prices and contracts were adjusted to them, and then one should rise so much as to go out of use, the consequences would be disastrous to debtors beyond anything now apprehended.

I proceed then to criticize the notions of a concurrent circulation, as to their common features. The error with them all is that they try to corner commodities the supply of which is beyond their control or knowledge. That is a fatal error in any corner, as I have already shown. If it were proposed that each nation should have a certain amount of circulation, composed of the two metals in equal parts, and then that the circulation should be closed, then the corner might work and there would be some sense in it. Suppose that a nation had two hundred millions of fixed circulation, half gold and half silver, and that this sum was not in excess of its requirement for money. Then I do not see how either half of the coinage should fall relatively to the other; but if silver did fall, every dollar of silver which was sought would involve the relinquishment of a dollar in gold and this exchange would act on equal and limited amounts of each metal. It would then depress one metal and raise the other to an exactly equal degree. The balance might, in that case, be retained. The hypothesis of a closed circulation is, however, preposterous. No one thinks of it.

The plan of a concurrent circulation with a free mint strikes, upon close examination, at every step, against difficulties of that sort which warn a scientific man that he is dealing with an empirical and impossible delusion. How is it to be brought about? The movement towards a bimetallic circulation would never begin unless the ratio of the coinage was the market ratio. It would not go on unless the mint ratio followed every fluctuation of the market. It would not be accomplished unless the mint ratio at last was that of the market. It would not remain unless the market ratio remained fixed. But the mint ratio cannot be changed from time to time. If it were, the result would be inextricable confusion in the coins, driving us back to the use of scales and weights with which to treat the coins as bullion.

If we pass over this difficulty, and suppose, for the sake of argument, that the system had been brought into activity, the reasons why it could not stand present themselves in numbers. They all come back to this, that the supply is beyond our knowledge and control. If the supply of either metal increased, it would overthrow the legal rating at the point at which it was put into the market, and would destroy the equality there. Its effects would spread according to the amount of the new supply and the length of time it continued. The bimetallists seem to forget that an increased demand counteracts an increased supply only by absorbing it under a price fluctuation. The same error is familiar in the plans for perpetual motion. Speculations to that end often overlook the fact that we cannot employ a force in mechanics without providing an escapement which is always exhausting the force at our disposal. So the bimetallists seem to think of their enhanced demand as acting on value without an actual action and reaction which consist in absorbing supply under a price fluctuation. The new metal would therefore pass into the circulation and would destroy the equilibrium of the metals in the coinage. If this new addition were only a mathematical increment it would suffice to establish the principle for which I contend and to overthrow the bimetallic theory, for if I see that any force has a certain effect I must infer that the same force increased or continued would go on to greater effects; and if the final effect is not reached it is because the force is not sufficient, not because there is an act of the legislature in the way. If then, silver entered the circulation, gold would leave it and be exported, if the exchanges allowed of any export, or would be hoarded and melted. The silver-producing countries would therefore gravitate towards a silver circulation only, and other countries towards a gold circulation.

Here another assumption of the bimetallists is involved. They assume that the metal to be exported would be the one which falls. Thus, if all nations had a bimetallic circulation, and if the supply of silver in the United States increased, it would be necessary that this silver should be proportionately distributed among all the nations in order to keep up the bimetallic system. No bimetallist has ever faced this question. They assume that Americans would pay their foreign debts with silver in that case, and they rely on the international legal tender law to secure this. This is one of the fallacies of legal tender referred to at the outset. Rates of exchange and prices would at once vary to counteract any such operation, just as they always counteract the injustice of a forced circulation and throw it back on those who try to perpetrate it. It may suffice to put the case this way. If we had both metals circulating together so that a merchant obtained both in substantially equal proportions, and if silver should fall ever so little in our markets, owing to increased production, and if a foreigner were selling his products here, intending to carry home his returns in metal, which metal would he retain to carry away? Obviously that one which at the time and prospectively had the higher value. Rates of exchange and prices would adjust themselves so as to bring about the same result through the mechanism of finance. This is one of the most subtle questions involved in the general issue, but it is vital to the bimetallic theory.

Some writers have satisfied themselves with general opinions — guesses, I am obliged to call them — that if the fluctuations were kept within certain limits the concurrent circulation would stand. They probably rely on an element analogous to friction which unquestionably acts in economy and finance. This element consists of habit, prejudice, passion, dislike of trouble. It acts with great force in retail trade, and in individual cases, and in small transactions. Its force diminishes as we go upwards towards the largest transactions, where the smallest percentages give very appreciable sums. It seems to me that the bimetallic system reduces this friction to a minimum. If a man has to spend a dollar he does not go to a broker to buy a trade dollar with a greenback dollar, and save a cent or two, but if he has both a gold dollar and a silver dollar in his pocket (and, under the bimetallic system, the chances are that when he has two dollars he will have one of each), it needs only the lightest shade of difference in value to determine him which to give and which to hold. A bank of issue, holding equal amounts of the two metals with which to redeem its notes, would find an appreciable profit in giving one and holding the other, and it would require nothing but a word of command to the proper officer, involving no risk at all. Hence I say this friction would be reduced to its minimum under the bimetallic system. It is astonishing what light margins of profit suffice to produce financial movements nowadays; and the tendency is to make the movements turn on smaller and smaller margins. Five in the thousand above par carries gold out of this country. Four in the thousand carries it from England to France. When the French suspended specie payments a depreciation of two in the thousand on the paper sufficed to throw gold out of circulation. A variation in the ratio of metals from $15.5:1$ to $15.6:1$ is a variation of six and one-half in the thousand. I do not see how small a variation must be in order to justify any one in saying that a bimetallic circulation could exist in spite of it. Therefore it seems to me that the more accurately the bimetallic system was established the more delicate and more easily overthrown it would be, while if it was not accurately established it would not come about at all. I submit that such a result is one of the notes of an absurdity in any science.

An analogy has been suggested in illustration and support of the bimetallic theory that two vessels of water connected by a tube tend to preserve a level. I have already indicated my suspicion of all analogies, but I will alter this one to make it fit my idea of bimetallism. Suppose two vessels capable of expansion and contraction to a considerable degree, under the operation of forces which act entirely independently of each other, so that the variations in shape and capacity of each may have all conceivable relations to the corresponding variations of the other. Suppose further that each is fed by a stream of water, each stream being variable in its flow and the variations of each having all possible relations to the variations of the other. The fluctuations in capacity may represent fluctuations of demand, and the fluctuations of inflow, fluctuations of supply. Would the water in the two vessels stand at the same level except temporarily and accidentally, even though the two vessels were connected by a tube? The analogy of the connecting tube could not be admitted even then, because it brings into play the natural law of the equilibrium of fluids, to which the legal tie between the metals is not analogous. If we desire to make the analogy approximately just, in this respect, we may suppose that each vessel has an outlet and that a man is stationed to open the outlet of the vessel in which the water is at the higher point so as to try to keep them both at a level. It is evident that his utmost vigilance would be unavailing to secure the object proposed. I do not borrow the analogy or adopt it. I only show how inadequate it is, in the form proposed.

There is another group of propositions which have many advocates amongst us, of which something ought to be said — propositions of those who want to use silver as a legal tender at its value, under some scheme or other. Some want a public declaration, by appointed persons, from time to time, of the market value. Any such plan would throw on the officers in question a responsibility which would be onerous in the extreme, so much so that no one could or would discharge it; and it would introduce a mischievous element of speculation into the payment of all debts. It is, besides, open to the objections which may be adduced against the other plan, which is to have either coins or bars of silver, assayed and stamped, legal tender for debts at the market quotation. Here we need to remember the definition of legal tender given at the outset. If these silver coins and bars are convenient for the purpose they will come into use by custom and consent at their value. If they really pass at their market value, there will be no advantage to the debtor. One who has silver and wants to pay a debt can do so at its value by selling the silver. In this sense every man who produces wheat, cotton, iron, or personal services, pays his debts with them at their value. One who produced something else than silver would have no object in selling it for silver, to pay his debt with at the value of silver. He would have the trouble of another transaction, he would have to buy silver at its selling price, and the creditor to whom he paid it would have to sell it for money at the broker's buying price, with no advantage to either, but only to the broker. If silver passes at its value, legal tender has no force for it; if it is to have forced circulation in some way, it will help the debtor, as all forced circulation does, by enabling him to keep part of what he borrowed. If then these schemes really mean that silver shall pass at its value, they are of no use. It does so now. If they mean that silver shall be enabled to pay debts in some other way than iron, wheat, cotton, etc., then we know what we are dealing with. There is just as much reason why the government should pay for elevators and issue certificates of the amount and quality of grain, which should be legal tender, as there is why it should assay and stamp silver for that purpose, and issue notes for it. These cases only serve to bring out the distinction between money and merchandise, and to show that the perfection of money does not lie in the direction of a multiple legal tender, but of a single standard, as sharp and definite as possible. Such a standard has the same advantages in exchange as the most accurate measures of length and weight have in surveying or in chemistry, and it is turning backward the progress of monetary science to introduce fluctuations and doubt into the standard of value, just as it would be to cultivate inaccuracy in weights and measures.

Here I am forced to notice another hasty and mischievous analogy. Some devices for composite measures of length have been adopted to avoid contraction and expansion, and it is urged that bimetallic money is a step in the same direction. I by no means assert that science can do nothing to reach a better standard of value than gold is. What progress in that direction may lie in the future no one can tell, and he would be rash who should ever presume to deny that progress can be made; but when any proposition is presented it will have to show what composite measures of length show, viz., that its action is founded on natural laws. Heat and cold act oppositely on the components of the composite measures of length, or the arrangement is such that the action of the natural forces neutralizes. No such scientific principle underlies bimetallic money. The forces determining the value of gold and silver act independently of each other and are not subject to common influences. They are complex, moreover, and their effects are not uniform in their different degrees. Therefore this analogy also fails.

The opinion that a concurrent circulation is not possible has led several of the leading nations of Europe (and, at the time of writing such is still the system of the United States) to adopt the plan of a permanently false rating of gold and silver, so as to use silver as a subsidiary coinage. Silver is permanently overrated, so that it obtains currency above its bullion value. If the civilized nations want to use silver for money, so that the total amount of metallic money in the Western world shall be greater than the amount of gold, and if they are not satisfied with the use of it as subsidiary, then there is only one way left, and that is for some nations to use gold and some to use silver. This was the solution of the bimetallic difficulty which China was forced to adopt a thousand years ago. Some provinces used iron and some copper. The question then arises as to who will take silver. This brings me to the last point of which I have to speak.

I have discussed my subject as if gold and silver stood on the same level of desirability for money, and as if there were no choice of convenience between them. Such is not the case in fact. It will be observed that gold and silver never have been used together. Gold has generally been subsidiary, being employed for large transactions. With the advance of prices and the increase in variety of commodities, as well as in the magnitude of transactions, nations have passed from copper money to silver and from silver to gold. This advance is dictated by convenience. Silver is no longer as convenient a money for civilized industrial and commercial nations as gold. We therefore see them gradually abandoning silver, and we saw the Latin Union set up a bar against silver so soon as the operation of the double legal tender threatened to take away gold and give it silver. Whether this movement from silver to gold can be accomplished without financial convulsions I am not prepared to say, especially in view of the extent to which the nations have depreciated gold by paper issues, but I regard the movement as one which must inevitably go forward. The nations which step into the movement first will lose least on the silver they have to sell. The nations which use silver until the last will lose most upon it, because they will find no one to take it off their hands. If we now abandon the gold standard and buy the cast-off silver of the nations which have been using it and are now anxious to get rid of it, we voluntarily subject ourselves to that loss, which we are in no respect called upon to share. The Dutch at New York kept up the use of wampum longer than the English in New England. When the Yankees were trying to get rid of it, they carried it to New York, adding some which they manufactured for the purpose, and they carried the goods of the Dutchmen away. The latter then found that they held a currency which they could only get rid of at great loss and delay to the Indians north and west of them. The Yankees thus early earned a reputation for smartness. The measure now proposed is a complete parallel, only that now this nation proposes to take the rôle of the Dutch. We shall have to give our capital for silver, and after we have suffered from years of experience with a tool of exchange inferior to that which our neighbors are using, we shall have to get rid of it and buy the best. Then we shall incur the loss — to all those who have anything — of the difference between the capital we gave and that which we can get for the silver. The dreams of getting silver and keeping gold too, so as to have a concurrent circulation, are all vain. At the rating proposed there is no difference of opinion on this point amongst any persons at all qualified to give an opinion. The real significance of the propositions before the country is to make us one of the nations to take silver in the distribution I have described. The notion of a coinage union is impracticable. It would be easier to get up an international union to do away with war. England is perfectly satisfied with her money. She appreciates the peril of monetary experiments and will make none. Germany, Sweden, Finland, Denmark, and Holland have just changed from silver to gold, and will not enter on any new changes for a long period, if ever. The coinage union is therefore out of the question. The issue before us is simply whether we, being a gold nation, will, under these circumstances, abandon gold and take up silver. No doubt the nations which want gold would be very glad to have us do it. We should render them a great service; we should, however, do ourselves great harm, as much so as if we should buy a lot of cast-off machinery from them. They are waiting to see whether we are ignorant and foolish enough to put ourselves in this position; and when they have seen, we shall hear no more of the coinage union.

I have now presented the views to which my study of this question has led me. It will be perceived that I direct my attack against the postulate of all the bimetallic theories. I have carefully discriminated between the alternate standard and bimetallism. I have said little about the former. It is very much a matter of opinion whether it would work or not. I do not believe that it would, under a coinage union, but I should not feel forced to take strong ground against any one who held the contrary opinion. My subject has been a concurrent circulation of gold and silver, and I have tried to controvert the notion that any such thing is possible, with or without a coinage union, because that notion contradicts the first great law of economic science. If that notion is true, then there is no science of political economy at all; there are no laws to be found out, a professional economist has nothing to teach, and he might better try to find some useful occupation. If that notion is true, we have no ground on which to criticize the Congressmen who are trying to pass the silver bill. We cannot predict any consequences or draw any inferences from past experience. If legislation can control value for definite results, then the whole matter is purely empirical. In that case, the Congressional experiment may turn out well for all the grounds we have to assert the contrary; its success would only be questionable, not impossible; if it failed it would not be because its supporters had attempted the impossible, but because they had not used sufficient means. They could go on to try the experiment again and again in other forms and with other means, and they would indeed be doing right to proceed with their experiments, like the old alchemists, in the hope of hitting it at last. No economist would have any ground upon which to step in and define the limits of the possible, or to prescribe the conditions of success, or to set forth the methods which must be pursued — if he could not appeal with confidence to the laws of his science as something to which legislature as well as individuals must bend. Therefore one who holds the views I have expressed in regard to economic forces, laws, and phenomena is compelled, as well by his faith in his science as by the public interests now at stake in the question, to maintain that a concurrent circulation of gold and silver, either with or without a coinage union, is impossible.

THE INFLUENCE OF COMMERCIAL CRISES ON OPINIONS ABOUT ECONOMIC DOCTRINES

THE INFLUENCE OF COMMERCIAL CRISES ON OPINIONS ABOUT ECONOMIC DOCTRINES

[1879]

ANY ONE who follows the current literature about economic subjects will perceive that it is so full of contradictions as to create a doubt whether there are any economic laws, or whether, if there are any, we know anything about them. No body of men ever succeeded in molding the opinions of others by wrangling with each other, and that is the present attitude in which the economists present themselves before the public. Like other people who engage in wrangling, the economists have also allowed their method to degenerate from argument to abuse, contempt, and sneering disparagement of each other. The more superficial and self-sufficient the opinions and behavior of the disputants, the more absolutely they abandon sober arguments and devote themselves to the method I have described. As I have little taste for this kind of discussion and believe that it only degrades the science of which I am a student, I have taken no part in it. In answer to your invitation, now, what I propose to do is to call your attention to some features of the economic situation of civilized nations at the present time with a view to establish two points:

1. To explain the vacillation and feebleness of opinions about economic doctrine which mark the present time, and

2. To show the necessity, just at this time, of calm and sober apprehension of sound doctrine in political economy.

At the outset let me ask you to notice the effects which

have been produced during the last century by the developments of science and of the industrial arts. Formerly, industry was pursued on a small scale, with little or no organization. Markets were limited to small districts, and commerce was confined to raw materials and colonial products. Producer and consumer met face to face. The conditions of the market were open to personal inspection. The relations of supply and demand were matters of personal experience. Production was carried on for orders only in many branches of industry, so that supply and demand were fitted to one another, as we may say, physically. Disproportionate production was, therefore, prevented and the necessity of redistributing productive effort was made plain by the most direct personal experience. Under such a state of things, much time must elapse between the formation of a wish and its realization.

Within a century very many and various forces have been at work to produce an entire change in this system of industry. The invention of the steam engine and of the machines used in the textile fabrics produced the factory system, with a high organization of industry, concentrated at certain centers. The opening of canals and the improvement of highways made possible the commerce by which the products were distributed. The cheapening of printing and the multiplication of means of advertising widened the market by concentrating the demand which was widely dispersed in place, until now the market is the civilized world. The applications of steam power to roads and ships only extended further the same development, and the telegraph has only cheapened and accelerated the means of communicating information to the same end.

What have been the effects on industry?

1. The whole industry and commerce of the world have been built up into a great system in which organization has become essential and in which it has been carried forward

and is being carried forward every day to new developments. Industry has been growing more and more impersonal as far as the parties to it are concerned. Our wants are satisfied instantaneously and regularly by the coöperation of thousands of people all over the world whom we have never seen or heard of; and we earn our living daily by contributing to satisfy the wants of thousands scattered all over the world, of whom we know nothing personally. In the place of actual contact and acquaintance with the persons who are parties to the transactions, we now depend upon the regularity, under the conditions of earthly life, of human wants and human efforts. The system of industry is built upon the constancy of certain conditions of human existence, upon the certainty of the economic forces which thence arise, and upon the fact that those forces act with perfect regularity under changeless laws. If we but reflect a moment, we shall see that modern industry and commerce could not go on for a day if we were not dealing here with forces and laws which may properly be called natural because they come into action when the conditions are fulfilled, because the conditions cannot but exist if there is a society of human beings collected anywhere on earth, and because, when the forces come into action, they work themselves out, according to their laws, without possible escape from their effects. We can divert the forces from one course to another; we can change their form; we can make them expend themselves upon one person or interest instead of upon another. We do this all the time, by bad legislation, by prejudice, habit, fashion, erroneous notions of equity, happiness, the highest good, and so on; but we never destroy an economic force any more than we destroy a physical force.

2. Of course it follows that success in the production of wealth under this modern system depends primarily on the correctness with which men learn the character of

economic forces and of the laws under which those forces act. This is the field of the science of political economy, and it is the reason why it is a science. It investigates the laws of forces which are natural, not arbitrary, artificial, or conventional. Some communities have developed a great hatred for persons who held different religious opinions from themselves. Such a feeling would be a great social force, but it would be arbitrary and artificial. Many communities have held that all labor, not mental, was slavish and degrading. This notion, too, was conventional, but it was a great social force where it existed. Such notions, either past or present, are worth studying for historical interest and instruction, but they do not afford the basis for a science whose object is to find out what is true in regard to the relations of man to the world in which he lives. The study of them throws a valuable sidelight on the true relations of human life, just as the study of error always throws a sidelight upon the truth, but they have no similarity to the law that men want the maximum of satisfaction for the minimum of effort, or to the law of the diminishing return from land, or to the law of population, or to the law of supply and demand. Nothing can be gained, therefore, by mixing up history and science, valuable as one is to the other. If men try to carry on any operation without an intelligent theory of the forces with which they are dealing, they inevitably become the victims of the operation, not its masters. Hence they always do try to form some theory of the forces in question and to plan the means to the end accordingly. The forces of nature go on and are true only to themselves. They never swerve out of pity for innocent error or well-intentioned mistakes. This is as true of economic forces as of any others. What is meant by a good or a bad investment, except that one is based on a correct judgment of forces and the other on incorrect judgment? How would sagacity, care, good judgment, and prudence meet their reward if the economic forces swerved out of pity for error? We know that there is no such thing in the order of nature.

I repeat, then, that the modern industrial and commercial system, dealing as it does with vast movements which no one mind can follow or compass in their ramifications and which are kept in harmony by natural laws, demands steadily advancing, clear, and precise knowledge of economic laws; that this knowledge must banish prejudices and traditions; that it must conquer baseless enthusiasms and whimsical hopes. If it does not accomplish this, we can expect but one result — that men will chase all sorts of phantoms and impossible hopes; that they will waste their efforts upon schemes which can only bring loss; and that some will run one way and some another until society loses all coherence, all unanimity of judgment as to what is to be sought and how to attain to it. The destruction of capital is only the least of the evils to be apprehended in such a case. I do not believe that we begin to appreciate one effect of the new civilization of the nineteenth century, *viz.*, that the civilized world of to-day is a unit, that it must move as a whole, that with the means we have devised of a common consent in regard to the ends of human life and the means of attaining them has come also the *necessity* that we should move onward in civilization by a common consent. The barriers of race, religion, language, and nationality are melting away under the operation of the same forces which have to such an extent annihilated the obstacles of distance and time. Civilization is constantly becoming more uniform. The conquests of some become at once the possession of all. It follows that our scientific knowledge of the laws which govern the life of men in society must keep pace with this development or we shall find our social tasks grow faster than our knowledge of social science, and our society will break to pieces under the burden. How, then, is this scientific knowledge to grow? Certainly not without controversy, but certainly also not without coherent, steady, and persistent effort, proceeding on the lines already cut, breaking new ground when possible, correcting old errors when necessary.

3. It is another feature of the modern industrial system that, like every high organization, it requires men of suitable ability and skill at its head. The qualities which are required for a great banker, merchant, or manufacturer are as rare as any other great gifts among men, and the qualities demanded, or the degree in which they are demanded, are increasing every day with the expansion of the modern industrial system. The qualities required are those of the practical man, properly so called: sagacity, good judgment, prudence, boldness, and energy. The training, both scientific and practical, which is required for a great master of industry is wide and various. The great movements of industry, like all other great movements, present subordinate phenomena which are apparently opposed to, or inconsistent with their great tendencies and their general character. These phenomena, being smaller in scope, more directly subject to observation and therefore apparently more distinct and positive, are well calculated to mislead the judgment, either of the practical man or of the scientific student. In nothing, therefore, does the well-trained man distinguish himself from the ill-trained man more than in the balance of judgment by which he puts phenomena in their true relative position and refuses to be led astray by what is incidental or subsidiary. If, now, the question is asked, whether we have produced a class of highly trained men, competent to organize labor, transportation, commerce, and banking, on the scale required by the modern system, as rapidly as the need for them has increased, I believe no one will answer in the affirmative.

4. Another observation to which we are led upon notic-

ing the character of the modern industrial system is that any errors or follies committed in one portion of it will produce effects which will ramify through the whole system. We have here an industrial organism, not a mere mechanical combination, and any disturbance in one part of it will derange or vitiate, more or less, the whole. The phenomena which here appear belong to what has been called fructifying causation. One economic error produces fruits which combine with those of another economic error, and the product of the two is not their sum, nor even their simple product, but the evil may be raised to a very high power by the combination. If a number of errors fall together the mischief is increased accordingly. Currency and tariff errors constantly react upon each other, and multiply and develop each other in this way. Furthermore, the errors of one nation will be felt in other nations through the relations of commerce and credit which are now so close. There is no limit to the interest which civilized nations have in each other's economic and political wisdom, for they all bear the consequences of each other's follies. Hence when we have to deal with that form of economic disease which we call a commercial crisis, we may trace its origin to special errors in one country and in another, and may trace out the actions and reactions by which the effects have been communicated from one to another until shared by all; but no philosophy of a great commercial crisis is adequate nowadays unless it embraces in its scope the whole civilized world. A commercial crisis is a disturbance in the harmonious operation of the parts of the industrial organism. During economic health, the system moves smoothly and harmoniously, expanding continually, and its health and vigor are denoted by its growth, that is, by the accumulation of capital, which stimulates in its turn the hope, energy, and enterprise of men. Industrial disease is produced by disproportionate production, a wrong distribution of labor, erroneous judgment in enterprise, or miscalculations of force. These all have the same effect, *viz.*, to waste and destroy capital. Such causes disturb, in a greater or less degree, the harmonious working of the system, which depends upon the regular and exact fulfillment of the expectations which have been based on coöperative effort throughout the whole industrial body. The disturbance may be slight and temporary, or it may be very serious. In the latter case it will be necessary to arrest the movement of the whole system and to proceed to a general liquidation, before starting again. Such was the case from 1837 to 1842, and such has been the case for the last five years. It is needless to add that this arrest and liquidation cannot be accomplished without distress and loss to great numbers of innocent persons, and great positive loss of capital, to say nothing of what might have been won during the same period but must be foregone.

The financial organization is the medium by which the various parts of the industrial and commercial organism are held in harmony. It is by the financial organization that capital is collected and distributed, that the friction of exchanges is reduced to a minimum, and that time is economized, through credit, between production and consumption. The financial system furnishes three indicators — prices, the rate of discount, and the foreign exchanges — through which we may read the operation of economic forces now that their magnitude makes it impossible to inspect them directly. Hence the great mischief of usury laws which tamper with the rate of discount, and of fluctuating currencies which falsify prices and the foreign exchanges. They destroy the value of the indicators, and have the same effect as tampering with the scales of a chemist or the steam-gauge of a locomotive.

In the matter of prices we have another difficulty to contend with, which is inevitable in the nature of things.

We must choose some commodity to be the denominator of value. We can find no commodity which is not itself subject to fluctuation in its ratio of exchange with other things. Great crises have been caused in past times by fluctuations in the value of the commodities chosen as money, and such an element is, no doubt, at hand in the present crisis, although it had nothing to do with bringing it about. It follows that any improvement in the world's money is worth any sacrifice which it can possibly cost, if it tends to secure a more simple, exact, and unchanging standard of value.

The next point of which I wish to speak is easily introduced by the last remark; that point is the cost of all improvement. The human race has made no step whatever in civilization which has not been won by pain and distress. It wins no steps now without paying for them in sacrifices. To notice only things which are directly pertinent to our present purpose: every service which we win from nature displaces the acquired skill of the men who formerly performed the service; every such step is a gain to the race, but it imposes on some men the necessity of finding new means of livelihood, and if those men are advanced in life, this necessity may be harsh in the extreme. Every new machine, although it saves labor, and because it saves labor, serves the human race, yet destroys a vested interest of some laborers in the work which it performs. It imposes on them the necessity of turning to a new occupation, and this is hardly ever possible without a period of distress. It very probably throws them down from the rank of skilled to that of unskilled labor. Every new machine also destroys capital. It makes useless the half-worn-out machines which it supersedes. So canals caused capital which was invested in turnpikes and state coaches to depreciate, and so railroads have caused the capital invested in canals and other forms to depreciate. I see no exception to the rule that the progress won by the race is always won at the expense of some group of its members.

Any one who will look back upon the last twenty-five years cannot fail to notice that the changes, advances, and improvements have been numerous and various. We are accustomed to congratulate each other upon them. There can be no doubt that they must and will contribute to the welfare of the human race beyond what any one can now possibly foresee or measure. I am firmly convinced, for my opinion, that the conditions of wealth and civilization for the next quarter of a century are provided for in excess of any previous period of history, and that nothing but human folly can prevent a period of prosperity which we, even now, should regard as fabulous. We can throw it away if we are too timid, if we become frightened at the rate of our own speed, or if we mistake the phenomena of a new era for the approach of calamity, or if the nations turn back to mediæval darkness and isolation, or if we elevate the follies and ignorances of the past into elements of economic truth, or if, instead of pursuing liberty with full faith and hope, the civilized world becomes the arena of a great war of classes in which all civilization must be destroyed. But, such follies apart, the conditions of prosperity are all provided.

We must notice, however, that these innovations have fallen with great rapidity upon a vast range of industries, that they have accumulated their effects, that they have suddenly altered the currents of trade and the methods of industry, and that we have hardly learned to accommodate ourselves to one new set of circumstances before a newer change or modification has been imposed. Some inventions, of which the Bessemer steel is the most remarkable example, have revolutionized industries. Some new channels of commerce have been opened which have changed the character and methods of very important branches of commerce. We have also seen a movement of several nations to secure a gold currency, which movement fell in with a large if not extraordinary production of silver and altered the comparative demand and supply of the two metals at the same time. This movement had nothing arbitrary about it, but proceeded from sound motives and reasons in the interest of the nations which took this step. There is here no ground for condemnation or approval. Such action by sovereign nations is taken under liberty and responsibility to themselves alone, and if it is taken on a sufficiently large scale to form an event of importance to the civilized world, it must be regarded as a step in civilization. It can only be criticized by history. For the present, it is to be accepted and interpreted only as an indication that there are reasons and motives of self-interest which can lead a large part of the civilized world to this step at this time.

The last twenty-five years have also included political events which have had great effects on industry. Our Civil War caused an immense destruction of capital and left a large territory with millions of inhabitants almost entirely ruined in its industry, and with its labor system exposed to the necessity of an entire re-formation. Part of the expenditures and losses of the war were postponed and distributed by means of the paper currency which, instead of imposing industry and economy to restore the losses and waste, created the foolish belief that we could make war and get rich by it. The patriotic willingness of the nation to be taxed was abused to impose taxes for protection, not for revenue, so that the industry of the country was distorted and forced into unnatural development. The collapse of 1873, followed by a fall in prices and a general liquidation, was due to the fact that every one knew in his heart that the state of things which had existed for some years before was hollow and fictitious. Confidence failed because every one knew that there were no real grounds for confidence. The Franco-Prussian war had, also, while it lasted, produced a period of false and feverish prosperity in England. It was succeeded by great political changes in Germany which, together with the war indemnity, led to a sudden and unfounded expansion of speculation, amounting to a mania. Germany undoubtedly stands face to face with a new political and industrial future, but she has postponed it by a headlong effort to realize it at once. In France, too, the war was followed by a hasty, and, as we are told, unwise extension of permanent capital, planned to meet the extraordinary demand of an empty market. In England the prosperity of 1870–1872 has been followed as usual by developments of unsound credit, bad banking, and needless investments in worthless securities.

Here then we have, in a brief and inadequate statement, circumstances in all these great industrial nations peculiar to each, yet certainly sufficient to account for a period of reaction and distress. We have also before us great features of change in the world's industry and commerce which must ultimately produce immeasurable advantages, but which may well, operating with local causes, produce temporary difficulty; and we have to notice also that the local causes react through the commercial and credit relations of nations to distribute the evil.

It is not surprising, under such a state of things, that some people should lose their heads and begin to doubt the economic doctrines which have been most thoroughly established. It belongs to the symptoms of disease to lose confidence in the laws of health and to have recourse to quack remedies. I have already observed that certain phenomena appear in every great social movement which are calculated to deceive by apparent inconsistency or divergence. Hence we have seen the economists, instead of holding together and sustaining, at the time when it was most needed, both the scientific authority and the positive truth of their doctrines, break up and run hither and thither, some of them running away altogether. Many of them seem to be terrified to find that distress and misery still remain on earth and promise to remain as long as the vices of human nature remain. Many of them are frightened at liberty, especially under the form of competition, which they elevate into a bugbear. They think that it bears harshly on the weak. They do not perceive that here "the strong" and "the weak" are terms which admit of no definition unless they are made equivalent to the industrious and the idle, the frugal and the extravagant. They do not perceive, furthermore, that if we do not like the survival of the fittest, we have only one possible alternative, and that is the survival of the unfittest. The former is the law of civilization; the latter is the law of anti-civilization. We have our choice between the two, or we can go on, as in the past, vacillating between the two, but a third plan — the socialist desideratum — a plan for nourishing the unfittest and yet advancing in civilization, no man will ever find. Some of the crude notions, however, which have been put forward surpass what might reasonably have been expected. These have attached themselves to branches of the subject which it is worth while to notice.

1. As the change in the relative value of the precious metals is by far the most difficult and most important of the features of this period, it is quite what we might have expected that the ill-trained and dilettante writers should have pounced upon it as their special prey. The dabblers in philology never attempt anything less than the problem of the origin of language. Every teacher knows that he has to guard his most enthusiastic pupils against precipitate attempts to solve the most abstruse difficulties of the science. The change in the value of the precious metals which is going on will no doubt figure in history as one of

the most important events in the economic history of this century. It will undoubtedly cost much inconvenience and loss to those who are in the way of it, or who get in the way of it. It will, when the currency changes connected with it are accomplished, prove a great gain to the whole commercial world. The nations which make the change do so because it is important for their interests to do it. Now, suppose that it were possible for those who are frightened at the immediate and temporary inconveniences, to arrest the movement — the only consequence would be that they would arrest and delay the inevitable march of improvement in the industrial system.

2. The second field, which is an especial favorite with the class of writers which I have described, is that of prognostications as to what developments of the economic system lie in the future. Probably every one has notions about this and every one who has to conduct business or make investments is forced to form judgments about it. There is hardly a field of economic speculation, however, which is more barren.

3. The third field into which these writers venture by preference is that of remedies for existing troubles. The popular tide of medicine is always therapeutics, and the less one knows of anatomy and physiology the more sure he is to address himself exclusively to this department, and to rely upon empirical remedies. The same procedure is followed in social science, and it is accompanied by the same contempt for scientific doctrine and knowledge and remedies. To bring out the points which here seem to me important, it will be necessary to go back for a moment to some facts which I have already described.

One of the chief characteristics of the great improvements in industry, which have been described, is that they bring about new distributions of population. If machinery displaces laborers engaged in manufactures, these laborers are driven to small shopkeeping, if they have a little capital; or to agricultural labor, if they have no capital. Improvements in commerce will destroy a local industry and force the laborers to find a new industry or to change their abode. When forces of this character coöperate on a grand scale, they may and do produce very important redistributions of population. In like manner legislation may, as tariff legislation does, draw population to certain places, and its repeal may force them to unwelcome change. We may state the fact in this way: let us suppose that, in 1850, out of every hundred laborers in the population, the economical distribution was such that fifty should be engaged in agriculture, thirty in manufacturing, and the other twenty in other pursuits. That is to say that, with the machinery and appliances then available, thirty manufacturing laborers could use the raw materials and food produced by fifty agricultural laborers so as to occupy all to the highest advantage. Now suppose that, by improvements in the arts, twenty men could, in 1880, use to the best advantage the raw materials and food produced by sixty in agriculture. It is evident that a redistribution would be necessary by which ten should be turned from manufacturing to land. That such a change has been produced within the last thirty years and that it has reached a point at which is setting in the counter movement to the former tendency from the land to the cities and towns, seems to me certain. There are even indications of great changes going on in the matter of distribution which will correct the loss and waste involved in the old methods of distribution long before any of the fancy plans for correcting them can be realized, and which are setting free both labor and capital in that department. Now if we can economize labor and capital in manufacturing, transportation, and distribution, and turn this labor and capital back upon the soil, we must vastly increase wealth, for that movement would enlarge the stream of wealth from its very source.

Right here, however, we need to make two observations.

1. The modern industrial system which I have described, with its high organization and fine division of labor, has one great drawback. The men, or groups of men, are dissevered from one another, their interests are often antagonistic, and the changes which occur take the form of conflicts of interest. I mean this: if a shoemaker worked alone, using a small capital of his own in tools and stock, and working for orders, he would have directly before him the facts of the market. He would find out without effort or reflection when "trade fell off," when there was risk of not replacing his capital, when the course of fashion or competition called upon him to find other occupation, and so on. When a journeyman shoemaker works for wages, he pays no heed to these things. The employer, feeling them, has no recourse but to lower wages. It is by this measure that, under the higher organization, the need of new energy, or of a change of industry, or of a change of place is brought home to the workman. To him, however, it seems an arbitrary and cruel act of the master. Hence follow trade wars and strikes as an especial phenomenon of the modern system. It is just because it is a system, or more properly still, an organism, that the readjustments which are necessary from time to time in order to keep its parts in harmonious activity, and to keep it in harmony with physical surroundings, are brought about through this play of the parts on each other.

2. A general movement of labor and capital towards land, throughout the civilized world, means a great migration towards the new countries. This does not by any means imply the abandonment or decay of older countries, as some have seemed to believe. On the contrary, it means new prosperity for them. When I read that the United

States are about to feed the world, not only with wheat and provisions, but with meat also, that they are to furnish coal and iron to mankind, that they are to displace all the older countries as exporters of manufactures, that they are to furnish the world's supply of the precious metals, and I know not what all besides, I am forced to ask what is the rest of the world going to do for us? What are they to give us besides tea, coffee, and sugar? Not ships, for we will not take them and are ambitious to carry away all our products ourselves. Certainly this is the most remarkable absurdity into which we have been led by forgetting that trade is an exchange. Neither can any one well expect that all mankind are to come and live here. The conditions of a large migration do, however, seem to exist. A migration of population is still a very unpopular idea in all the older states. The prejudice against it is apparent amongst Liberals and Tories, economists and sentimentalists. There is, however, a condition which is always suppressed in stating the social problem as it presents itself in hard times. That problem, as stated, is: "How are the population to find means of support?" and the suppressed condition is: "if they insist on staying and seeking support where they are and in pursuits to which they are accustomed." The hardships of change are not for one moment to be denied, but nothing is gained by sitting down to whine about them. The sentimental reasons for clinging to one's birthplace may be allowed full weight, but they cannot be allowed to counterbalance important advantages. I do not see that any but land owners are interested to hold population in certain places, unless possibly we add governing classes and those who want military power. When I read declamations about nationality and the importance of national divisions to political economy (observe that I do not say to political science), I never can find any sense in them, and I am very sure that the writers never put any sense into them.

We may now return to consider the remedies proposed for hard times. We shall see that although they are quack remedies, and although they set at defiance all the economic doctrines which have been so laboriously established during the last century, they are fitted to meet the difficulty as it presents itself to land owners, governments, military powers, socialists, and sentimentalists. The tendency is towards an industrial system controlled by a natural coöperation far grander than anybody has ever planned, towards a community of interest and welfare far more beneficent than any universal republic or fraternity of labor which the Internationalists hope for, and towards a free and peaceful rivalry amongst nations in the arts of civilization. It is necessary to stop this tendency. What are the means proposed?

1. The first is to put a limit to civil liberty. By civil liberty (for I feel at once the need of defining this much-abused word) I mean the status which is created for an individual by those institutions which guarantee him the use of his own powers for his own development. For three or four centuries now, the civilized world has been struggling towards the realization of this civil liberty. Progress towards it has been hindered by the notion that liberty was some vague abstraction, or an emancipation from some of the hard conditions of human life, from which men never can be emancipated while they live on this earth. Civil liberty has also been confused with political activity or share in civil government. Political activity itself, however, is only a means to an end, and is valuable because it is necessary to secure to the individual free exercise of his powers to produce and exchange according to his own choice and his own conception of happiness, and to secure him also that the products of his labor shall be applied to his satisfaction and not to that of any others. When we come to understand civil liberty for what it is, we shall probably

go forward to realize it more completely. It will then appear that it begins and ends with freedom of production, freedom of exchange, and security of property. It will then appear also that governments depart from their prime and essential function when they undertake to transfer property instead of securing it, and it may then be understood that legal tender laws, and protective tariffs as amongst the last and most ingenious devices for transferring one man's product to another man's use, are gross violations of civil liberty. At present the attempt is being made to decry liberty, to magnify the blunders and errors of men in the pursuit of happiness into facts which should be made the basis of generalizations about the functions of government, and to present the phenomena of the commercial crisis as reasons for putting industry once more in leading strings. It is only a new foe with an old face. Those who have held the leading strings of industry in time past have always taken rich pay for their services, and they will do it again.

2. The second form of remedy proposed is quite consistent with the last. It consists in rehabilitating the old and decaying superstition of government. It is called the state, and all kinds of poetical and fanciful attributes are ascribed to it. It is presented, of course, as a superior power, able and ready to get us out of trouble. If an individual is in trouble, he has to help himself or secure the help of friends as best he can, but if a group of persons are in trouble together, they constitute a party, a power, and begin to make themselves felt in the state. The state has no means of helping them except by enabling them to throw the risks and losses of their business upon other people who already have the burdens and losses of their own business to bear, but who are less well organized. The "state" assumes to judge what is for the public interest and imposes taxes or interferes with contracts to force individuals

to the course which will realize what it has set before itself. When, however, all the fine phrases are stripped away, it appears that the state is only a group of men with human interests, passions, and desires, or, worse yet, the state is, as somebody has said, only an obscure clerk hidden in some corner of a governmental bureau. In either case the assumption of superhuman wisdom and virtue is proved false. The state is only a part of the organization of society in and for itself. That organization secures certain interests and provides for certain functions which are important but which would otherwise be neglected. The task of society, however, has always been and is yet, to secure this organization, and yet to prevent the man in whose hands public power must at last be lodged from using it to plunder the governed—that is, to destroy liberty. This is what despots, oligarchs, aristocrats, and democrats always have done, and the latest development is only a new form of the old abuse. The abuses have always been perpetrated in the name of the public interest. It was for the public interest to support the throne and the altar. It was for the public interest to sustain privileged classes, to maintain an established church, standing armies, and the passport and police system. Now, it is for the public interest to have certain industries carried on, and the holders of the state power apportion their favor without rule or reason, without responsibility, and without any return service. In the end, therefore, the high function of the state to regulate the industrial organization in the public interest is simply that the governing group interferes to make some people give the products of their labor to other people to use and enjoy. Every one sees the evils of the state meddling with his own business and thinks that he ought to be let alone in it, but he sees great public interests which would be served if the state would interfere to make other people do what he wants to have them do.

Now if these two measures could be carried out — if
liberty could be brought into misapprehension and contempt, and if the state-superstition could be saved from
the decay to which it is doomed, the movements of population and the changes in industry, commerce, and finance,
could be arrested. The condemnation of all such projects
is, once and for all, that they would arrest the march of civilization. The joy and the fears which have been aroused on
one side and on the other by the reactionary propositions
which have been made during the last five years are both
greatly exaggerated. Such reactionary propositions are in
the nature of things at such a time. It must be expected
that the pressure of distress and disappointed hopes will
produce passionate reaction and senseless outcries. From
such phenomena to actual practical measures is a long step.
Every step towards practical realization of any reactionary
measures will encounter new and multiplying obstacles.
A war of tariffs at this time would so fly in the face of all
the tendencies of commerce and industry that it would
only hasten the downfall of all tariffs. Purely retaliatory
tariffs are a case of what the children call "cutting off your
nose to spite your face." Some follies have become physically
impossible for great nations nowadays. Germany has been
afflicted: first, by too eager hopes, second, by the great
calamity of too many and too pedantic doctors, third,
by a declining revenue, and fourth, by socialistic agitation
amongst the new electors. It appears that she is about to
abandon the free-trade policy although she does not embrace
protection with much vigor. The project already comes in
conflict with numerous and various difficulties which had
not been foreseen, and, in its execution, it must meet with
many more. The result remains to be studied. France
finds that the expiration of each treaty of commerce produces consequences upon her industry which are unendur-
able, and while the task of adjusting rival and contending

interests so as to create a new system drags along, she is
compelled to ward off, by temporary arrangements, the
revival of the general tariff which the treaties had super-
seded. In the meantime her economists, who are the most
sober and the best trained in the world, are opening a
a vigorous campaign on the general issue. If England
should think of reviving protection, she would not know
what to protect. If she wanted to retaliate, she could only
tax raw materials and food. The proposition, as soon as it is
reduced to practical form, has no footing. As for ourselves
we know that our present protective system never could
have been fastened upon us if it had not been concealed
under the war legislation, and if its effects had not been
confused with those of the war. It could not last now if
the public mind could be freed from its absorption in sec-
tional politics, so that it would be at liberty to turn to this
subject.

In conclusion, let me refer again to another important
subject on which I have touched in this paper — what we
call the silver question. It would, no doubt, be in the power
of civilized nations to take some steps which would alle-
viate the inconveniences connected with the transition of
several important nations from a silver to a gold currency.
For one nation, which has no share in the trouble at all,
to come forward out of "magnanimity" or any other motive
to save the world from the troubles incident to this step,
is quixotic and ridiculous. It might properly leave those
who are in the trouble to deal with it amongst themselves.
Either they or all might, however, do much to modify the
effects of the change. The effort to bring about an international union to establish a bimetallic currency at a fixed
ratio is quite another thing. It will stand in the history
of our time as the most singular folly which has gained
any important adherence. As a practical measure the
international union is simply impossible. As a scientific

proposition, bimetallism is as absurd as perpetual motion. It proposes to establish perpetual rest in the fluctuations of value of two commodities, to do which it must extinguish the economic forces of supply and demand of those commodities upon which value depends. The movement of the great commercial nations towards a single gold currency is the most important event in the monetary history of our time, and one which nothing can possibly arrest. It produces temporary distress, and the means of alleviating that distress are a proper subject of consideration; but the advantages which will be obtained for all time to come immeasurably surpass the present loss and inconvenience.

I return, then, to the propositions with which I set out. Feebleness and vacillation in regard to economic doctrine are natural to a period of commercial crisis, on account of the distress, uncertainty, and disorder which then prevail in industry and trade; but that is just the time also when a tenacious grasp of scientific principles is of the highest importance. The human race must go forward to meet and conquer its problems and difficulties as they arise, to bear the penalties of its follies, and to pay the price of its acquisitions. To shrink from this is simply to go back and to abandon civilization. The path forward, as far as any human foresight can now reach, lies in a better understanding and a better realization of liberty, under which individuals and societies can work out their destiny, subject only to the incorruptible laws of nature.

THE PHILOSOPHY OF STRIKES

THE PHILOSOPHY OF STRIKES[1]

THE progress in material comfort which has been
made during the last hundred years has not produced
content. Quite the contrary: the men of to-day are not
nearly so contented with life on earth as their ancestors
were. This observation is easily explainable by familiar
facts in human nature. If satisfaction does not reach to
the pitch of satiety, it does not produce content, but discontent; it is therefore a stimulus to more effort, and is
essential to growth. If, however, we confine our study of
the observation which we have made to its sociological
aspects, we perceive that all which we call "progress" is
limited by the counter-movements which it creates, and
we also see the true meaning of the phenomena which have
led some to the crude and silly absurdity that progress
makes us worse off. Progress certainly does not make
people happier, unless their mental and moral growth
corresponds to the greater command of material comfort
which they win. All that we call progress is a simple en-
largement of chances, and the question of personal happiness
is a question of how the chances will be used. It follows that
if men do not grow in their knowledge of life and in their
intelligent judgment of the rules of right living as rapidly
as they gain control over physical resources, they will not
win happiness at all. They will simply accumulate chances
which they do not know how to use.

The observation which has just been made about individual happiness has also a public or social aspect which
is important. It is essential that the political institutions,

[1] *Harper's Weekly*, September 15, 1883

the social code, and the accepted notions which constitute
public opinion should develop in equal measure with the
increase of power over nature. The penalty of failure to
maintain due proportion between the popular philosophy
of life and the increase of material comfort will be social
convulsions, which will arrest civilization and will subject
the human race to such a reaction toward barbarism as
that which followed the fall of the Roman Empire. It
is easy to see that at the present moment our popular
philosophy of life is all in confusion. The old codes are
breaking down; new ones are not yet made; and even
amongst people of standing, to whom we must look to
establish the body of public opinion, we hear the most
contradictory and heterogeneous doctrines about life and
society.

The growth of the United States has done a great deal
to break up the traditional codes and creeds which had
been adopted in Europe. The civilized world being divided
into two parts, one old and densely populated and the other
new and thinly populated, social phenomena have been
produced which, although completely covered by the same
laws of social force, have appeared to be contradictory.
The effect has been to disturb and break up the faith of
philosophers and students in the laws, and to engender
numberless fallacies amongst those who are not careful
students. The popular judgment especially has been dis-
ordered and misled. The new country has offered such
chances as no generation of men has ever had before. It
has not, however, enabled any man to live without work,
or to keep capital without thrift and prudence; it has not
enabled a man to "rise in the world" from a position of
ignorance and poverty, and at the same time to marry
early, spend freely, and bring up a large family of children.

The men of this generation, therefore, without distinction of class, and with only individual exceptions, suffer

from the discontent of an appetite excited by a taste of luxury, but held far below satiety. The power to appreciate a remote future good, in comparison with a present one, is a distinguishing mark of highly civilized men, but if it is not combined with powers of persevering industry and self-denial, it degenerates into mere day-dreaming and the diseases of an overheated imagination. If any number of persons are of this character, we have morbid discontent and romantic ambition as social traits. Our literature, especially our fiction, bears witness to the existence of classes who are corrupted by these diseases of character. We find classes of persons who are whining and fault-finding, and who use the organs of public discussion and deliberation in order to put forth childish complaints and impossible demands, while they philosophize about life like the *Arabian Nights*. Of course this whole tone of thought and mode of behavior is as far as possible from the sturdy manliness which meets the problems of life and wins victories as much by what it endures as by what it conquers.

Our American life, by its ease, exerts another demoralizing effect on a great many of us. Hundreds of our young people grow up without any real discipline; life is made easy for them, and their tastes and wishes are consulted too much; they grow to maturity with the notion that they ought to find the world only pleasant and easy. Every one knows this type of young person, who wants to find an occupation which he would "like," and who discusses the drawbacks of difficulty or disagreeableness in anything which offers. The point here referred to is, of course, entirely different from another and still more lamentable fact, that is, the terrible inefficiency and incapability of a great many of the people who are complaining and begging. If any one wants a copyist, he will be more saddened than annoyed by the overwhelming applications for the position. The advertisements which are to be found in the newspapers of widest circulation, offering a genteel occupation to be carried on at home, not requiring any previous training, by which two or three dollars a day may be earned, are a proof of the existence of a class to which they appeal. How many thousand people in the United States want just that kind of employment! What a beautiful world this would be if there were any such employment!

Then, again, our social ambition is often silly and mischievous. Our young people despise the occupations which involve physical effort or dirt, and they struggle "up" (as we have agreed to call it) into all the nondescript and irregular employments which are clean and genteel. Our orators and poets talk about the "dignity of labor," and neither they nor we believe in it. Leisure, not labor, is dignified. Nearly all of us, however, have to sacrifice our dignity, and labor, and it would be to the purpose if, instead of declamation about dignity, we should learn to respect, in ourselves and each other, work which is good of its kind, no matter what the kind is. To spoil a good shoemaker in order to make a bad parson is surely not going "up"; and a man who digs well is by all sound criteria superior to the man who writes ill. Everybody who talks to American schoolboys thinks that he does them and his country service if he reminds them that each one of them has a chance to be President of the United States, and our literature is all the time stimulating the same kind of senseless social ambition, instead of inculcating the code and the standards which should be adopted by orderly, sober, and useful citizens.

The consequences of the observations which have now been grouped together are familiar to us all. Population tends from the country to the city. Mechanical and technical occupations are abandoned, and those occupations which are easy and genteel are overcrowded. Of course the persons in question must be allowed to take their own choice, and seek their own happiness in their own way, but it is inevitable that thousands of them should be disappointed and suffer. If the young men abandon farms and trades to become clerks and bookkeepers, the consequence will be that the remuneration of the crowded occupations will fall, and that of the neglected occupations will rise; if the young women refuse to do housework, and go into shops, stores, telegraph offices and schools, the wages of the crowded occupations will fall, while those of domestic servants advance. If women in seeking occupation try to gain admission to some business like telegraphing, in competition with men, they will bid under the men. Similar effects would be produced if a leisure class in an old country should be compelled by some social convulsion to support themselves. They would run down the compensation for labor in the few occupations which they could enter.

Now the question is raised whether there is any remedy for the low wages of the crowded occupations, and the question answers itself: there is no remedy except not to continue the causes of the evil. To strike, that is, to say that the workers will not work in their chosen line, yet that they will not leave it for some other line, is simply suicide. Neither can any amount of declamation, nor even of law-making, force a man who owns a business to submit the control of it to a man who does not own it. The telegraphers have an occupation which requires training and skill, but it is one which is very attractive in many respects to those who seek manual occupation; it is also an occupation which is very suitable, at least in many of its branches, for women. The occupation is therefore capable of a limited monopoly. The demand that women should be paid equally with men is, on the face of it, just, but its real effect would be to keep women out of the business. It was often said during the telegraphers' strike that the demand of the strikers was just, because their wages were less than those of artisans. The argument has no force at all. The only question was whether the current wages for telegraphing were sufficient to bring out an adequate supply of telegraphers. If the growing boys prefer to be artisans, the wages of telegraphers will rise. If, even at present rates, boys and girls continue to prefer telegraphing to handicraft or housework, the wages of telegraphers will fall. Could, then, a strike advance at a blow the wages of all who are now telegraphers? There was only one reason to hope so, and that was that the monopoly of the trade might prove stringent enough and the public inconvenience great enough to force a concession — which would, however, have been speedily lost again by an increased supply of telegraphers.

Now let us ask what the state of the case would be if it was really possible for the telegraphers to make a successful strike. They have a very close monopoly; six years ago they nearly arrested the transportation of the country for a fortnight; but they were unable to effect their object. More recently the freight-handlers struck against the competition of a new influx of foreign unskilled laborers, and in vain. The printers might make a combination, and try to force an advance in wages by arresting the publication of all the newspapers on a given day, but there are so many persons who could set type, in case of need, that such an attempt would be quite hopeless. In any branch of ordinary handicraft there would be no possibility of creating a working monopoly or of producing a great public calamity by a strike. If we go on to other occupations we see that bookkeepers, clerks, and salesmen could not as a body combine and strike; much less could teachers do so; still less could household servants do so. Finally, farmers and other independent workers could not do it at all. In short, a striker is a man who says: "I mean to get my living by doing this thing and no other thing as my share of the social effort, and I do not mean to do this thing except on such and such terms." He therefore proposes to make a contract with his fellow-men and to dictate the terms of it. Any man who can do this must be in a very exceptional situation; he must have a monopoly of the service in question, and it must be one of which his fellow-men have great need. If, then, the telegraphers could have succeeded in advancing their wages fifteen per cent simply because they had agreed to ask for the advance, they must have been far better off than any of the rest of their fellow-men.

Our fathers taught us the old maxim: Cut your coat according to your cloth; but the popular discussions of social questions seem to be leading up to a new maxim: Demand your cloth according to your coat. The fathers thought that a man in this world must do the best he could with the means he had, and that good training and education consisted in developing skill, sagacity, and thrift to use resources economically; the new doctrine seems to be that if a man has been born into this world he should make up his mind what he needs here, formulate his demands, and present them to "society" or to the "state." He wants congenial and easy occupation, and good pay for it. He does not want to be hampered by any limitations such as come from a world in which wool grows, but not coats; in which iron ore is found, but not weapons and tools; in which the ground will produce wheat, but only after hard labor and self-denial; in which we cannot eat our cake and keep it; in which two and two make only four. He wants to be guaranteed a "market," so as not to suffer from "overproduction." In private life and in personal relations we already estimate this way of looking at things at its true value, but as soon as we are called upon to deal with a general question, or a phenomenon of industry in which a number of persons are interested, we adopt an entirely conventional and unsound mode of discussion. The sound gospel of industry, prudence, painstaking, and thrift is, of course, unpopular; we all long to be emancipated from worry, anxiety, disappointment, and the whole train of cares which fall upon us as we work our way through the world. Can we really gain anything in that struggle by organizing for a battle with each other? This is the practical question. Is there any ground whatever for believing that we shall come to anything, by pursuing this line of effort, which will be of any benefit to anybody? If a man is dissatisfied with his position, let him strive to better it in one way or another by such chances as he can find or make, and let him inculcate in his children good habits and sound notions, so that they may live wisely and not expose themselves to hardship by error or folly; but every experiment only makes it more clear that for men to band together in order to carry on an industrial war, instead of being a remedy for disappointment in the ratio of satisfaction to effort, is only a way of courting new calamity.

STRIKES AND THE INDUSTRIAL ORGANIZATON

STRIKES AND THE INDUSTRIAL
ORGANIZATION [1]

ANYONE who has read with attention the current
discussion of labor topics must have noticed that
writers start from assumptions, in regard to the doctrine
of wages, which are as divergent as notions on the same
subject-matter well can be. It appears, therefore, that
we must have a dogma of wages, that we cannot reason
correctly about the policy or the rights of the wages system
until we have such a dogma, and that, in the meantime,
it is not strange that confusion and absurdity should be
the chief marks of discussion carried on before this prime
condition is fulfilled.

Some writers assume that wages can be raised if the
prices of products be raised, and that no particular difficulty would be experienced in raising prices; others assume
that wages could be raised if the employers would be satisfied with smaller profits for themselves; still others assume
that wages could be raised or lowered according as the
cost of living rises or falls. These are common and popular
assumptions, and have nothing to do with the controversies
of professional economists about the doctrine of wages.
The latter are a disgrace to the science, and have the especial
evil at this time that the science cannot respond to the chief
demand now made upon it.

If the employer could simply add any increase of wages
to his prices, and so recoup himself at the expense of the
consumer, no employer would hold out long against a
strike. Why should he? Why should he undertake loss,

[1] *Popular Science News*, July, 1887.

worry, and war, for the sake of the consumers behind him?
If an employer need only submit to a positive and measurable curtailment of his profits, in order to avoid a strike and secure peace, it is probable that he would in almost every case submit to it. But if the employees should demand five per cent advance, and the employer should grant it, adding so much to his prices, they would naturally and most properly immediately demand another five per cent, to be charged to the consumers in the same way. There would be no other course for men of common sense to pursue. They would repeat this process until at some point or other they found themselves arrested by some resistance which they could not overcome. Similarly, if wages could be increased at the expense of the employer's gains, the employer who yielded one increase would have to yield another, until at some point he decided to refuse and resist. In either case, where and what would the limit be? Whenever the point was reached at which some unconquerable resistance was encountered, the task of the economist would begin.

There is no rule whatever for determining the share which any one ought to get out of the distribution of products through the industrial organization, except that he should get all that the market will give him in return for what he has put into it. Whenever, therefore, the limit is reached, the task of the economist is to find out the conditions by which this limit is determined.

Now it is the character of the modern industrial system that it becomes more and more impersonal and automatic under the play of social forces which act with natural necessity; the system could not exist if they did not so act, for it is constructed in reliance upon their action according to ascertainable laws. The condition of all social actions and reactions is therefore set in the nature of the forces which we have learned to know on other fields of scientific investigation, and which are different here only inasmuch as they act in a different field and on different material. The relations of parties, therefore, in the industrial organism is such as the nature of the case permits. The case may permit of a variety of relations, thus providing some range of choice.

A person who comes into the market, therefore, with something to sell, cannot raise the price of it because he wants to do so, or because his "cost of production" has been raised. He has already pushed the market to the utmost, and raised the price as high as supply and demand would allow, so as to win as large profits as he could. How, then, can he raise it further, just because his own circumstances make it desirable for him so to do? If the market stands so that he can raise his price, he will do it, whether his cost of production has increased or not. Neither can an employer reduce his own profits at will; he will immediately perceive that he is going out of business, and distributing his capital in presents.

The difficulty with a strike, therefore, is, that it is an attempt to move the whole industrial organization, in which all the parts are interdependent and intersupporting. It is not, indeed, impossible to do this, although it is very difficult. The organization has a great deal of elasticity in its parts — an aggressive organ can win something at the expense of others. Everything displaces everything else; but if force enough is brought to bear, a general displacement and readjustment may be brought about. An organ which has been suffering from the aggression of others may right itself. It is only by the collision of social pressure, constantly maintained, that the life of the organism is kept up, and its forces are developed to their full effect.

Strikes are not necessarily connected with violence to either persons or property. Violence is provided for by the criminal law. Taking strikes by themselves, therefore, it may be believed that they are not great evils; they are costly, but they test the market. Supply and demand does not mean that the social forces will operate of themselves; the law, as laid down, assumes that every party will struggle to the utmost for its interests — if it does not do so, it will lose its interests. Buyers and sellers, borrowers and lenders, landlords and tenants, employers and employees, and all other parties to contracts, must be expected to develop their interests fully in the competition and struggle of life. It is for the health of the industrial organization that they should do so. The other social interests are in the constant habit of testing the market, in order to get all they can out of it. A strike, rationally begun and rationally conducted, only does the same thing for the wage-earning interest.

The facts stare us plainly in the face, if we will only look at them, that the wages of the employees and the price of the products have nothing to do with each other; that the wages have nothing to do with the profits of the employer; that they have nothing to do with the cost of living or with the prosperity of the business. They are really governed by the supply and demand of labor, as every strike shows us, and by nothing else.

Turning to the moral relations of the subject, we are constantly exhorted to do something to improve the relations of employer and employee. I submit that the relation in life which has the least bad feeling or personal bitterness in it is the pure business relation, the relation of contract, because it is a relation of bargain and consent and equivalence. Where is there so much dissension and bitterness as in family matters, where people try to act by sentiment and affection? The way to improve the relation of employer and employee is not to get sentiment into it, but to get sentiment out of it. We are told that classes are becoming more separated, and that the poor are learning to hate the rich, although there was a time when no class hatreds existed. I have sought diligently in history for the time when no class hatreds existed between rich and poor. I cannot find any such period, and I make bold to say that no one can point to it.

TRUSTS AND TRADES–UNIONS

TRUSTS AND TRADES-UNIONS[1]

I HAVE attempted to show, in foregoing essays,[2] what an immense rôle is played by monopoly throughout the whole social life of mankind in all its stages. There would not be any struggle for existence if it were not true that the supply in nature of the things necessary for human existence is niggardly. The struggle for existence consists in a contest against the constraints by which human life is surrounded; the process by which men have won something in that contest, in the course of time, has consisted in playing off one of nature's monopolies against another — the process, namely, which we call "employing natural agents." On its social and political side, the advance has consisted in securing for the individual a chance in some degree to control his own destiny; not to be at the sport of natural and social forces, but to bring his own energy to bear to enlarge his own conditions of enjoyment and survival.

At every stage of history, however, the natural monopolies have formed the basis of social and political monopolies. The possession of those powers which, under the circumstances, were most efficient for the acquisition of what men want has always given superiority and dominion in human society, whether those powers were physical force, beauty, learning, virtue, capital, or anything else. Where does any one find ground to believe that the fact will ever be different, and that those who have the powers which are most potent in the society in which they live will use those powers, not to get the things which all men want for themselves, but to get those same things for other people?

[1] *The Independent*, April 19, 1888.
[2] "Earth Hunger, and Other Essays," pp. 217–270.

The fashion has always been in the past for those who possessed the essential powers to take control of the state and realize their monopoly in that way. If plutocracy should now prevail it would be simply a repetition of that experience. The only device which has ever given promise of wider and more humane organization of the state is constitutional liberty, which compels, by the intervention of institutions created to serve this purpose, the ruling class, whoever they were, to respect the recognized and defined rights of all the rest.

Now, democracy having sapped and dissolved all the inherited forms of social organizaton and reduced the social body to atoms, it is most interesting to observe the inevitable recurrence of all the old tendencies, in new forms fitted to the times. Some of us thought that liberty was won forever, and that the race was nevermore to be disturbed by its old problems, but it is already apparent that, when a society is resolved into its constituent atoms, the question under what forces, and upon what nuclei, it will crystallize into new forms, has acquired an importance never known before.

Just now public attention is all absorbed by the new name "trust" applied to one of these phenomena. I can see nothing new in a trust as compared with the rings, pools, etc., with which we have been familiar during this generation, except the guarantee which the trust secures to all the members of the same that no one inside of it shall play traitor to the rest. The greatest difficulty with modern combinations has been that there have been no sanctions by which the members could be bound, and that the profits of the insider who turned against his comrades have always been an irresistible temptation. In the mediæval guilds, which were "trusts" of the most solid construction, the sanctions were of the sternest kind — religious, political, and social — and yet they never succeeded in their purpose. In modern times, as is well known to all who are acquainted with the attempts which have been made, inside of various branches of industry, to arrange agreements which have not been large enough or public enough to get into the newspapers the difficulty of enforcing loyalty against those who felt strong enough to beat the rest if they should go alone, or against those who saw a chance to sell out on the rest, or against those who were in desperate straits for cash, has been the constant stumbling-block. Fifty years ago, in the last days of the United States Bank, Nicholas Biddle organized a cotton trust, to try to control the cotton market of the world. It was a complete failure. In general, combinations of this character are in constant dilemma: they must always grow bigger and bigger, in order to encompass a sufficient area to constitute a unit; but the bigger they grow, the less is their internal cohesion. The exception to this must be noted in a moment.

The great expansion of the market by modern inventions in transportation has broken up all the former local and petty monopolies, and is rapidly making of the industry and commerce of mankind a whole which cannot be divided by geographical lines. The conditions of competition in such a system are no doubt onerous to the last degree. The conditions that must be taken into account to win success are numerous and complicated. The nerve-strain of comprehending and of justly estimating the factors, and of following their constant variations, is too great for any one to endure. Foresight must be used, yet there are so many unknown quantities that foresight is impossible; if the attempt is made to master all the unknown quantities, then the task is so enormous that it cannot be accomplished. Furthermore, the relations with other persons in the industrial system are necessarily close. It is impossible to escape such relations, and it is impossible to avoid a share in the consequences of the mistakes and incompetence of the others. It must be added that, at a time when the advance in the arts has forced the whole industry of the globe into intimate relations which nothing can possibly cut off, legislative interferences have produced artificial and erratic currents in the industrial and commercial relations of all countries. The consequences are disappointing and disastrous incidents in the history of industry. At the same time the improvements in the communication of intelligence have made it possible for men farthest apart in space, language, and nationality, if they have confidence in each other's business ability and command of capital, to coöperate by personal agreements.

Trusts are an attempt to deal with this state of things. It is, of course, a jest when the makers of a trust affirm that they make it for the benefit of consumers, and it may very well be doubted whether a trust is a feasible and beneficial device in the interest of either party; but it is wrong to overlook the fact that the trust, in its efforts to deal with the case, and to secure orderly and rational development, instead of heats and chills in industry, has a real and legitimate task on hand. It is certain that there is room for the introduction of intelligent method into modern industry, under forms which shall be germane to modern conditions, and it is certain that this will never be done properly by legislation, but only by the voluntary and intelligent coöperation of the parties interested. It is also by no means certain that this systematization of industry, under intelligent coöperation of the parties conducting it, would cost consumers anything, provided always that there was no legislation to prevent the recourse at any time to any other sources of supply which might be available. The economies of management under intelligent administration are a source from which gains may be made which will cost the consumer nothing. The expenses of industrial war constitute a big fund for dividends to which the consumer does not contribute.

It is worth while to notice, by some familiar examples, what the motive of a trust is; it will be found a far more everyday matter than most people suppose. A man who owns a house and lot buys the vacant lot adjacent in order to control it. He and his neighbors buy up all the vacant lots on the street in order to prevent undesirable contact with anything which would deteriorate their property. They have already fallen victims to the spirit of monopoly, and are subject to all the denunciations heaped upon aristocrats and exclusivists. In their case already the practical difficulty of defining the unit to be comprehended, in order to attain the object and no more, is apparent. Examples are furnished every day in which capital is refused for certain enterprises because it is seen that the investment might no sooner be made than its profits might be destroyed by another enterprise parallel with it. The thing cannot be done at all until it is done on a scale sufficiently large to constitute a complete unit. We are familiar enough with the dilemma offered to us when, on the one hand, railroads which consolidate put themselves in a position to serve us far more efficiently, yet on the other hand, railroads which consolidate cease to compete with each other for our benefit. Which do we want them to do? The railroads themselves are familiar with the experience that they are constantly forced to make extensions in order to secure a certain territory, that is, to establish a closed unit, and that every extension, instead of attaining a finality, only makes further extension unavoidable. This is the class of facts in the industrial development of our time which has produced the trusts, and it is certain that they offer another motive than that of simple desire to secure means of extortion.

I am not yet able to see that any trust can succeed unless it is founded on a natural or legislative monopoly, and furthermore on a monopoly whose product cannot be produced in an amount exceeding the demand at the price which has been customary before the formation of the trust; and I cannot see any chance for legislation to do any good unless it is in the repeal of all such laws as are found to furnish a basis for the organization of an artificial monopoly.

It cannot have escaped the attention of the reader that trades-unions are a monopolistic organization on the side of labor entirely parallel with the trusts on the side of capital, "a product of the same age and of the same forces," and an endeavor to deal with the same problem from the standpoint of another interest. The motives of coercion, discipline, and strict internal organization are the same in both cases, and some of the sanctions are the same; for the pools and rings have tried the boycott until they have proved its worthlessness. There is a notion afloat that the modern trades-union is a descendant of the mediæval gild. It might, with equal truth, and equal futility, be asserted that the modern college, stock exchange, and joint stock company, are descended from the mediæval gild. The nineteenth-century trades-union is a nineteenth-century institution, as much or more so than the ring, pool, corner, or trust. They are all products of the same facts in the industrial development, and one is just as inevitable, and, in that sense, legitimate, as the other. There are some who, while vehemently denouncing trusts, offer us, with great complacency and satisfaction, as a solution of the "labor question," the assertion that the employers and employees ought to combine or coöperate in some way; they do not appear to see at all that if any such thing should be brought about it would be the most gigantic "trust" that could possibly be conceived.

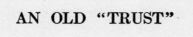

AN OLD "TRUST"

AN OLD "TRUST" [1]

IN the year 1579, Conrad Roth, a merchant of Augsburg, who had been interested in the trade in spices between Lisbon and Germany, proposed to an officer of the treasury of the Elector of Saxony a scheme for a company to monopolize the pepper trade. The Elector was one of the most enterprising and enlightened princes of his time, and the proposition was really intended to be made to him as the only person who could command the necessary capital and had, at the same time, courage and energy to undertake the enterprise.

A company was formed of officers of the treasury, called the Thuringian Company, and a warehouse was prepared at Leipzig. It was reckoned that if the company could raise the price of pepper one groschen per pound, the profits would be over 38,000 florins per annum. Roth and the Thuringian Company were to participate in the enterprise equally, but the Prince was to put up all the capital, and Roth was to do all the work. The latter also owned a very valuable contract with the King of Portugal, according to which he was, for five years, to send to India money enough to buy up all the pepper produced, so that none could come into Europe through Egypt and Italy. Before that time the Portuguese officers had illegally sold some of it, so that it did get into Europe that way; but by buying in India this was now to be stopped.

Roth proposed to divide Europe into three sections: Portugal, Spain, and the West; Italy and the South; Germany and the North. The Saxon company was to have the last as its share of the monopoly. It was hoped that the gains might be forced up to a much higher figure

[1] *The Independent*, June 13, 1889.

than the one above given, if only all pepper then in Frankfort, Venice, Nuremberg, and Hamburg could be bought up.

No sooner was the plan formed, however, than Roth began to reach out after extensions to it. He wanted to include the trade in other spices. He also proposed that the Elector should provide the capital for an exchange bank to do the exchange business between Leipzig and Lisbon. Next he found that the existing postal arrangements were entirely inadequate to the requirements of his business, and he proposed to the Elector a complete plan for a postal service between Italy, Germany, France, Spain, and Portugal. Then, having found the shipping facilities unsatisfactory, he proposed that the Elector should enter into a contract with the King of Denmark, by which the latter, who owned ships, should provide a regular service between Lisbon and the Elbe.

These plans all show the grand energy of this projector, and the Elector entered into them all. He could not carry out the postal service without the consent of the Emperor, and this he was unable to get. Roth and the Elector were ahead of their time; the Emperor was not; he said that the plan proposed "something new, which had never been in use in the time of their ancestors." The attempt to unite private merchants in the speculation also failed at Leipzig, and elsewhere the attitude toward it was extremely unfriendly.

When the stock of pepper began to accumulate at Leipzig, it was found that the article did not begin to be scarce elsewhere. Although the advances of the Prince were already far greater than he had promised when the plan was formed, it was found impossible to begin sales until all the pepper on the European market elsewhere could be bought up; and at the same time reports came that, in spite of Roth's contract, any one who had money could buy all the pepper he wanted in India, and that it was coming into Europe freely through Egypt and Venice. In the spring of 1580 the supply in the cities of Holland and Germany was ample. It appeared that Roth could not prevent the contractors for other parts of Europe from shipping to Germany, and the price was falling there; instead of being at fifteen groschen, where the speculators hoped to hold it, it was below twelve. At this point Roth's creditors began to put attachments on his property. All this led the Elector to say: "We fear that there has been a great mistake in Roth's original and still repeated assertion that all the pepper which comes into Europe comes through Lisbon."

In April Roth committed suicide upon hearing of the death of the King of Portugal. It was known that the King of Spain intended to claim the succession, and that the Portuguese would resist; this war and the possibility of a Spanish succession meant ruin to the speculation. The Elector was obliged to send agents in every direction to get possession of the assets of the company, in order to recover his funds. In the end it appears that he escaped without very serious loss; he sold the whole stock to a syndicate of South German merchants, at a price which restored all his capital. After moralizing on his experience he declared: "Inasmuch as I am now weary and sick, and am anxious to pass the remaining time which God vouchsafes me in quiet, I have firmly determined to have done with commerce, whether it would bring me gain or loss." "I have," he says again, "strengthened my head and I will have done with false commerce."[1]

This enterprise was plainly an attempt to exploit a natural monopoly, and to do it by an operation which should embrace the whole world; it was a purely money-making scheme, unrelieved by any social or industrial advantage. It shows how erroneous it is to suppose that

[1] Falke, "August von Sacheen."

the merchants of the fifteenth and sixteenth centuries were inferior in boldness to those of to-day, or superior to them in disposition to sacrifice themselves for the public good; it would be easy to accumulate any amount of evidence that they were, on the contrary, entirely unscrupulous in the pursuit of gain, and that they were bold beyond anything known to modern merchants. They might well be so. This story shows what great risks, dangers, perplexities, and disappointments they were subject to. The risk element was plainly enormous, but the gains corresponded, of course, and hence we find some of these men enormously rich; but it is plain that there was no routine to help the man who had less natural ability. There was no regularity in any of the contributory operations, such as shipping lines and post-office; there were no regular and adequate banking facilities. If by "trust" we mean a combination to exploit a monopoly, either natural or artificial, the men of that period had made an art of that sort of undertaking, and had a skill in it of which the moderns have no conception.

One cannot help admiring the courage and energy of this Roth. He had everything to contend with; he was far in advance of his age. If he had lived in our time he would have been a great captain of industry — we could have given him something better to do than making a corner on pepper.

In our current social discussions there is a special kind of fallacy which consists in quasi-historical assertions. For instance, it is said that the power of capital is increasing and is greater than it ever has been. This is in form an historical assertion, but those who make it never expect to be held to an historical responsibility for it. They throw it out with a kind of risk, because they are not very accurately informed as to the power of capital in former times, and have not heard that it used to act as it does now.

Capitalists never had less *irresponsible* power than now. It is said that monopoly is growing evil; that it never was so great. If people choose to pass laws to make monopolies, they must, of course, take the consequences; but there never was a time when the control of natural monopolies was so rational as now, and there never was a time when the efforts of cliques to make artificial monopolies could be so easily frustrated as now. It is said that trusts embracing the whole world are a new and threatening danger, never heard of before. It has seemed to me that, if we are to have history, it might be well for once to see some facts which illustrate "the good old times" as they really were. Of course nothing is thereby proved as to the good or ill of trusts; but something is proved as to the fallacy of that class of quasi-historical assertions which I have described.

SHALL AMERICANS OWN SHIPS?

SHALL AMERICANS OWN SHIPS ?[1]

SINCE the war, public attention has been drawn more or less to the marked decline in American shipping. It has been generally assumed and conceded that this was a matter for regret, and some discussion has arisen as to remedies — what to do, in fact, in order to bring it about that Americans should own ships. In these discussions, there has generally been a confusion apparent in regard to three things which ought to be very carefully distinguished from each other: ship-building, the carrying trade, and foreign commerce.

1. As to ship-building — Americans began to build ships, as an industry, within fifteen years after the settlement at Massachusetts Bay. Before the Revolution they competed successfully as ship-builders with the Dutch and English, and they sold ships to be used by their rivals. Tonnage and navigation laws played an important part in the question of separation between the colonies and England, and the same laws took an important place in the formation of the Federal Constitution. One generation was required for the people of this country to get over the hard logical twist in the notion that laws which were pernicious when laid by Great Britain were beneficial when laid by ourselves. The vacillation which has marked the history of our laws about tonnage and navigation is such that it does not seem possible to trace the effects of legislation upon ship-building. In the decade 1850–1860 a very great decline in the number of ships built, especially for ocean traffic, began to be marked. Sails began to give

[1] *The North American Review*, Vol. CXXXII, pp. 559-566.   (June, 1881.)

way to steam, but the building of steamships required great
advantages of every kind in the production of engines and
other apparatus — that is, it required the presence, in a
highly developed state, of a number of important auxiliary
and coöperating industries. As iron was introduced into
ship-building, of course the ship-building industry became
dependent upon cheap supplies of iron as it had before
been dependent on cheap supplies of wood. No doubt
these changes in the conditions of the industry itself have
been the chief cause of the decline in ship-building in this
country, and legislation has had only incidental effects.
It is a plain fact of history that the decline in ship-building
began before the war and the high tariff. Of course the
effects produced by changes in the conditions of an industry
are inevitable; they are not to be avoided by any legislation.
They are annoying because they break up acquired habits
and established routine, and they involve loss in a change
from one industry to another, but legislation can never do
anything but cause that loss to fall on some other set of
people instead of on those directly interested. Within the
last few years it has become certain that steel is to be the
material of ocean vessels — a new improvement which will
not tend to bring the industry back to this country. On
the whole, therefore, the decline in ship-building of the
last twenty-five years seems to indicate that somebody
else than ourselves must build the world's ships for the
present. We have, by legislative devices, forced the
production of a few ocean steamers, but these cases prove
nothing to the contrary of our inference. If this nation
has a hobby for owning some ships built in this country,
and is willing to pay enough for the gratification of that
hobby, no doubt it can secure the pleasure it seeks. A
fisherman who has caught nothing sometimes buys fish
at a fancy price; he saves himself mortification and gets
a dinner, but the possession of the fish does not prove that

he has profitably employed his time or that he has had sport.

2. The carrying trade differs from ship-building as carting differs from wagon-building. Carrying is the industry of men who own ships; their interests are more or less hostile to those of the ship-builders. Ship owners want to buy new ships at low prices; they want the number of competing ships kept small; they want freights high. In all these points the interest of the ship-builder is the opposite: the ship owner is indifferent where he gets his ships; he only wants them cheap and good. There is no sentiment in the matter any more than there is in the purchase of wagons by an express company, or carriages by a livery-stable keeper.

3. Foreign commerce is still another thing. It consists in the exchange of the products of one country for those of another. The merchant wants plenty of ships to carry all the goods at the lowest possible freights, but it is of no importance to him where the ships were built, or who owns and sails them.

A statement and definition of these three industries suffices to show what confusion must arise in any discussion in which they are not properly distinguished. It is plain that there are three different questions: (1) Can the farmer build a vehicle? (2) Can he get his crop carried to market? (3) Can he sell his crop? It is evident that a country which needs a protective tariff on iron and steel must give up all hopes of building ships for ocean traffic. For the country which, by the hypothesis, needs a protective tariff on iron and steel cannot produce those articles as cheaply as some other country. Its ships, however, must compete upon the ocean with those of the country which has cheap iron and steel. The former embody a larger capital than the latter, and they must be driven from the ocean. If, then, subsidies are given to protect the carrying trade, when prosecuted in ships built of protected iron, the loss is transferred from the ship owners to the people who pay taxes on shore. These taxes, however, add to the cost of production of all things produced in the country, and thereby lessen the power of the country to compete in foreign commerce. This lessens the amount of goods to be carried both out and in, lowers freights, throws ships out of use, and checks the building of ships; and the whole series of legislative aids and encouragements must be begun over again, with a repetition and intensification of the same results. As long as the system lasts it works down, and the statistics show, very naturally, that fewer and fewer ships are built in the country, and that less and less of the carrying trade is carried on under the national flag. In view of the three different and sometimes adverse interests which are connected by their relation to the shipping question, it is not strange that when the representatives of those interests meet to try to consider that question, there should simply be a scramble between them to see which can capture the convention. The last convention of this sort was captured by the owners of a lot of unsalable and unsailable old hulks, who had hit upon the brilliant idea of getting the nation to pay them an annual bounty for the use of their antiquated and dilapidated property. Strange to say, in a country which is charged with being too practical and hardheaded, this proposition received respectful attention and consideration. It is also strange that our people should believe that taxing farmers to force the production of iron, taxing farmers again to force the production of ships out of protected iron, and taxing farmers again to pay subsidies to enable protected ships to do business, is a way to make this country rich.

So soon as the three different industries, or departments of business, which I have described are distinguished from each other, it is apparent that the fundamental one of the three is foreign commerce. If we have no commerce we need no carrying, and it would be absurd to build ships; if we have foreign commerce its magnitude determines the amount of demand there is for freight and for ships. The circle of taxation which I have mentioned, and which is obviously only a kind of circuit, described from and upon the farmer as a center and fulcrum to bear the weight of the whole, is necessarily and constantly vicious, because it presses down on the foreign commerce, which is the proper source of support for carrying and ship-building. On the other hand, the emancipation of foreign commerce from all trammels of every sort is the only means of increasing the natural, normal, and spontaneous support of carrying and ship-building, assuming that the carrying trade and ship-building are ends in themselves.

It is, however, no object at all for a country to have either ship-building industry, or carrying trade, or foreign commerce; herein lies the fundamental fallacy of all the popular and Congressional discussions about ships and commerce. It is only important that the whole population should be engaged in those industries which will pay the best under the circumstances of the country. For the sake of exposing the true doctrine about the matter, we may suppose (what is not conceivable as a possible fact) that a country might not find greater profit in the exportation of any part of any of its products than in the home use of the same. If this could be true, and if it were realized, the proof of it would be that no foreign trade would exist. There would be no ground for regret since the people would be satisfied and better off than as if they had a foreign trade. Carrying trade and ship-building would not exist.

If a country had a foreign trade of any magnitude whatever, it would not be any object for that country to do its own carrying. The figures which show the amount paid by the people of the United States to non-American ship owners for freight, and the figures which show the small percentage of our foreign commerce which is carried under the American flag, in themselves prove nothing at all. The only question which is of importance is this: are the people of the United States better employed now than they would be if engaged in owning and sailing ships? If they were under no restraints or interferences, that question also would answer itself. If Americans owned no ships and sailed no ships, but hired the people of other countries to do their ocean transportation for them, it would simply prove that Americans had some better employment for their capital and labor. They would get their transportation accomplished as cheaply as possible. That is all they care for, and it would be as foolish for any nation to insist on doing its own ocean transportation, devoting to this use capital and labor which might be otherwise more profitably employed, as it would be for a merchant to insist on doing his own carting, when some person engaged in carting offered him a contract on more advantageous terms than those on which he could do the work.

Furthermore, the people of a country which had little foreign commerce might find it very advantageous to prosecute the carrying trade. In history, the great trading nations have been those which had a small or poor territory at home: the Dutch were the great carriers of the seventeenth and eighteenth centuries, when the foreign commerce of their own territory was insignificant; the New Englanders of the last century and of the first quarter of this century became the carriers of commodities to and fro between all parts of the world, especially between our middle and southern states and the rest of the world. They took to the sea because their land did not furnish them with products which could remunerate their capital and labor so well as the carrying trade did. They won a high reputation for the merchant service, which was in their hands, and they earned fortunes by energy, enterprise, promptitude, and fidelity. The carrying trade is an industry like any other; it is neither more nor less desirable in itself than any other. In any natural and rational state of things it would be absurd to be writing essays about it. If any one thought he could make more profit in that business than in some other he would set about it. When the census was taken he would be found busy at that business, would be so reported, and that would be the end of the matter as a phenomenon of public interest.

If a nation had foreign commerce, and some of its citizens found the carrying trade an advantageous employment for their labor and capital as compared with other possible industries in the country, it would not follow that some other citizens of that country ought to engage in shipbuilding. It is no object to build ships, but only to get such ships as are wanted, in the most advantageous manner. If a man should refuse to carry on a carting business unless he could make his own wagons, it would be such a reflection on his good sense that his business credit would be very low. If some Americans could buy and sail ships so as to make profits, what is the sense of saying that they shall not do it because some other Americans cannot build ships at a profit? Only one answer to this question has ever been offered by anybody, and that is the prediction that, some day, if we go without ships long enough, we shall, by the mere process of going without, begin to get some — a prediction for which the prophets give no guarantee, in addition to their personal authority, save the fact that we have fewer ships and worse ones every year.

I have said above that, if there were no restraints or interferences, we should simply notice whether any Americans took to the carrying trade or not, and should thence infer that they might or might not be better employed in some other industry. It is impossible, now, to say whether, if all restrictions were removed, the carrying trade or ship-building would be a profitable industry in the United States or not. Any opinion given by anybody on that point is purely speculative. The present state of the iron and steel industries, and of the manufacture of engines and machinery, is so artificial that no one can judge what would be the possibilities of those industries under an entirely different state of things. It is, however, just because the present state of things prevents a free trial that it is indefensible; we are working in the dark and on speculation all the time and have none of the natural and proper tests and guarantees for what we are doing. We are controlled by the predictions of prophets, the notions of dogmatizers, the crude errors of superficial students of history, the wrongheaded inferences of shallow observers, and the selfish machinations of interested persons. We can distinguish many forces which are at work on our ship-building and on our carrying trade, but none of them are genuine or respectable. We are submitting to restraints and losses, and we have no guarantee whatever that we shall ever win any compensation. The teaching of economic science is distinctly that we never shall win any. We are expending capital without any measurement or adjustment of the *quid pro quo;* we are spending without calculation, and receiving something or nothing — we do not know which. The wrong of all this is not in the assumption that we have not certain industries which we would have (for we cannot tell whether that is so or not), but the wrong is in the arbitrary interference which prevents us from having them, if any man wants to put his capital into them, and which prevents us from obtaining the proper facts on which to base a judgment about the state and relations of industries in the country.

Whenever the question of ships is raised, the clamor for subsidies and bounties is renewed, and we are told

again that England has established her commerce by
subsidies. It would be well if we could have an understanding, once for all, whether England's example is a good
argument or not. As she has tried, at some time or other,
nearly every conceivable economic folly, and has also
made experiment of some sound economic principles, all
disputants find in her history facts to suit them, and it
needs only a certain easily acquired skill in misunderstanding things to fashion any required argument from the
economic history of England. Some of our writers and
speakers seem to be under a fascination which impels them
to accept as authoritative examples the follies of English
history, and to reject its sound lessons. In the present case,
however, the matter stands somewhat differently. England
is a great manufacturing area; it imports food and raw
materials, and exports finished products; it has, therefore,
a general and public interest in maintaining communication
with all parts of the world. The analogy in our case is
furnished by the subsidized railroads in our new states, or,
perhaps even better, by the mail routes which we sustain
all over our territory, from general considerations of public
advantage, although many such routes do not pay at all.
Subsidies to ships for the mere sake of having ships, or
ocean traffic, when there is no business occasion for the subsidized lines, would have no analogy with English subsidies.

If then the question is put: Shall Americans own ships?
I do not see how any one can avoid the simple answer:
Yes, if they want them. Universally, if an American wants
anything, he ought to have it if he can get it, and if he hurts
no one else by getting it. To enter on the question whether
he is going to make it or buy it, and whether he is going
to buy it of A or of B, is an impertinence. We boast a
great deal of having a free country; our orators shout
themselves hoarse about liberty and freedom. Stop one
of them, however, and ask him if he means free trade and

free ships, and he will demur. No; not that; that will not
do. He is in favor of freedom for himself and his friends
in those respects in which they want liberty against other
people, but he is not in favor of freedom for other people
against restraints which are advantageous to him and his
political allies. He is in favor of freedom for those who are
being oppressed — by somebody else; not for those who
are being oppressed by himself. I heard it asserted not
long ago that we have no monopolies in this country,
because it is a free country. It is not a free country, because
there are more artificial monopolies in it than in any other
country in the world. The popular notion that it is free
rises from the fact that there are fewer natural monopolies
in it than in any other great civilized country. It is necessary, however, to go to Turkey or Russia to find instances
of legislative and administrative abuses to equal the existing
laws and regulations of the United States about ships,
the carrying trade, and foreign commerce. These laws
have been brought to public attention again and again,
but apparently with little effect in awakening popular
attention, while the newspapers carry all over the country
details about abuses in Ireland, Russia, and South Africa.
We should stop bragging about a free country and about
the enlightened power of the people in a democratic republic
to correct abuses, while laws remain which treat the buying,
importing, owning, and sailing of ships as pernicious actions,
or, at least, as doubtful and suspicious ones. I have no conception of a free man or a free country which can be satisfied
if a citizen of that country may not own a ship, if he wants
one, getting it in any legitimate manner in which he might
acquire other property; or may not sail one, if he finds
that a profitable industry suited to his taste and ability;
or may not exchange the products of his labor with that
person, whoever he may be, who offers the most advantageous terms.

POLITICS IN AMERICA, 1776–1876

POLITICS IN AMERICA, 1776–1876 [1]

WHEN the Continental Congress met in 1774, few persons in the colonies perceived that the ties to the mother country were about to be severed, and few, if any, were republicans in theory, or contemplated a "revolution" in the political system. The desire for independence was developed during 1775, and the question as to the form of government to be adopted came up by consequence. It presented no real difficulty. The political organization of some of the colonies was such already that there were no signs of dependence except the arms and flag, the form of writs, and a responsibility to the Lords of Trade which sat very lightly upon them. Necessary changes being made in these respects, those colonies stood as complete republics. The others conformed to this model.

In bringing about these changes great interest was developed in political speculations, an interest which found its first direction from Paine's "Common Sense," and was sustained by diligent reading of Burgh's "Political Disquisitions," and Macaulay's "History of England." The same speculations continued to be favorite subjects of discussion for twenty-five years afterwards. The journals of the time were largely made up of long essays by writers with fanciful *noms de plume*, who discussed no simple matters of detail, but the fundamental principles of politics and government. The method of treatment was not historical, unless we must except crude and erroneous generalizations on classical history, and it seemed to be believed that the colonial history of this country was es-

[1] *The North American Review*, vol. cxxii, pp. 47–87. (January, 1876.)

pecially unfit to furnish guidance for the subsequent period; but the disquisitions in question pursued an *a priori* method, starting from the broadest and most abstract assumptions. The same method has marked American political philosophy, so far as there has been any such thing, ever since. It is very much easier than the method which requires a laborious study of history.

The natural effect of the war, but still more of the doctrines in regard to liberty taught by Paine, and of the deplorable policy of local terrorism pursued by the Committees of Safety against Tories and Refugees, was to produce and bring into prominence a class of active, shallow men, who felt their new powers and privileges but not the responsibility which ought to go with these. The old colonial bureaucracy, which had enjoyed all the social preëminence that colonial life permitted, was gone. Office was open to many who, before the war, had little chance of attaining it. They sought it eagerly, expecting to enjoy the social advantages they had formerly envied. In the northern states a class of eager office-seekers arose who gained a great influence, saw their arena in the states especially, and jealously opposed the power of the Confederation. This class made hatred to England almost a religion, and testified to their political virtues by persecuting Tories and Refugees. They found popular grievances also ready to their hand as a means of advancement. The mass of the people had been impoverished by the war. The attempts at commercial war had reacted upon the nation with great severity. The paper issues of the Congress and the states had wrought their work to derange values, violate contracts, inflate credit, and destroy confidence. On the return of peace the industries which had been sustained only by war ceased to be profitable; the reduction of prices spread general ruin and left thousands indebted and impoverished. The consequence was discontent and disorder. All this was height-

ened by the contrast with another class which had been
enriched by privateering, contracts, and "financiering."
The soldier who returned in rags, bringing only a few bits
of scrip worth fifteen or twenty cents on the dollar, found
his family in want, and some of his neighbors, who had
borne few of the sacrifices of the war, enriched by it and
now enjoying its fruits. It seemed to this whole class that
they had not yet got liberty, or that they did not know what
it was. They did not look for it to a closer union.

This party, for it soon became a party, found an alliance
in a quarter where it would hardly have been expected, in
the slave-owning planters of the South — an alliance which
has been of immense importance in our political history.
The planters, at the outbreak of the war, had been heavily
indebted to English capitalists and merchants. They now
feared that they would be compelled to pay their debts, and
they saw in the treaty-making power of the general government the source from which this compulsion would come.
They therefore opposed any union which would strengthen
and give vigor to that power. To this party were added
those who had adopted, on theoretical and philosophical
grounds, the enthusiasm for liberty which was then prevalent in both hemispheres. It should be added to the
characteristics of this party that it looked with indifference
upon foreign commerce, cared little for foreign opinion,
would have been glad to be isolated from the Old World,
and had very crude opinions as to the status and relations
of European nations.

This party naturally went on to confound liberty with
equality, and political virtue with tenacity of rights. It
furthermore confounded power with privilege, and thought
that it must allow no civil power or authority to exist if it
meant really to exterminate aristocratic privilege. It was
not so clear in its conception of political duties, and certainly
failed to see that the best citizen is not the one who is

most tenacious of his political rights, but the one who is most faithful to his political duties; that envy and jealousy are not political virtues; and that equality can be attained only by cutting off every social advance and setting up as the standard, not what is highest, but what is a low average.

An opposing party gradually formed itself of men of wider information and superior training. These men understood the institutions of Great Britain and their contrast to those of any other country in Europe. They understood just what the war had done for the Colonies. They did not consider that it had altered the internal institutions inherited from the mother country, or set the Colonies adrift upon a sea of political speculation to try to find a political utopia. Some of them joined for a time in the prevalent opinion that the Americans were better and purer than the rest of mankind, but experience soon taught them their error. Tradition and experience still had weight with them; and in making innovations they sought development rather than destruction and reconstruction. They were conservative by property, education, and character.

To this party it was evident that the colonies had lost much by falling out of the place in the family of nations which they had filled as part of the British Empire, and they believed that a similar place must now be won on an independent footing. They understood the necessity of well-regulated foreign relations, of foreign commerce, and of public credit. Their general effort was, therefore, to secure order and peace in the internal relations of the country by establishing liberty indeed, but liberty under law; and to secure respectability and respect abroad by fidelity to treaties and pecuniary engagements, by a reputation for commercial integrity, and by a development of the arts of peace. The first requisite to all this was a more perfect union.

The two parties, therefore, formed about the issue of a revision of the Articles of Confederation, but it was not until the absolute necessity of the objects aimed at by the Federalists — objects which are in their nature less directly obvious and tangible — had been demonstrated by experience, that this revision was brought about. The Union was not the result of a free and spontaneous effort, but was "extorted from the grinding necessity of a reluctant people." A political party which resists a proposed movement by predicting calamitous results to flow from it must abide by the verdict of history. Tried by this test, the anti-Federalists are convicted of resisting the most salutary action in our political history. The victory was won, not by writing critical essays about the movement and the relations of parties, but by the direct and energetic activity of those men of that generation who had enjoyed the greatest advantages of education and culture.

Three evils were inherited under the new Constitution from the old system: slavery (which the framers of the Constitution tolerated, thinking it on the decline), paper money (which they thought they had eradicated), and the mercantile theories of political economy. These three evils, in their single or combined development, have given character to the whole subsequent political history of the country. One of them has been eliminated by a civil war. The other two confront us as the great political issues of to-day.

The framers of the Constitution, without having any precise definition of a republic in mind, knew well that it differed from a democracy. No one of them was a democrat. They were, at the time of framing the Constitution, under an especial dread of democracy, on account of the rebellion in Massachusetts. They meant to make a Constitution in order to establish organized or articulated liberty, giving guarantees for it which should protect it from popular tyranny as much as from personal despotism. Indeed, they recognized the former as a great danger, the latter as a delusion. They therefore established a constitutional republic. The essential feature of such a system of government (for it is a system of government, and not a political theory) is that political power be conferred under a temporary and defeasible tenure. That it be conferred by popular election is not essential, although it is convenient in many cases. This method was the one naturally indicated by the circumstances of the United States. The system which was established did not pretend to give direct effect to public opinion according to its fluctuations. It rather interposed delays and checks in order to secure deliberation, and it aimed to give expression to public opinion only after it was matured. It sought to eliminate prejudice and passion by prescribing beforehand methods which seemed just in themselves, independently of conflicting interests, in order that, when a case arose, no advantage of procedure might be offered to either party; and it aimed to subject action to organs whose operation should be as impersonal as it is possible for the operation of political organs to be.

Democracy, on the other hand, has for its essential feature equality, and it confers power on a numerical majority of equal political units. It is not a system of government for a state with any but the narrowest limits. On a wider field it is a theory as to the depositary of sovereignty. It seizes upon majority rule, which is only a practical expedient for getting a decision where something must be done and a unanimous judgment as to what ought to be done is impossible, and it makes this majority the depositary of sovereignty, under the name of the sovereignty of the people. This sovereign, however, is as likely as any despot to aggrandize itself, and to promulgate the unformulated doctrines of the divine right of the

sovereign majority to rule, the duty of passive obedience
in the minority, and that the majority can do no wrong.

Opposition to the Federal Constitution died out in a
year or two, and no one could be found who would confess
that he had resisted its adoption. Parties divided on
questions of detail and of interpretation, and the points
on which they differed were those by which the Constitution imposed delays and restraints upon the popular will.
The administrations of Washington and Adams threw
continually increasing weight in favor of constitutional
guarantees, as the history of the French Revolution seemed
to the Federalists to furnish more and more convincing
proofs of the dangers of unbridled democracy. The opposition saw nothing in that history save the extravagant
ebullitions of a people new to freedom — saw rather examples to be imitated than dangers to be shunned. Sympathy and gratitude came in to exercise a weighty influence
on political issues. The personal executive and the judiciary were the chief subjects of dislike, and General
Washington himself finally incurred abuse more wanton
and severe than any President since, except the elder
Adams, has endured, because the fact was recognized that
Washington's personality was the strongest bulwark which
the system possessed at the outset.

Democracy, however, was, and still is, so deeply rooted
in the physical and economic circumstances of the United
States, that the constitutional barriers set up against it
have proved feeble and vain. Fears of monarchy have now
almost ceased or are ridiculed. Monarchist and aristocrat are now used only as epithets to put down some over-
bold critic of our political system; but in the early days
of the Republic the mass of the people believed that the
supporters of the first two administrations desired aristocracy and monarchy. In a new country, however, with
unlimited land, the substantial equality of the people in

property, culture, and social position is inevitable. Political equality follows naturally. Democracy is given in the circumstances of the case. The yeoman farmer is the prevailing type of the population. It is only when the pressure of population and the development of a more complex social organization produce actual inequality in the circumstances of individuals, that a political aristocracy can follow and grow upon a social aristocracy. The United States are far from having reached any such state as yet. These facts were felt, if not distinctly analyzed and perceived, even by those who might on theory have preferred monarchical institutions; and, as Washington said, there were not ten men in the country who wanted a monarchy.

The Federalists repaid their opponents with a no less exaggerated fear of their principles and intentions, regarding them as Jacobins and *sans culottes*, who desired to destroy whatever was good and to produce bloodshed and anarchy. Party spirit ran to heights seldom reached since. Partisan abuse outstripped anything since. It was an additional misfortune that the questions at issue were delicate questions of foreign policy and international law. It is a great evil in a republic that parties should divide by sympathy with two foreign nations, and it is the greatest evil possible that they should not believe in each other's loyalty to the existing constitution.

The deeper movement which was stirring to affect the general attitude or standpoint from which the Constitution was viewed (a matter, of course, of the first importance under a written constitution), and which was changing the constitutional republic into a democratic republic, did not escape the observation of the most sagacious men of the earliest days. Fisher Ames wrote to Wolcott in 1800: "The fact really is, that over and above the difficulties of sustaining a free government, and the freer the more difficult, there is a want of accordance between our system and the state of our public opinion. The government is republican; opinion is essentially democratic. Either events will raise public opinion high enough to support our government, or public opinion will pull down the government to its own level." The fact was that the government could not, under the system, long remain above the level of public opinion. The Federalists, assisted by the prestige of Washington's name, held it there for twelve years; but they probably never, on any of the party issues, even with a restricted suffrage, had a majority of the voters. Dating the rise of parties from the time of Jay's Treaty, they had a majority of the House of Representatives only under the excitement of French insult in 1798.

The leading men of 1787–1788, as has been said, worked industriously and energetically for political objects. The first decade of the Republic had not passed by, however, before men began to estimate the cost and sacrifices of public life and the worry of abuse and misrepresentation, to compare this with what they could accomplish in politics, and to abandon the contest. To the best public men professions and other careers offered fame, fortune, honorable and gratifying success. In public life they struggled against, and were defeated by, noisy, active men who could not have competed with them in any other profession. Their best efforts were misunderstood and misrepresented. They had no reward but the consciousness of fulfilling a high public duty. Furthermore they lacked, as a class, the tact and sagacity which the system indispensably requires. The leaders of the Federal party committed a political blunder of the first magnitude in quarrelling with John Adams, whatever may have been his faults. They thereby separated themselves from the mass of their own party, and at a time when parties were so evenly balanced that they required harmony for any chance of success; and they put themselves in the position of a junto or cabal, trying to dictate to the party without guiding its reason. Those of them who had withdrawn from, or had been thrown out of political life by the causes above mentioned were most active in this work of disorganization. They had abandoned that sort of task which they had engaged in at the outset, and which, difficult as it is, is permanently incumbent on the cultured classes of the country — to make the culture of the nation homogeneous and uniform by imparting and receiving, by living in and of and for the nation, contributing to its thought and life their best stores, whatever they are. A breach was opened there which has gone on widening ever since, and which has been as harmful to our culture as to our politics. On the one side it has been left to anti-culture to control all which is indigenous and "American"; and on the other hand American culture has been like a plant in a thin soil, given over to a sickly dilettantism and the slavish imitation of foreign models, ill understood, copied for matters of form, and, as often as not, imitated for their worst defects.

An actual withdrawal of the ablest men from political life, such as we have come to deplore, began, then, at this early day. Many others were thrown out for too great honesty and truth in running counter to the popular notions of the day. John Adams incurred great unpopularity for having said that the English Constitution was one of the grandest achievements of the human race — an assertion which Callender disputed, with great popular success, by dilating upon the corruption of the English administration under George III, but an assertion which, in the sense in which it was made, no well-informed man would question. Sedgwick laid down the principle that the government might claim the last man as a soldier and the last dollar in taxation — an abstract proposition which is unquestionable, but which Callender disputed, once more

with great popular success, by arguing as if it were a proposition to take the last man and the last dollar.   Dexter
lost a reëlection by opposing a clause of the naturalization
law, that a foreign nobleman should renounce his titles on
being naturalized.   It was opposed as idle and frivolous,
and favored as if every foreign nobleman would otherwise
become by naturalization a member of Congress.   Hamilton and Knox abandoned the public service on account of
the meagerness of their salaries.   Pickering, who left office
really insolvent, and with only a few hundred dollars in
cash, was pursued by charges of corruption on the ground
of unclosed accounts.   Wolcott, at the end of long and
faithful service, was charged with the responsibility for a
fire which broke out in his office, as if he had sought to
destroy the records of corrupt proceedings.

It is no wonder that these men abandoned public life,
and that their examples deterred others, unless they were
men born to it, who could not live out of the public
arena; but it is true now, as it was then, that men of true
culture, high character, and correct training can abandon
public political effort only by the surrender of some of the
best interests of themselves and their posterity.   The pursuit of wealth, which is the natural alternative, has always
absorbed far too much of the ambition of the nation, and
under such circumstances there could be no other result
than that a wealthy class should arise, to whom wealth
offers no honorable social power, in whom it awakens no
intellectual or political ambition, to whom it brings no
sense of responsibility, but for whom it means simply the
ability to buy what they want, men or measures, and to
enjoy sensual luxury.   A class of men is produced which
mocks at the accepted notions while it uses them, and
scorns the rest of us with a scorn which is so insulting only
because it is so just.   It is based on the fact that we will
not undergo the sacrifices necessary to self-defense.   This

pursuit of wealth was almost the only pursuit attractive to able men who turned their backs on the public service in the early days. In later years professional careers and scientific and literary pursuits have disputed to a great and greater extent the dominion of wealth over the energies of the nation; but politics have not yet won back their due attraction for able and ambitious men.

The Federalists also held a defective political philosophy. They did not see that the strength of a constitutional republic such as they desired must be in the intelligent approval and confidence of the citizens. Adams and Hamilton agreed in supposing that some artificial bond must be constructed to give strength to the system. Hamilton looked for it in the interest of the wealthy class, which he wanted to bind up in the system — a theory which would have changed it into a plutocracy. Adams sought the bond in ambition for social eminence, and did not see that, where such eminence sprang only from wealth or official rank, the very principle of human nature which he invoked would, under the form of envy, counteract his effort.

The presidential election of 1801 having been thrown into the House of Representatives, the Federalists added to their former blunder another far more grave. Abandoning their claims to principle and character, they took to political intrigue and bargaining, in the attempt to elect Burr over Jefferson. Their exit from power might otherwise have been honorable, and they might, as an opposition party, have made a stand for inflexible principle and political integrity; but it was hard for them after this to talk of those things, especially as Burr went on to develop the character which Hamilton had warned them that he possessed. They fell into the position of "independent voters," throwing their aid now with one and now with the other faction of the majority; but history does not show that they ever forced either one or the other to "adopt good measures," for the obvious reason that the majority possessed the initiative. The purchase of Louisiana seemed to them to transfer the power of the Union to the southern and frontier states, the seat of the political theories which they regarded as reckless and lawless. They feared that the power of the Union would be used to sacrifice commerce and to put in operation wild theories by which the interests of the northern and eastern states would be imperiled, and the inherited institutions of constitutional liberty, which they valued as their best possessions, would be overthrown. The Embargo and Non-intercourse Acts seemed only the fulfillment of these fears. The recourse of a minority has always been to invoke the Constitution and to insist upon the unconstitutionality of what they could not resist by votes, each party in turn thereby bearing witness to the truth that the Constitution is the real safeguard of rights and liberty. In the last resort also the minority, if it has been local, and has seen the majority threatening to use the tremendous power of the Confederation to make the interests of the minority subservient to the interests of the rest, has felt its loyalty to the Union decline. How far the Federalists went in this direction it is difficult to say, but they certainly went farther than they were afterwards willing to confess or remember. They gradually faded out of view as a political power after the second war and in the twenties "Federalist" became a term of reproach.

The opposite party, called by themselves Republicans after 1792, took definite form in opposition to Washington's administration on the question of ratifying Jay's Treaty. They were first called Democrats in 1798, the name being opprobrious. They adopted it, however, first in connection with the former name; and the joint appellation, Democratic Republicans, or either separately, was used indifferently down to the middle of this century.

Jefferson was the leader of this party. He did not write any political disquisitions or aid in the attempts which have been mentioned to form public opinion; but his expressions in letters and fugitive writings struck in with the tide of Democracy so aptly and exactly that he seemed to have put into people's mouths just the expression for the vague notions which they had not yet themselves been able to get into words. Jefferson, in fact, was no thinker. He was a good specimen of the *a priori* political philosopher. He did not reason or deduce; he dogmatized on the widest and most rash assumptions, which were laid down as self-evident truths. He did not borrow from the contemporaneous French schools, for his democracy is of a different type; but both sprang from the same germs and pursued the same methods of speculation. Freneau, Bache, Callender, and Duane wrought continually upon public opinion, and Jefferson entered into the leadership of the party they created, by virtue of a certain skill in giving watchwords and dogmatic expressions for the ideas which they disseminated.

The dogmas which Jefferson taught, or of which he was the exponent, were not without truth. Their fallacy consisted in embracing much falsehood, and also in excluding the vast amount of truth which lay outside of them. For instance, the dogma that the voice of the people is the voice of God is not without truth, if it means that the enlightened and mature judgment of mankind is the highest verdict on earth as to what is true or wise. This is the truth which is sought to be expressed in the ecclesiastical dogma of Catholicity, but the political and the ecclesiastical dogma have the same limitation. This verdict of mankind cannot be obtained in any formal and concrete expression, and is absolutely unattainable on grounds of speculation antecedent to experiment. It is in history only; or, rather, it constitutes history. In Jefferson's doctrine and practice

it resolved itself simply into this practical rule: the test
of wisdom for the statesman and of truth for the philosopher
is popularity.   When the statesman has a difficult practical question before him as to what to do, according to this
theory he puts forward what seems to him best as a proposition.   If, then, the return wave of popular sympathy
comes back to him with promptitude and with the intensity
to which he is accustomed, he infers that he has proposed
wisely, and goes forward.   If there is delay or uncertainty
in the response, he draws back.   The actual operation of
this theory is that, if the statesman in question is the idol
of a popular majority, the approving response is quick and
sure, because the proposition comes from him, not because
the tribunal of appeal has considered or can consider the
question.   If an unpopular man endeavors to use the same
test, the answer is doubtful, feeble, hesitating, or impatient, because those to whom he appeals have not the
necessary preparation, or time, or interest to judge in the
matter.   In general, the theory is popular, because it
flatters men that they can decide anything offhand, by the
light of nature, or by some prompt application of assumptions as to "natural rights," or by applying the test of a
popular dogma or prejudice.   It tramples study and
thought and culture under foot and turns their boasts to
scorn.   On the other hand, it makes statesmanship impossible.   Study and thought go for nothing.   There can
be no authority derived from information or science or
training, and no leadership won by virtue of these.   If the
decision is to come from a popular vote, why not abandon
useless trouble and trust to that alone?

Such has been the outcome in history, as will appear
further on, of the doctrines which are associated with the
name of Jefferson, although they really had their origin in
the great social tendencies of the time and in the circumstances of the American people.   The love of philosophiz-

ing about government was a feature in the life of the second half of the eighteenth century. The method of philosophizing on assumptions was the only one employed. The Americans, with meager experience and high purposes, readily took refuge in abstractions. The habit of pursuing two or three occupations at once destroyed respect for special or technical knowledge. There seemed to be nothing unreasonable in referring a question of jurisprudence or international law to merchants, farmers, and mechanics, for them to give an opinion on it as a mere incident in their regular occupations. Jefferson himself could sit down and develop out of his own consciousness a plan for fortifications and a navy, for a nation in imminent danger of war, with no more misgivings, apparently, than if he was planning an alteration on his estate.

"The further democracy was pushed, first in theory, then in practice, the more completely was the belief in the equality of all [in rights and privileges] converted, in the minds of the masses, into the belief in the equal ability of all to decide political questions of every kind. The principle of mere numbers gradually supplanted the principle of reflection and study." This tendency reaches its climax in the popular doctrines that every man has a right to his opinion and that one man's opinion is as good as another's. We have abundant illustration of the might which it gives to "the phrase."

It has been well said that "men can reason only from what they know" — a doctrine which would reduce the amount of reasoning to be done by anybody to a very little. The common practice is to reason from what we do not know, which makes every man a philosopher.

Jefferson's election was the first triumph of the tendency towards democracy — a triumph which has never yet been reversed. The old conservatism of the former administrations died out, and it is important to observe that, from this time on, we have in conflict not the same two parties as before, but only factions or subdivisions of the one party which, under Washington and Adams, was in opposition to the administration.

The event did not justify the fears which were entertained before the election. Jefferson did not surrender any of the power of the executive. He aggrandized it as neither of his predecessors would have dared to do. He did not surrender the central power in favor of states' rights; and his foreign policy, governed by sympathy to France and hatred to England, was only too sharp and spirited. It seldom happens to an opposition party, coming into power, to have the same question proposed to it as to its predecessor, and to put its own policy to trial. This happened to Jefferson. Jay's Treaty was hesitatingly signed by Washington, and it gave the country ten years of peace and neutrality. Pinckney and Monroe's Treaty was rejected by Jefferson, and in six years the country was engaged in a fruitless war.

Madison's administration revived many of the social usages which Jefferson had ostentatiously set aside, in consistency with the general spirit of preference, on the ground of republican simplicity, for what is common over what is elegant and refined. The natural tendency of the party in power to think that what is is right, and that while they are comfortable other people ought to be so, was apparent here. It went on so far during Madison's first term, that the leaders thought it necessary to break the monotony and to secure again, in some way, the readiness and activity of political life which had prevailed under Jefferson. They forced Madison into the war with England — a war which brought disturbance into the finances and spread distress amongst the people, which won some glory at sea only by vindicating the old Federalist policy in regard to a navy, but which was marked by disaster on land until the battle of New Orleans. At the return of peace in Europe, England was left free to deal with the United States, and a peace was hastily made in which the question of impressment, the only question at issue, was left just where it had been at the beginning.

There ensued in our internal politics an "era of good feeling." The old parties no longer had any reason to exist. Some of the Federal doctrines had been adopted. The navy was secure in its popularity. The Federal financial system had been adopted by the party in power. They had contracted a debt, laid direct taxes, and enlisted armies. When confronted by problems of war and debt, they had found no better way to deal with them than the ways which had been elaborated by the older nations, and which they had blamed the Federalists for adopting. The questions of neutrality had disappeared with the return of peace in Europe. The fears of Jacobinism on the one hand and of monarchy on the other were recognized as ridiculous. If, however, any one is disposed to exaggerate the evils of party, he ought to study the history of the era of good feeling. Political issues were gone, but personal issues took their place. Personal factions sprang up around each of the prominent men who might aspire to the Presidency, and, in their struggles to advance their favorites and destroy their rivals, they introduced into politics a shameful series of calumnies and personal scandals. Every candidate had to defend himself from aspersions, from attacks based upon his official or private life. The newspapers were loaded down with controversies, letters, documents, and evidence on these charges. The character of much of this matter is such as to awaken disgust and ridicule. Mr. A. tells Mr. B that, when in Washington, he was present at a dinner at the house of Mr. C at which Mr. D said that he came on in the stage with Mr. E, who told him that Mr. F had seen a letter from Mr. G, a supposed friend of one candidate, to Mr. H, the friend of another candidate, making charges against the first candidate, which he (Mr. G) felt bound in honor to make known. Mr. B publishes his information, and then follow long letters from all the other gentlemen, with explanations, denials, corroborative testimony, and so on, in endless reiteration and confusion. It was another noteworthy feature of this period, that every public man seemed to stand ready to publish a "vindication" at the slightest provocation, and that in these vindications a confusion between character and reputation appears to be universal.

These faction struggles culminated in the campaign of 1824. The first mention of General Jackson for the Presidency seems to be in a letter from Aaron Burr to his son-in-law, Alston of South Carolina, in 1815. An effort was being made to form a party against the Virginia oligarchy. Those who were engaged in it sought a candidate who might be strong enough to secure success. Burr justified his reputation as a politician by pointing out the man, but it was yet too soon. The standard of what a Federal officer ought to be was yet too high. The Albany *Argus* said of the nomination, in 1824: "He [Jackson] is respected as a gallant soldier, but he stands in the minds of the people of this state at an immeasurable distance from the executive chair." The name of Jackson was used, however, in connection with the Presidency, by various local conventions, during 1822 and 1823; and, although the nomination was generally met with indifference or contempt in the North and East, it soon became apparant that he was the most dangerous rival in the field. The nominations had hitherto been made by caucuses of the members of Congress of either party. Until Jefferson's second nomination, these had been held under a decent veil of secrecy. Since that time they had exerted more and more complete and recognized control. Crawford was marked for the succession, although he was under some discipline for having allowed his name to be used in the caucus of 1816 against Monroe. The opposing candidates now discovered that caucus nominations were evil, and joined forces in a movement to put an end to them. This movement gained popular approval on general principles. When the caucus was called, naturally only the friends of Crawford attended — sixty-six out of two hundred and sixteen Republican members. The nomination probably hurt him. It was proudly said that King Caucus was now dethroned, but never was there a greater mistake. He had only just come of age and escaped from tutelage. He was about to enter on his inheritance.

General Jackson obtained the greatest number of votes in the electoral college; and when the election came into the House, a claim was loudly put forward which had been feebly heard in 1801, that the House ought simply to carry out the "will of the people" by electing him. This claim distinctly raised the issue which has been described, of democracy against the Constitution. Does the Constitution give the election to the House in certain contingencies, or does it simply charge it with the duty of changing a plurality vote into an election? No one had a majority, but the House was asked really to give to a major vote the authority which, even on the democratic theory, belongs to a majority.

The election could not but result in the discontent of three candidates and their adherents, but the Jackson party was by far the most discontented and most clamorous. They proceeded to organize and labor for the next campaign. They were shrewd, active men, who knew well the arena and the science of the game. They offered to Adams's administration a ruthless and relentless opposition. There were no great party issues; indeed, the country was going through a period of profound peace and prosperity which offered little material for history and little occasion for active political combat. The administration was simple and businesslike and conducted the affairs of the government with that smoothness and quiet success which belong to the system in times of peace and prosperity. Mr. Adams was urged to consolidate his party by using the patronage of the executive, and the opinion has been expressed that, if he had done so, he could have won his reëlection. He steadfastly refused to do this.

The truth was that a new spirit had come over the country, and that the candidacy of Jackson was the form in which it was seeking admission into the Federal administration. Here we meet with one of the great difficulties in the study of American political history. The forces which we find in action on the Federal arena have their origin in the political struggles and personal jealousies of local politicians, now in one state and now in another; and the doctrines which are propounded at Washington, and come before us in their maturity, have really grown up in the states. Rotation in office began to be practiced in New York and Pennsylvania at the beginning of the century. The Federalists then lost power in those states, and their political history consists of the struggles of factions in the Republican party. Jefferson and Madison taught Democracy in Virginia, but it never entered their heads that the "low-down whites" were really to meddle in the formative stage of politics. They expected that gentlemen planters would meet and agree upon a distribution of offices, and that then the masses should have the privilege of electing the men they proposed. The Clintons and Livingstones in New York were Democrats, but they likewise understood that, in practice, they were to distribute offices around their dinner-tables.

In the meantime men like Duane were writing essays for farmers and mechanics, which were read from one end of the Union to the other, in which they were preaching hostility to banks and the "money power," hostility to the judiciary and to the introduction of the common law of England, the election of judicial officers, rotation in office, and all the dogmas which we generally ascribe to a much later origin. These notions even found some practical applications, as in the political impeachment of judges in Pennsylvania in 1804 — acts which fortunately did not become precedents. The new constitutions which were adopted from time to time during the first quarter of this century show the slow working of this leaven, together with the gradual adoption of improvements far less questionable.

After 1810 began also the series of great inventions which have really opened this continent to mankind. The steamboat was priceless to a country which had grand rivers but scarcely any roads. In 1817 De Witt Clinton persuaded New York to commence the Erie Canal, and before it was finished scores of others were projected or begun. Politically and financially the system of internal improvements has proved disastrous, but those enterprises helped on the events which we are now pursuing, for they assisted in opening the resources of the continent to the reach of those who had nothing. The great mass of the population found themselves steadily gaining in property and comfort. Their independence and self-reliance expanded. They developed new traits of national character, and intensified some of the old ones. They had full confidence in their own powers, feared no difficulties, made light of experience, were ready to deal offhand with any problems, laughed at their own mistakes, despised science and study, overestimated the practical man, and overesteemed material good. To such a class the doctrines of democracy seemed axiomatic, and they ascribed to democracy the benefits which accrued to them as the first-comers in a new country. They generally believed that the political system created their prosperity; and they never perceived that the very bountifulness of the new country, the simplicity of life, and the general looseness of the social organism, allowed their blunders to pass without the evil results which would have followed in an older and denser community. The same causes have produced similar results ever since.

Political machinery also underwent great development during the first quarter of the century. In New York there was perhaps the greatest amount of talent and skill employed in this work, and the first engine used was the appointing power. The opposing parties were only personal and family factions, but they rigorously used power, when they got it, to absorb honors and places. That conception of office arose, under which it is regarded as a favor conferred on the holder, not a position in which work is to be done for the public service. Hence the office-holder sat down to enjoy, instead of going to work to serve. If some zealous man who took the latter view got into office, he soon found that he could count upon being blamed for all that went amiss, but would get little recognition or reward while things went well, and that the safest policy was to do nothing. The public was the worst paymaster and the most exacting and unjust employer in the country, and it got the worst service. The consequence was that the early political history of New York is little more than a story of the combinations and quarrels of factions, annual elections, and lists of changes in the office-holders. The Clintons and Livingstones united against Burr, who was the center of an eager and active and ambitious coterie of young men, who already threatened to apply democratic doctrines with a consistency for which the aristocratic families were not prepared. Then they began to struggle with each other until the Livingstones were broken up. Then the "Martling men" and the Clintonians, the Madisonians and the Clintonians, the "Bucktails" and the Clintonians, with various subdivisions, kept up the conflict until the Constitution of 1821 altered the conditions of the fight, and Regency and Anti-regency, or Regency and People's Party, or Regency and Workingmen's Party became the party headings. The net result of all this for national politics was the production of a class of finished "politicians," skilled in all the work of "organization" which in any wide democracy must be the first consideration. Some of these gentlemen entered the national arena in 1824. The Regency was then supporting Crawford as the regular successor. On its own terms it could have been won for Adams, but this arrangement was not brought about. It did not require the astuteness of these men to see on reflection, that Jackson was the coming man. He was in and of the rising power. He represented a newer and more rigorous application of the Jeffersonian dogmas. His manners, tastes, and education, had nothing cold or aristocratic about them. He had never been trained to aim at anything high, elegant, and refined, and had not been spoiled by contact with those who had developed the art of life. He had, moreover, the great advantage of military glory. He had bullied a judge, but he had won the battle of New Orleans. He had hung a man against the verdict of a court-martial, but the man was a British emissary. It was clear that a tide was rising which would carry him into the Presidential chair, and it behooved other ambitious men to cling to his skirts and be carried up with him.

It is in and around the tariff of 1828 that the conflict centers in which these various forces were combined or neutralized to accomplish the result. The student of our economic or political history cannot pay too close study to that crisis. For the next fifteen years the financial and political questions are inextricably interwoven.

The election of Jackson marks a new era in our political history. A new order of men appeared in the Federal administration. The whole force of local adherents of the new administration, who had worked for it and therefore had claims upon it, streamed to Washington to get their reward. It seems that Jackson was forced by the rapacity of this crowd into the "reformation" of the government. The political customs which had grown up in New York and Pennsylvania were transferred to Washington. Mr. Marcy, in a speech in the Senate, January 24, 1832, on Van Buren's nomination as minister to England, boldly stated the doctrine that to the victors belong the spoils, avowing it as a doctrine which did not seem to him to call for any delicacy on the part of politicians. In fact, to men who had grown up as Mr. Marcy had, habit in this respect must have made that doctrine seem natural and necessary to the political system. The New York politicians had developed an entire code of political morals for all branches and members of the political party machine. They had studied the passions, prejudices, and whims of bodies of men. They had built up an organization in which all the parts were adjusted to support and help one another. The subordinate officers looked up to and sustained the party leaders while carrying the party machinery into every nook and corner of the state, and the party leaders in turn cared for and protected their subordinates. Organization and discipline were insisted upon throughout the party as the first political duty. There is scarcely a phenomenon more interesting to the social philosopher than to observe, under a political system remarkable for its looseness and lack of organization, the social bond returning and vindicating itself in the form of party tyranny, and to observe under a political system where loyalty and allegiance to the Commonwealth are only names, how loyalty and allegiance to party are intensified. It is one of the forms under which the constant peril of the system presents itself, namely, that a part may organize to use the whole for narrow and selfish ends. The idea of the commonwealth is lost and the public arena seems only a scrambling-ground for selfish cliques. In the especial case of the New York factions, this was all intensified by the fact that there were no dignified issues, no real questions of public policy at stake, but only factions of the ins and the outs, struggling for the spoils of office. Naturally enough, the contestants thought that to the victors belong the spoils —otherwise the contest had no sense at all. In this system, now, fidelity to a caucus was professed and enforced. Bolting, or running against a regular nomination, were high crimes which were rarely condoned. On the other hand, the leaders professed the doctrine that a man who surrendered his claims for the good of the party, or who stood by the party, must never be allowed to suffer for it. The same doctrines had been accepted more or less at Washington, but in a feeble and timid way. From this time they grew into firm recognition. Under their operation politics became a trade. The public officer was, of necessity, a politician, and the work by which he lived was not service in his official duty, but political party labor. The tenure of office was so insecure and the pay so meager, that few men of suitable ability could be found who did not think that they could earn their living more easily, pleasantly, and honorably in some other career. Public service gravitated downwards to the hands of those who, under the circumstances, were willing to take it. It presented some great prizes in the form of collectorships, etc., the remuneration for which was in glaring contrast with the salaries of some of the highest and most responsible officers in the government; but, for the most part, the public service fell into the hands of men who were exposed to the temptation to make it pay.

After the general onslaught on the caucus, in 1824, it fell into disuse as a means of nominating state officers, and conventions took its place. At first sight this seemed to be a more complete fulfillment of the democratic idea. The people were to meet and act on their own motion. It was soon found, however, that the only change was in the necessity for higher organization. In the thirties there was indeed a fulfillment of the theory which seems now to have passed away; there was a spontaneity and readiness in assembling and organizing common action which no longer exists; there was a public interest and activity far beyond what is now observable. One is astonished at the slight occasion on which meetings were held, high excitement developed, and energetic action inaugurated. The anti-Masonic movement, from 1826 to 1832, is a good instance. The "Liberty party" (Abolitionists), the "Native Americans," the "Anti-renters," all bear witness to a facility of association which certainly does not now exist. It is, however, an indispensable prerequisite to the pure operation of the machinery of caucus and convention. The effort to combine all good men has been talked about from the beginning, but it has always failed on account of the lack of a bond between them as strong as the bond of interest which unites the factions.

During the decade from 1830 to 1840 a whole new set of machinery was created to fit the new arrangements. This consisted in committees, caucuses, and conventions, ramifying down finally into the wards of great cities, and guided and handled by astute and experienced men. Under their control the initiative of "the people" died out. The public saw men elected whom they had never chosen, and measures adopted which they had never desired, and themselves, in short, made the sport of a system which cajoled and flattered while it cheated them. If a governor had been elected by some political trickery a little more flagrant than usual, he was very apt, in his inaugural, to draw a dark picture of the effete monarchies of the Old World, and to congratulate the people on the blessings they enjoyed in being able to choose their own rulers.

This period was full of new energy and turbulent life. Railroads were just beginning to carry on the extension of production which steamboats and canals had begun. Immigration was rapidly increasing. The application of anthracite coal to the arts was working a revolution in them. On every side reigned the greatest activity. Literature and science, which before had had but a meager existence, were coming into life. The public journals, which had formerly been organs of persons and factions, or substitutes for books, now began to be transformed into the modern newspaper. The difficulties and problems presented by all this new life were indeed great, and the tasks of government, as well to discriminate between what belonged to it and what did not, as to do what did belong to it, were great. On the general principles of the Democratic party of the day in regard to the province of government, history has already passed the verdict that they were sound and correct. On the main questions which divided the administration and the opposition, it must pass a verdict in favor of the administration. These issues were not indeed clear and the parties did not, as is generally supposed, take sides upon them definitely. Free trade, so far as it was represented by the compromise tariff, was the result of a coalition between Clay and Calhoun against the administration, after Calhoun's quarrel with Jackson had led the latter to revoke the understanding in accordance with which Calhoun retired from the contest of 1824 and took the second place. The South was now in the position in which the northeastern states had found themselves at the beginning of the century. The Southerners considered that the tariff of 1828 had subjected their interests to those of another section which held a majority in the general government, and that the Union was being used only as a means of so subjecting them. They seized upon the Kentucky and Virginia resolutions of 1798, which Jefferson and Madison had drawn when in opposition, as furnishing them a ground of resistance, and threw into the tariff question no less a stake than civil war and disunion. On this issue there were no parties. South Carolina stood alone.

Banks had been political questions in the states and in the general government from the outset. The history of Pennsylvania and New York furnishes some great scandals under this head. From time to time, the methods of banking employed had called down the condemnation of the most conservative and sensible men, and had aroused some less well-balanced of judgment to indiscriminate hostility. Jackson's attack on the Bank of the United States sprang from a political motive, and he proposed instead of it a bank on the "credit and revenues of the government" — a proposition too vague to be understood, but which suggested a grand paper-machine, at a time when the Bank of the United States was at its best. This attack rallied to itself at once all the local banks; the great victory of 1832 was not a victory for hard money so much as it was a victory of the state banks over the national bank. The removal of the deposits was a reckless financial step, and the crash of 1837 was its direct result.

The traditional position of the Democratic party on hard money has another source. In 1835 a party sprang up in New York City, as a faction of Tammany, which took the name of the "Equal Rights party," but which soon received the name of the "Locofoco party" from an incident which occurred at Tammany Hall, and which is significant of the sharpness of party tactics at the time. This party was a radical movement inside of the administration party. It claimed, and justly enough, that it had returned to the Jeffersonian fountain and drawn deeper and purer waters than the Jacksonian Democrats. It demanded equality with a new energy, and in its denunciations of monopolies and banks went very close to the rights of property. It demanded that all charters should be repealable, urgently favored a metallic currency, resisted the application of English precedents in law courts and legislatures, and desired an elective judiciary. It lasted as a separate party only five or six years, and then was cajoled out of existence by superior political tactics; but it was not without reason that the name spread to the whole party, for, laying aside certain extravagances, two or three of its chief features soon came to be adopted by the Democrats.

On the great measures of public policy, therefore, the position of the administration was not clear and thorough, but the tendency was in the right direction, especially when contrasted with the policy urged by the Whigs. In regard to internal improvements, the administration early took up a position which the result fully justified, and in its opposition to the distribution of the surplus revenue its position was unassailable. In its practical administration of the government there is less ground for satisfaction in the retrospect. Besides the general lowering of tone which has been mentioned, there were scandals and abuses which it is not necessary to specify. General Jackson's first cabinet fell to pieces suddenly, under the effect of a private scandal and of the President's attempt to coerce the private social tastes of his cabinet, or rather of their wives. He held to the doctrine of popularity, and its natural effect upon a man of his temper, without the sobriety of training and culture, was to stimulate him to lawless self-will. He regarded himself as the chosen representative of the whole people, charged, as such, with peculiar duties over against Congress. The "will of the people" here received a new extension. He found it in himself, and what he found there he did not hesitate to set in opposition to the will of the people as this found expression through their constitutional organs. At the same time the practice of "instructions" marked an extension, on another side, of the general tendency to bring public action closer under the control of changing majorities.

Van Buren's election was a triumph of the caucus and convention, which had now been reduced to scarcely less exactitude of action than the old congressional caucus. Van Buren, however, showed more principle than had been expected from his reputation. He had to bear all the blame for the evil fruits resulting from the mistakes made during the last eight years. Moving with the radical or Locofoco tendency, he attempted to sever bank and state by the independent treasury, and in so doing he lost the support of the "Bank Democrats." This, together with the natural political revulsion after a financial crisis, lost him his re-election.

The Whig party was rich in able men, which makes it the more astonishing that one cannot find, in their political doctrines, a sound policy of government. The national bank may still be regarded as an open question, and favoring the bank was not favoring inconvertible paper money; but their policy of high tariff for protection, of internal improvements, and of distribution of the surplus revenue, has been calamitous so far as it has been tried. They also present the same lack of political sagacity which we have remarked in the Federalists, whose successors in general they were. They oscillated between principle and expediency in such a way as to get the advantages of neither; and they abandoned their best men for available men at just such times as to throw away all their advantages. The campaign of 1840 presents a pitiful story. There are features in it which are almost tragic. An opportunity for success offering, a man was chosen who had no marks of eminence and no ability for the position. His selection bears witness to an anxious search for a military hero. It resulted in finding one whose glory had to be exhumed from the doubtful tradition of a border Indian war. The campaign was marked by the introduction of mass meetings and systematic stump-speaking, and by the erection of "log-cabins," which generally served as barrooms for the assembled crowd, so that many a man who went to a drunkard's grave twenty or thirty years ago dated his ruin from the "hard-cider campaign." After the election it proved that hungry Whigs could imitate the Democrats of 1829 in their clamor for office, and, if anything, better the instruction.   The President's death was charged partly to worry and fatigue.   It left Mr. Tyler President, and the question then arose what Mr. Tyler was — a question to which the convention at Harrisburg, fatigued with the choice between Clay and Harrison, had not given much attention.   It was found that he was such that the Whig victory turned to ashes.   No bank was possible, no distribution was possible, and only a tariff which was lame and feeble from the Whig point of view.   The cabinet resigned, leaving Mr. Webster alone at his post.   In vain, like a true statesman, he urged the Whigs to rule with Mr. Tyler, since they had got him and could not get rid of him or get anybody else.   Like a true statesman, again, he remained at his post, in spite of misrepresentation, until he could finish the English treaty, and it was another feature of the story that he lost position with his party by so doing.   The system did not allow Mr. Webster the highest reward of a statesman, to plan and mold measures so as to impress himself on the history of his country.   It allowed him only the work of reducing to a minimum the harm which other people's measures were likely to do.   In the circumstances of the time war with England was imminent, and there was good reason for fear if the negotiation were to fall into the hands of the men whom Mr. Tyler was gathering about him.   The Whigs were broken and discouraged, and as their discipline had always been far looser than that of their adversaries, they seemed threatened with disintegration. The other party, however, was divided by local issues and broken into factions. Its discipline had suffered injury, and its old leaders had lost their fire while new ones had not arisen to take their places. The western states were growing into a size and influence in the confederation which made it impossible for two or three of the old states to control national politics any longer.

In this state of things the southern leaders came forward to give impetus and direction to the national administration. They had, what the southern politicians always had, leisure for conference. They had also character and social position, and a code of honor which enabled them to rely on one another without any especial bond of interest other than the general one. They had such a bond, common and complete, in their stake in slavery. They could count, without doubt or danger, on support throughout their entire section. They had a fixed program also, which was an immense advantage for entering on the control of a mass of men under no especial impetus. They had besides their traditional alliance with the Democrats of the North — an alliance which always was unnatural and illogical, and which now turned to the perversion of that party. They prepared their principles, doctrines, and constitutional theories to fit their plans.

Difficulties with Mexico in regard to Texas had arisen during Jackson's administration. These difficulties seemed to be gratuitous and unjust on the part of the United States, and they seemed to be nursed by the same power. The diplomatic correspondence on this affair is not pleasant reading to one who would see his country honorable and upright, as unwilling to bully as to be bullied. Such was not the position of the United States in this matter.

It was determined by the southern leaders to annex Texas to the United States, and to this end they seized upon the political machinery and proceeded to employ it.

The election of Polk is another of the points to which the student of American politics should give careful attention. The intrigues which surrounded it have never been more than partially laid bare, but, if fairly studied, they give deep insight into the nature of the forces which operate in the name of the will of the people. The slavery issue was here introduced into American politics; and when that question was once raised, it "could not be settled until it was settled right." For ten years efforts were made to keep the issue out of politics and to prevent parties from dividing upon it. What was desired was that the old parties should stand in name and organization, in order that they might be used, while the actual purposes were obtained by subordinate means. A party with an organization and discipline, and a history such as the Democratic party had in 1844, is a valuable property. It is like a well-trained and docile animal which will go through the appointed tasks at the given signal. It disturbs the discipline to introduce new watchwords and to depart from the routine, in order to use reason instead of habit. Hence the effort is to reduce the new and important issues to subordinate places, to carry them incidentally, while the old commonplaces hold together the organization. It is safe to say, however, that, in the long run, the true issues are sure to become the actual issues, and that delay and deceit only intensify the conflict.

Upon Polk's election the independent treasury and comparative free trade were fixed in the policy of the government for fifteen years, with such beneficial results as to render them the proudest traditions of the party which adopted them.

Mr. Calhoun had abandoned the opposition during Van Buren's administration, and had begun to form and lead the southern movement. His own mind moved too rapidly for his adherents, and he could not bring them to support

him up to the positions which he considered it necessary
to take; but, even as it was, the steps of the southern
program came out with a rapidity, and were of a character,
to shock the imperfectly prepared northern allies. The
Democratic party of the North was not a proslavery party.
Whigs and Democrats at the North united in frowning
down Abolition excitements, and in maintaining the compromises of the Constitution. Old-line Whigs and hunker
Democrats agreed in the conservatism which resisted the
introduction of this question; but when, in 1844, Van
Buren was asked, as a test question to a candidate, whether
he would favor the annexation of Texas, the subject of
slavery in the territories was thrown into the political
arena from the southern side. It was not then a question
of abolishing slavery in the southern states, which could
not have obtained discussion except in irresponsible newspapers and on irresponsible platforms. It was not a question of spreading slavery into the old territories, for Texas
and the Indian Territory barred the way to all which the
Missouri Compromise left open. It was now a question of
taking or buying or conquering new territory for slavery,
and every one knew well that the chief reason for the revolt of Texas was that Mexico had abolished slavery. The
South indeed claimed to have suffered aggressions and en-
croachments in regard to slavery ever since the adoption
of the Constitution, and the attempt was now to be made
to secure recompense. In the form in which the proposition came up it was no slight shock to those who had always
been in alliance with the South. Party men like Van Buren
and Benton drew back. Southerners like Clay resisted.
The actual clash of arms, fraudulently brought about and
speciously misrepresented, put an end to discussion, and
aroused a war fever under the pernicious motto, "Our
country, right or wrong." If we are a free people and
govern ourselves, our country is ourselves, and we have

no guaranty of right and injustice if we throw those standards behind us the moment we have done wrong enough
to find ourselves at war. The war ended, moreover, in an
acquisition of territory, which, of course, was popular;
and it proved that this territory was rich in precious metals,
which added to the popular estimate of it. The antecedents of the war were forgotten.

Its political results, however, were far more important.
Calhoun now came forward to ward off a long conflict in
regard to slavery in these territories, by the new doctrine
that the Constitution extended to all the national domain,
and carried slavery with it — a doctrine which his fol-
lowers did not, for ten years afterwards, dare to take up
and rigorously apply, and which divided the Democratic
party of the North. The repeal of the Missouri Compromise and the enactment of the Fugitive Slave Law were
only steps in the conflict which was as yet confused, but
which was clearing itself for a crisis. The South, like every
clamorous suitor, reckless of consequences, obtained wide
concessions from an adversary who sought peace and con-
tentment, and who saw clearly the dangers of a struggle
outside the limits of constitution and law.

The Abolitionists, from their first organization, pursued
an "irreconcilable" course. They refused to vote for any
slaveholder, or for any one who would vote for a slaveholder, and refused all alliances which involved any concession whatever. They more than once, by this course,
aided the party most hostile to them, and, in the view of
the ordinary politician, were guilty of great folly. They
showed, however, what is the power of a body which has
a principle and has no ambition, and is content to remain
in a minority. Probably if the South had been more moderate, the Abolitionists would have attracted little more
notice than a fanatical religious sect; but, as events marched

on, they came to stand as the leaders in the greatest political movement of our history. The refusal of the Whig Convention of 1848 to adopt an antislavery resolution, and the great acts above mentioned, together with the popular reaction against a party which, if it had had its way, would never have won the grand territories on the Pacific, destroyed the Whig party. The party managers, enraged at the immense foreign element which they saw added year by year to their adversaries, forming a cohort, as it appeared, especially amenable to party discipline and the dictation of party managers, took up the Native American movement, which had had some existence ever since the great tide of immigration set in. The effort was wrecked on the obvious economic follies involved in it. How could a new country set hindrances against the immigration of labor? Politically, the effect was great in confirming the allegiance of naturalized voters, as a mass, to the Democratic party as the party which would protect their political privileges against malicious attacks. The formation of the Free-Soil party or its development into the Republican party, brought the extension of slavery into the territories, and the extension of its influence in the administration of the government, distinctly forward as the controlling political issue.

On this issue the Democratic party, as a political organization, made up traditionally of the southern element which has been described, of so much of the old northern Democratic party as had not been repelled by the recent advances in Southern demands, and of the large body of immigrants who regarded that party as the poor man's and the immigrant's friend, fell out of the place it had occupied as the representative of the great democratic tide which flows through and forms our political history. This movement has been in favor of equality. It has borne down and obliterated all the traditions and prejudices

which were inherited from the Old World. It has eliminated from our history almost all recollection of the old
Federal party, with its ideas of social and political leadership. It has crushed out the prestige of wealth and education in politics. It has, by narrow tenures, and by cutting
away all terms of language and ceremonial observances
tending to mark official rank, restrained the respect and
authority due to office. The Northern hatred of slavery in the
later days was due more to the feeling that it was undemocratic than to the feeling that it was immoral. It was always an anomaly that the Virginians should be democrats
par excellence, and should regard the yeomen farmers of
New England as aristocrats, when, on any correct definitions or standards, the New England States were certainly
the most democratic commonwealths in the world. Slavery was an obvious bar to any such classification; and when
slavery became a political issue, the parties found their consistent and logical position. The rise and victory of the
Republican party was only a continuation of the same
grand movement for equality. The old disputes between
Federalists and Jeffersonians had ended in such a complete
victory for the latter, that the rising generation would have
enumerated the Jeffersonian doctrines as axioms or definitions of American institutions. Every schoolboy could
dogmatize about natural and inalienable rights, about the
conditions under which men are created, about the rights
of the majority, and about liberty. The same doctrines
are so held to-day by the mass of the people, and they are
held so implicitly that corollaries are deduced from them
with a more fearless logic than is employed upon political
questions anywhere else in the world. Even scholars and
philosophers who reflect upon them and doubt them are
slow to express their dissent, so jealous and quick is the
popular judgment of an attempt upon them. The Democratic party of the fifties was, therefore, false to its funda-

mental principle of equality when it followed its alliance with the South and allowed itself to be carried against equality for negroes. Whether there were not subtle principles of human nature at work is a question too far-reaching to be followed here.

With the rise of the Republican party there came new elements into American politics. The question at stake was moral in form. It enlisted unselfish and moral and religious motives. It reached outside the proper domain of politics — the expedient measures to be adopted for ends recognized as desirable — and involved justice and right in regard to the ends. It enlisted, therefore, heroic elements: sacrifice for moral good, and devotion to right in spite of expediency. At the same time, the issue was clear, simple, single, and distinct. The organization upon it was close and harmonious, not on account of party discipline, but on account of actual concord in motive and purpose. The American system was here seen in many respects at its best, and it worked more nearly up to its theoretical results in the election of Lincoln, a thoroughly representative man out of the heart of the majority, than in any other election in our history. It is probably the recollection and the standard of this state of things which leads men now on the stage to believe that corruption is spreading and that the political system is degenerating. It is one of the peculiarities of the government of the United States, that it has little historical continuity. If it had more, or if people had more knowledge of their own political history, the above-mentioned opinion would find little ground. The student of history who goes back searching for the golden age does not find it.

All the heroic elements in the political issue of 1860 were, of course, intensified by the war. There was the consciousness of patriotic sacrifice in submitting to loss, bloodshed, and taxation for the sake of an idea, for the further extension of political blessings long enjoyed and highly esteemed. After the war, national pride and consciousness of power expanded naturally, but the questions which then arose were of a different order. They were properly political questions. They concerned taxation, finance, the reconstruction of the South, the status of the freedmen. The war fervor, or the moral fervor of the political contest, could not remain at the former high pitch. There followed a natural reaction. Questions which touched the results of the war brought a quick and eager response. It would not be in human nature that that response should not be tinged by hatred of rebels and by the worse passions which war arouses. For war is at best but a barbarous makeshift for deciding political questions. Let them be never so high and pure in their moral aspects, war drags them down into contact with the lowest and basest passions — with cruelty, rapacity, and revenge. Moreover, it was natural that people should want rest and quiet after the anxiety and excitement of war. Every householder desired to enjoy in peace the political system which he had defended and established by war; he did not care to renew the excitement on the political arena. The questions which arose were no longer such as could be decided by reference to a general political dogma or a moral principle or a text of Scripture. They were such as to perplex and baffle the wisest constitutional lawyer or the ablest financier or the wisest statesman. The indifference and apathy which ensued were remarkable, and they probably had still other causes. The last twenty-five years have seen immense additions to the number and variety of subjects which claim a share of the interest and attention of intelligent men. Literature has taken an entirely new extension and form. Newspapers bring daily information of the political and social events of a half-dozen civilized countries. New sciences appeal to the

interest of the entire community. Educational, ecclesiastical, sanitary, and economic undertakings, in which the
public welfare is involved, demand a part of the time and
effort of every citizen. At the same time trade and industry have undergone such changes in form and method that
success in them demands far closer and more exclusive
application than formerly. The social organization is
becoming more complex, the division of labor is necessarily
more refined, and the value of expert ability is rapidly rising.

It follows from all this that, while public interests are
becoming broader and weightier, the ability of the average
voter to cope with them is declining. It is no wonder that
we have not the political activity of the first half of this
century. Instead of grasping at the right to a share in
deciding, we shrink from the responsibility. We are more
inclined to do here what we should do in any other affair
— seek for competently trained hands into which to commit the charge. The frequent elections, instead of afford-
ing a pleasurable interest to the ordinary voter, appear
to be tiresome interruptions. What he wants is good government, honorable and efficient administration, business-
like permanence, and exactitude. He recognizes in the
short terms and continual elections, not an opportunity
for him to control the government, but an opportunity for
professional hangers-on of parties to make a living, and a
continually recurring opportunity for schemers of various
grades to enter and carry out their plans when people are
too busy to watch them. The opinion seems to be gaining
ground that, for fear of power, we have eliminated both
efficiency and responsibility; that if power is united with
responsibility, it will be timid and reluctant enough; and
that the voter needs only reserve the right of supervision
and interference from time to time. The later state constitutions show a reaction from those of the first half of
the century in the length of terms of office, and in the gen-

eral tendency of the people to take guaranties against themselves or their representatives. There seems also to be a tendency to investigate the theory of appointments or elections to office as a means of devising measures more satisfactory to that end. No system will ever give a self-governing people a government which is better than they can appreciate; but the very belief, to which we have before referred, that the government is degenerating, is the best proof that the public standards as to the *personnel* and the methods of the government are rising. It seems to be perceived that the plan of popular selection is applicable to executive and legislative officers, but that it is not applicable to the judiciary or to administrative officers. In the one case, broad questions of policy control the choice; in the other case, personal qualifications and technical training, in regard to which the mass of voters cannot be informed and cannot judge. In some quarters, an unfortunate effort has been made to charge the duty of making certain appointments upon the judges, because, as a class, they retain the greatest popular confidence and because the restraints of their position are the weightiest. This, however, seems to be using up our last reserves. There has been abundant criticism of political movements and circumstances of late years. At first sight, it does not appear to be very fruitful. People seem to pay as little heed to it as devout Catholics do to the asserted corruptions of the Church; but other and deeper signs point to a conservative movement, slow, as all popular movements must be, but nevertheless real.

The political party system which had been developed previous to the war underwent no change during the heroic period. The doctrines of spoils and of rotation in office were indeed condemned, but it appeared (as it must appear to any new party coming into office) that the interests at stake were too great to be risked by leaving any part of the administration in the hands of disaffected men, and, with some apologies, the changes were made. It is the fate of the party in power to draw to itself all the unprincipled men who seek to live by politics, and to lose its principled adherents as, on one question after another, they disapprove of its action. The moral and heroic doctrines or sentiments of the Republican party were just the political principles which offered the best chance to the unprincipled. A man of corrupt character could "hate slavery" when that was the line of popularity and success, and could be "loyal" when only loyal men could get offices. The political machinery whose growth has been traced was adopted by the new party as a practical necessity, and the men "inside politics" still teach the old code wrought out by Tammany Hall and the Albany Regency, not only as the only rules of success for the ambitious politician, but also as the only sound theories on which the Republic can be governed. In those quarters where hitherto the refinements of the system have all been invented, a new and ominous development has recently appeared in the shape of the "Boss." He is the last and perfect flower of the long development at which hundreds of skilful and crafty men have labored, and into which the American people have put by far the greatest part of their political energy. It has been observed that the discipline or coercion which we dread for national purposes and under constitutional forms appears with the vigor of a military despotism in party; and that the conception of loyalty, for which we can find no proper object in our system, is fully developed in the party. Under this last development, also, we find leadership, aristocratic authority of the ablest, nay, even the monarchical control of the party king. He is a dictator out of office. He has power, without the annoyance or restraints of office. He is the product of a long process of natural selection. He has arisen from the ranks, has been tried by various tests, has been trained in subordinate positions, and has come up by steady promotions — all the processes which, when we try to get them into the public service, we are told are visionary and aristocratic. With the now elaborate system of committees rising in a hierarchy from the ward to the nation, with the elaborate system of primaries, nominating committees, caucuses, and conventions, not one citizen in a thousand could tell the process by which a city clerk is elected. It becomes a special trade to watch over and manage these things, and the power which rules is not the "will of the people," but the address with which "slates" are made up. Organization is the secret by which the branches of the political machinery are manipulated, when they are not, by various devices, reduced, as in the larger cities, to mere forms. In these cases the ring and the "Boss" are the natural outcome. Any one who gets control of the machine can run it to produce what he desires, with the exception, perhaps, that if he should try to make it produce good, he might find that this involved a reverse action of the entire mechanism, under which it would break to pieces. These developments are as yet local, for the plunder of a great city is a prize not to be abandoned for any temptation which the general government can offer. In some cases they are hostile to the power of the Federal office-holders where that is greatest and most dangerous, so that they neutralize each other. At the same time some of the Federal legislation in the way of "protection" and subsidies offers high inducements and abundant opportunities for debauching the public service. There are afforded by the system in great abundance means of rewarding adherents, distributing largess, collecting campaign funds, and performing favors; and it tends to bind men together in cliques up and down through the service, on the basis of mutual assistance and support and protection. Suppose that the ring and the "Boss" should ever be ingrafted upon this system!

It cannot be regarded as a healthful sign that such a state of things creates only a laugh or a groan of disgust or at best a critical essay. It seems sometimes as if the prophecy of Calhoun had turned into history: "When it comes to be once understood that politics is a game, that those who are engaged in it but act a part, and that they make this or that profession, not from honest conviction or an intent to fulfil them, but as a means of deluding the people, and, through that delusion, acquiring power, — when such professions are to be entirely forgotten, the people will lose all confidence in public men. All will be regarded as mere jugglers, the honest and patriotic as well as the cunning and profligate, and the people will become indifferent and passive to the grossest abuses of power, on the ground that those whom they may elevate, under whatever pledges, instead of reforming, will but imitate the example of those whom they have expelled."

In the final extension of the conception of the "will of the people," and of the position of Congress in relation to it, Congress has come to be timid and faltering in the face of difficult tasks. It knows how to go when the people have spoken, and not otherwise. The politician gets his opinions from the elections, and the legislature wants to be pushed, even in reference to matters which demand promptitude and energy. Statesmanship has no positive field and has greatly declined. The number of able men who formerly gave their services to mold, correct, and hinder legislation, and upon whom the responsibility for leading on doubtful and difficult measures could be thrown, has greatly decreased. The absence of "leaders" has often been noticed. The fact seems to be that able men have observed that such statesmen as have been described bore the brunt of the hard work, and were held responsible for what they had done their best to hinder; that they cherished a vain hope and ambition their whole lives long, and saw inferior men without talent or industry perferred before them. It is a sad thing to observe the tone adopted towards a mere member of Congress as such. When one reflects that he is a member of the grand legislature of the nation, it is no gratifying sign of the times that he should be regarded without respect, that a slur upon his honor should be met as presumptively just, and that boys should turn flippant jests upon the office, as if it involved a dubious reputation. If the Republic possesses the power to meet and conquer its own tasks, it cannot too soon take measures to secure a representative body which shall respect itself and be respected, without doubt or question, both at home and abroad; for the times have changed and the questions have changed, and we can no longer afford to govern ourselves by means of the small men. The interests are now too vast and complex, and the greatest question now impending, the currency, contains too vast possibilities of mischief to this entire generation to be left the sport of incompetents. The democratic Republic exults in the fact that it has, against the expectations of its enemies, conducted a great civil war to a successful result. A far heavier strain on democratic-republican self-government lies in the questions now impending: can we ward off subsidy-schemers? can we correct administrative abuses? can we purify the machinery of elections? can we revise erroneous financial systems and construct sound ones? The war appealed to the simplest and commonest instincts of human nature, especially as human nature is developed under democratic institutions. The questions before us demand for their solution high intellectual power and training, great moderation and self-control, and perhaps no less disposition to endure sacrifices than did the war itself.

Such a review as has here been given of the century of
American politics must raise the question as to whether the
course has been upward or downward, and whether the
experiment is a success or not. On such questions opinions
might fairly differ, and I prefer to express upon them only
an individual opinion.

The Federal political system, such as it is historically in
the intention and act of its framers, seems to me open to
no objection whatever, and to be the only one consistent
with the circumstances of the case. I have pursued here a
severe and exact criticism of its history, as the only course
consistent with the task before me, and the picture may
seem dark and ungratifying. I know of no political history
which, if treated in the same unsparing way, would appear
much better. I find nothing in our history to throw doubt
upon the feasibility and practical advantage of a constitutional Republic. That system, however, assumes and imperatively requires high intelligence, great political sense,
self-sacrificing activity, moderation, and self-control on the
part of the citizens. It is emphatically a system for sober-
minded men. It demands that manliness and breadth of
view which consider all the factors in a question, submit
to no sophistry, never cling to a detail or an objection or
a side issue to the loss of the main point, and, above all,
which can measure a present advantage against a future
loss, and individual interest against the common good.
These requirements need only be mentioned to show that
they are so high that it is no wonder we should have fallen
short of them in our history. The task of history is to show
us wherein and why, so that we may do better in future.

If the above sketch of our political history has been
presented with any success, it shows the judgment which
has been impressed upon my mind by the study of it,
namely, that the tenor of the Constitution has undergone
a steady remolding in history in the direction of democ-

racy. If a written constitution were hedged about by all the interpretations conceivable, until it were as large as the Talmud, it could not be protected from the historical process which makes it a different thing to one generation from what it is to another, according to the uses and needs of each. I have mentioned the forces which seem to me to produce democracy here. They are material and physical, and there is no fighting against them. It is, however, in my judgment, a corruption of democracy to set up the dogma that all men are equally competent to give judgment on political questions; and it is a still worse perversion of it to adopt the practical rule that they must be called upon to exercise this ability on all questions as the regular process for getting those questions solved. The dogma is false, and the practical rule is absurd. Caucus and wire-pulling and all the other abuses are only parasites which grow upon these errors.

Reform does not seem to me to lie in restricting the suffrage or in other arbitrary measures of a revolutionary nature. They are impossible, if they were desirable. Experience is the only teacher whose authority is admitted in this school, and I look to experience to teach us all that the power of election must be used to select competent men to deal with questions, and not to indirectly decide the questions themselves. I expect that this experience will be very painful, and I expect it very soon.

On the question whether we are degenerating or not, I have already suggested my opinion that we are not degenerating. The lamentations on that subject have never been silent. It seems to me that, taking the whole community through, the tone is rising and the standard is advancing, and that this is one great reason why the system seems to be degenerating. Existing legislation nourishes and produces some startling scandals, which have great effect on people's minds. The same legislation has demoralized the people, and perverted their ideas of the functions of government even in the details of town and ward interests. The political machinery also has been refined and perfected until it totally defeats the popular will, and has produced a kind of despair in regard to any effort to recover that of which the people have been robbed; but I think that it would be a great mistake to suppose that there are not, behind all this, quite as high political standards and as sound a public will as ever before. An obvious distinction must be made here between the administration of the government, or the methods of party politics, and the general political morale of the people. Great scandals are quickly forgotten, and there are only too many of them throughout our history. Party methods have certainly become worse and worse. The public service has certainly deteriorated; but I should judge that the political will of the nation never was purer than it is to-day. That will needs instruction and guidance. It is instructed only slowly and by great effort, especially through literary efforts, because it has learned distrust. It lacks organization, and its efforts are spasmodic and clumsy. The proofs of its existence are not very definite or specific, and any one in expressing a judgment must be influenced by the circle with which he is most familiar; but there are some public signs of it, which are the best encouragement we have to-day.

THE ADMINISTRATION OF
ANDREW JACKSON

THE ADMINISTRATION OF [1]
ANDREW JACKSON
[1880]

YOU must have observed that the social sciences, including politics and political economy, are the favorite arena of those who would like to engage in learned discussion without overmuch trouble in the way of preparation. I doubt not that you have also been struck by the fact that these sciences are now the refuge of the conceited dogmatism which has been expelled from the physical sciences. It follows that the discussions in social science are the widest, the most vague, the most imperative in form of statement, the most satisfactory to the writers, the least convincing to everybody else; and that the social sciences make very little progress. The harm does not all come from the amateurs and volunteers who meddle in these subjects. It comes also from false methods and want of training on the part of those of higher pretensions. If, however, the methods which have hitherto been pursued are correct, if any one is able without previous care or study to strike out the solution of a difficult social problem, for which solution, however, he can give no guarantee to anybody else, then the social sciences are given over to endless and contemptible wrangling, and are unworthy of the time and attention of sober men. Such, however, is not the case. The Science of Life, which teaches us how to live together in human society, and has more to do with our happiness here than any other science, is not a mere structure of *a priori* whims. It is not a mass of guesses which the guesser tries to render plausible. It is not a tangle of dog-

[1] Address before the Kent Club of the Yale Law School.

mas which are incapable of verification. It is not a bundle of sentiments and enthusiasms and soft-hearted wishes bound together either by religious or by irreligious prejudices. It is not a heap of statistical matter without logic. Whether you regard the social science under the form of law, politics, political economy, or social science in its narrower application, these negatives all apply. It is only under some application of scientific methods and scientific tests that, in this department as in others, any results worth our notice can be won.

Now the materials, the facts, and the phenomena of social science are presented to us under two forms: first, as a successive series, *viz.*, in history, in which we see social forces at work and the social evolution in progress; secondly, in statistics, in which the contemporaneous phenomena are presented in groups.[1] Under this view social science has promise, at least, of issuing from its present condition and taking on a steady progress, while it also becomes evident what history ought to be and how we ought to use it.

I have thought it necessary to preface the present lecture with this bare suggestion of the standpoint from which I take up my subject. For the study of politics, some questions in political economy, and some social problems, the history of the United States has greater value than that of any other country. All the greater is the pity that its history is as yet unwritten, or all the greater is the humiliation that the only attempts in that direction which are worth mentioning have been made by foreign scholars, and are not even in the English language. In American history also, for the study of politics and finance, no period equals in interest the administration of Andrew Jackson. I propose, therefore, in the limited time I can now com-

---

[1] Statistics means here, what it ought to mean, much more than tables of figures.

mand, to point out to you the reasons why this period of our history is worthy of the most attentive study. I may say here that Professor Von Holst of Freiburg has perceived the importance and interest of this period and published a lecture in regard to it which I regard as thoroughly sound and correct in its standpoint and criticism. His views coincide with those which I have been accustomed to present in my lectures on the History of American Politics, and I have profited, for my present purpose, by some suggestions of his.

Mr. Monroe was the last of the public men of the first generation of the republic who succeeded to the presidential chair by virtue of a certain standing before the public. During his administration the old parties died out or were merged in a new party, a compromise between the two. There followed during his second administration what was called the "era of good feeling," during which there were no party divisions and no strong party feeling. This period was very instructive, however, for any one who is disposed to see the evils of party in an exaggerated light, for there sprang up no less than five aspirants to the succession, whose interests were pushed by personal arguments solely. These arguments took the form also, not of enumerating the services of the candidate favored, but of spreading scandals about his rivals. The newspapers were loaded down with weary "correspondence" about "charges and countercharges" against each of the candidates.

Mr. Crawford of Georgia obtained the nomination of the democratic congressional caucus in 1824, but loud complaints were raised against this method of nominating candidates. It was demanded that the people should be free from the dominion of King Caucus, and should nominate and elect freely. No machinery for accomplishing this was yet at hand, and none was proposed, but the outcry which was partly justified by the evils of the congressional caucus system and partly consisted of phrases which were sure of great popular effect, greatly injured Mr. Crawford. He had been Secretary of the Treasury during the financial troubles of the years following the war, and had managed that thankless office on the whole very well, but he had not performed the impossible. He had not brought the finances of the country into a sound condition while allowing the banks to do as they chose. He had not kept up the revenue while trade was prostrated, and he had not crushed the United States Bank while preserving the business interest of the country. He had many enemies amongst those who, on the one side and on the other, thought that he ought to have done each of these things. Hostility to the Bank was not as great in 1824 as in 1820, but there was a large party which was determined in this hostility. Mr. Crawford was also said to be broken in health, and this came to be believed so firmly that it has generally passed into history as one of the chief causes of his defeat. It is so accepted by Von Holst. Mr. Crawford was disabled from September, 1823, to September, 1824, but he lived until 1834, spending the last years of his life as a circuit judge, and he was well enough in 1830 to ruin John C. Calhoun's chances of succeeding General Jackson.

The next candidate was Mr. Adams, Secretary of State under Mr. Monroe. He enjoyed the support of New England. There was no question of Mr. Adams's abilities, or of his great public services, or of his character; but he was not popular. I do not, of course, think this at all derogatory to him, but you observe that it is hard for a man to despise popularity and at the same time have enough of it to be elected to office in a democracy. Mr. Adams really liked popularity and wanted it, and there was a continual strife within him between the aristocrat who sought independent and isolated activity to please himself and the politician who must please others. It is the explanation of much in his conduct which seemed erratic and inconsistent to his contemporaries.

Mr. Clay was the candidate of the West, and Mr. Calhoun of a portion of the South.

These men were all in prominent positions, three of them in the Cabinet, and one speaker of the House. On the 20th of August, 1822, the House of Representatives of Tennessee presented another candidate in the person of General Jackson. This gentleman had been educated for a lawyer and had been on the bench of Tennessee. He was in Congress during the administration of Washington and voted against a clause in the address of Congress to Washington on his retirement, in which a hope was expressed that Washington's example might be imitated by his successors.[1] As a member of Congress he had been noticeable only for violence of speech and action. At New Orleans he had won a creditable military success at the close of a war which had brought little glory on land. While there he came into collision with the civil court on refusing to obey a writ of habeas corpus. Some incidents of this event are especially characteristic of the man. He came into court March 31, 1815, surrounded by the populace, and refused to answer interrogatories. Then, pointing to the crowd, he said to the judge, alluding to the previous judicial inquiry: "I was then with these brave fellows in arms; you were not, sir!" He interrupted the judge while he was reading his decision, saying: "Sir, state facts and confine yourself to them, since my defence is and has been precluded; let not censure constitute a part of this sought-for punishment." The judge replied: "It is with delicacy, general, that I speak of your name or character. I consider you the savior of the country, but for your contempt of court authority, or to that effect, you will pay a fine of $1000." The general drew his check for the sum and re-

---

[1] Niles, XLVI, 407.

tired. The crowd dragged his carriage to the French coffee-house, with acclamations and waving flags. He there made a speech.[1] The fine, amounting with interest to $2,700, was refunded by Congress in 1844.

In 1818 he had violated the territory of Florida, then a province of Spain, with whom we were at peace. He claimed, in 1830, that he had done this with the conniv-ance of Mr. Monroe. During the same campaign against the Seminoles he captured two men who were aiding the enemy and were said to be British subjects. A court-martial condemned one of them to death and the other to less punishment. He ordered both executed, thus over-ruling the verdict on the side of severity.

The people might have been divided into two great classes according to the opinion of Jackson which was entertained in 1822. The more sober and intelligent considered him a violent, self-willed, ignorant, and untrained man. They thought that he had perhaps the soldier's virtues and that he had done the country good service as a soldier but they doubted if he had the first qualification of a ruler, *viz.*, to know how to obey. They thought him quarrelsome, vain, untutored in the forms of civilized life which teach men to ignore much, to endure more, and to reserve the stake of personal feeling and personal struggle for the last and highest emergencies. They perceived, on the contrary, that he never distinguished great things from small, es-pecially where his own pride was involved, and that he had no reserve at all about throwing his personality into unseemly controversies, which he never shunned but seemed to like. I have already said that these personal criminations and recriminations were common at the time; Mr. Webster is the only prominent public man of the time who succeeded in avoiding newspaper controversies, and he did not altogether escape altercations in the Senate. Public

[1] Niles, VIII, 246.

men were continually scenting attacks on their character and setting vigorously to work to vindicate the same, not perceiving that such vindications always derogate from the man who makes them.   This much ought to be said in excuse for General Jackson if this fault was especially prominent in him.   You may imagine how incredible it seemed to persons who formed this estimate of Jackson that any one could soberly propose him for the chair which had hitherto been filled by Washington, Adams, Jefferson, Madison, and Monroe.   The Federalists of New England had had little affection or admiration for the last three Presidents, but they had never been ashamed of them as public men.

The other of the two great classes to which I have referred held a very opposite opinion of General Jackson. To them he was a military hero and a popular idol.   They liked him better for taking Pensacola in defiance of international law.   They liked him for bearding the judge who wanted to enforce the habeas corpus.   They thought it spirited in him to hang two Englishmen to solve a doubt. I do not mean that they reasoned much about it, for they did not; at bottom they were actuated by an instinct of fellowship.   They recognized a man with the same range of ideas and feelings, the same contempt for history, law, Old-World forms, and traditions by which they themselves were actuated.   His bluntness, his rollicking, untamed manner, his hit-or-miss arguments, his respect for the popular whim or emotion as the only control he would admit, his plump ignorance which exceeded omniscience in its boldness, all flattered the populace and won its favor. Here was a hero from amongst themselves, using their methods, despising the restrictions of the cultivated and the learned, a virtuoso in negligence and carelessness of manner, aiming at rudeness and bluntness as things worth cultivating, and elevating want of culture into a qualification for greatness and a title to honor.

In order to understand the full importance of this you must look at some facts in social and political development which had immediately preceded. At the adoption of the Constitution property qualifications limiting the suffrage were general, but they had been removed steadily and gradually until by 1820 the suffrage was universal throughout almost all the states. The Jeffersonian ideas of government and policy had also spread steadily and rapidly and had received more and more extended interpretation. They were fallacious and only half true at best, that is to say, they were of the most mischievous order of propositions possible in politics; but in popular use and interpretation they had become worn into a kind of political cant, in which the moiety of truth had disappeared and the residuum of falsehood had become the highest political truth and the badge of political orthodoxy. To use the ballot was held synonymous with freedom; the rule of the numerical majority was made equivalent to the republic; the "will of the people" was held paramount to the Constitution — which is nothing more than saying that to do as you choose is superior to doing as you have agreed. And it had become a political dogma that, if there are only enough of you together, when you do as you have a mind to, you are sure to do right.

I use the past sense here, but you will at once perceive that I am describing what is still strong amongst us.

Of course there was, outside of these two classes, a large body of persons, scattered, as to their political opinions, all the way between the two extremes; but the second class was large and was growing very rapidly from social and industrial causes which are yet to be specified.

During the European wars the people of the New England states made great gains from commerce. In the middle states manufactures began under the protection of embargo and war. In the South there was less wealth,

but the possession of land and slaves created an aristocracy
of large political influence over poorer neighbors. In New
York something of the same kind existed, two or three
of the great families struggling with one another for the
political control of the state. These were all democrats
of a peculiar type well worthy of study. They professed
popular principles while they scorned the populace and led
cohorts of uneducated men whom they handled and disposed of as they chose. After the war the commerce and
industry of the country suffered a heavy reverse from which
it did not recover until 1820 or 1821; but then came the
influence of steam navigation, as the first of the great inventions, together with the factory system and some great
improvements in machinery, and the position of the artisan, in spite of the protective policy to which the result
was generally attributed as a cause, underwent a steady
and very great improvement. In 1825 the Erie Canal was
opened and, together with the application of steam to
lake and river navigation, led to an unparalleled development west of the Alleghanies. In the southwestern states
the immense profits of cotton culture led to rapid settlement and development. As early as 1816 the tide of immigration had become marked. It was interrupted during
the hard times but went on again increasing steadily. Thus
you see that the material prosperity of this country was
just taking its great start at the beginning of the twenties.
The natural consequence was that there was a great body
of persons here who had been used to straitened circumstances, but who now found themselves prosperous, every
year improving their condition. Such a state of things is
of course eminently desirable. Economists and statesmen
are continually trying to bring it about. Observe, however,
some of the inevitable social, political, and moral effects.
This class expanded under the sun of prosperity both its
virtues and its vices. It became self-reliant and independ-

ent. It feared no mishap. It took reckless risks. It laughed at prudence. It had overcome so many difficulties that it took no forethought for any yet to come. It loved dash and bravado and high spirit. It admired energy and enterprise as amongst the highest human virtues. It scorned especially theory, or philosophy, and professed exaggerated faith in the practical man. It never estimated science very highly until science began to lead to patent mixtures for various purposes and to mining engineering. Then it took to business colleges and technical schools for the dissemination of the same. Especially did this class despise any historical or scientific doctrines which came from the other side of the water. It was a general premise that the new country needed new systems throughout the whole social and political fabric, and that what was enforced by European experience was surely inapplicable here. As against England this assumption was considered especially strong. In the writings of some of the men who greatly influenced public opinion from 1820 to 1830 this amounted almost to fanaticism. "Home industry," and "Internal Improvements," owed much of their success over the mind of the nation to the industrious use of this prejudice. These subjects were not political issues until 1830.

Of course I have nothing to do with the question which to many would seem to be here the only important one, *viz.*, whether these traits are not noble and praiseworthy and do not constitute the Americans the first nation in the world. Those are idle questions. Political institutions are not framed to produce noble and praiseworthy men. If any are planned to that end they always fail. But political institutions follow the social and industrial conditions, if the people adapt themselves to the facts of the case. So it has been here; and, although I have used the past tense in this description of the effects of rapid prosperity, you observe that the features are those which still mark our

American society as a whole. I have simply to take cognizance of these effects as facts inseparable from the conditions of that society.

Here, then, I come to the assertion to which I desire especially to call your attention under my present subject: that is, that General Jackson's personal popularity and his political influence were not created by him at all, but were simply the results of the fact that he exactly fitted in as a leader into the rising class of persons of small property, low education, and crude notions of politics and finance. Of this class he was the leader as long as he lived. You will recognize here an illustration of the wider historical generalization, that the prominent man and his surroundings always act and react on one another and the old question as to which "causes" the other is idle.

Such being the circumstances in 1822, when Jackson's name was first mentioned in connection with the Presidency, the class of persons whom I first described as considering this a bad joke soon discovered their mistake. In the following year the people of Blount County, Tennessee held a meeting at which they passed strong resolutions in his support,[1] and it was soon evident to the aspirants at Washington that he was the most dangerous competitor of all. Calhoun hastened to retire into the second place, with the understanding that he was to succeed in four years, Jackson having pronounced for one term only. Pending the contest, in 1823, Jackson was elected United States Senator from Tennessee. The result of the election of 1824 was that Jackson got 99 votes in the electoral college, Adams 84, Crawford 41, and Clay 37. Clay was thus excluded from the contest in the House. His friends voted for Adams, who got 13 states, Jackson 7, and Crawford 4. The states which voted for Jackson were New Jersey, Pennsylvania, South Carolina, Tennessee, Indiana,

[1] Niles, XXIV, 247.

Alabama, and Mississippi. This election was in many respects important for the history of politics in the country. I leave aside all but the relation to Jackson and the political movement which he represented. His friends were by no means content, and they were not quiet in their discontent. They accused Clay of carrying his votes over to Adams by a corrupt bargain, according to which he was to be Secretary of State in the new Cabinet. There was less ground for this accusation than for almost any other personal calumny to be found in our political history, but it clung to Mr. Clay as long as he lived.

The most significant feature, however, for the political movement of the time was this: General Jackson's supporters claimed that, as he had a plurality of the votes of the Electoral College, it was shown to be the will of the people that he should be President, and that the House of Representatives ought simply to have carried out the popular will, thus expressed, to fulfillment. You observe the full significance of the doctrine thus affirmed. The Constitution provides that the House shall elect a President when the Electoral College fails to give any candidate a majority. It confers an independent choice between the three highest candidates upon the House. Already the independent choice which the Constitution intended to give to the Electoral College had been abrogated by Congressional caucus nominations and pledged elections. It was now claimed that the House should simply elevate the plurality of the highest candidate in the College to a majority in the House. Thus the antagonism between the permanent specification of the Constitution and the momentary will of the people was sharply defined. It was the antagonism between the general law and the momentary impulse, between sober dispassionate judgment as to what is generally wise and a special inconvenience or disappointment. I strive to put it into everyday language because it is a phenomenon of human life which is the same whether it is seen in the character of an individual striving to control his wayward impulses by general principles, or in the political history of a great democratic republic seeking to obtain dignity, stability, and imperial majesty by binding the swaying wishes of the hour under broad and sacred constitutional provisions. It was the opening of that issue which is vital to this republican issue which cleaves down through our entire political and social fabric, the issue to which parties must ever return and about which they will always form so long as this experiment lasts — the issue, namely, of constitutionalism *versus* democracy, of law *versus* self-will; the question whether we are a constitutional republic whose ultimate bond is the loyalty of the individual citizen to the Constitution and the laws or a democracy in which at any time the laws and the Constitution may give way to what shall seem, although not constitutionally expressed, to be the will of the people. General Jackson was from the time of this election the exponent of the latter theory.

I do not mean to say that the issue was clearly defined at the time, or that the parties ranged themselves upon it with logical consistency. Any student of history knows that political parties never do that. Still less do I mean to say that parties since that time have kept strictly to the position on one side or the other of this issue which their traditions would require. Political history and political tradition have little continuity with us, and the fact has been that the Jacksonian doctrine has permeated our whole community far too deeply. We have had some who merely grubbed in a mole-eyed way in the letter of the Constitution, as indeed Jackson and his fellows did, and we have had others who were and are restive under any invocation of the Constitution. True constitutionalism, however, the grand conception of law, of liberty under law, of the free obedience of intelligent citizens, is what now needs explaining and enforcing as the key to any true solution of the great problems which, as we are told on every side, beset the republic.

I cannot now follow the history in detail to show the movements of parties during the next four years. Mr. Adams's administration was unfortunate in its attempts to settle the old misunderstanding with England about the West India trade. It got that question into one of those awkward corners, out of which neither party can first seek exit, which the diplomatist ought to avoid as the worst form of diplomatic failure. In its home policy it favored internal improvements and protection to the most exaggerated degree. But the administration was dignified, simple, and businesslike. It was a model in these respects of what an administration under our system ought to be. It presented no heroics whatever, neither achievements nor scandals, and approached, therefore, that millenial form of society in which time passes in peace and prosperity without anything to show that there is either government or history.

Nevertheless this administration did not receive justice from its contemporaries. Mr. Adams seemed always to feel a certain timidity, which he expressed in his letter to the House of Representatives on his election, because he had gone into office without a popular majority. In Congress he had to deal with an opposition which was factious, disappointed, and malignant, determined to make the worst of everything he did and to make capital at every step for General Jackson. It was a campaign four years long, and it was conducted by a new class of politicians who made light of principle and gloried in finesse. The end of the old system of family leadership in New York and the certainty that there would never be another congressional caucus, led to new forms of machinery for manipulating the popular power. These were set up under loud denunciations of dynasties, aristocracies, families, dictation, and so on. The most remarkable and most powerful of these new organs was the Albany Regency, which shaped our political history for the next ten or fifteen years. The intrigues of the period culminated in the tariff act of 1828, in which Pennsylvania and the South were brought into a strange coalition to support Jackson and a high tariff, leaving New England out of the golden shower of tariff-created wealth, as she held aloof from the support of the popular idol. I regret that I cannot now stop to analyze and expose this prime specimen of legislation in which tariff and politics were scientifically intermingled.

As for political principles, there were none at stake and none argued in the contest. The struggle was ruthlessly personal. A month before the election an editorial in *Niles's Register* used the following language: "We had much to do with the two great struggles of parties from 1797 to 1804 and 1808 to 1815, and we are glad that we are not so engaged in this, more severe and ruthless than either of the others, and, we must say, derogatory to our country, and detrimental to its free institutions and the rights of suffrage, with a more general grossness of assault upon distinguished individuals than we ever before witnessed."

Jackson was elected by 178 votes to 83 for Adams. The criticisms which had been made upon Adams's administration were now all used as a basis for representing the entire government as needing reform. This reform took the form of removing all persons in office and replacing them by friends of the new President. Up to this time the tenure of office in the public service had been during efficiency or good behavior, although instances of removals for political reasons had not been wanting and there had been many changes when Jefferson went into office. I will only say in passing that the complaints of inefficiency in office and of corruption during Jackson's administration steadily and

justly increased. According to a report by Secretary
Ewing, in 1841, there were lost, to the government between
1829 and 1841, over two millions and a half of dollars by
defalcations of public officials. The Cabinet selected by
Jackson at the outset consisted of obscure men remarkable
only for their loyalty to the person of the President. It may
be said in general of the new appointments to inferior offices
that they constituted a deterioration of the public service.
Two doctrines were now affirmed as democratic principles
which, if they should be accepted as such, would be the condemnation of democracy to all sober-minded men. The first
was that of rotation in office, which, if it is a democratic
principle, raises inefficiency and venality to permanent features of the public service. You will observe that its effect
has been, as a matter of history, to make thousands of
people believe despairingly that these things are inseparable from the public service and that elections only determine which set shall enjoy the opportunity. The other
doctrine or democratic principle was that to the victors
belong the spoils. This was distinctly enunciated by
William L. Marcy on the floor of the Senate. He said
that he did not hesitate to avow the principle as a principle. By this principle corruption in the public service
is made a matter of course. I think that these two "principles" are rotten, and by virtue of their own intrinsic
baseness. If any one is inclined to despair of the republic
now, he ought to remember that there was a time when
men shamelessly professed these doctrines as principles.
I doubt if any one would be bold enough to do it to-day.

Whether General Jackson went into office intending to
make war on the United States Bank, is a question which
has never yet found a solution, but the drift of the
evidence is for the negative. During the summer of 1829
some of the New Hampshire politicians of the new school
endeavored to obtain the removal of Mr. Jeremiah Mason

from the Presidency of the Portsmouth Branch of the United States Bank. They brought no charge whatever against him save that he was a friend of Mr. Webster, and they urged that some friend of the administration might make the Branch useful in its service. The Secretary of the Treasury (Ingham) endeavored to induce the President of the Bank (Biddle) to remove Mr. Mason. Biddle refused to do this. In this controversy the administration men were in the position of striving to bring the Bank into politics on their side and the Bank was in the position of striving to remain neutral in politics. From this, however, dates the great conflict of Jackson's administration. You will greatly err in trying to form any judgment in this matter if you doubt the *bona fides* of General Jackson. Where his personal value was not at stake he was genial, good-natured, and generous. In questions of policy he was easily led up to the point at which he formed an opinion. His opinion might be crystallized, however, suddenly, by the most whimsical consid<del>er</del>atives, or under the most erratic motives. When he had formed what for him was an opinion, he clung to it with astonishing obstinacy. It rose before his mind as a fact of the most undeniable certainty. The echo of it, which came back to him by virtue of his popularity, seemed to him to sanction it with the highest authority. One who denied it was shameless and unpardonable, one who resisted it deserved any punishment which the fashions of the age allowed. You recognize the description of a strong and originally powerful mind destitute of training.

At the outset the Bank was guilty only of neutrality where he demanded support. At this time it had lived down much of the hatred it had justly incurred at the outset, but there was no difficulty in reviving it. The Bank was never in a stronger or sounder condition than in 1829, and it enjoyed high credit both at home and abroad. The word went out, however, that the Bank was a monopoly, the possession of the moneyed aristocracy, undemocratic, and hostile to liberty. The first blow fell, in spite of some vague premonitory rumors, with great suddenness. In the annual message of December, 1829, Jackson incorporated a short paragraph questioning the constitutionality of the Bank and proposing a Bank on the credit and revenues of the government. The alarm thus created was twofold, first on account of the Bank which was threatened, and second on account of the new institution which sounded like a government paper money bank. Parties did not as yet divide on this issue. The strongest partisans of Jackson took up the cry against the Bank, but not yet with vigor; the more intelligent supporters of the administration still favored it. In 1830 the message was much milder in regard to the Bank, and the Treasury Report was even favorable to it. In 1831, however, the message was once more strongly hostile.

In the meantime the President had vetoed an internal improvement bill and taken up a position of hostility to the policy of improvements. The tariff of 1828 had provoked the South to more and more energetic protests until South Carolina adopted the doctrine and policy of nullification. There never was a greater political error, for she alienated the vast body of the nation, even in the South, which might have been brought to oppose protection but would not favor nullification as a means of destroying it. It was in this connection that Jackson's traits availed to procure him, in his own day, the approval of men like Webster and has availed to give him a place amongst our political heroes and in the hearts of people who to-day know little more about him than that he prevented nullification. He certainly acted with very commendable firmness in giving it to be understood that nullification meant rebellion and war. His attitude and, far more, the legislation of the session of 1832–1833 including the compromise tariff of March 2, 1833, averted civil war. What part in all this drama was played by his hostility to Mr. Calhoun it is difficult to say. They were now sworn enemies, General Jackson having been informed (by Mr. Crawford) that Mr. Calhoun, instead of being his friend in the cabinet of Mr. Monroe, had been one of those who disapproved of his acts in the Seminole war in 1878. General Jackson upon this diverted the succession from Mr. Calhoun and, after taking a second term himself, gave the succession to Martin Van Buren, a weak and unpopular candidate, who had, by virtue of his position in the Albany Regency, given New York to Jackson. Mr. Van Buren was Secretary of State in Jackson's first cabinet, which suddenly exploded in 1831 on a question of social etiquette. He was next nominated to the English mission and went out, but failed of confirmation, an incident only worth mentioning because the hotter partisans of Jackson proposed to abolish the Senate for rejecting one of his nominations.

All these and other personalities which it is impossible to group in any way, and which I cannot follow into detail, played their part in the great drama which was opening. The popular democratic party was gaining ground every day. A consciousness of power, a desire to assume public duties from which they had hitherto held aloof, was taking stronger possession of them. On the other hand, an opposition was forming under the name of the National Republican party which had a certain vague legitimacy of descent from the old Federal party. It adopted as its principles protection, internal improvements, distribution of the public lands, and the National Bank. This party first began to be called Whigs in Connecticut, in 1834.[1] It always seemed strangely lacking in political sagacity. It offered to its enemies the very strongest arguments against itself. It

[1] Niles, XLVI, 101.

had managed to get on the side, which will pass into history as the wrong side, of at least three great questions and perhaps also of the fourth. It forced the administration into an impregnable position in regard to free trade, hard money, and an opposition to the distribution of land or revenue; and it managed in the end to put itself unequivocally in the wrong and the opposite party in the right on the sub-treasury and the public finances.

It commenced its career as a party by a great blunder — an act which was recognized as such immediately afterwards — and that was the effort to re-charter the Bank in 1832. It had been the strongest answer of the Bank to Jackson's early attacks that its charter did not expire until March 3, 1836, that he had forced the issue of a re-charter on the country six and a half years before the time, and that he had nothing to do with the re-charter unless he assumed that he was to be reëlected. The National Republican convention was held at Baltimore on December 12, 1831. Mr. Clay was nominated for President. The petition for a re-charter was presented January 9, 1832, as a manœuvre in the campaign. Forthwith the charge of anticipating an exciting question was turned against the opposition. They were charged with bringing the Bank into politics, and the Bank was forced into the political campaign to defend its existence. The re-charter was passed July 4, 1832, and vetoed July 10. Up to this time there had been plenty of administration men who favored the Bank. This issue, thus forced by the opposition on the eve of election, and thus accepted by the President for his own person, raised Bank on Anti-Bank to a test of political orthodoxy, and, in the political language of the time, many were forced to "turn a sharp corner." The issue was now also Jackson *versus* the Bank, and then first did it become apparent to what extent the Jackson party had gained and how thorough was its devotion. The current party names were Jackson and Anti-Jackson, and candidates were so designated down to the lowest town officers. The Whigs protested in vain against the folly of this. They argued with men who would not argue, and assumed the force of motives the powerlessness of which was proved by the fact that men could profess such personal political allegiance. They did not truly appreciate the democracy in which they lived. They suffered themselves to be isolated as a body and they lost the proper conservative power of an opposition by failing to go with the sentiment of the vast energetic, growing (if you choose to call it so), vulgar democracy. It is a danger which always besets the conservative party here, whose members will always be a minority, and will always find much to offend their refinement in a new community like this. They will always be tempted to withdraw from contact with it and to gratify their vanity at the expense of all public influence.

The consequence of the issue as it was made in 1832 was that Jackson got 219 and Clay 49 votes in the Electoral College.[1] Things now entered on a new stage. The lower class which I have hitherto endeavored to characterize fairly, but without timidity, now took on the character of a genuine proletariat. It has been only at few periods that any development of the lowest sections of our population has produced what could properly be called by that name. The period of Jackson's second administration was the most marked of these. In the large cities trades-unions arose, and in certain sections agrarian doctrines were advocated, while there was a general dissemination of socialistic notions. In 1836 there were formal riots and public disturbances of lesser grade. Partly this was due to the arrogance of class success, partly to the flattery of demagogues, and partly to industrial changes and to currency disturbances which are to be mentioned in a moment.

[1] For Clay, Massachusetts, Rhode Island, Connecticut, Delaware, Maryland.

The National Bank being doomed if Jackson should be reëlected, a large moneyed class had been drawn into the administration party, *viz.*, those who wanted to found local banks. The administration party, therefore, included these two branches, to the former or lower of which the nickname Locofoco was given.

General Jackson regarded his reëlection as a sanction of all that he had done or proposed. According to his principles the question of wisdom in banking and currency did not come from history or science, but from a majority vote of the people. What is to be noticed, however, is that the people simply assented to whatever he proposed and ratified whatever he did, because it was he that did it. There resulted a state of things paralleled in our history only in the case of Mr. Jefferson, that is, an action and reaction between the executive and a popular majority in which each stimulated the other by ready sympathy and mutual support. The President pursued his way without a misgiving, and the opposition in Congress while they saw their members dwindling and the majority becoming more and more overwhelming, could only express their astonishment at the sudden acts and irregular methods of procedure of the executive. The subservient majority, consisting largely of professional politicians of the new type, recognized that for the time being their occupation of plotting and controling was gone. Their hopes lay in no independent action, but in loyalty to the chief.

I feel here how much I am saying which under other circumstances would require proof, but the proof lies before any one who will throw aside Benton and Parton and look into the Congressional debates and the newspapers of the time.

The President now pushed on his hostility to the Bank, being doubly enraged by the efforts it had made to fight its own battle in contending against him during the campaign.

He avowed his determination to make the "experiment" of using local banks as fiscal agents of the government. Naturally enough, the banking and commercial world was frightened at experiments, carried on without skill or knowledge and running athwart the financial and business interests of the country. Up to this time, you must remember, the administration had not pronounced for specie currency at all, but it was supposed that the President favored a government paper bank. In his Bank veto message he had said that a charter for a Bank which would have been free from objection might have been obtained by coming to him beforehand. In his first message after his reëlection he raised the question whether the public deposits were safe in the Bank and whether the government shares in the Bank ought not to be sold. In spite of all that had gone before these were startling questions. A majority of the Committee of Ways and Means found the deposits safe. The minority made some strong and undeniable points against the Bank.

During the summer of 1833 Amos Kendall was appointed agent to see what banks could be engaged to take the public deposits. On August 19 of that year the five government directors of the Bank made a report showing the amount expended by the Bank in printing during the campaign, and on September 18, 1833, the President read to his cabinet a paper setting forth the reasons why the public deposits should be removed from the United States Bank. The Secretary of the Treasury, Mr. Duane, refused to give the order for removal and was dismissed. Mr. Taney was made Secretary and he ordered that no further sums should be deposited in the Bank by collectors or others. December 3, 1833, he reported to Congress his reasons for doing this. On December 9, the government directors sent in a memorial to Congress saying that they had been shut out from a knowledge of the affairs of the Bank. On March 28,

1834, the Senate, after having tried in vain to pass a more specific censure, resolved that the President had "assumed upon himself authority and power not conferred by the Constitution and the laws." On April 15, the President sent in a protest against this resolution, saying that if he had been guilty of violating the Constitution he ought to be impeached, not censured by resolution. This protest the Senate refused to register. They could not impeach him, and the House was far from thinking of such a thing. In fact, the question of status of the Secretary of the Treasury is a delicate one. Some independent responsibility is laid upon him, according to the laws of 1789 and 1800, but, as he is liable to be dismissed by the President, he cannot have an independent responsibility. The resolution of censure was "expunged" on January 16, 1837. In the House of Representatives, on April 4, 1834, it was resolved that the Bank ought not to be re-chartered, that the deposits ought not to be restored, that the state banks ought to be made depositories of the public funds, and that a select committee on the Bank should be raised. The majority of this committee reported, on May 22, that the Bank had refused to submit to investigation, while the minority (Everett and Ellsworth) reported that the majority had made unreasonable demands. On February 4, 1834 the Senate had referred to the Finance Committee an inquiry in regard to the Bank; and at the next session, on December 18, 1834, the Committee reported, by John Tyler, favorably to the Bank in every respect. In the message of December, 1834, the President reviewed the whole war against the Bank and summed up the charges against it. Therewith the political and congressional war over the old Bank came to an end with a full victory for the administration.

The earliest announcement of the policy of the administration in favor of a metallic currency was in a reply made by the President [1] in February, 1834, to a deputation from

[1] Niles, March 1, 1834.

Philadelphia who came to complain of the hard times. According to the report they gave, the President was very rude and violent.   He ascribed all the trouble to the "monster," as he called the Bank over and over again.   He declared that he would introduce a specie currency and that the government should use no other.   He evidently knew little of the laws of money and finance, and, although much which he and his supporters afterwards urged in support of this policy was as true and sound as any propositions in physical science, yet it was mixed up with fallacies which neutralized it, and it degenerated into a kind of fanaticism about the precious metals.   The measure of distributing the deposits amongst local banks, and thereby stimulating bank credits, was destructive to the other measure of introducing a specie currency.   The distribution of the surplus revenue, which had accumulated in the banks amongst the states, was an opposition measure that was passed on account of the foolish belief, which so often leads our politicians astray, that there was political capital in it.   Jackson signed the bill, but he criticized it in his next message, giving plain and statesmanlike reasons against it.

I must mention one other institution which took its rise in this period, and that is the national convention. I have already mentioned the Convention of the National Republicans at Baltimore in 1831.   The Jackson men held one at Baltimore on May 21, 1832.   With this invention our political institutions entered on a new phase, and "politician" acquired a new meaning.   The power of party, the binding force of caucus agreements, the conception of bolting a regular nomination as the highest political crime, were developed first in the ranks of the Jackson party, but speedily followed to the best of their ability by the opposition.   The Tammany Club of New York was the school in which these political arts were cultivated to the highest pitch, to be imitated elsewhere.   There had been loud shouts over the downfall of "King Caucus" when, in 1824, the candidate of the congressional caucus was defeated, but the fact was that King Caucus had only just come of age and was entering into his inheritance. Behind the convention speedily arose the class of politicians vulgarly known as wire-pullers who spent their time between elections in intriguing and plotting and distributing. The Albany Regency found that its power slipped away into the hands of these more secret operators. There sprang up men who did not care for office, who lived no one knew how, or who took offices which to them were sinecures while they wielded the real political power. The convention proved to be an engine well adapted to the purposes of this class. It had all the forms of freedom, publicity, and popular initiative, while the real manipulation was astonishingly easy for two or three shrewd and experienced men. I am using the past tense here again for decency's sake. I wish that I could do so because the things I describe were really matters of history.

You see now that I have spared nothing whatever here, neither national pride, nor party prejudice, nor hereditary family feeling. My business is simply with the truth of history so far as it is attainable, and so far as I am able faithfully to state it. It would be very easy now to say that Andrew Jackson demoralized American politics, and to throw upon his memory the blame for all the political troubles, shames, and problems of which we are every day reminded. Such, however, would be very far from the inference I want to draw. I have tried to emphasize the fact that Jackson himself was only a typical and representative man in and of his time, that it is often difficult to say whether he led or was carried forward. His administration, in the view I have tried to present, was only the time at which a certain tendency came to victory. It was only a case of the conflict which constitutes great political parties under all governments, the conflict between the radical and conservative tendencies. The radical tendency had won one victory under Jefferson, and, coming into office, had become conservative. In Jackson's elevation a new radical tendency, more excessive than the first, came to victory. I have shown also in my criticism on the Whig party how it fell out of sympathy with the great movement which was going on and which was inevitably conditioned in the social and economic circumstances of the country.

This tendency has still pursued its way down to our own times. The party which organized under Jackson became involved in the slavery question by combinations which it would be most interesting to study; but this will be only a passing phase, a temporary issue in our political life, and only a feature of the history of the concrete Democratic party, not of the great democratic tendency. The doctrines of the Jacksonian democracy have permeated nearly the whole country. They have come to be popularly regarded as postulates or axioms of civil liberty. Those who deny them are the scholars, the historians, the philosophers, the book-men of every grade; and they deny them under their breath, at the penalty of sacrificing all share in public life. It is certain, however, that the issue must come back to its permanent form and that the political strife must be waged between the conservative and the radical theories of politics — between those who lay the greater stress on law and those who lay the greater stress on liberty, between those who see political health chiefly in the social principle and those who see it chiefly in the individual, between constitutionalism and democracy.

This will not come about by any critical reflections of mine or by those of any other political philosopher. It will come about by experience, and by instinct rather than by reflection. For the evils and corruptions of which we daily complain arise from democratic theories of politics, developed and applied without reference to the actual circumstances of the case, and under assumptions which are false. Experience has convinced nearly all of us who are willing to think about the matter that rotation in office is mischievous to the public interest and demoralizing to the men who enter the public service. Experience has long since brought home to us the shame of the doctrine that to the victors belong the spoils. Experience has shown us the evils of frequent elections and short terms of office, and it is continually opening the eyes of more and more of us to the evils of electing a large number of administrative officers and making them independent of each other. Experience has shown us the inapplicability of the principle of election to the selection of judges. Experience is showing that the notion of the responsibility of a party is a delusion and that the notion of responsibility to the people is only a jingle of words; and as new constitutions are formed we find that they continually take more guarantees from the people against themselves.

On the contrary the path of reform lies in the direction of stronger constitutional guarantees and greater reverence for law as law. Any conservative party which fulfills its function in this country will have to take its stand on that platform. Its reforms must be historical, not speculative. They must be founded in the genius and history of the country. The democracy here, in the sense of the widest popular participation in public affairs, is inevitable until the land is taken up and the population begins to press upon the means of subsistence, that is to say, for a future far beyond what we need take into consideration. Our whole history shows this, and the part which I have discussed shows conclusively what we may also all see in our own daily observation — that the men, the parties, the

theories which oppose themselves to this tendency are
swept down like seeds before a flood. It is idle to ask
whether is it a good tendency. It is a fact — a fact
whose causes arise from the deepest and broadest social
and economic circumstances of the country. But there
is a foundation for true constitutionalism in the traditions
of our race and in our inherited institutions — in our inherited reverence for law, which is all that keeps us from
going the way of Mexico and Peru.

The philosophers and book-men have no great rôle offered
them in a new country. They will always be a minority,
they will always be holding back in the interest of law,
order, tradition, history, and they will rarely be entrusted
with the conduct of affairs; but, since their lot is cast here,
if they withdraw from the functions which fall to them in
this society, such as it is, they do it at the sacrifice not only
of duty but also of everything which makes a fatherland
worth having, to them or to their posterity. The fault
which they commit is the complement of that committed
by their opponents. For the notion which underlies democracy is that of rights, tenacity in regard to rights, the
brutal struggle for room for one's self, and, still more
specifically, for *equal* rights, the root principle of which is
envy. This was abundantly illustrated in Jackson's day.
The opposition of his supporters to bank and tariff had no
deeper root than this, and the name they chose for themselves as descriptive of their aims was "The Equal
Rights Party." But the principle of political life lies not
in rights but in duties. The struggle for rights is at best
war. The subjection to duty reaches the same end, reaches
it far better, and reaches it through peace. Still less is
there any principle of political health in the idea of *equality*
of rights, much as some people seem to believe the opposite. In political history it has been the melancholy
province of France to show us that if you emphasize

equality you reduce all to a dead level of slavery, with a succession of revolutions to bring about a change of masters.

If, then, the classes which are by education and position conservative withdraw from public activity, pride themselves on their cleanness from political mire, and satisfy themselves at most with a negative and destructive interference at the polls from time to time, the conception of political duty with them must be as low as with their opponents; and I will add that they will at best turn from one set of masters to another, under a general and steady deterioration in the political tone of the country. If we have to-day a society in which we go our ways in peace, freedom, and security, a society from the height of which we look back upon the life of the sixteenth and seventeenth centuries with a shudder, we owe it to no class of men who wrote satirical essays on contemporary politics and said to one another: "What is the use?" Elliott and Hampden and Sydney and these revolutionary heroes whose praise we are just now chanting did not win for us all the political good we owe them by any such policy as that. There was no use, as far as any one could see, in their cases. They risked persecution, imprisonment, the axe, and the scaffold, and their puny efforts seemed ridiculous in the face of the task they undertook; but they never stopped to think of that. They saw that it was the right thing to do then to speak or to resist, and they did it and let the end take care of itself.

Now we Americans of to-day have no heroic deeds to perform. We have no fear of the stake or the axe for political causes. We are not called upon to do any grand deeds. Perhaps it would be easier if we were. If we had a Cæsar at Washington I would warrant him his Brutus within a fortnight. But we have need of the same sense of duty which has animated all the heroes of constitutional government and civil liberty, and I am not sure but we need some of their courage also, for it demands at least as much moral courage to beard King Majority as it ever did to beard King Cæsar. Nothing less than the experiment of self-government is at stake in the question whether thousands of citizens are capable of that form of duty which makes a man work on without results and without reward, even, it may be, in the face of misrepresentation and abuse, simply because he sees a certain direction in which his efforts ought to be expended.

Such, however, I conceive to be the calling of the conservative classes of this country, at least for this generation. We have undertaken to govern ourselves, and we are just finding, now that the country is filling up and its cities growing large, that it is a great task, that it takes time and thought, that we need any and all resources of science and experience which we can call to our aid; and we are finding especially that the forms of law and of the Constitution are every year more essential, and the untamed forces of society more dangerous. No supernatural interference will come to our assistance. No man, no committee, no party, no centralized organization of the general government, can rid us of our difficulties and yet leave us self-government. Nor can we invent any machinery of elections or of government which will do the work for us. We have got to face the problems like men, animated by patriotism, acting with business-like energy, standing together for the common weal. Whenever we do that we cannot fail of success in getting what we want; so long as we do not do that, our complaints of political corruption are the idlest and most contemptible expressions which grown men can utter.

THE COMMERCIAL CRISIS OF 1837

THE COMMERCIAL CRISIS OF 1837

[1877–1878]

THE decade from 1830 to 1840 is the most important and interesting in the history of the United States. The political, social, and industrial forces which were in action were grand, and their interaction produced such complicated results, that it is difficult to obtain a just and comprehensive view of their relations and influences. In the first place, the United States advanced between the second war with England and 1830 to a position of full and high standing in the family of nations. The security and stability of the government were accepted as established. England and France, on the other hand, just before and after 1830, were involved in social and political troubles of an alarming kind. By contrast, the United States, with a rapidly increasing population, expanding production and trade, a contented people, and a surplus revenue offered great attractions to both laborers and capital. At the same time the pride of the Americans in their country produced self-reliance, energy, and enterprise which laughed at difficulties. New means of transportation by steamboats and canals were opening up the country and assuring to the population the advantages of a new and unbounded continent. Production therefore offered high returns to both labor and capital.

The advantages of a new country were credited to the political institutions of democracy, and increasing prosperity, due to the fresh resources brought within reach, was held to be proof of the truth of the political dogmas entertained by the workers. A sort of boyish exuberance, compounded of inexperience, ignorance, and fearless enterprise, marked politics as well as industry. Jackson's election in 1828 brought to power a party which had been produced by these circumstances.

The war debt of 1812 became payable in the years after 1824 and was distributed over the period down to 1835. With growth and increasing prosperity, the revenue increased with such rapidity that the debt could be paid almost as fast as it became payable. The chief purposes for which the Bank of the United States had been founded in 1816 were to provide a sound and uniform paper currency convertible with specie, of uniform value throughout the Union, and to act as fiscal agent for the government, holding the revenue wherever collected and disbursing the expenditures wherever they were to be made. The interest of the government and the people was the motive, and the bank charter was a contract with the Bank to perform the services for specified considerations. One of the considerations was the right of the Bank to use the deposits as loanable capital. The government was not bound to keep any balance over expenditure, but the revenue was so large that the Bank came to hold annually increasing average deposits of from five to eight or nine millions of public money, which it used for profit. From this vicious arrangement two consequences followed: first, public attention was directed to the deposits, not as existing for the public service, but for the profit of the Bank; and, second, the public considered itself entitled to claim something of the Bank besides true business credit, in the matter of discounts.

Jackson opened the war on the Bank publicly in his first message. Sharp correspondence had been going on already between the Secretary of the Treasury and the Bank, which had reached such a point that the Secretary had referred to the removal of the deposits as a power in his hands to coerce the Bank. Generally speaking, the state of the Bank and the state of the currency were satisfactory in 1830, but the Bank had begun in 1827 to issue branch drafts which stimulated credit and soon produced mischief. Of the war on the Bank it is not necessary to speak in detail. In December, 1831, Clay was nominated for President by the National Republicans, and he and his friends determined to bring on the question of the re-charter of the Bank as a campaign issue. The re-charter was passed by Congress and vetoed by the President in 1832. The issue in the campaign was thus made up between the personal popularity of Jackson and of the Bank. The former won an overwhelming victory which he construed to mean that the people had weighed the question of re-chartering the Bank and had decided against it.

In September, 1833, he removed the deposits from the National Bank on his own responsibility, and placed them in selected state banks which would agree to keep one-third of their note circulation in coin, redeem all notes on demand, and issue no notes under a five-dollar denomination. This was to be an experiment. In the meantime the administration was eagerly pressing on the extinction of the public debt. The consequences were such as to prove that, however popular such a policy may be, it may easily be carried too far. The public deposits were loaned by the Bank to merchants, then recalled and paid to the public creditors, and then reinvested by them, so that the money market was subjected to recurrent and sudden shocks. The withdrawal and transfer of the deposits constituted another and more violent operation of the same kind, so that there was a crisis and panic in the spring of 1834. The eight or nine millions of public deposits were a continual source of mischief to the money market. By the contraction of the Bank of the United States to pay the deposits, and the contraction of the state banks to put themselves within the rule for receiving the same, the currency, in the summer of 1834, was perhaps better than ever before. The coinage act of June, 1834, turned the standard over from silver to gold.

The deposit banks were urged to discount freely so as to satisfy the public with the change. Banks were organized in great numbers all over the country to take the place of the great Bank and to get a share in the profits of handling the public money. On January 1, 1835, the debt was all paid and the government had no further use for its surplus revenue. There was but one correct and straightforward course to pursue in such a case and that was to lower taxes so as not to collect any surplus, but this the Compromise Act forbade. The surplus revenue was the greatest annoyance to the protectionists who wanted to keep duties high for "incidental protection," and they proposed scheme after scheme for distributing the lands, or the proceeds of the lands, or, finally, the surplus revenue itself, so as to cut down the revenue without reducing the import duties.

With the increase of banks and bank issues speculation began. It became marked in the spring of 1835 and went on increasing for two years. Cotton was rising in price, for the new machinery, and new means of transportation in England, together with the extension of joint stock banks there, had given a great stimulus to the cotton manufacturer. There was an increasing demand for the raw material. It followed that the cities in which the exchange and banking of all this industry were carried on also enjoyed great prosperity. Railroads were just being introduced and ships were needed to transport the products. Thus from natural causes the period was one of immense industrial development. The great need for carrying it on was capital, and the political incidents which brought about or encouraged the bank expansion may be regarded as accidental. The combination of the two in fact, however, produced a wild speculation. The banks furnished credit, not capital, and being restrained by usury laws from exerting through the rate of discount the proper check upon an inflated or speculative market they embarked with the business community on a course where all landmarks were soon lost.

No sooner, however, was this condition of the commercial and banking community well established than a new shock was given by another political interference. The administration had now advanced to the point of desiring to establish a specie currency for the country. The object was laudable and the means taken were proper, but, following as they did in the train of the events already mentioned, they produced new confusion. In 1836 various acts were passed to bring about a specie currency, and in July of that year the Secretary of the Treasury ordered the receivers of public money to take only gold and silver for lands. The circumstances warranted this order. The sales of lands had risen from two or three to twenty-four million dollars in a year, and the amount was paid in the notes of "banks"[1] which deserved no credit. If the nation was not to be swindled out of the lands the measure was necessary. It then became necessary for the purchasers of land to carry specie to the West and vast amounts of it accumulated in the offices of the receivers, or were transferred at great trouble and expense to deposit banks. The specie was obtained from the eastern banks, and inasmuch as the whole existing system had pushed them to the utmost limit of expansion, these demands for specie were embarrassing. Two points here deserve notice. It is strange to see what a superstition about "specie" had taken

[1] Some counterfeiters were arrested at New York in a garret where they had $20,000 in notes of the "Ottawa Bank" and $800 in specie. They were very indignant — said they were a "bank" and were printing their notes at New York for economy. They came so nearly within the definition of a "bank" current at this time that they escaped on this plea.

possession of the public mind. It was regarded as a good thing to have, but too good to use. A specie dollar was regarded as an excuse for its owner to print and circulate from three to twenty paper ones, but it was not regarded as having any other use. The withdrawal of the specie basis from an inflated paper was no doubt a serious blow to the whole fabric, but, if the paper had not been redundant the transfer of specie to the West could only have forced an importation of so much more. This superstition about specie also prevented any demand upon the banks for specie for any purpose. Such a demand was regarded as a kind of social or business crime. Hence the "convertibility" of the notes was a polite fiction. The second point worth noticing is that the bank advocates continually talked about "the credit system" when they meant the system of issuing credit bank notes; and they grew eloquent about the advantages of credit, as if those advantages could only be won by using worthless bank notes and not by lending gold or silver or capital in any form.

We are not yet, however, at the end of the political acts which threw the money market into convulsions. The opposition succeeded, in the summer of the presidential election year, 1836, in passing an act to *deposit* with the states the surplus over a balance of five millions in the Treasury on January 1, 1837. The amount was thirty-seven millions. This sum was scattered in eighty-nine deposit banks all over the country. Its distribution was, therefore, controlled by local pressure and political favoritism, not by the needs of the government (for it did not need the money at all) or by the demand and supply of capital. The banks had regarded it as a permanent deposit and had loaned it in aid of the various public and private enterprises which were being pushed on every hand at such a rate that labor was said to be drawn away from agriculture so that the country was importing bread stuffs. It was now to be withdrawn and transferred once more, and this time it was said that, if these "deposits" were such an advantage, the states ought to have it, and could then, as well as the banks, be called on to give back the money whenever it might be needed. The deposit took place in 1837, in three installments, January, April, and July, and amounted to twenty-eight millions. The fourth installment was never paid. The money was all squandered or worse.

The charter of the Bank of the United States was to expire on the 3d of March, 1836. One year before that time the directors ordered the "exchange committee" to loan the capital, as fast as it should be released, on stocks, so as to prepare for winding up. From this resolution dates the subsequent history of the Bank, for the exchange committee consisted of the President and two directors selected by him, to whose hands the whole business of the Bank was hereby entrusted. The branches were sold and the capital gradually released throughout 1835, but in February, 1836, an act was suddenly passed by the Pennsylvania legislature to charter the United States Bank of Pennsylvania, continuing the old Bank. The act was said to have been obtained by bribery, but investigation failed to prove it. The most open bribery was on the face of it, for it provided for several pet local schemes of public improvement, for a bonus and loans to the state by the Bank, and for abolishing taxes — provisions which secured the necessary support to carry it.

During the year 1836 the money market was very stringent. The enterprises, speculations, and internal improvements demanded continual new supplies of capital. The amount of securities exported grew greater and greater and kept the foreign exchanges depressed. American importing houses contracted larger and longer debts to foreign agents. The money market in England became very stringent likewise, and these long credits became harder and harder to carry. Three English houses, Willson, Wildes, and Wiggins, had become especially engaged in these American credits which they found it necessary to curtail. The winter was one of continual stringency, aggravated by popular discontent, riots, and trades-union disturbances, arising from high prices and high rents. The failures commenced on the fourth of March, 1837, the day that Van Buren was inaugurated, in Mississippi and Louisiana. Hermann, Briggs & Co., of New Orleans, failed, with liabilities said to be from four to eight millions. As soon as this was known in New York, their correspondents, J. L. & S. Joseph & Co. failed. The first break in the expanded fabric of credit therefore came in connection with cotton. The price had advanced so much during the last three or four years as to draw many thousands of persons who had no capital into cotton production, but the profits were so great that a good crop or two would pay for all the capital. The planters of Mississippi especially had accordingly organized themselves into banking corporations and issued notes as the easiest way to borrow the capital they wanted. From 1830 to 1839 the banking capital of Mississippi increased from three to seventy-five millions, which of course represented one credit built upon another, on renewed and extended debt, as the old planters bought more slaves and took up more land instead of paying for the old, or as new settlers came in. Mississippi was therefore indebted to the Northeast for the redemption of their immense bank debt, or for the capital bought with it. The high rates for money in England and this country at last checked the rise in cotton in 1836. Bad harvests and high prices for food fell in with a glut of manufactured cotton, and when cotton began to fall ruin was certain. As soon as the revulsion came it ran through the whole speculative system. The new suburbs which had been laid out in every city and village never came to anything.

Western lands lost all speculative value, and railroad and canal stock fell with rapidity.

The first resort for help was to Mr. Biddle. The calamity most apprehended was a shipment of specie, and the effort was to gain an extension of credit or the substitution of a better for a less known credit. The Bank of the United States had high credit in Europe, and indeed all over the world. Ultimately payment must be made by crops yet to be produced or forwarded. Biddle entered into an agreement with the New York banks which seems to have been only partially carried out, but he sold post notes payable one year from date at Barny's in London. He received one hundred and twelve and one-half for these, specie being at one hundred and seven. The bonds were discounted in England at five per cent. United States Bank stock was at one hundred and twenty.

The situation in England was so serious that all seemed to depend on remittances from the United States. The Bank of England extended aid to "the three W's" to the extent of five hundred thousand pounds on a guarantee made up in the city, and opened a credit of two million pounds for the United States Bank, if one-half the amount should be shipped in specie. To this condition the United States Bank would not agree. The proposition attributed to the Bank of the United States a strength which it did not possess. The management of the Bank of England in this and the two following years was bad, and did much to enhance the mischief in both countries. France participated in the distress although there had been no speculation there.

A delegation of New York merchants was sent to Washington on May 3 to ask the President to recall the specie circular, to defer the collection of duty bonds, and to call an extra session of Congress. In their address to him they sum up the situation: in six months at New York, real estate had shrunk forty millions; in two months two hundred and fifty firms had failed, and stocks had shrunk twenty millions; merchandise had fallen thirty per cent, and within a few weeks twenty thousand persons had been thrown out of employment.

Early in May three banks at Buffalo failed. On May 8, the Dry Dock Bank (New York) failed. On the tenth all the New York City banks suspended. The militia were under arms and there were fears of a riot. On the eleventh the Philadelphia banks suspended, because the New York banks had, and because, although they had plenty of specie for themselves, they had not enough for the whole "Atlantic seaboard." They said, however, that they were debtors, on balance, to New York. As the news spread through the country, the banks, with few exceptions, suspended. It was one of the notions born of the bank war that the United States Bank was guilty of oppression when it called on state banks for their balances, and the state banks had practiced "leniency" towards each other. Bank statements of the period show enormous sums as due to and from other banks. This was what carried them all down together, for one could not stand alone unless its debits and credits were with the same banks.

During the summer the governors of several states called extra sessions of the legislatures. The President had refused to recall the specie circular, or to call an extra session of Congress, but the embarrassments of the Treasury forced him to do the latter. The collection of duty bonds was deferred and the revenue thereby cut off. The public money was in the suspended banks, and the Treasury, nominally possessed of forty millions, at the very time when part of this sum was being paid to the states, had to drag along from day to day by the use of drafts on its collectors for the small sums received or by chance left over in their hands since the suspension. As notes under five dollars had been forbidden by nearly all the states, and as specie was at ten per cent premium, all small change disappeared, and the towns were flooded with notes and tickets for small sums, issued by municipalities, corporations, and individuals.

The most interesting fact connected with this commercial credit is that New York and Philadelphia took opposite policies in regard to it, and thus offered, in their differing experience, an experimental test of those policies. The New York legislature passed an act allowing suspension for one year. The New York policy then was to contract liabilities and prepare for resumption at the date fixed. The Philadelphia policy, in which Mr. Biddle was the leader, was to wait without active exertions for things to get better. In his letter of May 13 to Adams, Biddle said that the Bank could have gone on without trouble, but that consideration for the rest forced him to go with them. What especially moved him was that, if the Pennsylvania banks had not suspended, Pennsylvanians would have had to do business with a better currency than the New Yorkers, which would have been unfair. Mr. Biddle knew perfectly well that the exchanges would arrange all that. He was an adept at writing plausible letters. The truth, which was not known until four years later, was that the capital of the Bank had never been withdrawn from the stock loans, that the chief officers of the Bank were plundering it, and that suspension was not more welcome to any institution in the country than to the great Bank. The jealousy between New York and Philadelphia was very great at this time. Mr. Biddle's personal vanity seems to have been greatly flattered when, in March, he was called on by the New Yorkers to help them. He was still the leading financier of the country. The business men could not spare him, even if the government had thrown him off. There seems also to be some evidence that he hoped that a

great and universal revulsion would force the general government to re-charter his Bank. The success of his post notes
in England and France was another source of gratified
vanity to him. In his theory of banking he was one of
those who believe that the redemption of the bank note is
effected by the merchandise. Hence banking was, for him,
an art by which the banker regulated commerce through
expansions and contractions of the circulation according to
the circumstances which he might observe in the market.

The first effect of the opposite courses taken by New York
and Philadelphia was very favorable to his views. The
southern trade was transferred from New York to Philadelphia. Southern notes were at a discount of twenty or
twenty-five per cent. Receiving these notes from the
merchants, the Bank employed them through Bevan and
Humphreys in buying cotton. This operation began in
July and was intended to move the cotton to Europe in
order to meet the post notes of the Bank when they should
become due. The firm of Biddle and Humphreys was also
formed and established at Liverpool as the agent of this
operation. In the extension of the transaction cotton was
bought and paid for by drafts on Bevan and Humphreys
of Philadelphia, which drafts were discounted by the
Bank. Biddle and Humphreys, having sold the cotton,
remitted the proceeds to Mr. Jandon, former cashier of the
Bank, sent to England as its agent in July. To all this it
must be added that the Bank assumed the function of
securing, for its producers, a good or fair price for cotton.
Jandon's instructions were to protect the interests of the
bank, and "of the country at large."

If the Bank had simply been a strong, sound bank, intent on earning profits, it would have sent two or three
millions to Europe, selling exchange at one hundred and
twelve, and would not have suspended. The rest of the
story would then have been very different for all con-

cerned. The arrival in June of a ship in England with one hundred thousand dollars specie sufficed to sustain American credit and to revive American securities. When the credit of a debtor is tainted, nothing revives it like payment.

The extra session of Congress met on September 4. The fourth installment of the State Deposit Fund was postponed until January 1, 1839, but it was locked up in the suspended banks and, as the former installments had been drawn from the better banks, the balance due was all in the worst banks of the country, those of the southwestern states. As they had loaned it to their customers, it was, in fact, amongst the people of those states. A law was passed to institute suit against these banks unless they paid on demand, or gave bonds to do so in three installments before July 1, 1839. There were only six deposit banks then paying specie; one was new, four had not suspended, and one had resumed. Power to call on the states for the funds "deposited" with them was taken from the Secretary of the Treasury and held by Congress. Interest-bearing Treasury notes were provided for one year, to meet expenses, and an extension of nine months was given on duty bonds. At this session the sub-treasury system was brought forward as an administration measure. It split the party. The "bank democrats" (state bank interest which joined the Jackson party in 1832 to break down the United States Bank) went into opposition. The advocates of the "credit system" said the sub-treasury scheme, by giving the government control of the specie in the country, would give it control of all credit. Meanwhile Benton said that the eighty million specie in the country was its bulwark against adversity, and the Locofocos said that any one who exported specie was a British hireling. So that there was a fine confusion of financial notions.

In the fall the English money market became much easier, and the same tendency appeared here. Specie at

New York was at about seven per cent premium, but steadily declining. Prices of breadstuffs remained very high (flour nine dollars to nine dollars and a half at New York) and the stagnation of industry was complete. Migration to the West was large.

On August 18 the New York banks called a convention of banks to deliberate on resumption. The Philadelphia banks frustrated the proposition by refusing. A convention met in October but adjourned without action until April. On the 7th of April the New York banks had assets two and a half times their liabilities, excluding real estate, and were creditors of the Philadelphia banks for $1,200,000. They had reduced their liabilities from $25,400,000 on January 1, 1837 to $12,900,000 on January 1, 1838, and the foreign exchanges were favorable.

The bank convention met April 1, 1838, and voted by states to resume January 1, 1839, without precluding an earlier day. New York and Mississippi alone voted nay, the former because the date was too remote; the latter because it was too early. New England joined Philadelphia and Baltimore for the later day. Mr. Biddle published another letter in which he blamed the rigor of the contraction at New York; he wanted to remain "prepared to resume but not resuming," and looked to Congress to do the work. The exchange between New York and Philadelphia was then four and a half per cent against the latter. The southwestern exchanges were growing worse On May 1, the Philadelphia banks resolved to pay specie for demands under one dollar. The Bank of England engaged to send one million pounds in specie to support resumption, and did send one hundred thousand pounds, but then receded from the undertaking; its stock of specie was now very large and increasing. The New York banks resumed during the first week in May, the Boston and New England banks generally at the same time. Specie was coming into

New York. On May 31 Congress repealed the specie circular, whereupon Mr. Biddle published another letter saying that since Congress had acted, he saw his way to resumption and would "coöperate." The Bank had, at this time, over thirteen millions loaned on "bills receivable," that is, on securities put in the teller's drawer, as cash to replace cash taken out.

After the adjournment of Congress on July 9 there was a much better feeling, especially on account of the defeat of the sub-treasury bill, and on July 10, Governor Ritner of Pennsylvania published a proclamation requiring the banks to resume on August 13, and to pay and withdraw all notes under five dollars. On July 23 a bank convention composed of delegates from the middle states met at Philadelphia. It was agreed to resume on August 13. The Philadelphia banks were obliged to contract very suddenly and money was very dear there. As soon as they resumed there were demands on them from New York, exchange being against them. This caused excitement and indignation. The banks generally declared dividends as soon as they resumed. Elsewhere, here and in England, money was easy and the times rapidly improving. There was, however, a feverish and uncertain market for cotton. Biddle and Humphreys were carrying an immense stock, and buyers and sellers differed as to prices.

On December 10, 1838, Biddle published another letter to Adams in which he reviewed his policy of the last two years, and withdrew the Bank from all its former public activity. He says: "It abdicates its involuntary power." He defended the cotton speculations, saying that he had saved the great staple of our country from being sacrificed, by introducing a new competitor into the market. Here then was a buyer who had gone into the market on purpose to "bull" some one else's property. His fate could not be very doubtful. At this same time the Liverpool market was very dull and the spinners were curtailing their demands because the supply was under the control of speculators. It was true, as was asserted, that the crop was short, but the buyers took this for a speculator's story, and, anticipating a break in the corner and a fall in price, they refused to buy. The speculation no doubt unduly depressed the price. The southwestern agents of the Bank of the United States were offering advances of from two to five cents above the market price to secure consignments to Biddle and Humphreys, and Mr. Jandon, because he had lost instead of winning confidence, was paying ruinous rates for money to carry on his operations.

During the winter most of the southern and western banks resumed, at least nominally, but as the spring of 1839 approached the southern exchanges again fell and many of the banks suspended again. On March 29 Biddle resigned the presidency of the Bank, saying that he left it strong and prosperous. The stock fell from one hundred and sixteen to one hundred and twelve, but soon recovered. The money market became stringent again, influenced by fears of the South.

In March, by speculative sales, by the diminution of stock, and by the real shortness of the crop, cotton was forced up one and one-fourth pence at Liverpool, and Biddle and Humphreys sold out their entire stock. The net profit was six hundred thousand dollars. This was regarded as a great triumph, and as a complete vindication of Biddle's policy. In July, 1839, the Bank of the United States paid a semi-annual dividend of four per cent — its last one.

The success of the cotton speculation led to a plan for renewing it on a grander scale. On June 6, an unsigned circular was published at New York, which proposed a scheme for advancing three-fourths of the value at fourteen cents on all cotton consigned to Biddle and Humphreys.

They were to "hold on until prices vigorously rally." The agent, Mr. Wilder, declared that this had nothing to do with the United States Bank, so far as he knew. It was, however, a scheme of the Bank. The Southwestern notes were falling lower and lower, and the post notes issued in the Southwest the year before were now falling due, and were not paid. The pressure of this fell on Philadelphia, where money was up to fifteen per cent and the banks were curtailing. The news from England was also bad. Cotton was down two cents. The specie of the Bank of England was rapidly declining and money was at five per cent. The arrangements from this side in 1837 had simply consisted in renewals or extensions, and as yet few payments had been made. Stocks, etc., were sent over, but they fell upon a glutted and stringent market and the prices declined. These securities therefore did not furnish means of payment, and specie shipments were found to be necessary. The Bank of the United States had prevented any shipment of specie by offering all the bills demanded at one hundred and nine and a half, and Mr. Jandon had been obliged to adopt the most reckless means to meet these bills. In August he wrote to Biddle and Humphreys to supply him with money at any sacrifice of cotton. "Life or death to the Bank of the United States is the issue." The Bank here urged Bevan and Humphreys to direct their agents to meet Jandon's demands and the Bank assumed the loss. In August the Bank sent an agent to New York, to draw all the bills he could sell on Hottinguer at Paris, to draw the proceeds in specie from the New York banks, and to ship it to meet the bills, the object being to force the New York banks to suspend in order that their example might again be quoted. The Bank also sold its post notes at a discount of eighteen per cent per annum in Boston, New York, Baltimore, and smaller places, and gathered up capital to meet the emergency at Philadelphia caused by the failure of the Southern remittances. The money markets in all these cities were very stringent until October. On the ninth of that month the Bank of the United States failed on drafts from New York, and on the tenth the news was received that the drafts on Hottinguer had been protested. He had given notice that he would not pay unless he was covered, and the drafts arrived before the specie did. Jandon succeeded in getting Rothschild to take up the bills. The amount was seven million francs.

The banks south and west of New York and some of the Rhode Island banks now suspended again. Specie at Philadelphia was at one hundred and seven to one hundred and seven and one-half. United States Bank stock at seventy. On October 15, it was at eighty, and sold at New York at one-fourth premium. Scarcely any New York City notes were in circulation.

This suspension was the real catastrophe of the speculative period which preceded. A great and general liquidation now began. Perhaps as many as two hundred of these banks never resumed. The stagnation of industry lasted for three or four years. The public improvements so rashly begun were suspended or abandoned. The states were struggling with the debts contracted. Some repudiated; some suspended the payment of interest. The New England states and New York escaped all the harsher features of this depression and emerged from it first. In proportion as we go further south and west we find the distress more intense and more prolonged. The recovery was never marked by any distinct point of time, but came gradually and imperceptibly.

The credit of the Bank of the United States bore up wonderfully under the shock of its second suspension. Its friends were ready to attribute its misfortunes to conspiracies, jealousy, or any other cause but its own faults.

They did not indeed know its internal history. It might have recovered if it had not been ruined from within. The cotton speculations showed a loss, in the summer of 1840, after saddling the Bank with all possible charges, of $630,000 for the speculators. The legislature of Pennsylvania ordered the banks to resume January 15, 1841. On the first of January, 1841, a statement of the assets of the Bank was made, when it appeared that they consisted of a mass of doubtful and worthless securities. The losses to date were over five millions, according to the report of the directors, but over seventeen millions, taking the stocks at their market value. The Bank resumed January 15, with the other Philadelphia banks, and the great Bank loaned the state four hundred thousand dollars, agreeing to loan as much more. In twenty days the Philadelphia banks lost eleven millions in specie, of which six millions were taken from the Bank of the United States. On February 4 the Bank failed for the third and last time. Its final failure was said to be due to stock jobbers. Suits were at once begun in such numbers that all hope of ever resuscitating it had to be abandoned. Its deposits, when it failed, were one million one hundred thousand dollars and its notes in circulation two million eight hundred thousand dollars. Twenty-seven millions out of the thirty-five of its capital were held in Europe. The stock, in March, 1841, was at seventeen. A committee of the stockholders reported in April, showing the internal history of the Bank for five years. This brought out from Mr. Biddle six letters of explanation, defense, and recrimination, which are valuable chiefly for the further insight they give into the history. As to the winding up of the Bank it is very difficult to obtain information. Private inquiries lead to the following results. Three trusts were constituted: one for the city banks to which the Bank owed five or six millions; one for the note-holders and depositors; and one for the other creditors. The city banks, the note-holders, and the depositors were ultimately paid in full. The other claims were bought up by one or two persons who took the assets. What they made of them is not matter of history.

The attempt of the Pennsylvania banks to resume in January, 1841, had been the signal for similar attempts in the other states. The banks on the seaboard as far south as South Carolina generally resumed, and in the Western and Gulf states some took the same step. All were indebted to the Northeast, and were asked to pay as soon as they said they were ready to pay. Like the Philadelphia banks they succumbed to this demand. The Virginia banks held out until April, when the suspension was once more universal south of New York.

All the states except New Hampshire, Vermont, Rhode Island, Connecticut, and Delaware had debts, amounting in all to nearly two hundred millions. The Southern States had generally contracted these debts to found banks. The Middle and Western States had contracted debts for public works. In the former case the profits of the banks were expected to cover the interest on the debt. In the latter case the works were expected to be remunerative in a short time, and the interest was provided for in the meantime by bank dividends (on stocks owned by the state, which only constituted another debt), by taxes on banks, and by royalties. Both schemes were plausible and might have been successful if managed with good judgment and moderation. Under the actual circumstances they were subject to political control, the methods of which were reckless and ignorant. The consequence was that when credit collapsed and the English market no longer absorbed the state stocks with avidity, the states found themselves heavily indebted, bound to pay large interest charges, and without the anticipated revenue. The state banks of the South had loaned their borrowed capital to legislators and politicians, and had no assets but "suspended debt." The improvement states had become heavily indebted to their own banks and depended on bank dividends to pay interest. The state banks all held state stocks as assets, and when these declined in value, the banks became insolvent. Thus the banking system was interlocked with the state finances and with the mania for improvements unwisely planned and attempted without reference to the capital at command. The aversion to taxation was very strong, and as taxation was delayed, one state after another defaulted on its interest. The delinquent states were Pennsylvania (which laid taxes in 1840, but inadequate to meet the deficiency), Michigan (of which the Bank of the United States held two millions in bonds not paid for when it failed), Mississippi (of which the same bank held five millions in bonds the obligation of which was disputed and never met), Indiana (whose debt was one-fifth of the total valuation), Illinois, Louisiana, Maryland and Arkansas, and Florida territory — total amount, one hundred and eleven millions. In five years the Bank of the United States gave to Pennsylvania three millions, subscribed nearly half a million to public improvements by corporations, and loaned the state eight and one-half millions. In 1857–1858 Pennsylvania sold out her works, which had cost thirty-five millions, for eleven millions. The bonds deposited in New York to secure circulation had a par value of four and six-tenths millions, but were worth only one and six-tenths millions on the first of January, 1843. As early as March, 1841, this decline caused a panic in "Safety Fund" and "Free Bank" notes at New York.

Pennsylvania now entered on another experiment which threatened to ruin her remaining banks as the reckless demands on the Bank of the United States had helped to ruin that institution. On May 3, 1841, the legislature passed, over a veto, a "Relief Act." The object was to secure a loan of three millions from the banks. The Act allowed them to issue that amount in small notes which they were to subscribe to a five per cent loan. They were to redeem the notes in five per cent stock on demand in amounts over one hundred dollars. The stocks were then at eighty and specie at seven per cent premium.

The best financial writer in the country at that time (Gouge) said of this Act: Pennsylvania, "after having borrowed as much as she could in the old-fashioned way from banks and brokers, and domestic and foreign capitalists, resolved to extort a loan of a dollar a head from every washerwoman and woodsawyer and everybody else within her limits who had a dollar to lend. But as washerwomen and woodsawyers and other dollar people cannot long dispense with the use of their funds, it was necessary to give these certificates of loan in a circulating form, so that the burden might be shifted from one to another day by day, or, if necessary, two or three times a day."

The summer of 1841 was marked by intense distress in Pennsylvania. A table of the best investment stocks of Philadelphia shows a shrinkage between August, 1838, and August, 1841, from sixty million to three and one-half millions. The wages class was exposed to the bitterest poverty and distress. The Pennsylvanians attributed the trouble to the want of a protective tariff. For a time, in the autumn, the Relief notes seemed to act beneficially. The banks took them and they circulated at par with the rest of the state currency. In January, 1842, the Girard Bank failed, and about the same time the Pennsylvania and three others less important, and by March a crisis was reached worse than anything which had preceded. A bill was suddenly passed by the legislature commanding immediate resumption. An amendment was proposed that the banks should no longer be bound to receive the Relief notes, although the state should do so. The amendment was afterwards withdrawn, but the Relief notes were ruined. They fell, some to seventy-five and some to fifty in state currency and then became merchandise, after six months and three days of use. Capital was now not to be had at four per cent per month, but this bankruptcy had cleared the situation. The eleven banks which had not failed agreed to resume on March 18. The exchanges with New York turned in favor of Philadelphia. The years 1842 and 1843 were years of great depression. The banks throughout the west and south were liquidating, after which they either perished or resumed. From 1843 a new sound and healthy development of industry and credit began. The recovery, however, was very slow, and banks sprang up again sooner and faster than anything else.

The total amount of Relief notes issued in Pennsylvania was two and one tenth millions. In January, 1843, the amount outstanding was, of depreciated $639,834, of specie value (issued by banks which had resumed) $240,801. Bicknell's *Reporter* said: "If any one can devise an immediate plan whereby the people can get rid of about $700,000 of paper trash, he will be entitled to the name of a public benefactor." In February, 1843, the Legislature ordered the Treasurer to cancel $100,000 of Relief notes at once and $100,000 monthly until all were destroyed, but in June, 1843, there were still $684,521 out.

This is certainly a melancholy story of the way in which people who enjoy the most exceptional chances of wealth and prosperity can squander them by ignorance of political economy and recklessness in political management. Banks were regarded as means of borrowing capital, not as institutions for lending it. If there was anywhere a group of needy speculators, they secured a bank charter, elected themselves directors, gave their notes for the stock, printed a lot of bank notes, loaned the notes to themselves, and

went out and with the notes bought the capital they
wanted. Bank after bank failed with an immense circulation afloat and no assets but the notes of its directors,
who had failed too. When the United States had thirty
or forty millions surplus on hand and these banks could get
the custody and handling of it for an indefinite period,
because the country had no need for it, it can readily be
understood why banks multiplied. The banks were encouraged to lend this deposit freely to the public, which they
were by no means loath to do, for that was the only way
to gain a profit on it. They lent it, not once but two or
three times over. The New York bank commissioners
pointed out the danger of a system in which the borrower
came directly into contact with the bank which issued the
currency. If a man was eager to borrow and pay high interest and the bank had only to print the notes to accommodate him, there was every stimulus to over-issue. If
the borrower engaged in any enterprise he raised the price
of everything he bought. When he became engaged in
his enterprise and wanted more capital, he went back to the
bank more eager and more ready to pay high interest than
ever, and the operation was repeated. In 1836, on the top
of the inflation, the rates for money were twelve and fifteen per cent throughout the year, with a very tight money
market. The banks and the business community could not
throw the blame on each other. They stimulated each other
and went on in their folly hand in hand. The penalties,
however, were not fairly distributed. The banks "suspended," as they called it; that is, when asked to pay their
debts, they said they would not; and they enjoyed a complete immunity in this respect, while people outside who
could not pay had to fail.

I have tried, within the limits to which I am bound, to
show how many elements were combined in this period
and how they were all interwoven. There are the political

elements, the tariff element, the movement of population
to the new land, the fiscal operations of the general government, the revolution in the coinage, the mania for public
improvements, the reckless creation of state debts, and the
war on the United States Bank. Any one of these might
have accounted for a financial crisis in an old country,
and the fact that the catastrophe produced by all combined
was not greater here is a striking proof of the vitality of
the country and the wonderful advantages which it was
wasting.

On the four or five years of inflated prosperity there
followed four or five years of the most slow and grinding
distress. 1843 is the year of lowest prices in our history,
and the year of severest restriction in industry. In 1842
the United States Treasury was under protest and actually
bankrupt, and American credit was so low that an agent of
the general government who was sent to Europe to try
to place a loan of only twelve million dollars there could
not do it at all. In that same year, however, out of what
income it did have, the general government distributed six
hundred thousand dollars, which came from land, amongst
the states. As for calling back any of the twenty-eight
millions deposited with the states, no effort of the kind
was ever made. The states were complaining that the
fourth installment, to which they had a right, had never
been paid to them. The question is sometimes mooted
whether a national debt is a curse or a blessing. There can
be no doubt whatever that a national surplus is a curse.

In the years before 1837 there had been a great deal of
eloquence spent upon "the credit system." After 1837
this matter was dropped. By the credit system they meant
the multiplication of bank notes which were false promises.
The notion was that the system of using these in business
gave poor men an easier chance to get rich. At first they
were loaned easily at low rates. Then, as prices rose and

speculation became active, interest advanced. The "poor men" found themselves forced to submit to more and more ruinous renewals, all the heavier because of the usury law, until they lost all they had ever really owned. The question, then, is how much better off than they were would the poor men of 1830 have been in 1845 if they had gone on slowly earning and saving capital and making no use of credit at all. As it was, the poor men of 1830, after supposing themselves rich in 1836, were all bankrupt in 1845. Such is the course of every inflation of the currency. It is proved by hundreds of instances; and there is no delusion which it seems so hard to stamp out of the minds of men as this, that in business we can make something out of nothing, although we cannot in chemistry or mechanics. Nothing more surely tempts the man without capital to his ruin than the easy credit which accompanies the first stages of inflation.

It is worth while also to reflect for a moment on the results of the two plans for dealing with the crisis: the New York plan and the Philadelphia plan. When an error has been committed in this world, we always have to bear the penalty for it. If we do not like the stripes on one side we can turn and take them on the other, but when nature inflicts penalties for her broken laws we never can squirm out of the way. In this case, then, when the folly had been perpetrated the punishment had to be suffered. The only choice was whether to take it quick and heavy, or light and long. The New Yorkers chose the former way. The contraction was severe and painful while it lasted, but it was soon over. From May, 1838, the New York banks resumed and held on without further default and the New York business recovered and entered upon a new course of growth from that time. The Philadelphians took the other course. They made it easy for the debtors and waited for the storm to blow over. The consequence was that the

debts increased still further. The advantage in trade over
New York proved shortlived and terribly expensive, for
the goods were not paid for. The confusion and distress
lasted for four years longer than in New York, and the
total loss was very much greater. For the last five years
we have been under the same necessity as that which
oppressed the country in 1837. We have been following
the Philadelphia plan and I may give you my opinion that
we have not been wise. I think that we might have escaped three years ago with far less loss, and might have
been three years further on the road to new prosperity.

In conclusion let me draw your attention to the lesson
of this history in regard to resumption. There was no
resumption, you see, until the currency had been reduced to
the limits of the actual specie necessity of the country or
even below it. Either voluntarily or by bankruptcy the
redundant paper had to be withdrawn. Such has been
the case in every other instance of resumption that I know
of, which has been real and permanent. Applying this to
our own present circumstances I ask myself whether the
amount of paper now in circulation is in excess of the requirement of the country, and there seems to me every
reason to believe that it is. If that is so, resumption
cannot be real and permanent until a portion of it has
been redeemed and withdrawn. The interest in resumption
of the great body of industrious, sober, and thrifty citizens
cannot be exaggerated. Renewed prosperity on a solid
basis is impossible until after a complete return to specie
value. There are those, however, who want to live by
anything but honest labor, who find their best chance
when prices are fluctuating and currency is continually
changing in value. They have schemes and interests
which resumption must destroy. They have done all
they could to make it fail and they are watchful and eager
to see it fail. If it does fail it will be a great national

calamity, on account of the authority which it will offer to these prophets of evil if for no other reason. Resumption with us now stands at just that point where the lightest preponderance of force may turn it one way or the other — may insure its success or cause its failure. It is a great gain to get our faces set in the right direction. It arouses the national pride in the success of resumption. It silences opposition and malevolent efforts against it. It makes it very much easier to take the requisite steps to insure success, for they involve no pain at all, nothing but economy and prudence in the national finances; the avoidance of unnecessary expenditure and the postponement for a time of certain expenditures proper in themselves. If the country needs six hundred million dollars to do its business with, then the withdrawal of a portion of the paper would simply bring gold into circulation, and resumption would be placed beyond a doubt. If the country does not want six hundred million dollars to do its business with, then we cannot sustain specie payments with that amount afloat, and we have still before us more of the experience of 1842 and 1843.

THE SCIENCE OF SOCIOLOGY

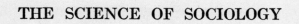

THE SCIENCE OF SOCIOLOGY [1]

IN the present state of the science of sociology the man who has studied it at all is very sure to feel great self-distrust in trying to talk about it. The most that one of us can do at the present time is to appreciate the promise which the science offers to us, and to understand the lines of direction in which it seems about to open out. As for the philosophy of the subject, we still need the master to show us how to handle and apply its most fundamental doctrines. I have the feeling all the time, in studying and teaching sociology, that I have not mastered it yet in such a way as to be able to proceed in it with good confidence in my own steps. I have only got so far as to have an almost overpowering conviction of the necessity and value of the study of that science.

Mr. Spencer addressed himself at the outset of his literary career to topics of sociology. In the pursuit of those topics he found himself forced (as I understand it) to seek constantly more fundamental and wider philosophical doctrines. He came at last to fundamental principles of the evolution philosophy. He then extended, tested, confirmed, and corrected these principles by inductions from other sciences, and so finally turned again to sociology, armed with the scientific method which he had acquired. To win a powerful and correct method is, as we all know, to win more than half the battle. When so much is secured, the question of making the discoveries, solving the problems, eliminating the errors, and testing the results, is only a question of time and of strength to collect and master the data.

[1] Speech at the Farewell Banquet to Herbert Spencer, held November 9, 1882.

We have now acquired the method of studying sociology scientifically so as to attain to assured results. We have acquired it none too soon. The need for a science of life in society is urgent, and it is increasing every year. It is a fact which is generally overlooked that the great advance in the sciences and the arts which has taken place during the last century is producing social consequences and giving rise to social problems. We are accustomed to dwell upon the discoveries of science and the development of the arts as simple incidents, complete in themselves, which offer only grounds for congratulation. But the steps which have been won are by no means simple events. Each one has consequences which reach beyond the domain of physical power into social and moral relations, and these effects are multiplied and reproduced by combination with each other. The great discoveries and inventions redistribute population. They reconstruct industries and force new organization of commerce and finance. They bring new employments into existence and render other employments obsolete, while they change the relative value of many others. They overthrow the old order of society, impoverishing some classes and enriching others. They render old political traditions grotesque and ridiculous, and make old maxims of statecraft null and empty. They give old vices of human nature a chance to parade in new masks, so that it demands new skill to detect the same old foes. They produce a kind of social chaos in which contradictory social and economic phenomena appear side by side to bewilder and deceive the student who is not fully armed to deal with them. New interests are brought into existence, and new faiths, ideas, and hopes, are engendered in the minds of men. Some of these are doubtless good and sound; others are delusive; in every case a competent criticism is of the first necessity. In the upheaval of society which is going on, classes and groups are thrown against each other in such a way as to produce class hatreds and hostilities. As the old national jealousies, which used to be the lines on which war was waged, lose their distinctness, class jealousies threaten to take their place. Political and social events which occur on one side of the globe now affect the interests of population on the other side of the globe. Forces which come into action in one part of human society rest not until they have reached all human society. The brotherhood of man is coming to be a reality of such distinct and positive character that we find it a practical question of the greatest moment what kind of creatures some of these hitherto neglected brethren are. Secondary and remoter effects of industrial changes, which were formerly dissipated and lost in the delay and friction of communication, are now, by our prompt and delicate mechanism of communication, caught up and transmitted through society.

It is plain that our social science is not on the level of the tasks which are thrown upon it by the vast and sudden changes in the whole mechanism by which man makes the resources of the globe available to satisfy his needs, and by the new ideas which are born of the new aspects which human life bears to our eyes in consequence of the development of science and the arts. Our traditions about the science and art of living are plainly inadequate. They break to pieces in our hands when we try to apply them to the new cases. A man of good faith may come to the conviction sadly, but he must come to the conviction honestly, that the traditional doctrines and explanations of human life are worthless.

A progress which is not symmetrical is not true; that is to say, every branch of human interest must be developed proportionately to all the other branches, else the one which remains in arrears will measure the advance which may be won by the whole. If, then, we cannot produce a science of life in society which is broad enough to solve all the new social problems which are now forced upon us by the development of science and art, we shall find that the achievements of science and art will be overwhelmed by social reactions and convulsions.

We do not lack for attempts of one kind and another to satisfy the need which I have described. Our discussion is in excess of our deliberation, and our deliberation is in excess of our information. Our journals, platforms, pulpits, and parliaments are full of talking and writing about topics of sociology. The only result, however, of all this discussion is to show that there are half a dozen arbitrary codes of morals, a heterogeneous tangle of economic doctrines, a score of religious creeds and ecclesiastical traditions, and a confused jumble of humanitarian and sentimental notions which jostle each other in the brains of the men of this generation. It is astonishing to watch a discussion and to see how a disputant, starting from a given point of view, will run along on one line of thought until he encounters some fragment of another code or doctrine, which he has derived from some other source of education; whereupon he turns at an angle, and goes on in a new course until he finds himself face to face with another of his old prepossessions. What we need is adequate criteria by which to make the necessary tests and classifications, and appropriate canons of procedure, or the adaptation of universal canons to the special tasks of sociology.

Unquestionably it is to the great philosophy which has now been established by such ample induction in the experimental sciences, and which offers to man such new command of all the relations of life, that we must look for the establishment of the guiding lines in the study of sociology. I can see no boundaries to the scope of the philosophy of evolution. That philosophy is sure to embrace all the interests of man on this earth. It will be one of its crowning triumphs to bring light and order into the social problems which are of universal bearing on all mankind. Mr. Spencer is breaking the path for us into this domain. We stand eager to follow him into it, and we look upon his work on sociology as a grand step in the history of science. When, therefore, we express our earnest hope that Mr. Spencer may have health and strength to bring his work to a speedy conclusion, we not only express our personal respect and good-will for himself, but also our sympathy with what, I doubt not, is the warmest wish of his own heart, and our appreciation of his great services to true science and to the welfare of mankind.

INTEGRITY IN EDUCATION

INTEGRITY IN EDUCATION[1]

IN addressing you on the present occasion, I am naturally led to speak of matters connected with education. We are met here amid surroundings which, to the great majority of us, are unfamiliar, but we are assembled in the atmosphere of our school days and under the inspiration of school memories. Some of us are rapidly approaching, if we have not already reached, the time when our interest in education re-arises in behalf of the next generation. Many are engaged in the work of teaching. Others have only just finished a stage in their education. I therefore propose to speak for a few minutes about integrity in education, believing that it is a subject of great importance at the present time, and one which may justly command your interest.

By integrity in education, I mean the opposite of all sensationalism and humbug in education. I would include under it as objects to be aimed at in education, not only the pursuit of genuine and accurate information and wide knowledge of some technical branch of study, but also real discipline in the use of mental powers, sterling character, good manners, and high breeding.

Modern sensationalism is conquering a wide field for itself. It is a sort of parasite on high civilization. Its motto is that seeming is as good as being. Its intrinsic fault is its hollowness, insincerity, and falsehood. It deals in dash, flourish, and meretricious pretense. It resides in the form, not in the substance; in the outward appearance, not in the reality. It arouses disgust whenever it is per-

[1] Address delivered in Hartford.

ceived; but the worst of it is that its forms are so various, its manifestations are sometimes so delicate, and it often lies so near to the real and the true, that is it difficult to distinguish it. Life hurries past us very rapidly. The interests which demand our attention are very numerous and important. We have not time to scrutinize them all. Then, too, the publicity of everything nowadays prevents modest retirement from being a sign of merit. We go on the principle that if anything is good, it is for the public. Publicity is honorable and proper recognition, and those who have charge of the public trumpets have not time, if they have the ability, to discriminate and criticize very closely.

These reflections account sufficiently for the growth of sensationalism in general. Probably each one sees the mischief which it does in his own circle or profession more distinctly than elsewhere. I have certainly been struck by its influence on education. I see it in common-school education as well as in the universities. It attaches to methods as well as to subjects. It develops a dogmatism of its own. Men without education, or experience as teachers, often take up the pitiful rôle of another class which has come to be called "educators." They start off with a whim or two which they elaborate into theories of education. These they propound with great gravity in speech and writing, producing long discussions as to plans and methods. They are continually searching for a patent method of teaching, or a royal road to learning, when, in fact, the only way to learn is by the labor of the mind in observing, comparing, and generalizing, and any patent method which avoids this irksome labor produces sham results and fails of producing the mental power and discipline of which education consists.

Persons of this class are generally impatient until they have attained some opportunity of putting their notions in practice, and then it is all over with any institution which becomes subject to their wild empiricism.

The saddest results of such proceedings are seen, of course, in the pupils. That a certain school should lose its pupils, or fall into debt, or be closed, is a comparatively small affair. The real mischief is that men should be produced who have no real education, but only a perverse training in putting forward plausible and meretricious appearances. Such education falls in with the outward phenomena of a sensational era and strengthens the impressions which a young and inexperienced observer gets from our modern society, that audacity is the chief of talents, that success or failure is the only measure of right or wrong, that the man to be admired is the one who invents clever tricks to circumvent a rival or opponent, or to skip over a troublesome principle. Young people are more acute in their observations, and they draw inferences and form generalizations more logically and consistently than their elders. They have not yet learned respect for dogmas, traditions, and conventionalities, and their "education" goes on silently but surely, developing a philosophy of life either of one kind or another. If, therefore, you have an educational system consisting of formal cram for recitation or examination, if there is a skimming of textbooks, an empty acquisition of terms, a memorizing of results only, you may pursue high-sounding studies and "cover a great deal of ground," you may have an elaborate curriculum and boast of your proficiency in difficult branches, but you will have no education. You may produce men who can spend a lifetime dawdling over trifles, or men who always scatter their force when they try to think, but you will not have intelligent men with minds well-disciplined and well under control, who are able to apply their full force to any new exigency, or any new problem, and to grasp and conquer it.

The fault here is plain enough.   People forget, or do not perceive, that simplicity and modesty are the first requisites in scientific pursuits.   We have to begin humbly and with small beginnings if we want to go far.   Inflation and pretense only lead to vanity and dilletantism, not to strength and fruitful activity.   If we advance eagerly, we deceive ourselves by the notion that we are making grand progress. We are only leaving much undone which we shall have to go back and repair.   If, on the other hand, we proceed slowly and with painstaking, every step of advance is sure and genuine.   It forms a great vantage-ground for the next step.   It strengthens and confirms the mental powers. They come to act with certainty by scientific processes, not by guesses, and this mental discipline enables us to apply our powers wherever we need them.   A new task is not a dead wall which is impassable to us because we have never seen one like it before.   It is only a new case for the application of old and familiar processes.   I never see anything more pitiable than the helpless floundering in a new subject of a young man far on in his education who has never yet learned to use his mind.

In what I have already said about the philosophy of life which a young person forms during the process of education, I have suggested that education must exert a great influence on character.   It is sometimes asserted that education ought to mold character — ought to have that object and work towards it, of set purpose.   I do not deny this, but I beg you to observe that it obscures the truth. The truth is that education inevitably forms character one way or the other.   The error is in speaking as if academical instruction could be carried on without training character, unless the set purpose were entertained.   One might read many books on mathematics and the sciences without any very direct moral culture, but everything we learn about this world in which we live reacts in some sort of principle for the regulation of our conduct here. This, however, is not the most important thing. A school is a miniature society. Do we not all know how it forms an atmosphere of its own, how the members make a code of their own, and a public opinion of their own? And then, what a position the teacher holds in this little community. What a dangerous and responsible eminence he occupies. What criticism he undergoes. What an authority his example exerts. So, in this little society, general notions of conduct are unconsciously formed, principles are adopted, habits grow. Every member in his place gives to, and takes from, the common life. It may be well doubted whether there is any association of life which exerts greater influence on character than does the school, and its influence comes, too, just as the formative period, when impressions are most easily received and sink deepest.

Here then is where sensationalism may do its greatest harm, and where integrity of method is most important. The untruthfulness of sensationalism here becomes a germinal principle, which develops into manifold forms of untruthfulness in character. Young people cannot practice show and pretense and yet be taught to believe that the only important thing is what you are, and not at all what people think about you. They cannot practice the devices which give a semblance of learning, and yet be taught to believe that shams are disgraceful and that the frank honesty which owns the worst is a noble trait. They may learn to be ashamed when caught in a false pretense, but they will not learn shame at deceit. I do not say that they will lie or steal, but it is a pitiful code which defines honesty as refraining from seizing other people's property. Honesty is a far wider virtue than not-stealing. It embraces rectitude of motive and purpose, completeness and consistency of principle, and delicacy of responsibility. Truthfulness is the very cornerstone of character, and an instinct of dislike for whatever is false or meretricious is one of the feelings which all sound education must inculcate. It cannot do so, however, unless its *personnel* and its methods are all animated by unflinching integrity.

I mentioned also, at the outset, amongst those things which are embraced in education and to which I desire to see the principle of integrity applied, good manners. Some people make an ostentatious display of neglect for good manners. They think it democratic, or a sign of good fellowship, to be negligent in this respect. They think it something to be boasted of that they have no breeding. Some others make manners supersede education and training and even character. It is the latter error which most invades the sphere of education. We are familiar with its forms. It gives us the mock gentleman of the drawing-room under the same coat with the rowdy of the bar-room. When this system triumphs, it fits our young people out with a few fashionable phrases, which suffice for the persiflage of the drawing-room, when a scientific subject by chance comes up. Girls are the victims of this system far more than boys, but in "cultivated circles" cases are common of this kind, in which a smattering of books has been engrafted on the culture of the dancing school. Young men and young women who have tacked together a few miscellaneous phrases current amongst the learned will deliver you their opinions roundly on the gravest problems of philosophy and science. The phrases which stick in their minds the longest are those which are epigrammatic and paradoxical, whether true or not. In fact, they could not analyze or criticize their mental stock if they should try. They have never learned to consider a subject and form an opinion.

It does not follow, however, that boorishness is erudition, or that it does not belong to education to teach the good manners which are good simply because they are the spontaneous expression of a sound heart and a well-trained mind. Envy, malice, and selfishness are the usual springs of bad manners. They belong to the untrained and brutish man, and it is the province of true education to eradicate them. Hence it is that where true education is wanting we may often find the worst manners with the greatest social experience, and the truest courtesy where there has been genuine discipline, but little acquaintance with social forms.

I have not started this train of thought in order to tell you now that we have enjoyed the true method of education, and that others have not, but there are some things connected with this institution which we may remember with pleasure in view of the reflections which I have presented.

This school was founded so long ago that it already has a body of graduates who are useful and influential men in this city, and many others are scattered up and down the country, useful and honorable, if not celebrated citizens. It was not founded without some struggle, but the more enlightened views prevailed and the results have vindicated those views, I suppose to the satisfaction of everybody. The enterprise enjoyed at the outset the patronage of a body of men of remarkably broad views and sound public spirit. We who profited by its instruction in our time may properly remember those men on this occasion with gratitude and respect. One of them, surpassed by none in zeal to work for and intelligence to plan such an institution, has only just passed away. Your city has been fortunate in possessing such citizens.

The plan on which the school was founded was remarkably wise and farseeing. It has placed the highest education within the reach of every boy in your city who had sufficient industry and self-denial to seek it. Many of you are now in the position of active and responsible citizens.

You must regard this institution as one of the boasts of your city. Guard it well. You may not boast of it only. You owe it a debt which you must pay. Every boy and girl who has graduated here owes a debt to the common school system of America. Every man for whom this school has opened a career which would otherwise have been beyond his reach, owes a tenfold debt, both to the common school system and to the class in which he was born. Sectarian interests, private school interests, property interests, and some cliques of "culture" falsely so called, are rallying against the system a force which people as yet underrate. There is no knowing how soon the struggle may open, and you may be called upon to pay the allegiance you owe.

This school has also been remarkably fortunate in the selection of the teachers who have presided over it. We cannot exaggerate the value of this selection. It is by the imperceptible influence of the teacher's character and example that the atmosphere of a school is created. It is from this that the pupils learn what to admire and what to abhor, what to seek and what to shun. It is from this that they learn what methods of action are honorable and what ones are unbecoming. They learn all this from methods of discipline as well as from methods of instruction. They may learn craft and intrigue, or they may learn candor and sincerity. They may learn to win success at any cost, or they may learn to accept failure with dignity, when success could only be won by dishonor.

You know well what has always been the tone impressed on this institution by the teachers we had here. We had many, both gentlemen and ladies, whom we remember with respect and affection. Our later experience of the world and of life has only served to show us more distinctly, in the retrospect, how elevated was their tone, how sincere their devotion, how simple and upright their methods of dealing with us. They were not taskmasters to us, and their work was not a harsh and ungrateful routine to them.

One figure will inevitably arise before the minds of all when these words are said, the figure of one who died with the harness on. I have never seen anywhere, in my experience, a man of more simple and unconscious high-breeding, one who combined more thoroughly the dignity of official authority with the suavity of unrestrained intercourse with his pupils. It is a part of the good fortune which came to us and to this city from this institution that so many young people here enjoyed his personal influence.

It follows, as a natural consequence, from these facts, that we enjoyed here to a high degree what I have described as integrity in education. Sensationalism of any kind has always been foreign to the system here. It must perish in such an atmosphere. We had instruction which was real and solid, which conceded nothing to show and sacrificed nothing to applause. We learned to work patiently for real and enduring results. We learned the faith that what is genuine must outlast and prevail over what is meretricious. We learned to despise empty display. We had also a discipline which was complete and sufficient, but which was attained without friction. There was no sentimentality, no petting, no affectation of free and easy manners. Discipline existed because it was necessary, and it was smooth because it was reasonable.

Now there is nothing to which people apply more severe criticism, as they grow old, than to their education. They find the need of it every day, and they have to ask whether it was sufficient and suited to the purpose or not. It is because we find, I think, that our education here does stand this test that we are able to meet here on an occasion like this with genuine interest and sympathy. The years in their flight have sacttered us and brought us weighty cares and new interests. We could not lay these aside to come back here for purposes of mere sentiment, or to repeat conventional phrases. We meet on the ground of grateful recollection of benefits received, benefits which we can specify and weigh and measure.

This school must be regarded as a local institution. It belongs to this city and its advantages are offered to the young people who grow up here. I have referred to the exceptional wisdom and enlightenment which presided over its foundation and have nourished its growth. In conclusion, let me refer to what concerns its present and its future. We are reminded by all we see about us here that its building and its appliances are far better than they were in our day. Its prosperity bears witness to its present good management. But, gentlemen, these good things are not to be preserved without vigilance and labor. The same wisdom and enlightenment must preside over the future as over the past. I doubt not that the value of this institution to your city is so fully appreciated, and the methods by which it has been developed are so well understood, that any peril to it or to them would arouse your earnest efforts for its defence. Keep it as it has been, devoted to correct objects by sound methods. Sacrifice nothing to the *éclat* of hasty and false success. Concede nothing to the modern quackery of education. Resist the specious schemes of reckless speculators on educational theories. It is not to be expected that you can escape these dangers any more than other people, and you have to be on your guard against them. You want here an educational institution which shall, in its measure, instruct your children in the best science and thought of the day. You want it to make them masters of themselves and of their powers. You want it to make them practical in the best and only true sense, by making them efficient in dealing intelligently with all the problems of life. The country needs such citizens to-day. The state needs them. Your city needs them. They are needed in all the trades and professions. You must look to such institutions as this to provide them, and you must keep it true to its methods and purpose if you want it to turn out men of moral courage, high principle, and devotion to duty.

DISCIPLINE

DISCIPLINE

IT occurs very frequently to a person connected as a teacher with a great seat of learning to meet persons who, having completed a course of study and having spent a few years in active life, are led to make certain reflections upon their academical career. There is a great uniformity in the comments which are thus made, so far as I have heard them, and they enforce upon me certain convictions. I observe that an academical life is led in a community which is to a certain extent closed, isolated, and peculiar. It has a code of its own as well for work as for morals. It forms a peculiar standpoint, and life, as viewed from it, takes on peculiar forms and peculiar colors. It is scarcely necessary to add that the views of life thus obtained are distorted and incorrect.

I should not expect much success if I should undertake to correct those views by description in words. It is only in life itself, that is, by experience, that men correct their errors. They insist on making experience for themselves. They delude themselves with hopes that they are peculiar in their persons and characters, or that their circumstances are peculiar, and so that in some way or other they can perpetrate the old faults and yet escape the old penalties. It is only when life is spent that these delusions are dispelled and then the power and the opportunity to put the acquired wisdom to practice is gone by. Thus the old continually warn and preach and the young continually disregard and suffer.

Although I could not expect better fortune than others if I should thus preach, yet there are some things which, as I have often been led to think, young men in your situation might be brought to understand with great practical advantage, and which, if you did understand them, and act upon them, would save you from the deepest self-reproach and regret which I so often hear older men express; and the present occasion seems a better one than I can otherwise obtain, for presenting those things. I allude to some wider explanations of the meaning and purpose of academical pursuits. I do not mean theories of education about which people dispute, but I mean the purposes which any true education has in view, and the responsibilities it brings with it. It surely is not advisable that men of your age should pursue your education as a mere matter of routine, learning prescribed lessons, performing enforced tasks, resisting, unintelligent, and uninterested. Such an experience on your part would not constitute any true education. It would not involve any development of capability in you. It could only render you dull, fond of shirking, slovenly in your work, and superficial in your attainments. Unless I am greatly mistaken, some counteraction to such a low and unworthy conception of academical life may be secured by showing its relation to real life, and attaching things pursued here to practical and enduring benefits. I have known men to get those benefits without knowing it; and I believe that you would get them better if you got them intelligently, and that you would appreciate them better if you got them consciously.

In the first place, it will be profitable to look at one or two notions in regard to the purpose of education which do not seem to be sound. One is that it is the purpose of education to give special technical skill or dexterity and to fit a man to get a living. We may admit at once that the object of study is to get useful knowledge. It was, indeed, the error of some old systems of academical pursuits that they gave only a special dexterity and that too in such a direction as the making of Greek and Latin verses, which is a mere accomplishment and not a very good one at that. It must be ranged with dancing and fencing; it is not as high as drawing, painting, or music. There is, moreover, a domain in which special technical training is proper. It is the domain of the industrial school, for giving a certain theoretical knowledge of persons who will be engaged for life in the mechanic arts. With this limitation, however, we have at once given to us the bounds which preclude this notion from covering the true conception of an academic career. It does not simply provide technical training for a higher class of arts which require longer preparation. You know that this conception is widely held through our American community, and that it is laid down with great dogmatic severity by persons who sometimes, unfortunately, are in a position to turn their opinions into law. It is one of the great obstacles against which all efforts for higher education amongst us have to contend.

I pass on, however, to another opinion just now much more fashionable and held by people who are, at any rate, much more elegant than the supporters of the view just mentioned, that is, the opinion that what we expect from education is "culture." Culture is a word which offers us an illustration of the degeneracy of language. If I may define culture, I have no objection to admitting that it is the purpose of education to produce it; but since the word came into fashion, it has been stolen by the dilettanti and made to stand for their own favorite forms and amounts of attainments. Mr. Arnold, the great apostle, if not the discoverer, of culture, tried to analyze it and he found it to consist of sweetness and light. To my mind, that is like saying that coffee is milk and sugar. The stuff of culture is all left out of it. So, in the practice of those who accept this notion, culture comes to represent only an external smoothness and roundness of outline without regard to intrinsic qualities.

We have got so far now as to begin to distinguish different kinds of culture. There is chromo culture, of which we heard much a little while ago, and there is bouffe culture, which is only just invented. If I were in the way of it, I should like to add another class, which might be called sapolio culture, because it consists in putting a high polish on plated ware. There seems great danger lest this kind may come to be the sort aimed at by those who regard culture as the end of education.

A truer idea of culture is that which regards it as equivalent to training, or the result of training, which brings into intelligent activity all the best powers of mind and body. Such a culture is not to be attained by writing essays about it, or by forming ever so clear a literary statement or mental conception of what it is. It is not to be won by wishing for it, or aping the external manifestations of it. We men can get it only by industrious and close application of the powers we want to develop. We are not sure of getting it by reading any number of books. It requires continual application of literary acquisitions to practice and it requires a continual correction of mental conceptions by observation of things as they are. For the sake of distinguishing sharply between the true idea of culture and the false, I have thought it better to call the true culture discipline, a word which perhaps brings out its essential character somewhat better.

Here let me call your attention to one very broad generalization on human life which men continually lose sight of, and of which culture is an illustration. The great and heroic things which strike our imagination are never attainable by direct efforts. This is true of wisdom, glory, fame, virtue, culture, public good, or any other of the great ends which men seek to attain. We cannot reach any of these things by direct effort. They come as the refined result, in a secondary and remote way, of thousands of acts which have another and closer end in view. If a man aims at wisdom directly, he will be very sure to make an affectation of it. He will attain only to a ridiculous profundity in commonplaces. Wisdom is the result of great knowledge, experience, and observation, after they have all been sifted and refined down into sober caution, trained judgment, skill in adjusting means to ends.

In like manner, one who aims at glory or fame directly will win only that wretched caricature which we call notoriety. Glory and fame, so far as they are desirable things, are remote results which come of themselves at the end of long and repeated and able exertions.

The same holds true of the public good or the "cause," or whatever else we ought to call that end which fires the zeal of philanthropists and martyrs. When this is pursued directly as an immediate good, there arise extravagances, fanaticisms, and aberrations of all kinds. Strong actions and reactions take place in social life, but not orderly growth and gain. The first impression no doubt is that of noble zeal and self-sacrifice, but this is not the sort of work by which society gains. The progress of society is nothing but the slow and far remote result of steady, laborious, painstaking growth of individuals. The man who makes the most of himself and does his best in his sphere is doing far more for the public good than the philanthropist who runs about with a scheme which would set the world straight if only everybody would adopt it.

This view cuts down a great deal of the heroism which fills such a large part of our poetry, but it brings us, I think, several very encouraging reflections. The first is that one does not need to be a hero to be of some importance in the world. Heroes are gone by. We want now a good supply of efficient workaday men, to stand each in his place and do good work. The second reflection to which we are led is that we do not need to be straining our eyes continually to the horizon to see where we are coming out, or, in other words, we do not need to trouble ourselves with grand theories and purposes. The determination to do just what lies next before us is enough. The great results will all come of themselves and take care of themselves. We may spare ourselves all grand emotions and heroics, because the more simply and directly we take the business of life, the better will be the result. The third inference which seems to be worth mentioning is that we come to understand the value of trifles.

All that I have said here about wisdom, fame, glory, "public good," as ends to be aimed at, holds good also of culture. It becomes a sham and affectation when we make it an immediate end, and comes in its true form only as a remote and refined result of long labor and discipline.

Before I speak of it, however, in its direct relation to education, let me introduce one other observation on the doctrine I have stated that we cannot aim at the great results directly. That is this: the motive to all immediate efforts is either self-interest or the desire to gratify one's tastes and natural tendencies. I say that all the grand results which make up what we call social progress are the results of millions of efforts on the part of millions of people, and that the motive to each effort in the heart of the man who made it was the gratification of a need or a tendency of his nature. I know that some may consider this a selfish doctrine, eliminating all self-sacrifice and martyr or missionary spirit, but to me it is a pleasure to observe that we are not at war with ourselves, and that the intelligent pursuit of our best good as individuals is the surest means to the good of society. Moreover, do you imagine that if you set out to make the most of yourself in any position in which you are placed, that you will have no chance for self-sacrifice, and no opportunity of martyrdom offered you? Do you think that a man who employs thoroughly all the means he possesses to make his one unit of humanity as perfect as possible, can do so without at every moment giving and receiving with the other units about him? Do you think that he can go on far without finding himself stopped by the question whether his comrades are going in the same direction or not? Will he not certainly find himself forced to stand against a tide which is flowing in the other direction? It will certainly be so. The real martyrs have always been the men who were forced to go one way while the rest of the community in which they lived were going another, and they were swept down by the tide. I promise you that if you pursue what is good for yourself, you need not take care for the good of society; I warn you that if you pursue what is good, you will find yourself limited by the stupidity, ignorance, and folly of the society in which you live; and I promise you also that if you hold on your way through the crowd or try to make them go with you, you will have ample experience of self-sacrifice and as much martyrdom as you care for.

Now, if I have not led you too deep into social philosophy, let us turn again to culture. We find that culture comes from thought, study, observation, literary and scientific activity, and we find that men practice these for gain, for professional success, for immediate pleasure, or to gratify their tastes. The great motive of interest provides the energy and this culture is but a secondary result. It is a significant fact to observe that when the motive of interest is removed, culture becomes flaccid and falls into dilletantism.

I think that we have gained a standpoint now from which we can study undergraduate life and make observations on it which have even scientific value. During an undergraduate career, the motive of interest in each successive step is wanting. There is no immediate object of pleasure or gain in the lesson to be learned next. Only exceptionally is it true that the learning of the lesson will gratify a taste or fill a desire. The university honors are only artificial means of arousing the same great motive, which is in the social body what gravitation is in physics. The penalties which are here to be dreaded are but imitations of life's penalties. I think that many who have undertaken to give advice and rebuke and warning to young men in a state of pupilage have failed because they have not fully analyzed or correctly grasped this fact, that the academical world is a little community by itself in which the great natural forces which bind older men to sobriety and wisdom act only imperfectly. Life is far less interesting when the successive steps are taken under compulsion or for a good which is remote and only known by hearsay, than it is when every step is taken for an immediate profit. I doubt very much whether the hope of culture or self-sacrificing zeal for the public good would make older men toil in lawyer's offices and counting-houses, unless there were such immediate rewards as wealth and professional success. In real life it is true that men must do very many things which are disagreeable and which they do not want to do, but there too the disagreeable things are made easier to bear. The troubles of academical life seem to be arbitrary troubles, inflicted by device of foolish or malicious men. Troubles of that kind always rouse men to anger and rankle in their hearts. But there is no railing against those ills of life which are inherent in the constitution of things. A man who rails at those is laughed at. So the man just emancipated from academical life finds himself freed from conventional rules but subjected to penalties for idleness and extravagance and folly infinitely heavier than any he has been accustomed to, and inflicted without warning or mercy or respite. On the other hand, he finds that life presents opportunities and attractions for him to work, where work has a zest about it which comes from contact with living things. His academical weapons and armor are stiff and awkward at first and he may very probably come to despise them, but longer experience will show that his education, if it was good, gave him rather the power to use any weapons than special skill in the use of particular ones. Special technical skill always tends to routine. Although it is an advantage in itself, it may under circumstances become a limitation. The only true conception of a "liberal" education is that it gives a broad discipline to the whole man, which uses routine without being conquered by it and can change its direction and application when occasion requires.

This brings me then to speak of the real scope and advantage of a disciplinary education. A man who has enjoyed such an education has simply had his natural powers developed and reduced to rule, and he has gained for himself an intelligent control of them. Before an academical audience it is not necessary for me to stop to clear away the popular notions about untutored powers and self-made men. It is enough to say that the "self-made" man is, by the definition, the first bungling essay of a bad workman. An undeveloped human mind is simply a bundle of possibilities. It may come to much or little. If it is highly trained by years of patient exercise, judiciously imposed, it becomes capable of strict and methodical action. It may be turned to any one of a hundred tasks which offer themselves to us men here on earth. It may have gained this discipline in one particular science or another, and it may have special technical acquaintance with one more than another. Such will almost surely be the case, but there is not a more mistaken, one-sided, and mischievous controversy than that about *the* science which should be made the basis of education. Every science has, for disciplinary purposes, its advantages and its limitations. The man who is trained on chemistry will become a strict analyst and will break up heterogeneous compounds of all kinds, but he will be likely also to rest content with this destructive work and to leave the positive work of construction or synthesis to others. The man who is trained on history will be quick to discern continuity of force or law under different phases, but he will be content with broad phases and heterogeneous combinations such as history offers, and will not be a strict analyst. The man who is trained on mathematics will have great power of grasping purely conceptional relations, or abstract ideas, which are, however, most sharply defined; but he will be likely to fasten upon a subordinate factor in some other kind of problem, especially if that factor admits of more complete abstraction than any of the others. The man who is trained on the science of language approaches the continuity and development of history with a guiding thread in his hand, and his comparisons, furnishing stepping-stones now on the right and now on the left, lead him on in a course where induction and deduction go so close together that they can hardly be separated; but the study of language again always threatens to degenerate into a cram of grammatical niceties and a fastidiousness about expression, under which the contents are forgotten. Now, in individual affairs, family, social, and political affairs, all these powers of mind find occasion for exercise. They are needed in business, in professions, in technical pursuits; and the man best fitted for the demands of life would be the man whose powers of mind of all these diverse orders and kinds had all been harmoniously developed. How shallow then is the idea that education is meant to give or can give a mass of monopolized information, and how important it is that the student should understand what he may expect and what he may not expect from his education. As your education goes on, you ought to gain in your power of observation. Natural incidents, political occurrences, social events, ought to present to you new illustrations of general principles with which your studies have made you familiar. You ought to gain in power to analyze and compare, so that all the fallacies which consist in presenting things as like, which are not like, should not be able to befog your reason. You ought to become able to recognize and test a generalization, and to distinguish between true generalizations and dogmas on the one hand, or commonplaces on another, or whimsical speculations on another. You ought to know when you are dealing with a true law which you may follow to the uttermost; when you have only a general truth; when you have an hypothetical theory; when you have a possible conjecture; and when you have only an ingenious assumption. These are most important distinctions on either side. Some people are affected by a notion, fashionable just now, that it belongs to culture never to go too far. Mr. Brook, in "Middlemarch," you remember, is a type of that culture. He believed in things up to a certain point and was always afraid of going too far. We have a good many aspirants after culture nowadays whose capital consists in a superficial literary tradition and the same kind of terror of going too far. They would put a saving clause in the multiplication table, and make reservations in the rule of three. On the other hand, we have those who can never express anything to which they are inclined to assent without gushing. A simple opinion must be set forth in a torrent fit to enforce a great scientific truth. One is just as much the sign of an imperfect training as the other, and you meet with both, as my description shows, in persons who pride themselves on their culture. I will not deny that they are cultivated; I only say that they are not well disciplined, that is, not well educated.

Your education, if it is disciplinary, ought also to teach

you the value of clear thinking, that is, of exact definitions,
clear propositions, well-considered opinions. What a flood
of loose rhetoric, distorted fact, and unclear thinking is
poured out upon us whenever a difficult question falls into
popular discussion! You cannot find that people who
assume to take part in the discussion have a clear definition in their minds of even what they conceive the main
terms in the discussion to mean. They do not seem able
to make a proposition which will bear handling so as to
see what it is, and whether it is true or not. They cannot
analyze even such facts as they have collected, and hence
cannot draw inferences which are sound. It needs but
little discussion of any great political or social question to
show instances of this, and to show the immense importance of having in the community men of trained and disciplined intellects, who can think with some clearness and
resist plain confusion of terms and thought. For instance,
I saw the other day a long argument on an important
public topic which turned upon the assertion and belief
on the part of the writer that a mathematical ratio and a
subjective opinion were things of the same nature and
value. Perhaps, when he was at school, his father thought
there was no use in studying algebra and geometry. It
would not make so much difference if he would not now
meddle with things for which he did not prepare himself,
but it is this kind of person who is the pest of every science,
traversing it with his whims and speculations; and perhaps
I feel the more strongly the importance of this point because the political, economic, and social sciences suffer
from the want of high discipline more than any others.

I ought not to pass without mention here the mischief
which is done in every science by its undisciplined advocates who, while admitted to its inner circle, distract its
progress and throw it into confusion by neglect of strict
principles, by incorrect analyses or classifications, or by

flinching in the face of fallacies. They render the ranks unsteady and delay the march, and the reason is because they have never had rigorous discipline either before or since they enlisted.

If your education is disciplinary, it ought also to teach you how to organize. I add this point especially because I esteem it important and it is rarely noticed. It is really a high grade of discipline which enables men to organize voluntarily. If men begin to study and think, they move away from tradition and authority. The first effect is to break up and dissolve their inherited and traditional opinions as to religion, politics, and society. This is a necessary process of transition from formal and traditional dogma to intelligent conviction. It applies to all the notions of religion, as has often been noticed, but it applies none the less to politics and to one's notions of life. The commonplaces of patriotism, the watchwords of parties and tradition, the glib and well-worn phrases and terms have to be analyzed again, and under the process much of their dignity and sanctity evaporates. So too one's views of life, of the meaning of social phenomena, and of the general rules for men to pursue with each other, undergo a recasting. Now during this process, men diverge and break up. They do not agree. They differ by less and more, and also by the various recombinations of the factors which they make. Pride, vanity, and self-seeking come in to increase this divergence, it being regarded as a sign of independence of thought.

It is not too much to say that so long as this divergence exists, it is a sign of a low and imperfect development of science. If pride and vanity intermingle, they show that discipline has not yet done its perfect work. It is only on a higher stage of culture or discipline that self is so overborne in zeal for the scientific good that opinions converge and organization becomes possible. But you are well aware that without organization we men can accomplish very little. It is not the freedom of the barbarian who would rather live alone than undergo the inevitable coercion of the neighborhood of others that we want. We want only free and voluntary coördination, but it belongs to discipline itself to teach us that we must have coördination in order to attain to any high form of good.

I have now tried to show you the scope, advantages, and needs of a disciplinary education. I have one remark more to make in this connection. A man with a well-disciplined mind possesses a tool which he can use for any purpose which he needs to serve. I do not consider it an important question by the study of what sciences he shall get this discipline, for, if he gets it, the acquisition of information in any new department of learning will be easy for him, and he will be strong, alert, and well equipped for any exigency of life.

Before quitting the subject, I desire to point out its relation to one other matter, that is, to morals, or manners. It is a common opinion that the higher man attains, the freer he becomes. A moment's reflection will show that this is not true — but rather quite the contrary. The rowdy has far less restraints to consider than the gentleman. "Noblesse oblige" was perverted in its application, perhaps, before the Revolution, but it contains a sound principle and a great truth. The higher you go in social attainments, the greater will be the restraints upon you. The gait, the voice, the manner, the rough independence, of one order of men is unbecoming in another. Education above all brings this responsibility. Discipline in manners and morals does not belong to the specific matter of education, but it follows of itself on true education. The educated man must work by himself without any overseer over him. He finds his compulsion in himself and it holds him to his task longer and closer than any external compulsion.

This responsibility to self we call honor, and it is one of the highest fruits of discipline when discipline, having wrought through intellect, has reached character. Honor falls under the rule which I mentioned early in this lecture. You cannot reach it because you want it. You cannot reach it by direct effort. It cannot be taught to you as a literary theory. True honor can only grow in men by the long practice of conduct which is good and noble under motives which are pure. We laugh at the artificial honor of the Middle Ages and despise that of the dueling code, but let us not throw away the kernel with the shell. Honor is a tribunal within one's self whose code is simply the best truth one knows. There are no advocates, no witnesses, and no technicalities. To feel one's self condemned by that tribunal is to feel at discord with one's self and to sustain a wound which rankles longer and stings more deeply than any wound in the body. It is the highest achievement of educational discipline to produce this sense of honor in minds of young men, which gives them a guide in the midst of temptation and at a time when all codes and standards seem to be matter of opinion. I have said some things about lack of discipline in thought and discussion, but that is nothing compared with the lack of discipline in conduct which you see in a man who has never known what honor is, whose whole moral constitution is so formless and flabby that it can perform none of its functions, and who is continually seeking some special plea, or sophistry, or deceptive device for paying homage to the right while he does the wrong. Education ought to act against all this and in favor of a high code of honor, not simply the education of schools and academies, but that together with the education of home and family. Our great educational institutions ought to have an atmosphere of their own and impose traditions of their own, for the power which controls in the academic community is not the voice of

authority but the voice of academic public opinion. That
might root out falsehood and violence and meanness of
every kind, which no penalties of those in authority could
ever reach; and I submit that such a public opinion would
be becoming in a body of young men of good home advantages and the best educational opportunities the country
affords. Call it high training, or culture, or discipline, or
high breeding, or what you will, it is only the sense of
what we owe to ourselves, and it is greater and greater
according to our opportunities.

THE COÖPERATIVE COMMONWEALTH

THE COÖPERATIVE COMMONWEALTH

NOTE BY THE EDITOR

AMONG Professor Sumner's papers there turned up a curiosity which I do not like to pass over altogether, although it is more appropriate, perhaps, to the purposes of the biographer. Apparently Sumner amused himself, along in the seventies or early eighties, in figuring to himself the state of the world under a socialistic régime of the sort which he was always ridiculing and opposing. He did this by imagining the contents of a socialist newspaper, the *New Era*, of the date July 4, 1950, consisting of editorials, news notes, public announcements, criminal cases, and even a book review. The whole caricatures in high colors the phenomena attending such a régime in its period of exuberance. "The following," he writes, "is a complete and verbatim copy of a [New York City] newspaper of the date given. It is printed on a small quarter sheet of coarse paper. The printing is so bad that it is hard to read, and the typographical errors, all of which have been corrected, are inexcusable."

The motto of the paper is: "Let the Rich Pay! Let the Poor Enjoy!" The responsible editor is Lasalle Smith, and the proprietors Marx Jones, Chairman of the New York City Board of Ethical Control, Cabet Johnson, Chairman of the Board of Arbitration for Wages and Prices, Babœuf Brown, Chairman of the Board of Control for Rents and Loans, and Rousseau Peters, President of the Coöperative Bank. A notice warns readers that "This paper is published strictly under the coöperative rules

441

established by the Typographical Union in our office and under the direction of the council of the same. The Committee of Grievances gives its assent and approval to each number before it is published. All subscriptions are payable monthly in advance to the Treasurer of the Typographical Union. The Typographical Union, being a member of the organized Coöperative Commonwealth, has police powers for the collection of all sums due to it."

A special notice reads as follows:

We send copies of this edition of our paper to a large number of persons who have not hitherto coöperated in our enterprise but whom we have enrolled until they signify their refusal. We call especial attention to the names and standing in the Coöperative Commonwealth of the proprietors of this journal. We believe that many of those whom we now invite to coöperate, and who have been under suspicion of being monopolists, capitalists, recalcitrants, and reactionists, will see that they cannot better establish their credit for civism than by accepting our invitation.

The following extracts are from the editorials:

Our reports of the Ethical Tribunal show that our noble Board of Ethical Control needs to guard diligently our interests. Another pestilent preacher has been condemned to the chain gang. At least we make sure that our streets will be cleaned, a task which no coöperators could be asked to perform, since all the ancient lawyers, professors, and preachers are now condemned to this business. The stubbornness and incorrigibility of these classes towards the Commonwealth is astonishing.

The Board of Ethical Control announce as the result of the plébiscite which was taken on April 1 last, that, by a vote of 5319 to 782, the Commonwealth voted to retain the present Board of Ethical Control for ten years, instead of reëlecting them annually as heretofore. This is as it should be. Why disturb the tranquillity of our happy state by constant elections when our affairs are entrusted to such competent hands?

The agents of the Board of Ethical Control reported 213 persons found dead in the streets at the dawn of day, 174 bearing marks of violence; the rest, not having coöperators' tickets, were ancient monopolists who had apparently perished of want. The Grand Coöperator said that he should submit to the Board of Ethical Control the question whether it is edifying to continue these reports.

———————

There follow extracts from the inaugural of G. P. M. C.[1] Lasalle Brown, which begin with the sentiment:

Of old ye were enslaved by those who said: Work! Save! Study! We emancipate you by saying: Enjoy! Enjoy! Enjoy!

The first right of everyone born on this earth is the right to enjoy. The Coöperative Commonwealth assures this right to all its members.

We have not abolished private property. We only hold that every man is considered to have devoted his property to public use. We have not abolished landlords, capitalists, employers, or captains of industry. We retain and use them. Such members of a society are useful and necessary if only they be held firmly in check and forced to contribute to the public good.

We need "history" and "statistics" to batter down all the old system, but we should be the dupes of our own

———

[1] These initials, as will be seen below, mean Grand Passed Master Coöperator, while G. C. indicates the lower grade of Grand Coöperator.

processes if we used them against ourselves. All sensible coöperators should know that history and statistics are far greater swindles than science.

There are dangers in the Coöperative Commonwealth which demand vigilance. There is danger of jealousy and division amongst coöperators. Harmony is essential to the Coöperative Commonwealth and we must have it at any price.

Some say that our Commonwealth is weak. It is the strongest state that ever existed. No one before our time ever knew the power of a "mob," as it used to be called. At a tap of the bell, every coöperator is at hand. Our only danger is factious division of this power. Let every co-operator have rewards for harmony and penalties for faction — strict, sure, and heavy!

There is danger from science. The evolution heresy is a worse foe to coöperation than the old Christian dogma. Stamp it out!

There is danger from the virus of the old anarchism — worst of all because it is often enough like the truth to deceive the elect. It means liberty and individualism. Stamp it out!

Under the heading "Domestic News" occurs the following:

The Commissioners of Emigration have detected several persons striving to leave the city for Long Island, carrying gold with them. It is well known that many rich persons, animated by selfishness and disregarding their duties as trustees of their wealth for the public, have escaped to the wilds of Long Island beyond the Commune of Brooklyn, carrying with them all the gold which they could obtain. Hence the Commissioners of Emigration have arranged to patrol the East River by the Commonwealth galleys and have limited the ferry transits to the Fulton ferry between 8 and 9 A.M. and 5 and 6 P.M. Any persons found carrying away gold will be sent to the galleys and the gold confiscated. Gold is needed to buy supplies for the Commonwealth.

No dispatches from Philadelphia have been received for a fortnight. A steamboat of 100 tons burden is cruising in the Hudson River, taking toll of all goods in transit across the river. Reports disagree as to the character of the persons on this boat. By some it is asserted to be manned by coöperators who, being poor, are putting into effect ethical claims against material goods. By others it is said to be manned by a gang of monopolist scoundrels and vagabonds, who, driven to desperation by the boycott and plan of campaign, seek this means to perpetuate their existence. It behooves the Board of Ethical Control to learn which of these reports is correct before taking action.

A report comes from the West that the Indians have seized Illinois, killing the whites and taking possession of the improvements. They have imbibed the ancient capitalistic notions and are impervious to ethical and coöperative doctrines. They are rapidly increasing in numbers, strange as it may seem, for we have read in ancient books that they were dying out a century ago. It is suggested that they now increase because they are conquering, and that they will go on doing so until they exterminate all whites from the continent. In the absence of private mails, we humbly suggest that our Board of Ethical Control should communicate with similar boards of the communes to the westward.

Under the heading "Industrial":

The Board of Equalization of Production have set the amounts of various commodities which may be produced during the coming fall season. Those whom it concerns are to call at the office of the Board at once, pay the fees, and obtain their instructions. The penalty of over-production is fixed at 100 coöperative units per unit of product, half to the informer.

The Board of Arbitration for Contracts will sit daily at their office in Coöperative Hall from 10 to 12 A.M. to approve of contracts. The fee is 1000 coöperative units from each party. Notice is called to the ordinance of the Board of Ethical Control: "If two or more persons make a contract without the presence and approval of the Board of Arbitration or otherwise than in conformity with the regulations of said Board, they may be fined according to the circumstances of the case."

The Coöperative Railroad Commission, having found a mechanic to repair the locomotive, announce that they will recommence regular weekly trips to Yonkers on next Monday. A train will start at 9 A.M., or as soon thereafter as convenient. Accommodation for twenty-five passengers. Passports may be obtained until noon on Saturday. They must be viséd by the Railroad Commission and by the Coöperative Guardians of Public Morals at their office in the Coöperative Workhouse not later than two o'clock on the same time. The fare to Yonkers will be 10,000 coöperative units. On account of the inter-county commerce law, all freight and passengers will be trans-shipped at Yonkers. To prevent vexatious inquiries, the Commission hereby announce that they are not informed whether or when trains will be dispatched to points beyond.

Since the Commonwealth was founded, as our readers know, coöperators have refused to work in coal mines. No great harm has come of this since the factories and machinery have been abolished and railroads and steamers have almost gone out of use. Some coal, however, is a convenience, and our readers will see with pleasure that delinquents in considerable numbers are being sent to these mines under an agreement with our Board of Ethical Control with the similar authority of the Lehigh Commune in the ancient state of Pennsylvania.

We are informed that a number of ancient capitalists and monopolists, being in a starving condition, recently applied to the Board of the said Commune for leave to go into an abandoned coal mine and work it for their own support.

A week ago yesterday, Coöperative Association 2391, A. P. D., bricklayers, 7824, M. X. H., plasterers, 4823 N. K. J., hodcarriers, F. L. M. 8296, joiners, met to consider the state of the building trades. On account of the decrease in the population, by which great numbers of houses are vacant, building has ceased for years past and these once great associations have dwindled down. The Board of Ethical Control has caused public buildings to be constructed in order to give them work and has ordered landlords to make repairs to the same end. The conference on Friday, a week ago, was to consider further measures of relief. It was decided that no vacant house ought to be allowed to stand. Some maintained that no repairs ought to be allowed at all, in order that new houses might become necessary, but others thought that this would take away what little work is now obtained. G. C. Marx Rogers, former professor of political economy, made a speech in which he proposed that all houses now vacant and all ruins now standing which give shelter to unregistered vagabonds and boycotted persons should be destroyed; also that a committee be appointed to inspect all existing dwellings, mark those which are out of repair and unfit for coöperative residences, and that these latter should then be razed to the ground. This would cause an immediate demand for new houses. This proposition was unanimously adopted.

On Wednesday last the coöperative associations aforesaid met to hear the report of the committee. Twelve hundred and forty-seven houses had been noted so far as unfit for residences. The joint associations passed a decree against said houses, as a beginning, and ordered the committee of the whole to proceed to execute it.

They marched in a body to Bleecker Street, the northernmost limit of the ruined houses and demolished them entirely. They then moved southerly, destroying all vacant houses. Gradually, a number of persons gathered to look on. The agents of Ethical Supervision kept this crowd at a distance and secured the joint Coöperative Associations full independence in the execution of their decree.

In East Canal Street, Nonconformist Jonathan Merritt, lessee of a block of tenements, tried to dissuade or prevent the destruction of his buildings. He was roughly handled, his skull split open and his arm broken by the coöperators. The agents of Ethical Supervision took him in on a charge of disturbing the public peace.

When it came to the destruction of occupied buildings, the tenants objected. By the ordinance of the Board of Lodgings and Rents, each had been allotted to his domicile and was, of course, bound to keep it until allowed to change. It was also feared that no lodgings could be found. The Board of Lodgings and Rents immediately convened and issued new allotments of domicile. Suspects, nonconformists, recalcitrants, and reactionists were sent to lodge in the ancient churches and the coöperators were assigned to their tenements.

The revival and prosperity of the building trades is now assured.

Under the heading "Misdemeanors":

Of all forms of incivism, the most reprehensible is hoarding gold. All good coöperators who know of cases of this criminal selfishness are bound to report it at the Bureau of Ethical Supervision under penalty of incivism on the one hand and a reward of ten per cent of the sum on the other. All gold must be exchanged at the bank of G. C. Cabet Rogers for coöperative units.

An audacious lampoon has been printed at some secret press, the authors of which must be discovered at all cost. It is a blasphemous parody of the Coöperative Catechism. The Commission of Ethical Inquiry has directed all its powerful machinery to detect the authors of this outrage. Let every coöperator oppoint himself a detective to help. Search every house in your neighborhood! Trust nobody! Every person found in possession of a copy of this pamphlet will be summarily removed from the Commonwealth.

The supply of potatoes which forms the staple food of the mass of our population is obtained from the northern part of the commune, in what was formerly Westchester County. The great fields there are tilled by the delinquents under taxes and fines, incorrigible monopolists, survival capitalists and others under judicial sentence, under the direction of the Board of Ethical Control. The convicts work from sunrise to sunset, in order to mark the distinction between them and honorable coöperators, who work but five hours per day. The product of the fields on its way to the town is subjected to toll by the free coöperative associations of the suburbs. Hence it always threatens to be inadequate. Good coöperators cannot better serve the Commonwealth than by ferreting out violators of the ordinances and other persons guilty of incivism.

Karl Marx Jones, agent of the Board of Equalization of Distribution, has disappeared. It is thought that he has gone towards Boston. He reported to the Board, it will be remembered, two weeks ago, a case of hoarding of gold. He was sent to collect it and was made custodian of it. It has disappeared. The Board count upon the aid of communes to the eastward to recover the gold, but not very confidently. He left all his coöperative units behind him.

Ordinances of the Committee of Inquiry appears as follows :

Boycotts are declared against Robert Dorr, for saying that the Coöperative Commonwealth is only a scheme to let a few exploit all the rest; Matthew Brown, for saying that it is all a woman's honor is worth to appear on the street of the Coöperative Commonwealth, even thickly veiled, for she runs the risk of attracting the attention of someone against whom no one can defend her; James Rowe, for refusing to aid the agents of the society in taking from her home without public scandal a woman charged with incivism; John White, for hiding gold coin; William Peck, for saying that Grand Coöperator Lasalle Brown secured the boycott of Elihu Snow to get his property away from him; Edward Grant, for saying that the Coöperative Commonwealth is only slavery in disguise and the treatment of persons convicted of incivism is slavery without disguise; Peter Moon, for saying that the Plan of Campaign is only a scheme to allow a man's debtors to rob him of a small fraction of their debts if they will let some of the Grand Coöperators rob him of all the remainder.

A considerable number of minor offences are tried before Grand Coöperator Rodbertus Pease, Member of the Board of Ethical Control:

George Wood, aged sixty, was arraigned for carrying a pistol at night, not being a member of any coöperative club and therefore not entitled so to do. He declared that the streets were unsafe at night and that he never went out after dark if he could help it, but that he was compelled to go for a doctor for his sick grandchild and took the pistol for security. He was met by two coöperators who asked him to contribute to the Aged Coöperators' Retreat. On his declaring that he had nothing, they searched him and found the pistol. They then demanded his coöperator's ticket. As he had none, they took him to the Bureau of Ethical Supervision, where he was detained until morning. The two complainants appeared against him. They declared that they were poor men. On examination it appeared that he was an incorrigible adherent of the ancient monopolism. He was fined 10,000 coöperative units, half to the informers. He began to lament at this, saying that he was very poor — poorer than the complainants; but the Grand Coöperator declared that no man could be a poor man who was not a coöperator.

The Emigration Commissioners whose sole duty is to prevent any immigrants from coming into our commune put at the bar Fritz Meyer, charged with immigrating. He pretended to be a sailor on the *Ferdinand Lasalle*, but did not return on board of her before she sailed. In defence he pleaded that he was left by accident. He was condemned to serve on the yacht of the Board of Ethical Control at the pleasure of said Board.

Ulysses Perkins and others, some of whom were coöperators and some not, complained that their neighborhood was annoyed by the Coöperative Brotherhood who hold their evening festivals at Coöperative Hall. They declared that there was shouting and singing and that windows were broken in spite of the heavy shutters. Their complaint was dismissed as an attempt to oppress organized labor, and the coöperators amongst them were especially reprimanded. The Grand Coöperator remarked that the prejudice against beer which was manifested in ancient prohibitory and license laws was not respected by the ethical judgment of our time.

On Monday last, several persons appeared to complain that the roads outside of the city are infested by robbers. They were detained and the Board of Ethical Control sent out delegates to inquire. They reported yesterday, when the complainants were brought before the tribunal to hear their report. They denied that there was any robbery, since robbery means undue exaction of rent or of work for wages. The word was used by the complainants in the ancient capitalistic sense. The delegates found many coöperators enjoying holiday in the fields and by the wayside. Some of them were playful and resented the exclusive manner of passers-by who did not engage in sport. They asked for treats, and they had appointed a committee to solicit funds for their games. Some bands of banished monopolists were reported to be infesting the woods, living by chance or by tilling some small fields which have not been allotted to them, and plotting against the Commonwealth. The Grand Coöperator said that such persons would be promptly dealt with and dispatched a force of guardians of Ethical Order against them. The complainants were discharged with a reprimand for misrepresenting the innocent enjoyment of the coöperators in the suburb.

William Johnson, employer, was arraigned for contumacy. The Board of Arbitration ordered him to pay 1000 coöperative units per day of six hours. He closed his works. The Grand Coöperator ordered a second charge for malicious lockout and fined him 10,000 coöperative units per day until he should reopen his works.

Eliza Marcy, cook, actress, 26, was charged with defamation of Emily Wilson, coöperative seamstress. The accused presented a certificate of patronage from G. M. C. Brissot Robinson and was discharged from custody, a rescript of the charge being transmitted to G. M. C. Robinson for such action as he should deem proper.

Maria Waters, arraigned for working at type-setting below man's rates, pleaded poverty and distress as an excuse. She is the daughter of an ancient monopolist from whom she inherited $100,000 before the abolition of inheritance. She had therefore been denied admittance to any coöperative society. She was fined 1000 coöperative units and sent to the Ethical Workhouse to work it out.

Patrick Boyle, coöperative bricklayer, for mending his own table, he not being a member of the furniture-makers' union, was arraigned as a scab and sentenced to forfeit his coöperative ticket, be graded as a non-conformist, and pay 1000 coöperative units fine. Being unable to pay, he was put under G. M. C. Scroggs to work it out.

Under "Benefits and Amusements":

In addition to the three regular Labor Days of July, the 10th, 20th, and 30th, the Board of Ethical Control has decreed an extra one on the 18th, with full wages. Commonwealth galleys will be ready to convey coöperators and their families to Blackwell's Island, where the dancing and dining rooms in the ancient prisons of despotism will be arranged for their entertainment. There will be a free circus at 3 P.M. and a free variety entertainment in the evening. The two latter have been provided by the liberality of G. P. M. C. Lasalle Brown.

Rents remitted for June and all arrears before January 1.

All coöperators in good standing are entitled to pensions of 100 coöperative units per week, with rations of coöperative bread and beer.

The agents of the Board of Equalization of Distribution will begin next Monday the distribution of July pensions to all coöperators in good and regular standing. The agents will call at the residences of coöperators. There has been some delay which has occasioned just murmurs. It has been due to delinquencies of tax-payers, amongst whom not a little old capitalistic virus remains.

Masked Ball on every Sunday evening in the ancient Trinity Church. Coöperative Enjoyment Association. Admission 100 c. u. All persons must wear coöperative medals displayed.

" Foreign News " reports the following débâcle:

It will be remembered that about three years ago the last remnant of English landlords was exiled to Guiana. The Commune of London granted them a ship, of which an immense number blocked the Thames, not having occupation, and they were allowed to navigate it if they could. Their children were taken away from them, to be educated in the principles of coöperation. From this mistaken complaisance a series of evil consequences have flowed.

Some of the exiles have had yachting experience and most of them, being trained in the ancient athletic sports, were able to navigate the ship. Instead of obeying the law, they sailed to Gibraltar and captured the ancient fortress. There they obtained arms and cannons, of which they put a number on board their ship and returned to London. Their first step was to seize the *Columbus*, a fine steamer of 1000 tons burden, one of the newest and in best repair of those lying in the river. They then filled her bunkers with coal and wood which they took by force from the Commonwealth barges in the river. They next seized the arsenals at Greenwich and Norwich, carried off a great number of repeating rifles and ammunition, and destroyed all the rest. The coöperators of London, being taken unawares and being prepared only to cope with the city monopolists, who had been disarmed, were unable to interfere.

The pirates moored their vessel opposite the city and sent a message of the G. P. M. C. by a captured coöperator that they would bombard the city if their children were not all delivered to them. A hundred of them landed with repeating rifles and revolvers and marched to the coöperative factories, where they set free all who chose to join them. In short, they departed after securing their children, a vast quantity of tools and machinery, arms, supplies, and ammunition. A large number of flunkies and snobs joined them, sufficient to man one or two other vessels.

It now appears that they have taken possession of the Island of Sicily and made it a base of concentration for a grand political reaction. They have proclaimed as far as possible that their island is a refuge for landlords, monopolists, and capitalists, and the roads of Europe are crowded with vagabonds seeking to reach this nest of pirates. The pirate state is growing. It is a republic like one of our ancient states. It has an army of 5000 men who boast that with the arms which they possess they can march from one end of Europe to another. They control the Mediterranean and all its coasts. They have served notice on the communal commonwealths of the Continent that they will avenge any coercion exercised against any persons who seek to join them, and six months ago they sent a force of 6000 men to Lyons to set free a band of aristocrats who were imprisoned there and were threatened with the guillotine.

It is said that there are no artisans now who are able to manufacture repeating rifles like those which these robbers possess, except amongst themselves — they having hired mechanics to recover the art. Even the guns yet remaining on the Continent cannot be used because the art of making the ammunition is lost. It was a great mistake to let these pestilent scoundrels loose. Their state threatens the whole coöperative movement. Its existence has greatly strengthened the collectivists among coöperators, for it is said that the big empires must be restored (on coöperative principles) to cope with them.

"Personal Items" record the following:

G. P. M. C. Lasalle Brown last evening gave a grand ball and house-warming in his new house on Fifth Avenue. By demolishing and removing the unsightly ruined houses in the neighborhood, a beautiful park and garden have been added to this fine tenement. It was illuminated last evening by thousands of lamps and torches carried by the convicts who are under discipline in the household of the G. P. M. C. The guests were members of the Board of Ethical Control and their families, some of whom, remembering their own antecedents, observed with interest amongst the convicts sons and daughters of ancient monopolists, and in some cases white-haired survivals from the age of bankers, railroad kings, and merchant princes. Such are the revenges of history!

One hundred new carriages for the Board of Ethical Control have just arrived. They are of the most superb workmanship and cost $5000 in gold each. They belong, of course, to the Commonwealth and can only be used under permission of the Board of Ethical Control. They have been put, one each, under the care of separate members of the Board, as no private individual is allowed to violate equality by owning a carriage. We noticed with pleasure yesterday the families of Grand Coöperators in these carriages in the park.

Non-conformists and others like them outside the pale of the Commonwealth have, of late years, when they found their position disagreeable, adopted the plan of attaching themselves voluntarily as retainers or vassals to coöperators, especially to the leading members of the Board of Ethical Control. In this way they secure some of the advantages of coöperation. In order to show their position and relationship, they wear special tokens or marks. The clients of the newly inaugurated G. P. M. C. have just been put into uniform or livery. They attended him in a body on his recent visit to his country seat at Riverdale, where they did guard duty. Added to his personal bodyguard of coöperators and friends, they made an imposing body. This country-seat, by the way, has just been surrounded by a high stone wall.

There occurs an obituary of one of the community's leading lights :

G. C. Brissot Cunningham died at 01 Fifth Avenue on Wednesday last. He was born May 16, 1905 and was educated for a lawyer. In 1930, putting himself in the foremost rank of the coöperative movement and identifying himself with the most radical section, he was admitted to the bar. By the abolition of inheritance, he found himself, on the death of his father in the following year, thrown entirely on his own resources. He then passed through some years of obscurity and great poverty, which taught him to feel for the poor.

Allying himself with the noble band which supported our present G. P. M. C., he helped to bring about the foundation of the coöperation in 1940 and was elected member of the Board of Ethical Control. In the Board he filled many of the most important and responsible positions on the several committees and was regularly reëlected. He devoted himself to securing the Commonwealth, flinching from no measure to establish it. He believed thoroughly in the motto "Enjoy." After he became a member of the Board of Ethical Control, the former mansion of the ——s on Fifth Avenue was allotted to him and furnished from the Commonwealth storehouse of forfeited property. He there kept up a munificent hospitality on the most altruistic principles. He neither cared to know whence his income came nor whither it went. In the spirit of a true coöperator, whatever belonged to the Commonwealth was his and whatever was his was free to any coöperator. His popularity with the masses was shown yesterday when they turned out in a body for his funeral. The non-coöperators who had felt his scourge were naturally absent. A few of them who could not conceal their joy at his death were summarily corrected by the coöperators. By his death at the early age of forty-five, our Commonwealth has lost a valuable supporter.

[According to the ordinance adopted by the Board of Ethical Control, February 10, 1945, since he died a member of the Board, his family will have a pension of $15,000 per annum in gold for twenty-five years and the use of his house for the same time. The Board will fill the vacancy next week. — Editor of this paper.]

The *Text-book of Coöperation*, ordained by the Board of Ethical Control for schools, is reviewed as follows:

This book is an authoritative exposition of the Coöperative Commonwealth in the commune form. It is to supersede all other books except the primer, writing-book, and elementary arithmetic. We have done with all the ancient rubbish. All the books which have not been destroyed are under the control of the Board of Ethical Control. Especially we are now rid of all pernicious trash about history, law, and political economy. The present book contains all that a good coöperator needs to know. Its tone is strictly ethical. By separating all children of incorrigibles and survivals from their parents and educating them on this book, we may soon hope to bring all capitalistic tradition to an end.

It is plainly proved here that the first right of every man and woman is the right to capital. This right is valid up to the time when he or she gets capital, when it becomes ethically subject to the similar right of someone else, who has no capital as yet, to have some. This principle carried out is the guarantee of justice and equality and is the fundamental principle of the Coöperative Commonwealth in the middle of the twentieth century.

The text-book describes the organization of our Commonwealth, with the duties of coöperators, and gives a list of the ordinances of the Board of Control.

There are now 1000 members of the Board of Ethical Control and 10,000 agents in their employ, chosen by lot monthly from all coöperators. The Board is divided into ten Boards of 100 each for various branches of duty. The members receive no salary but are remunerated by fees. They enjoy no privileges or rights in the Commonwealth, but have the duty of regulating all coöperative affairs according to their conscientious convictions of justice. The ten chairmen of Boards form an exclusive commission which decrees boycotts and plans of campaign. There are no laws or lawyers in the system and no courts or juries of the ancient type, now happily almost forgotten. There are no police, no detectives, no army, no militia, and no prisons. The ancient prison at Sing Sing, which is now within the limits of this commune, is turned into a Coöperators' Retreat. Under this happy régime no coöperator can do wrong. Our only culprits are recalcitrants, suspects, incorrigibles, survivals, and other would-be perpetuators of the old régime of monoply and capitalistic extortion. Such persons are compelled to expiate their selfishness and incivism by hard labor, but they are taken for this purpose into the households or factories of the members of the Board of Ethical Control, where they are subject to ethical discipline and produce those things which are essential to the community and which the Board of Ethical Control contracts to provide. The employments are such as free coöperators consider disagreeable, unhealthy, or degrading.

The Committee of Inquiry into Incivism is a committee of the Board of Ethical Control and has the high and important duty of watching over coöperative duties. Its number and members are unknown, lest they should be objects of malice. Its sessions and procedure are secret. It employs 100 agents but has a right to command the services at any time of all coöperators. Complaints of incivism may be lodged night or day by any coöperator in the lion's mouth in the court of the Coöperative Hall (ancient United States postoffice).

The Committee proceeds against persons guilty of incivism by boycotts chiefly. This measure puts the culprit outside the pale of the Commonwealth which he has maligned or in which he has refused to take his share. Such persons become vagabonds, and disappear or perish.

The chapter on coöperative religion is in the form of a catechism and is to be thoroughly learned by heart by all pupils. It inculcates the doctrines of our social creed by which each one is bound to serve the health, wealth, and happiness of every other. Those who have the means of material enjoyment shall put them at the disposition and use of those who have them not. It impresses above all the great duty of civism, or conformity to coöperative organization and obedience to the Board of Ethical Control.

There is complete equality and no distinction of class in the Coöperative Commonwealth. Every man, woman, and child is eligible to the Board of Ethical Control. The only distinction is of merit and service to the Commonwealth. In this the members of the Board of Ethical Control stand first. There is no second. Outside of the Coöperative Committee are, in order of demerit and detestation, probationers (coöperators who have forfeited their coöperative tickets for fault but who may be restored to membership), survivals (employers, capitalists, landlords, usurers, subject to the Commonwealth and continuing the ancient functions of such persons), nonconformists (stubborn persons who refuse to conform to the new order), recalcitrants (any of the former who have been subject to discipline five times), incorrigibles (after twenty cases of discipline), suspects (so decreed if charged but not convicted of incivism), reactionists (once coöperators but convicted of disorganization) and convicts (under boycott or plan of compaign). Every person must be registered and have always on his person a brass medal hung by a chain about his neck, bearing his designation and number, with the letters designating his group, domicile, also district, ward, and arrondissement. This constitutes his social designation. These medals are given out by the Board of Ethical Supervision. The fee is 1000 coöperative units, repeated each time that the person is re-classified and a new medal issued.

Advertisements are included, as, for example:

John Moon, licensed to sell pistols and ammunition. A few revolvers newly imported from the commune of Hartford at great difficulty and expense. Bliss Bldg.

Henry Black, pistols and bowie-knives. Sales strictly

within the ordinances. Every purchaser required to show coöperator's ticket, and sales registered. 268 Felicity Boulevard.

Elias Israel, pawn broker, loans at 10% per month on coöperative private property only. Sales of forfeited goods every Sunday. 618 Joy Avenue.

The editor has no compunction about publishing these extracts, though it may be objected that they can be at most of historical or personal interest. Perhaps, in the light of the antics of the Bolsheviki, even such a parody as the foregoing may seem less wide of the potentialities of the socialistic system. In any case, if modern socialism has renounced some of the wild dreams of its past, that is largely owing to the criticism and ridicule poured upon them by vigorous opponents of the Sumner type. Says a prominent American, writing to the editor subsequently to the publication of one of the foregoing volumes of this series: "I have for many years publicly and privately urged socialists to read — *really* read — Sumner — as the most doughty and competent foe with whom they have to reckon."

THE FORGOTTEN MAN

THE FORGOTTEN MAN

[1883]

I PROPOSE in this lecture to discuss one of the most subtile and widespread social fallacies. It consists in the impression made on the mind for the time being by a particular fact, or by the interests of a particular group of persons, to which attention is directed while other facts or the interests of other persons are entirely left out of account. I shall give a number of instances and illustrations of this in a moment, and I cannot expect you to understand what is meant from an abstract statement until these illustrations are before you, but just by way of a general illustration I will put one or two cases.

Whenever a pestilence like yellow fever breaks out in any city, our attention is especially attracted towards it, and our sympathies are excited for the sufferers. If contributions are called for, we readily respond. Yet the number of persons who die prematurely from consumption every year greatly exceeds the deaths from yellow fever or any similar disease when it occurs, and the suffering entailed by consumption is very much greater. The suffering from consumption, however, never constitutes a public question or a subject of social discussion. If an inundation takes place anywhere, constituting a public calamity (and an inundation takes place somewhere in the civilized world nearly every year), public attention is attracted and public appeals are made, but the losses by great inundations must be insignificant compared with the losses by runaway horses, which, taken separately, scarcely obtain mention in a local newspaper. In hard times insolvent debtors are a large class. They constitute an interest and are able to attract public attention, so that social philosophers discuss their troubles and legislatures plan measures of relief. Insolvent debtors, however, are an insignificant body compared with the victims of commonplace misfortune, or accident, who are isolated, scattered, ungrouped and ungeneralized, and so are never made the object of discussion or relief. In seasons of ordinary prosperity, persons who become insolvent have to get out of their troubles as they can. They have no hope of relief from the legislature. The number of insolvents during a series of years of general prosperity, and their losses, greatly exceed the number and losses during a special period of distress.

These illustrations bring out only one side of my subject, and that only partially. It is when we come to the proposed measures of relief for the evils which have caught public attention that we reach the real subject which deserves our attention. As soon as A observes something which seems to him to be wrong, from which X is suffering, A talks it over with B, and A and B then propose to get a law passed to remedy the evil and help X. Their law always proposes to determine what C shall do for X or, in the better case, what A, B and C shall do for X. As for A and B, who get a law to make themselves do for X what they are willing to do for him, we have nothing to say except that they might better have done it without any law, but what I want to do is to look up C. I want to show you what manner of man he is. I call him the Forgotten Man. Perhaps the appellation is not strictly correct. He is the man who never is thought of. He is the victim of the reformer, social speculator and philanthropist, and I hope to show you before I get through that he deserves your notice both for his character and for the many burdens which are laid upon him.

No doubt one great reason for the phenomenon which I bring to your attention is the passion for reflection and generalization which marks our period. Since the printing press has come into such wide use, we have all been encouraged to philosophize about things in a way which was unknown to our ancestors. They lived their lives out in positive contact with actual cases as they arose. They had little of this analysis, introspection, reflection and speculation which have passed into a habit and almost into a disease with us. Of all things which tempt to generalization and to philosophizing, social topics stand foremost. Each one of us gets some experience of social forces. Each one has some chance for observation of social phenomena. There is certainly no domain in which generalization is easier. There is nothing about which people dogmatize more freely. Even men of scientific training in some department in which they would not tolerate dogmatism at all will not hesitate to dogmatize in the most reckless manner about social topics. The truth is, however, that science, as yet, has won less control of social phenomena than of any other class of phenomena. The most complex and difficult subject which we now have to study is the constitution of human society, the forces which operate in it, and the laws by which they act, and we know less about these things than about any others which demand our attention. In such a state of things, over-hasty generalization is sure to be extremely mischievous. You cannot take up a magazine or newspaper without being struck by the feverish interest with which social topics and problems are discussed, and if you were a student of social science, you would find in almost all these discussions evidence, not only that the essential preparation for the discussion is wanting, but that the disputants do not even know that there is any preparation to be gained. Consequently we are bewildered by contradictory dogmatizing. We find in all these discussions only the application of pet notions and the clashing of contradictory "views." Remedies are confidently proposed for which there is no guarantee offered except that the person who prescribes the remedy says that he is sure it will work. We hear constantly of "reform," and the reformers turn out to be people who do not like things as they are and wish that they could be made nicer. We hear a great many exhortations to make progress from people who do not know in what direction they want to go. Consequently social reform is the most barren and tiresome subject of discussion amongst us, except æsthetics.

I suppose that the first chemists seemed to be very hardhearted and unpoetical persons when they scouted the glorious dream of the alchemists that there must be some process for turning base metals into gold. I suppose that the men who first said, in plain, cold assertion, there is no fountain of eternal youth, seemed to be the most cruel and cold-hearted adversaries of human happiness. I know that the economists who say that if we could transmute lead into gold, it would certainly do us no good and might do great harm, are still regarded as unworthy of belief. Do not the money articles of the newspapers yet ring with the doctrine that we are getting rich when we give cotton and wheat for gold rather than when we give cotton and wheat for iron?

Let us put down now the cold, hard fact and look at it just as it is. There is no device whatever to be invented for securing happiness without industry, economy, and virtue. We are yet in the empirical stage as regards all our social devices. We have done something in science and art in the domain of production, transportation and exchange. But when you come to the laws of the social order, we know very little about them. Our laws and institutions by which we attempt to regulate our lives under the laws of nature which control society are merely a series

of haphazard experiments. We come into collision with
the laws and are not intelligent enough to understand
wherein we are mistaken and how to correct our errors.
We persist in our experiments instead of patiently setting
about the study of the laws and facts in order to see where
we are wrong. Traditions and formulæ have a dominion ·
over us in legislation and social customs which we seem
unable to break or even to modify.

For my present purpose I ask your attention for a few
moments to the notion of liberty, because the Forgotten
Man would no longer be forgotten where there was true
liberty. You will say that you know what liberty is.
There is no term of more common or prouder use. None
is more current, as if it were quite beyond the need of
definition. Even as I write, however, I find in a leading
review a new definition of civil liberty. Civil liberty the
writer declares to be "the result of the restraint exercised
by the sovereign people on the more powerful individuals
and classes of the community, preventing them from availing
themselves of the excess of their power to the detriment of
the other classes." You notice here the use of the words
"sovereign people" to designate a class of the population,
not the nation as a political and civil whole. Wherever
"people" is used in such a sense, there is always fallacy.
Furthermore, you will recognize in this definition a very
superficial and fallacious construction of English constitutional history. The writer goes on to elaborate that
construction and he comes out at last with the conclusion
that "a government by the people can, in no case, become
a paternal government, since its law-makers are its manda-
taries and servants carrying out its will, and not its fathers
or its masters." This, then, is the point at which he
desires to arrive, and he has followed a familiar device in
setting up a definition to start with which would produce
the desired deduction at the end.

In the definition the word "people" was used for a class or section of the population. It is now asserted that if *that* section rules, there can be no paternal, that is, undue, government. That doctrine, however, is the very opposite of liberty and contains the most vicious error possible in politics. The truth is that cupidity, selfishness, envy, malice, lust, vindictiveness, are constant vices of human nature. They are not confined to classes or to nations or particular ages of the world. They present themselves in the palace, in the parliament, in the academy, in the church, in the workshop, and in the hovel. They appear in autocracies, theocracies, aristocracies, democracies, and ochlocracies all alike. They change their masks somewhat from age to age and from one form of society to another. All history is only one long story to this effect: men have struggled for power over their fellow-men in order that they might win the joys of earth at the expense of others and might shift the burdens of life from their own shoulders upon those of others. It is true that, until this time, the proletariat, the mass of mankind, have rarely had the power and they have not made such a record as kings and nobles and priests have made of the abuses they would perpetrate against their fellow-men when they could and dared. But what folly it is to think that vice and passion are limited by classes, that liberty consists only in taking power away from nobles and priests and giving it to artisans and peasants and that these latter will never abuse it! They will abuse it just as all others have done unless they are put under checks and guarantees, and there can be no civil liberty anywhere unless rights are guaranteed against all abuses, as well from proletarians as from generals, aristocrats, and ecclesiastics.

Now what has been amiss in all the old arrangements? The evils of the old military and aristocratic governments was that some men enjoyed the fruits of other men's labor;

that some persons' lives, rights, interests and happiness were sacrificed to other persons' cupidity and lust. What have our ancestors been striving for, under the name of civil liberty, for the last five hundred years? They have been striving to bring it about that each man and woman might live out his or her life according to his or her own notions of happiness and up to the measure of his or her own virtue and wisdom. How have they sought to accomplish this? They have sought to accomplish it by setting aside all arbitrary personal or class elements and introducing the reign of law and the supremacy of constitutional institutions like the jury, the habeas corpus, the independent judiciary, the separation of church and state, and the ballot. Note right here one point which will be important and valuable when I come more especially to the case of the Forgotten Man: whenever you talk of liberty, you must have *two* men in mind. The sphere of rights of one of these men trenches upon that of the other, and whenever you establish liberty for the one, you repress the other. Whenever absolute sovereigns are subjected to constitutional restraints, you always hear them remonstrate that their liberty is curtailed. So it is, in the sense that their power of determining what shall be done in the state is limited below what it was before and the similar power of other organs in the state is widened. Whenever the privileges of an aristocracy are curtailed, there is heard a similar complaint. The truth is that the line of limit or demarcation between classes as regards civil power has been moved and what has been taken from one class is given to another.

We may now, then, advance a step in our conception of civil liberty. It is the status in which we find the true adjustment of rights between classes and individuals. Historically, the conception of civil liberty has been constantly changing. The notion of rights changes from one generation to another and the conception of civil liberty changes with it. If we try to formulate a true definition of civil liberty as an ideal thing towards which the development of political institutions is all the time tending, it would be this: Civil liberty is the status of the man who is guaranteed by law and civil institutions the exclusive employment of all his own powers for his own welfare.

This definition of liberty or civil liberty, you see, deals only with concrete and actual relations of the civil order. There is some sort of a poetical and metaphysical notion of liberty afloat in men's minds which some people dream about but which nobody can define. In popular language it means that a man may do as he has a mind to. When people get this notion of liberty into their heads and combine with it the notion that they live in a free country and ought to have liberty, they sometimes make strange demands upon the state. If liberty means to be able to do as you have a mind to, there is no such thing in this world. Can the Czar of Russia do as he has a mind to? Can the Pope do as he has a mind to? Can the President of the United States do as he has a mind to? Can Rothschild do as he has a mind to? Could a Humboldt or a Faraday do as he had a mind to? Could a Shakespeare or a Raphael do as he had a mind to? Can a tramp do as he has a mind to? Where is the man, whatever his station, possessions, or talents, who can get any such liberty? There is none. There is a doctrine floating about in our literature that we are born to the inheritance of certain rights. That is another glorious dream, for it would mean that there was something in this world which we got for nothing. But what is the truth? We are born into no right whatever but what has an equivalent and corresponding duty right alongside of it. There is no such thing on this earth as something for nothing. Whatever we inherit of wealth, knowledge, or institutions from the past has been paid for by the labor and sacrifice of preceding generations; and the fact that these gains are carried on, that the race lives and that the race can, at least within some cycle, accumulate its gains, is one of the facts on which civilization rests. The law of the conservation of energy is not simply a law of physics; it is a law of the whole moral universe, and the order and truth of all things conceivable by man depends upon it. If there were any such liberty as that of doing as you have a mind to, the human race would be condemned to everlasting anarchy and war as these erratic wills crossed and clashed against each other. True liberty lies in the equilibrium of rights and duties, producing peace, order, and harmony. As I have defined it, it means that a man's right to take power and wealth out of the social product is measured by the energy and wisdom which he has contributed to the social effort.

Now if I have set this idea before you with any distinctness and success, you see that civil liberty consists of a set of civil institutions and laws which are arranged to act as impersonally as possible. It does not consist in majority rule or in universal suffrage or in elective systems at all. These are devices which are good or better just in the degree in which they secure liberty. The institutions of civil liberty leave each man to run his career in life in his own way, only guaranteeing to him that whatever he does in the way of industry, economy, prudence, sound judgment, etc., shall redound to his own welfare and shall not be diverted to some one else's benefit. Of course it is a necessary corollary that each man shall also bear the penalty of his own vices and his own mistakes. If I want to be free from any other man's dictation, I must understand that I can have no other man under my control.

Now with these definitions and general conceptions in mind, let us turn to the special class of facts to which, as I said at the outset, I invite your attention. We see that under a régime of liberty and equality before the law, we get the highest possible development of independence, self-reliance, individual energy, and enterprise, but we get these high social virtues at the expense of the old senti-mental ties which used to unite baron and retainer, master and servant, sage and disciple, comrade and comrade. We are agreed that the son shall not be disgraced even by the crime of the father, much less by the crime of a more distant relative. It is a humane and rational view of things that each life shall stand for itself alone and not be weighted by the faults of another, but it is useless to deny that this view of things is possible only in a society where the ties of kinship have lost nearly all the intensity of poetry and romance which once characterized them. The ties of sentiment and sympathy also have faded out. We have come, under the régime of liberty and equality before the law, to a form of society which is based not on status, but on free contract. Now a society based on status is one in which classes, ranks, interests, industries, guilds, associations, etc., hold men in permanent relations to each other. Custom and prescription create, under status, ties, the strength of which lies in sentiment. Feeble remains of this may be seen in some of our academical societies to-day, and it is unquestionably a great privilege and advantage for any man in our society to win an experience of the sentiments which belong to a strong and close association, just because the chances for such experience are nowadays very rare. In a society based on free contract, men come together as free and independent parties to an agreement which is of mutual advantage. The relation is rational, even rationalistic. It is not poetical. It does not exist from use and custom, but for reasons given, and it does not endure by prescription but ceases when the reason for it ceases. There is no sentiment in it at all. The fact is that, under the régime of liberty and equality before the law, there is no place for sentiment in trade or politics as public interests. Sentiment is thrown back into private life, into personal relations, and if ever it comes into a public discussion of an impersonal and general public question it always produces mischief.

Now you know that "the poor and the weak" are continually put forward as objects of public interest and public obligation. In the appeals which are made, the terms "the poor" and "the weak" are used as if they were terms of exact definition. Except the pauper, that is to say, the man who cannot earn his living or pay his way, there is no possible definition of a poor man. Except a man who is incapacitated by vice or by physical infirmity, there is no definition of a weak man. The paupers and the physically incapacitated are an inevitable charge on society. About them no more need be said. But the weak who constantly arouse the pity of humanitarians and philanthropists are the shiftless, the imprudent, the negligent, the impractical, and the inefficient, or they are the idle, the intemperate, the extravagant, and the vicious. Now the troubles of these persons are constantly forced upon public attention, as if they and their interests deserved especial consideration, and a great portion of all organized and unorganized effort for the common welfare consists in attempts to relieve these classes of people. I do not wish to be understood now as saying that nothing ought to be done for these people by those who are stronger and wiser. That is not my point. What I want to do is to point out the thing which is overlooked and the error which is made in all these charitable efforts. The notion is accepted as if it were not open to any question that if you help the inefficient and vicious you may gain something for society or you may not, but that you lose nothing. This is a complete mistake. Whatever capital you divert to the support of a shiftless and good-for-nothing person is so much diverted from some other employment, and that means from somebody else. I would spend any conceivable amount of zeal and eloquence if I possessed it to try to make people grasp this idea. Capital is force. If it goes one way it cannot go another. If you give a loaf to a pauper you cannot give the same loaf to a laborer. Now this other man who would have got it but for the charitable sentiment which bestowed it on a worthless member of society is the Forgotten Man. The philanthropists and humanitarians have their minds all full of the wretched and miserable whose case appeals to compassion, attacks the sympathies, takes possession of the imagination, and excites the emotions. They push on towards the quickest and easiest remedies and they forget the real victim.

Now who is the Forgotten Man? He is the simple, honest laborer, ready to earn his living by productive work. We pass him by because he is independent, self-supporting, and asks no favors. He does not appeal to the emotions or excite the sentiments. He only wants to make a contract and fulfill it, with respect on both sides and favor on neither side. He must get his living out of the capital of the country. The larger the capital is, the better living he can get. Every particle of capital which is wasted on the vicious, the idle, and the shiftless is so much taken from the capital available to reward the independent and productive laborer. But we stand with our backs to the independent and productive laborer all the time. We do not remember him because he makes no clamor; but I appeal to you whether he is not the man who ought to be remembered first of all, and whether, on any sound social theory, we ought not to protect him against the burdens of the good-for-nothing. In these last years I have read hundreds of articles and heard scores of sermons and speeches which were really glorifications of the good-for-nothing, as if these were the charge of society, recommended by right reason to its care and protection. We are addressed all the time as if those who are respectable were to blame because some are not so, and as if there were an obligation on the part of those who have done their duty towards those who have not done their duty. Every man is bound to take care of himself and his family and to do his share in the work of society. It is totally false that one who has done so is bound to bear the care and charge of those who are wretched because they have not done so. The silly popular notion is that the beggars live at the expense of the rich, but the truth is that those who eat and produce not, live at the expense of those who labor and produce. The next time that you are tempted to subscribe a dollar to a charity, I do not tell you not to do it, because after you have fairly considered the matter, you may think it right to do it, but I do ask you to stop and remember the Forgotten Man and understand that if you put your dollar in the savings bank it will go to swell the capital of the country which is available for division amongst those who, while they earn it, will reproduce it with increase.

Let us now go on to another class of cases. There are a great many schemes brought forward for "improving the condition of the working classes." I have shown already that a free man cannot take a favor. One who takes a favor or submits to patronage demeans himself. He falls under obligation. He cannot be free and he cannot assert a station of equality with the man who confers the favor on him. The only exception is where there are exceptional bonds of affection or friendship, that is, where the sentimental relation supersedes the free relation. Therefore, in a country which is a free democracy, all propositions to do something for the working classes have an air of patronage and superiority which is impertinent and out of place. No one can do anything for anybody else unless he has a surplus of energy to dispose of after taking care of himself. In the United States, the working classes, technically so called, are the strongest classes. It is they who have a surplus to dispose of if anybody has. Why should anybody else offer to take care of them or to serve them? They can get whatever they think worth having and, at any rate, if they are free men in a free state, it is ignominious and unbecoming to introduce fashions of patronage and favoritism here. A man who, by superior education and experience of business, is in a position to advise a struggling man of the wages class, is certainly held to do so and will, I believe, always be willing and glad to do so; but this sort of activity lies in the range of private and personal relations.

I now, however, desire to direct attention to the public, general, and impersonal schemes, and I point out the fact that, if you undertake to lift anybody, you must have a fulcrum or point of resistance. All the elevation you give to one must be gained by an equivalent depression on some one else. The question of gain to society depends upon the balance of the account, as regards the position of the persons who undergo the respective operations. But nearly all the schemes for "improving the condition of the working man" involve an elevation of some working men at the expense of other working men. When you expend capital or labor to elevate some persons who come within the sphere of your influence, you interfere in the conditions of competition. The advantage of some is won by an equivalent loss of others. The difference is not brought about by the energy and effort of the persons themselves. If it were, there would be nothing to be said about it, for we constantly see people surpass others in the rivalry of life and carry off the prizes which the others must do without. In the cases I am discussing, the difference is brought about by an interference which must be partial, arbitrary, accidental, controlled by favoritism and personal preference. I do not say, in this case, either, that we ought to do no work of this kind. On the contrary, I believe that the arguments for it quite outweigh, in many cases, the arguments against it. What I desire, again, is to bring out the forgotten element which we always need to remember in order to make a wise decision as to any scheme of this kind. I want to call to mind the Forgotten Man, because, in this case also, if we recall him and go to look for him, we shall find him patiently and perseveringly, manfully and independently struggling against adverse circumstances without complaining or begging. If, then, we are led to heed the groaning and complaining of others and to take measures for helping these others, we shall, before we know it, push down this man who is trying to help himself.

Let us take another class of cases. So far we have said nothing about the abuse of legislation. We all seem to be under the delusion that the rich pay the taxes. Taxes are not thrown upon the consumers with any such directness and completeness as is sometimes assumed; but that, in ordinary states of the market, taxes on houses fall, for the most part, on the tenants and that taxes on commodities fall, for the most part, on the consumers, is beyond question. Now the state and municipality go to great expense to support policemen and sheriffs and judicial officers, to protect people against themselves, that is, against the results of their own folly, vice, and recklessness. Who pays for it? Undoubtedly the people who have not been guilty of folly, vice, or recklessness. Out of nothing comes nothing. We cannot collect taxes from people who produce nothing and save nothing. The people who have something to tax must be those who have produced and saved.

When you see a drunkard in the gutter, you are disgusted, but you pity him. When a policeman comes and picks him up you are satisfied. You say that "society" has interfered to save the drunkard from perishing. Society is a fine word, and it saves us the trouble of thinking to say that society acts. The truth is that the policeman is paid by somebody, and when we talk about society we forget who it is that pays. It is the Forgotten Man again. It is the industrious workman going home from a hard day's work, whom you pass without noticing, who is mulcted of a percentage of his day's earnings to hire a policeman to save the drunkard from himself. All the public expenditure to prevent vice has the same effect. Vice is its own curse. If we let nature alone, she cures vice by the most frightful penalties. It may shock you to hear me say it, but when you get over the shock, it will do you good to think of it: a drunkard in the gutter is just where he ought to be. Nature is working away at him to get him out of the way, just as she sets up her processes of dissolution to remove whatever is a failure in its line. Gambling and less mentionable vices all cure themselves by the ruin and dissolution of their victims. Nine-tenths of our measures for preventing vice are really protective towards it, because they ward off the penalty. "Ward off," I say, and that is the usual way of looking at it; but is the penalty really annihilated? By no means. It is turned into police and court expenses and spread over those who have resisted vice. It is the Forgotten Man again who has been subjected to the penalty while our minds were full of the drunkards, spendthrifts, gamblers, and other victims of dissipation. Who is, then, the Forgotten Man? He is the clean, quiet, virtuous, domestic citizen, who pays his debts and his taxes and is never heard of out of his little circle. Yet who is there in the society of a civilized state who deserves to be remembered and considered by the legislator and statesman before this man?

Another class of cases is closely connected with this last. There is an apparently invincible prejudice in people's minds in favor of state regulation. All experience is against state regulation and in favor of liberty. The freer the civil institutions are, the more weak or mischievous state regulation is. The Prussian bureaucracy can do a score of things for the citizen which no governmental organ in the United States can do; and, conversely, if we want to be taken care of as Prussians and Frenchmen are, we must give up something of our personal liberty.

Now we have a great many well-intentioned people among us who believe that they are serving their country when they discuss plans for regulating the relations of employer and employee, or the sanitary regulations of dwellings, or the construction of factories, or the way to behave on Sunday, or what people ought not to eat or drink or smoke. All this is harmless enough and well enough as a basis of mutual encouragement and missionary enterprise, but it is almost always made a basis of legislation. The reformers want to get a majority, that is, to get the power of the state and so to make other people do what the reformers think it right and wise to do. A and B agree to spend Sunday in a certain way. They get a law passed to make C pass it in their way. They determine to be teetotallers and they get a law passed to make C be a teetotaller for the sake of D who is likely to drink too much. Factory acts for women and children are right because women and children are not on an equal footing with men and cannot, therefore, make contracts properly. Adult men, in a free state, must be left to make their own contracts and defend themselves. It will not do to say that some men are weak and unable to make contracts any better than women. Our civil institutions assume that all men are equal in political capacity and all are given equal measure of political power and right, which is not the case with women and children. If, then, we measure political rights by one theory and social responsibilities by another, we produce an immoral and vicious relation. A and B, however, get factory acts and other acts passed regulating the relation of employers and employee and set armies of commissioners and inspectors traveling about to see to things, instead of using their efforts, if any are needed, to lead the free men to make their own conditions as to what kind of factory buildings they will work in, how many hours they will work, what they will do on Sunday and so on. The consequence is that men lose the true education in freedom which is needed to support free institutions. They are taught to rely on government officers and inspectors. The whole system of government inspectors is corrupting to free institutions. In England, the liberals used always to regard state regulation with suspicion, but since they have come to power, they plainly believe that state regulation is a good thing — if *they* regulate — because, of course, they want to bring about good things. In this country each party takes turns, according as it is in or out, in supporting or denouncing the non-interference theory.

Now, if we have state regulation, what is always forgotten is this: Who pays for it? Who is the victim of it? There always is a victim. The workmen who do not defend themselves have to pay for the inspectors who defend them. The whole system of social regulation by boards, commissioners, and inspectors consists in relieving negligent people of the consequences of their negligence and so leaving them to continue negligent without correction. That system also turns away from the agencies which are close, direct, and germane to the purpose, and seeks others. Now, if you relieve negligent people of the consequences of their negligence, you can only throw those consequences on the people who have not been negligent. If you turn away from the agencies which are direct and cognate to the purpose, you can only employ other agencies. Here, then, you have your Forgotten Man again. The man who has been careful and prudent and who wants to go on and reap his advantages for himself and his children is

arrested just at that point, and he is told that he must go
and take care of some negligent employees in a factory or
on a railroad who have not provided precautions for themselves or have not forced their employers to provide precautions, or negligent tenants who have not taken care of
their own sanitary arrangements, or negligent householders
who have not provided against fire, or negligent parents
who have not sent their children to school. If the Forgotten Man does not go, he must hire an inspector to go.
No doubt it is often worth his while to go or send, rather
than leave the thing undone, on account of his remoter
interest; but what I want to show is that all this is unjust
to the Forgotten Man, and that the reformers and philosophers miss the point entirely when they preach that it is
his duty to do all this work. Let them preach to the
negligent to learn to take care of themselves. Whenever
A and B put their heads together and decide what A, B and
C must do for D, there is never any pressure on A and B.
They consent to it and like it. There is rarely any pressure
on D because he does not like it and contrives to evade it.
The pressure all comes on C. Now, who is C? He is
always the man who, if let alone, would make a reasonable
use of his liberty without abusing it. He would not constitute any social problem at all and would not need any
regulation. He is the Forgotten Man again, and as soon as
he is brought from his obscurity you see that he is just that
one amongst us who is what we all ought to be.

Let us look at another case. I read again and again
arguments to prove that criminals have claims and rights
against society. Not long ago, I read an account of an
expensive establishment for the reformation of criminals,
and I am told that we ought to reform criminals, not merely
punish them vindictively. When I was a young man, I
read a great many novels by Eugene Sue, Victor Hugo,
and other Frenchmen of the school of '48, in which the

badness of a bad man is represented, not as his fault, but as the fault of society. Now, as society consists of the bad men plus the good men, and as the object of this declaration was to show that the badness of the bad men was not the fault of the bad men, it remains that the badness of the bad men must be the fault of the good men. No doubt, it is far more consoling to the bad men than even to their friends to reach the point of this demonstration.

Let us ask, now, for a moment, what is the sense of punishment, since a good many people seem to be quite in a muddle about it. Every man in society is bound in nature and reason to contribute to the strength and welfare of society. He ought to work, to be peaceful, honest, just, and virtuous. A criminal is a man who, instead of working with and for society, turns his efforts against the common welfare in some way or other. He disturbs order, violates harmony, invades the security and happiness of others, wastes and destroys capital. If he is put to death, it is on the ground that he has forfeited all right to existence in society by the magnitude of his offenses against its welfare. If he is imprisoned, it is simply a judgment of society upon him that he is so mischievous to the society that he must be segregated from it. His punishment is a warning to him to reform himself, just exactly like the penalties inflicted by God and nature on vice. A man who has committed crime is, therefore, a burden on society and an injury to it. He is a destructive and not a productive force and everybody is worse off for his existence than if he did not exist. Whence, then, does he obtain a right to be taught or reformed at the public expense? The whole question of what to do with him is one of expediency, and it embraces the whole range of possible policies from that of execution to that of education and reformation, but when the expediency of reformatory attempts is discussed we always forget the labor and expense and who must pay.

All that the state does for the criminal, beyond forcing him to earn his living, is done at the expense of the industrious member of society who never costs the state anything for correction and discipline. If a man who has gone astray can be reclaimed in any way, no one would hinder such a work, but people whose minds are full of sympathy and interest for criminals and who desire to adopt some systematic plans of reformatory efforts are only, once more, trampling on the Forgotten Man.

Let us look at another case. If there is a public office to be filled, of course a great number of persons come forward as candidates for it. Many of these persons are urged as candidates on the ground that they are badly off, or that they cannot support themselves, or that they want to earn a living while educating themselves, or that they have female relatives dependent on them, or for some other reason of a similar kind. In other cases, candidates are presented and urged on the ground of their kinship to somebody, or on account of service, it may be meritorious service, in some other line than that of the duty to be performed. Men are proposed for clerkships on the ground of service in the army twenty years ago, or for custom-house inspectors on the ground of public services in the organization of political parties. If public positions are granted on these grounds of sentiment or favoritism, the abuse is to be condemned on the ground of the harm done to the public interest; but I now desire to point out another thing which is constantly forgotten. If you give a position to A, you cannot give it to B. If A is an object of sentiment or favoritism and not a person fit and competent to fulfill the duty, who is B? He is somebody who has nothing but merit on his side, somebody who has no powerful friends, no political influence, some quiet, unobtrusive individual who has known no other way to secure the chances of life than simply to deserve them. Here we have the Forgotten Man again, and once again we find him worthy of all respect and consideration, but passed by in favor of the noisy, pushing, and incompetent.   Who ever remembers that if you give a place to a man who is unfit for it you are keeping out of it somebody, somewhere, who is fit for it?

Let us take another case.   A trades-union is an association of journeymen in a certain trade which has for one of its chief objects to raise wages in that trade.   This object can be accomplished only by drawing more capital into the trade, or by lessening the supply of labor in it.   To do the latter, the trades-unions limit the number of apprentices who may be admitted to the trade.   In discussing this device, people generally fix their minds on the beneficiaries of this arrangement.   It is desired by everybody that wages should be as high as they can be under the conditions of industry.   Our minds are directed by the facts of the case to the men who are in the trade already and are seeking their own advantage.   Sometimes people go on to notice the effects of trades-unionism on the employers, but although employers are constantly vexed by it, it is seen that they soon count it into the risks of their business and settle down to it philosophically.   Sometimes people go further then and see that, if the employer adds the trades-union and strike risk to the other risks, he submits to it because he has passed it along upon the public and that the public wealth is diminished by trades-unionism, which is undoubtedly the case.   I do not remember, however, that I have ever seen in print any analysis and observation of trades-unionism which takes into account its effect in another direction.   The effect on employers or on the public would not raise wages.   The public pays more for houses and goods, but that does not raise wages.   The surplus paid by the public is pure loss, because it is only paid to cover an extra business risk of the employer.   If their trades-unions raise wages, how do they do it?   They do it by lessening the supply of labor in the trade, and this they do by limiting the number of apprentices. All that is won, therefore, for those in the trade, is won at the expense of those persons in the same class in life who want to get into the trade but are forbidden. Like every other monopoly, this one secures advantages for those who are in only at a greater loss to those who are kept out. Who, then, are those who are kept out and who are always forgotten in all the discussions? They are the Forgotten Men again; and what kind of men are they? They are those young men who want to earn their living by the trade in question. Since they select it, it is fair to suppose that they are fit for it, would succeed at it, and would benefit society by practicing it; but they are arbitrarily excluded from it and are perhaps pushed down into the class of unskilled laborers. When people talk of the success of a trades-union in raising wages, they forget these persons who have really, in a sense, paid the increase.

Let me now turn your attention to another class of cases. I have shown how, in time past, the history of states has been a history of selfishness, cupidity, and robbery, and I have affirmed that now and always the problems of government are how to deal with these same vices of human nature. People are always prone to believe that there is something metaphysical and sentimental about civil affairs, but there is not. Civil institutions are constructed to protect, either directly or indirectly, the property of men and the honor of women against the vices and passions of human nature. In our day and country, the problem presents new phases, but it is there just the same as it ever was, and the problem is only the more difficult for us because of its new phase which prevents us from recognizing it. In fact, our people are raving and struggling against it in a kind of blind way, not yet having come to recognize it. More than half of their blows, at present, are misdirected and fail of their object, but they will be aimed better by and by. There is a great deal of clamor about watering stocks and the power of combined capital, which is not very intelligent or well-directed. The evil and abuse which people are groping after in all these denunciations is jobbery.

By jobbery I mean the constantly apparent effort to win wealth, not by honest and independent production, but by some sort of a scheme for extorting other people's product from them. A large part of our legislation consists in making a job for somebody. Public buildings are jobs, not always, but in most cases. The buildings are not needed at all or are costly far beyond what is useful or even decently luxurious. Internal improvements are jobs. They are carried out, not because they are needed in themselves, but because they will serve the turn of some private interest, often incidentally that of the very legislators who pass the appropriations for them. A man who wants a farm, instead of going out where there is plenty of land available for it, goes down under the Mississippi River to make a farm, and then wants his fellow-citizens to be taxed to dyke the river so as to keep it off his farm. The Californian hydraulic miners have washed the gold out of the hillsides and have washed the dirt down into the valleys to the ruin of the rivers and the farms. They want the federal government to remove this dirt at the national expense. The silver miners, finding that their product is losing value in the market, get the government to go into the market as a great buyer in the hope of sustaining the price. The national government is called upon to buy or hire unsalable ships; to dig canals which will not pay; to educate illiterates in the states which have not done their duty at the expense of the states which have done their duty as to education; to buy up telegraphs which no longer pay; and to provide the capital for enterprises of

which private individuals are to win the profits. We are
called upon to squander twenty millions on swamps and
creeks; from twenty to sixty-six millions on the Mississippi
River; one hundred millions in pensions — and there is
now a demand for another hundred million beyond that.
This is the great plan of all living on each other. The
pensions in England used to be given to aristocrats who
had political power, in order to corrupt them. Here the
pensions are given to the great democratic mass who have
the political power, in order to corrupt them. We have
one hundred thousand federal office-holders and I do not
know how many state and municipal office-holders. Of
course public officers are necessary and it is an economical
organization of society to set apart some of its members
for civil functions, but if the number of persons drawn
from production and supported by the producers while
engaged in civil functions is in undue proportion to the
total population, there is economic loss. If public offices
are treated as spoils or benefices or sinecures, then they
are jobs and only constitute part of the pillage.

The biggest job of all is a protective tariff. This device
consists in delivering every man over to be plundered by his
neighbor and in teaching him to believe that it is a good
thing for him and his country because he may take his turn
at plundering the rest. Mr. Kelley said that if the internal
revenue taxes on whisky and tobacco, which are paid to
the United States government, were not taken off, there
would be a rebellion. Just then it was discovered that
Sumatra tobacco was being imported, and the Connecticut
tobacco men hastened to Congress to get a tax laid on it
for their advantage. So it appears that if a tax is laid on
tobacco, to be paid to the United States, there will be a
rebellion, but if a tax is laid on it to be paid to the farmers
of the Connecticut Valley, there will be no rebellion at all.
The tobacco farmers having been taxed for protected manu-

factures are now to be taken into the system, and the workmen in the factories are to be taxed on their tobacco to protect the farmers. So the system is rendered more complete and comprehensive.

On every hand you find this jobbery. The government is to give every man a pension, and every man an office, and every man a tax to raise the price of his product, and to clean out every man's creek for him, and to buy all his unsalable property, and to provide him with plenty of currency to pay his debts, and to educate his children, and to give him the use of a library and a park and a museum and a gallery of pictures. On every side the doors of waste and extravagance stand open; and spend, squander, plunder, and grab are the watchwords. We grumble some about it and talk about the greed of corporations and the power of capital and the wickedness of stock gambling. Yet we elect the legislators who do all this work. Of course, we should never think of blaming ourselves for electing men to represent and govern us, who, if I may use a slang expression, give us away. What man ever blamed himself for his misfortune? We groan about monopolies and talk about more laws to prevent the wrongs done by chartered corporations. Who made the charters? Our representatives. Who elected such representatives? We did. How can we get bad law-makers to make a law which shall prevent bad law-makers from making a bad law? That is, really, what we are trying to do. If we are a free, self-governing people, all our misfortunes come right home to ourselves and we can blame nobody else. Is any one astonished to find that men are greedy, whether they are incorporated or not? Is it a revelation to find that we need, in our civil affairs, to devise guarantees against selfishness, rapacity, and fraud? I have ventured to affirm that government has never had to deal with anything else.

Now, I have said that this jobbery means waste, plunder,

and loss, and I defined it at the outset as the system of
making a chance to extort part of his product from somebody else. Now comes the question: Who pays for it all?
The system of plundering each other soon destroys all that [sic]
it deals with. It produces nothing. Wealth comes only
from production, and all that the wrangling grabbers,
loafers, and jobbers get to deal with comes from somebody's toil and sacrifice. Who, then, is he who provides
it all? Go and find him and you will have once more
before you the Forgotten Man. You will find him hard at
work because he has a great many to support. Nature has
done a great deal for him in giving him a fertile soil and an
excellent climate and he wonders why it is that, after all,
his scale of comfort is so moderate. He has to get out of
the soil enough to pay all his taxes, and that means the
cost of all the jobs and the fund for all the plunder. The
Forgotten Man is delving away in patient industry, supporting his family, paying his taxes, casting his vote,
supporting the church and the school, reading his newspaper, and cheering for the politician of his admiration, but
he is the only one for whom there is no provision in the
great scramble and the big divide.

Such is the Forgotten Man. He works, he votes, generally
he prays — but he always pays — yes, above all, he pays.
He does not want an office; his name never gets into the
newspaper except when he gets married or dies. He keeps
production going on. He contributes to the strength of
parties. He is flattered before election. He is strongly
patriotic. He is wanted, whenever, in his little circle,
there is work to be done or counsel to be given. He may
grumble some occasionally to his wife and family, but he
does not frequent the grocery or talk politics at the tavern.
Consequently, he is forgotten. He is a commonplace man.
He gives no trouble. He excites no admiration. He is
not in any way a hero (like a popular orator); or a problem

(like tramps and outcasts); nor notorious (like criminals); nor an object of sentiment (like the poor and weak); nor a burden (like paupers and loafers); nor an object out of which social capital may be made (like the beneficiaries of church and state charities); nor an object for charitable aid and protection (like animals treated with cruelty); nor the object of a job (like the ignorant and illiterate); nor one over whom sentimental economists and statesmen can parade their fine sentiments (like inefficient workmen and shiftless artisans). Therefore, he is forgotten. All the burdens fall on him, or on her, for it is time to remember that the Forgotten Man is not seldom a woman.

When you go to Willimantic, they will show you with great pride the splendid thread mills there. I am told that there are sewing-women who can earn only fifty cents in twelve hours, and provide the thread. In the cost of every spool of thread more than one cent is tax. It is paid, not to get the thread, for you could get the thread without it. It is paid to get the Willimantic linen company which is not worth having and which is, in fact, a nuisance, because it makes thread harder to get than it would be if there were no such concern. If a woman earns fifty cents in twelve hours, she earns a spool of thread as nearly as may be in an hour, and if she uses a spool of thread per day, she works a quarter of an hour per day to support the Willimantic linen company, which in 1882 paid 95 per cent dividend to its stockholders. If you go and look at the mill, it will captivate your imagination until you remember all the women in all the garrets, and all the artisans' and laborers' wives and children who are spending their hours of labor, not to get goods which they need, but to pay for the industrial system which only stands in their way and makes it harder for them to get the goods.

It is plain enough that the Forgotten Man and the Forgotten Woman are the very life and substance of society.

They are the ones who ought to be first and always remembered. They are always forgotten by sentimentalists, philanthropists, reformers, enthusiasts, and every description of speculator in sociology, political economy, or political science. If a student of any of these sciences ever comes to understand the position of the Forgotten Man and to appreciate his true value, you will find such student an uncompromising advocate of the strictest scientific thinking on all social topics, and a cold and hard-hearted skeptic towards all artificial schemes of social amelioration. If it is desired to bring about social improvements, bring us a scheme for relieving the Forgotten Man of some of his burdens. He is our productive force which we are wasting. Let us stop wasting his force. Then we shall have a clean and simple gain for the whole society. The Forgotten Man is weighted down with the cost and burden of the schemes for making everybody happy, with the cost of public beneficence, with the support of all the loafers, with the loss of all the economic quackery, with the cost of all the jobs. Let us remember him a little while. Let us take some of the burdens off him. Let us turn our pity on him instead of on the good-for-nothing. It will be only justice to him, and society will greatly gain by it. Why should we not also have the satisfaction of thinking and caring for a little while about the clean, honest, industrious, independent, self-supporting men and women who have not inherited much to make life luxurious for them, but who are doing what they can to get on in the world without begging from anybody, especially since all they want is to be let alone, with good friendship and honest respect. Certainly the philanthropists and sentimentalists have kept our attention for a long time on the nasty, shiftless, criminal, whining, crawling, and good-for-nothing people, as if they alone deserved our attention.

The Forgotten Man is never a pauper. He almost always

has a little capital because it belongs to the character of the man to save something. He never has more than a little. He is, therefore, poor in the popular sense, although in the correct sense he is not so. I have said already that if you learn to look for the Forgotten Man and to care for him, you will be very skeptical toward all philanthropic and humanitarian schemes. It is clear now that the interest of the Forgotten Man and the interest of "the poor," "the weak," and the other petted classes are in antagonism. In fact, the warning to you to look for the Forgotten Man comes the minute that the orator or writer begins to talk about the poor man. That minute the Forgotten Man is in danger of a new assault, and if you intend to meddle in the matter at all, then is the minute for you to look about for him and to give him your aid. Hence, if you care for the Forgotten Man, you will be sure to be charged with *not* caring for the poor. Whatever you do for any of the petted classes wastes capital. If you do anything for the Forgotten Man, you must secure him his earnings and savings, that is, you legislate for the security of capital and for its free employment; you must oppose paper money, wildcat banking and usury laws and you must maintain the inviolability of contracts. Hence you must be prepared to be told that you favor the capitalist class, the enemy of the poor man.

What the Forgotten Man really wants is true liberty. Most of his wrongs and woes come from the fact that there are yet mixed together in our institutions the old mediæval theories of protection and personal dependence and the modern theories of independence and individual liberty. The consequence is that the people who are clever enough to get into positions of control, measure their own rights by the paternal theory and their own duties by the theory of independent liberty. It follows that the Forgotten Man, who is hard at work at home, has to pay both ways.

His rights are measured by the theory of liberty, that is, he has only such as he can conquer. His duties are measured by the paternal theory, that is, he must discharge all which are laid upon him, as is always the fortune of parents. People talk about the paternal theory of government as if it were a very simple thing. Analyze it, however, and you see that in every paternal relation there must be two parties, a parent and a child, and when you speak metaphorically, it makes all the difference in the world who is parent and who is child. Now, since we, the people, are the state, whenever there is any work to be done or expense to be paid, and since the petted classes and the criminals and the jobbers cost and do not pay, it is they who are in the position of the child, and it is the Forgotten Man who is the parent. What the Forgotten Man needs, therefore, is that we come to a clearer understanding of liberty and to a more complete realization of it. Every step which we win in liberty will set the Forgotten Man free from some of his burdens and allow him to use his powers for himself and for the commonwealth.

BIBLIOGRAPHY

BIBLIOGRAPHY

BIBLIOGRAPHICAL NOTE

The following bibliography is as nearly exhaustive as we have been able to make it. There are doubtless other articles which have not come under our notice; and there are certainly a number of contributions to the press, signed and unsigned, to which we have no clue. The distribution of those which we have found will indicate the task of any one who should aim at exhaustiveness.

It has seemed best to us to include the titles of certain unpublished writings, especially where these are to be made accessible to students by the deposit of the manuscripts with the Yale University Library (under Sumner Estate). Sumner had a way of writing something out very carefully, perhaps as a lecture, and then laying it away with apparently no thought of publishing it; a number of such manuscripts have been printed for the first time in this series of volumes. There are also a few of Sumner's printed utterances which we possessed in the form of clippings, but could not locate; the titles of such have been included as accessible at the Yale Library.

There is a good deal of Sumner's writing in the reports of the Connecticut State Board of Education. We have been informed that his services to that Board, extending over twenty years, included much committee work and many carefully written reports. As these are of a somewhat special nature, we refer simply to the documents of the Board.

It is the intention of the publishers to make of the volumes now in print under uniform style a set of four, to be numbered in the order of their appearance. For the sake of brevity, then, War and Other Essays is referred to below as Vol. I; Earth Hunger and Other Essays, as Vol. II; The Challenge of Facts and Other Essays, as Vol. III; and The Forgotten Man and Other Essays, as Vol. IV.

There are in these volumes a few numbers not written by Sumner, but about him, such as the Memorial Addresses in Vol. III.

A. G. K.
M. R. D.

1872. THE BOOKS OF THE KINGS, by K. C. W. F. Bähr. Translated, Enlarged, and Edited . . . Book 2, by W. G. Sumner, in Lange, J. P., A commentary on the Holy Scripture . . . New York, Scribner, Armstrong & Co., 1866–1882, 26 vols., VI, 312 pp.

THE CHURCH'S LAW OF THE INTERPRETATION OF SCRIPTURE. Unpublished manuscript on scientific criticism of the Bible. April 3. 61 pp. (Sumner Estate.)

MEMORIAL DAY ADDRESS. Delivered at Morristown, May 30. Printed for the first time in Vol. III, pp. 347–362.

1873. THE SOLIDARITY OF THE HUMAN RACE. Unpublished manuscript of an address on the influence of ideas and events in one country on conditions in other countries, delivered at the Sheffield Scientific School, January 11. 40 pp. (Sumner Estate.)

RELATION OF PHYSICAL TO MORAL GOOD. An address. Unpublished manuscript probably of this date, 35 pp. (Sumner Estate.)

INTRODUCTORY LECTURE TO COURSES IN POLITICAL AND SOCIAL SCIENCE. Printed for the first time in Vol. III, pp. 391–403.

HISTORY OF PAPER MONEY. Paper money in China, England, Austria, Russia, and the American Colonies. Unpublished manuscript, 109 pp. (Sumner Estate.)

SOCIALISM. Three unpublished manuscripts written between 1873 and 1880 which appear to be preliminary sketches to the essay entitled The Challenge of Facts. 38, 12, and 31 pp. respectively.

1874. A HISTORY OF AMERICAN CURRENCY, with chapters on the English Bank Restriction and Austrian Paper Money, to which is appended "The Bullion Report." New York, H. Holt & Co., iv, 391 pp., twofold diagram.

THE LESSON OF THE PANIC (of 1873). Unpublished manuscript advocating a return to a sound currency, 20 pp. (Sumner Estate.)

HAVE WE HAD ENOUGH? Unpublished manuscript on the evils of paper money, written soon after the panic of 1873, 15 pp. (Sumner Estate.)

POLITICAL ECONOMY. From 300 to 400 pp. of lecture notes for classroom use. (Sumner Estate.)

1874. TAXATION. What it is, what its relation to other departments of political economy is, and what are the general
principles by which it must be controlled. Unpublished
manuscript probably of this date, 24 pp. (Sumner
Estate.)

1875. AMERICAN FINANCE. Boston, Williams.

THE CURRENCY QUESTION. An address delivered about
this time opposing the issue of irredeemable paper money.
Unpublished manuscript, 96 pp. (Sumner Estate.)

1876. MONETARY DEVELOPMENT. (In Woolsey, T. D., and
others, First Century of the Republic. New York,
Harper & Bros.)

POLITICS IN AMERICA, 1776–1876. North American Review, January, Vol. CXXII, Centennial number, pp. 47–
87. Reprinted in Vol. IV, pp. 285–333.

SHALL THE "HARD TIMES" CONTINUE? A review of the
address of Professor Sumner before the New Haven
Chamber of Commerce. The Woonsocket Patriot,
May 19.

BOURBONISM. "Real Issues of the Day." New York
World, May 19.

FREE PIG-IRON. Letter to the New York Mercantile
Journal, June 3.

FOR PRESIDENT? New Haven Palladium, September 12.
Reprinted in Vol. III, pp. 365–379.

IS THE WAR OVER? "Real Issues of the Day." New
York World, October 9.

FEARS OF A SOLID SOUTH. "Real Issues of the Day."
New York World, October 10.

POLITICAL STATUS OF THE SOUTHERN STATES. Letter to
the New York World, October 16.

WHAT HAS BECOME OF REFORM? "Real Issues of the
Day." New York World, October 23.

THE DEMOCRATIC REPLY. To the visiting Republicans in
New Orleans who refused to enter into a conference upon
the subject of the counting of the election returns.
New York Tribune, November 17.

"PROFESSOR SUMNER ON LOUISIANA." Letter to the
New York World, November 21, in answer to Governor
Ingersoll's request to express his views on the political
situation in that state after his visit to New Orleans.

1876. IMPRESSIONS IN NEW ORLEANS. Letter to the New
York Herald, November 22.

1877. LECTURES ON THE HISTORY OF PROTECTION IN THE UNITED
STATES. Delivered before the International Free-trade
Alliance. Reprinted from "The New Century." Pub-
lished for the International Free-trade Alliance by
G. P. Putnam's Sons, New York, 64 pp. Contents:
The National Idea and the American System, Broad
Principles Underlying the Tariff Controversy, The
Origin of Protection in this Country, The Establishment
of Protection in this Country, Vacillation of the Pro-
tective Policy in this Country.
REPUBLICAN GOVERNMENT. The Chicago Tribune, Janu-
ary 1. Reprinted in Vol. III, pp. 223–240.
PROTECTION AND PIG-IRON. Letter to the Courier,
February 12.
DEMOCRACY AND RESPONSIBLE GOVERNMENT. Address
at Providence, R. I., June 20, before the Phi Beta Kappa
Society of Brown University. The Providence Evening
Press, June 21. Reprinted in Vol. III, pp. 243–286.
SILVER. Address before the Senior Class of Yale Uni-
versity. The New Haven Union, December 12.
THE SILVER QUESTION. What it is and how it should be
dealt with. New York World, December 12.
THE COMMERCIAL CRISIS OF 1837. Written in 1877 or
1878. (There are indications on the manuscript that
it was once printed, but efforts to find where have
failed.) Published, probably for the first time, in
Vol. IV, pp. 371–398.

1878. OUR REVENUE SYSTEM, by A. L. EARLE. Preface by W. G.
Sumner. New York, published for the New York Free-
trade Club by G. P. Putnam's Sons, 47 pp. (Economic
Monograph No. V.)
MONEY AND ITS LAWS. International Review, January
and February, Vol. V, pp. 75–81.
WHAT IS FREE TRADE? Chicago News, January 7.
SILVER. Address in Chicago. The Chicago Tribune,
January 9.
THE SILVER QUESTION. Lecture before the Manhattan
Club of New York City, January 25, on the disastrous

1878   results of remonetization. The New York World, January 26.

A FEW PLAIN ANSWERS. Letter to the New Haven Register, February 28, on the tariff.

PROTECTION AND REVENUE IN 1877. Lecture delivered before the New York Free-trade Club, April 18. New York, published for the New York Free-trade Club by G. P. Putnam's Sons. (Economic Monograph No. VIII.)

SOCIALISM. Scribner's Monthly, October, Vol. XVI, No. 6, pp. 887–893.

RELATION OF LEGISLATION TO CURRENCY. Unpublished manuscript written about this time dealing with the nature of money, coining, paper money, legal tender acts, the monetary experience of England and France, etc., and opposing the abuses of legislation in regard to currency. 45 pp. (Sumner Estate.)

A CONCURRENT CIRCULATION OF GOLD AND SILVER. Printed for the first time in Vol. IV, pp. 183–210.

1879. BIMETALLISM. Princeton Review, November, pp. 546–578.

AMORTIZATION OF PUBLIC DEBTS. Unpublished manuscript, chiefly historical, written about this time. 35 pp. (Sumner Estate.)

THE INFLUENCE OF COMMERCIAL CRISES ON OPINIONS ABOUT ECONOMIC DOCTRINES. An address probably of this date. Printed for the first time in Vol. IV, pp. 213–235.

THE CO-OPERATIVE COMMONWEALTH. Written in the seventies or eighties. Extracts printed for the first time in Vol. IV, pp. 441–462.

1880. WHAT OUR BOYS ARE READING. Combined with "Books and Reading for the Young," by J. H. Smart. Chas. Scribner's Sons. Reprinted in Vol. II, pp. 367–377.

THE TRUE AIM OF LIFE. Address to the Seniors in Yale University. The New Haven Register, February 1. (Not in form for re-printing.)

THE THEORY AND PRACTICE OF ELECTIONS. Princeton Review, March, pp. 262–286, and July, pp. 24–41.

TWO LETTERS TO THE NEW YORK TIMES, April 3 and 4, giving his reasons for using Spencer's "Study of Sociology" as a text-book.

1880. THE ADMINISTRATION OF ANDREW JACKSON. Address before the Kent Club of the Yale Law School, briefly reported in the New York Tribune, April 29. Printed in full for the first time in Vol. IV, pp. 337–367.

THE REVIVAL OF OCEAN COMMERCE. A free-trade letter to the American Railroad Journal, September 10.

Professor Sumner's views respecting the tariff question. Letters to the New Haven Register, October 9, 12, and 14.

THE FINANCIAL QUESTIONS NOW BEFORE US. Unpublished manuscript written about this time, 8 pp. (Sumner Estate.)

1881. ELECTIONS AND CIVIL SERVICE REFORM. Princeton Review, January, pp. 129–148.

PANIC WITHOUT CAUSE. Lecture in Brothers' Hall, New Haven, on the recent panic in Wall Street. New Haven Register, January 14.

THE ARGUMENT AGAINST PROTECTIVE TAXES. Princeton Review, March, pp. 241–259.

SHALL AMERICANS OWN SHIPS? North American Review, June, Vol. 132, No. CCXCV, pp. 559–566. Reprinted in Vol. IV, pp. 273–282.

FORTUNES MADE IN THREAD. Letter to the New York Times, June 5, on the peculiar protection given to the manufacturers of thread.

SOCIOLOGY. Princeton Review, November, pp. 303–323. Reprinted in Vol. I, pp. 167–192.

1882. ANDREW JACKSON AS A PUBLIC MAN. What he was, what chances he had, and what he did with them. Boston, New York, Houghton Mifflin Company. vi, 402 pp. (American Statesmen Series.)

POLITICAL ECONOMY AND POLITICAL SCIENCE. Comp. by W. G. Sumner, D. A. Wells, W. E. Foster, R. L. Dugdale, and G. H. Putnam. New York Society for Political Education. Cover title, 36 pp. Economic Tracts No. 2.

PROTECTIVE TAXES AND WAGES. Philadelphia Tariff Commission, 21 pp. Caption title.

BANK CHECKS AND BLANKETS. A free-trade letter to the New Haven Register, June 2.

THE "AMERICAN SYSTEM." A letter to the American Free-trade League, June.

1882. WHY SHOULD THE MEN OF IOWA LEVY TAXES ON THEM-
SELVES TO BENEFIT PENNSYLVANIA? Iowa State Leader,
September 4.

THE FREE PLAY OF ECONOMIC FORCES. Letter to the
Nation regarding Jevons's "State in Relation to Labor,"
September 30.

LUMBER PRICES. Letter to the Northwestern Lumber-
man, October 14.

Professor Sumner's speech before the Tariff Commission,
reviewed by George Basil Dixwell, Cambridge, J. Wilson
& Son, 43 pp.

Professor Sumner's "Argument against Protective Taxes,"
reviewed by George Basil Dixwell, Cambridge, J.
Wilson & Son, 13 pp.

WAGES. Princeton Review, November, pp. 241–262.

1883. THE FORGOTTEN MAN. The original lecture on this
subject, delivered in New Haven February 8 or 9.
28 typewritten pp. Printed for the first time in Vol. IV,
pp. 465–495.

WHAT SOCIAL CLASSES OWE TO EACH OTHER. First appeared in Harper's Weekly, February–May, Vol. XXVII,
Nos. 1366–1376. New York, Harper & Brothers,
169 pp.

ON THE CASE OF A CERTAIN MAN WHO IS NEVER
THOUGHT OF. Reprinted in Vol. I, pp. 247–253, from
"What Social Classes Owe to Each Other," pp. 123–133.

THE CASE OF THE FORGOTTEN MAN FURTHER CONSIDERED.
Reprinted in Vol. I, pp. 257–268, from "What Social
Classes Owe to Each Other," pp. 134–152.

BEST PUBLIC OPINION. Letter to the Gazette and Free
Press, January 12, in reply to T. K. Beecher.

LET COMMERCIAL RELATIONS ALONE. Letter to W. H.
Knight in the Gazette and Free Press, January 16.

Letter to Mr. Earle of the American Free-trade League
regarding a speech of Mr. Evarts's. Printed in the
New York Times, February 6.

"PROFESSOR SUMNER ON MONETARY SCIENCE." Letter
to the editor of Bradstreet's in which he disagrees with
the theory of H. C. Adams that money laws in economics
are dependent on the nation's sentiment as expressed in
its legislative enactments. February 10.

1883. "Professor Sumner Replies." Letter to the New Haven Register, February 10, referring to his remarks about the protective tax on thread in his lecture on the "Forgotten Man."

"Professor Sumner's Presumption." A defense of his letter to Mr. Earle regarding a speech of Mr. Evarts's. New York Times, February 14.

Willimantic Linen Mills. Letter to the New York Times, February 16, defending his position as taken against the protective tax on thread.

Some Facts about Thread. Unpublished manuscript, 14 pp., referring to the controversy with the Willimantic Linen Co. (Sumner Estate.)

A Theorist Answered. A free-trade letter to the New Haven Register, February 26, in reply to a letter signed "Hardpan."

The Gain to the Country by Protection. Letter to the New York Times, February 27.

"Professor Sumner Instructs His Critics." A free-trade letter to the New York Times, March 1.

That Census Puzzle. New York Times, March 2.

Protective Taxes and Wages. North American Review, March, Vol. 136, No. CCCXVI, pp. 270–276.

A Course of Reading in Political Economy. Prepared for The Critic, March, 4 pp.

The Tariff on Thread. Letter to the New York Times, March 8.

Thread. Letter to the Boston Transcript, April 25, regarding the Willimantic Linen Co.

Thread at Three Cents a Spool. Letter to the New York Times, April 28.

The Willimantic Mills' Profit. Letter to the Boston Transcript, April 30.

Letter to the Palladium (New Haven), April 30, regarding the controversy with the Willimantic Linen Co.

"Professor Sumner's Views." Letter to the New Haven Register, May 26, in answer to Mr. Barrows of the Willimantic Linen Co.

The Philosophy of Strikes. Harper's Weekly, September 15, Vol. XXVII, No. 1395, p. 586. Reprinted in Vol. IV, pp. 239–246.

1883. Letter to the New Haven Register, October 18, regarding the development of our industries.

"PROFESSOR SUMNER'S VIEWS RESPECTING THE TARIFF QUESTION." New Haven Register, October 19.

"MIXED UP MR. SHELDON." Letter to the New Haven Register, October 30, showing Mr. Sheldon's ignorance of tariff laws.

THE SCIENCE OF SOCIOLOGY. A Speech at the Farewell Banquet to Herbert Spencer. Delivered November 9, 1882, published in "Herbert Spencer on the Americans and the Americans on Herbert Spencer," pp. 35–40. New York, D. Appleton & Company, 96 pp. Reprinted in Vol. IV, pp. 401–405.

SUGGESTIONS ON SOCIAL SUBJECTS. Passages selected from "What Social Classes owe to Each Other," in the Popular Science Monthly, December, Vol. XXIV, pp. 160–169.

AN AMERICAN CRITICISM OF BRITISH PROTECTIONIST THEORIES. A criticism of Professor Sidgwick's doctrine that protective taxes come out of the foreigner. The London Economist, December 1, Vol. XLI, No. 2,101, pp. 1397–1398.

THE DEMOCRATIC THEORY OF PUBLIC OFFICES. Address before the Civil Service Reform Association, Rochester, N. Y. Reasons for reform in the manner of selecting public officers. What would be gained by the change. Printed in the Rochester newspapers of the time. (Sumner Estate.)

1884. PROBLEMS IN POLITICAL ECONOMY. New York, 12 mo., 125 pp. H. Holt & Co.

OUR COLLEGES BEFORE THE COUNTRY. Princeton Review, March, pp. 127–140. Reprinted in Vol. I, pp. 355–373.

SOCIOLOGICAL FALLACIES. North American Review, June, Vol. 138, No. CCCXXXI, pp. 574–579. Reprinted in Vol. II, pp. 357–364.

EVILS OF THE TARIFF SYSTEM. North American Review, September, Vol. 139, No. CCCXXXIV, pp. 293–299.

1885. PROTECTIONISM. The -Ism which Teaches that Waste makes Wealth. New York, H. Holt & Company, October, 12mo., 170 pp. Reprinted in Vol. IV, pp. 9–111.

1885. COLLECTED ESSAYS IN POLITICAL AND SOCIAL SCIENCE.
New York, H. Holt & Company, 173 pp. Contents:
Bimetallism, Wages, The Argument against Protective
Taxes, Sociology, Theory and Practice of Elections,
Presidential Elections and Civil Service Reform, Our
Colleges Before the Country.

OUR CURRENCY FOR THE LAST TWENTY-FIVE YEARS.
Harper's Weekly, January 10– February 7, Vol. XXIX,
Nos. 1464–1468.

SHALL SILVER BE DEMONETIZED? North American Review, June, Vol. 140, No. CCCXLIII, pp. 485–489.

1886. REGULATION OF CONTRACTS. How far have modern
improvements in production and transportation changed
the principle that men should be left free to make their
own bargains? Science, March 5, Vol. VII, No. 161,
pp. 225–228.

WHAT IS FREE TRADE? In Good Cheer for April, p. 7.
Reprinted in Vol. IV, pp. 123–127.

CAN PROTECTION INCREASE THE WEALTH OF THE COUN-
TRY? The Tax-gatherer, May 22, No. 19.

INDUSTRIAL WAR. Forum, September, Vol. II, pp. 1–8.
Reprinted in Vol. III, pp. 93–102.

MR. BLAINE ON THE TARIFF. North American Review,
October, Vol. 143, No. CCCLIX, pp. 398–405.

WHAT IS THE "PROLETARIAT"? The Independent, October 28. Reprinted in Vol. III, pp. 161–165.

WHO WIN BY PROGRESS? The Independent, November
25. Reprinted in Vol. III, pp. 169–174.

THE NEW SOCIAL ISSUE. The Independent, December 23.
Reprinted in Vol. III, pp. 207–212.

SUBJECTS FOR THESES AND COMPOSITIONS. Prepared
with notes and references attached to the subjects for
Senior and Junior Classes, Yale College. I. Honor
Theses in Political Science. II. Subjects for Required
Compositions. 9 pp. (Sumner Estate.)

HISTORY OF THE UNITED STATES OF AMERICA, 1824–1876.
Notes taken by J. C. Schwab, 1886–1887. MS $17\frac{1}{2}$ x
$25\frac{1}{2}$ cm. Yale University Library.

POLITICAL ECONOMY. Notes of lectures taken by J. C.
Schwab, 1886–1887. MS $17\frac{1}{2}$ x $25\frac{1}{2}$ cm. Yale University Library.

1887. WHAT MAKES THE RICH RICHER AND THE POOR POORER?
Popular Science Monthly, January, Vol. XXX, pp.
289–296. Reprinted in Vol. III, pp. 65–77.

SOCIALISM. Speech before the Massachusetts Reform
Club, Boston, January 8. Boston Sunday Record,
January 9.

FEDERAL LEGISLATION ON RAILROADS. The Independent,
January 20. Reprinted in Vol. III, pp. 177–182.

LEGISLATION BY CLAMOR. The Independent, February 24.
Reprinted in Vol. III, pp. 185–190.

THE SHIFTING OF RESPONSIBILITY. The Independent,
March 24. Reprinted in Vol. III, pp. 193–198.

SOME POINTS IN THE NEW SOCIAL CREED. The Independent, April 21. Reprinted in Vol. II, pp. 207–211.

THE INDIANS IN 1887. Forum, May, Vol. III, pp. 254–262.

SPECULATIVE LEGISLATION. The Independent, May 19.
Reprinted in Vol. III, pp. 215–219.

UNRESTRICTED COMMERCE. Chautauquan, June.

THE BANQUET OF LIFE. The Independent, June 23.
Reprinted in Vol. II, pp. 217–221.

SOME NATURAL RIGHTS. The Independent, July 28.
Reprinted in Vol. II, pp. 222–227.

STRIKES AND THE INDUSTRIAL ORGANIZATION. Popular
Science News, July, Vol. XXI, No. 7, pp. 93–94. Reprinted in Vol. IV, pp. 249–253.

STATE INTERFERENCE. North American Review, August,
Vol. 145, No. CCCLXIX, pp. 109–119. Reprinted in
Vol. I, pp. 213–226.

THE ABOLITION OF POVERTY. The Independent, August 25. Reprinted in Vol. II, pp. 228–232.

THE STATE AS AN "ETHICAL PERSON." The Independent,
October 6. Reprinted in Vol. III, pp. 201–204.

THE BOON OF NATURE. The Independent, October 27.
Reprinted in Vol. II, pp. 233–238.

CIVIL SERVICE REFORM. Chautauquan, November, pp. 78–80.

IS LIBERTY A LOST BLESSING? The Independent, November 24. Reprinted in Vol. II, pp. 131–135.

ADVANTAGES OF FREE TRADE. The Christian Secretary.
(Sumner Estate.)

1888. LAND MONOPOLY. The Independent, January 12. Reprinted in Vol. II, pp. 239–244.

A GROUP OF NATURAL MONOPOLIES. The Independent, February 16. Reprinted in Vol. II, pp. 245–248.

THE FALL IN SILVER AND INTERNATIONAL COMPETITION. Rand McNally's Banker's Monthly, February, pp. 47–48.

THE FIRST STEPS TOWARDS A MILLENNIUM. Cosmopolitan, March, pp. 32–36. Reprinted in Vol. II, pp. 93–105.

ANOTHER CHAPTER ON MONOPOLY. The Independent, March 15. Reprinted in Vol. II, pp. 249–253.

TRUSTS AND TRADES-UNIONS. The Independent, April 19. Reprinted in Vol. IV, pp. 257–262.

THE FAMILY MONOPOLY. The Independent, May 10. Reprinted in Vol. II, pp. 254–258.

THE FAMILY AND PROPERTY. The Independent, June 14 and July 19. Reprinted in Vol. II, pp. 259–269.

TARIFF REFORM. The Independent, August 16. Reprinted in Vol. IV, pp. 115–120.

THE STATE AND MONOPOLY. The Independent, September 13 and October 11. Reprinted in Vol. II, pp. 270–279.

"A CONDITION NOT A THEORY." Free trade. Belford's Monthly Magazine, October, Vol. I, No. 5.

DEMOCRACY AND PLUTOCRACY. The Independent, November 15. Reprinted in Vol. II, pp. 283–289.

DEFINITIONS OF DEMOCRACY AND PLUTOCRACY. The Independent, December 20. Reprinted in Vol. II, pp. 290–295.

1889. THE CONFLICT OF PLUTOCRACY AND DEMOCRACY. The Independent, January 10. Reprinted in Vol. II, pp. 296–300.

PEASANT EMANCIPATION IN DENMARK. Based on a review of Stavnsbaands-løsningen og landboreformerne. Set fra nationaløkonomiens Standpunkt. Af V. Falbe Hansen, Copenhagen: Gad. 1888. The Nation, February 7, No. 1232, pp. 123–124.

PEASANTS AND LAND TENURE IN SCANDINAVIA. Unpublished manuscript, 20 typewritten pages, written in 1889 or later, covering the period from the earliest times to the eighteenth century. (Sumner Estate.)

1889. SEPARATION OF STATE AND MARKET. The Independent, February 14. Reprinted in Vol. II, pp. 306–311.

DEMOCRACY AND MODERN PROBLEMS. The Independent, March 28. Reprinted in Vol. II, pp. 301–305.

SOCIAL WAR IN DEMOCRACY. The Independent, April 11. Reprinted in Vol. II, pp. 312–317.

AN EXAMINATION OF A NOBLE SENTIMENT. The Independent, May 16. Reprinted in Vol. II, pp. 212–216.

SKETCH OF WILLIAM GRAHAM SUMNER. The Popular Science Monthly, June, Vol. XXXV, pp. 261–268. Reprinted in Vol. III, pp. 3–13.

AN OLD "TRUST." The Independent, June 13. Reprinted in Vol. IV, pp. 265–269.

WHAT IS CIVIL LIBERTY? The Popular Science Monthly, July, Vol. XXXV, pp. 289–303. Reprinted in Vol. II, pp. 109–130.

WHO IS FREE? IS IT THE SAVAGE? The Independent, July 18. Reprinted in Vol. II, pp. 136–140.

WHO IS FREE? IS IT THE CIVILIZED MAN? The Independent, August 15. Reprinted in Vol. II, pp. 140–145.

WHO IS FREE? IS IT THE MILLIONAIRE? The Independent, September 12. Reprinted in Vol. II, pp. 145–150.

WHO IS FREE? IS IT THE TRAMP? The Independent, October 17. Reprinted in Vol. II, pp. 150–155.

LIBERTY AND RESPONSIBILITY. The Independent, November 21. Reprinted in Vol. II, pp. 156–160.

LIBERTY AND LAW. The Independent, December 26. Reprinted in Vol. II, pp. 161–166.

DO WE WANT INDUSTRIAL PEACE? Forum, December, Vol. VIII, pp. 406–416. Reprinted in Vol. I, pp. 229–243.

FREE TRADE. Unpublished manuscript of about this date. I. Definitions of Protection and Protectionism. II. The Medieval Doctrine of Commerce. III. The Sixteenth Century. IV. The Dynastic States. V. Mercantilism and the Colonial System. VI. The New Doctrine. VII. Smithianismus. VIII. Protection in the United States. IX. Nineteenth-century Protectionism. X. The Present Situation. About 64 typewritten pages. (Sumner Estate.)

1889. THE STRIKES. Unpublished manuscript written sometime in the eighties, 21 typewritten pages. A general survey of the "labor question." (Sumner Estate.)

A PARABLE. Written in the eighties. Printed for the first time in Vol. III, pp. 105–107.

THE SPHERE OF ACADEMICAL INSTRUCTION. Address delivered at the celebration of a school anniversary. To judge "what an academy is, what it ought to do, and how it ought to do it; and to judge of its achievements by true standards." Unpublished manuscript of the eighties, 27 pages. (Sumner Estate.)

INTEGRITY IN EDUCATION. An address delivered in Hartford probably in the eighties. Printed for the first time in Vol. IV, pp. 409–419.

DISCIPLINE. Probably in the eighties. Printed for the first time in Vol. IV, pp. 423–438.

THE CHALLENGE OF FACTS. Written sometime in the eighties. Original title was Socialism. Printed for the first time in Vol. III, pp. 17–52.

1890. ALEXANDER HAMILTON. ("Makers of America.") New York, 12mo., 280 pp., Dodd, Mead & Co.

LIBERTY AND DISCIPLINE. The Independent, January 16. Reprinted in Vol. II, pp. 166–171.

DOES LABOR BRUTALIZE? The Independent, February 20. Reprinted in Vol. II, pp. 187–193.

LIBERTY AND PROPERTY. The Independent, March 27. Reprinted in Vol. II, pp. 171–176.

LIBERTY AND OPPORTUNITY. The Independent, April 24. Reprinted in Vol. II, pp. 176–181.

WHY I AM A FREE TRADER. Twentieth Century, April 24, pp. 8–10.

CAN WE GET MORE MONEY? Frank Leslie's Illustrated Newspaper, May 3, Vol. LXX, No. 1807.

LIBERTY AND LABOR. The Independent, May 22. Reprinted in Vol. II, pp. 181–187.

PROPOSED SILVER LEGISLATION. Frank Leslie's Illustrated Newspaper, May 24, Vol. LXX, No. 1810, p. 330.

LIBERTY AND MACHINERY. The Independent, June 12. Reprinted in Vol. II, pp. 193–198.

THE DISAPPOINTMENT OF LIBERTY. The Independent, July 17. Reprinted in Vol. II, pp. 198–203.

1890. WHAT EMANCIPATES. The Independent, August 14. Reprinted in Vol. III, pp. 137–142.

THE DEMAND FOR MEN. The Independent, September 11. Reprinted in Vol. III, pp. 111–116.

THE SIGNIFICANCE OF THE DEMAND FOR MEN. The Independent, October 16. Reprinted in Vol. III, pp. 119–123.

WHAT THE "SOCIAL QUESTION" IS. The Independent, November 20. Reprinted in Vol. III, pp. 127–133.

1891. THE FINANCIER AND THE FINANCES OF THE AMERICAN REVOLUTION. New York, 2 vols., 8vo., 309 and 330 pp.

LIBERTÉ DES ÉCHANGES. Nouveau Dictionnaire d'Économie Politique, vol. 2, pp. 138–166, Guillaumin et Cie., Paris.

POWER AND PROGRESS. The Independent, January 15. Reprinted in Vol. III, pp. 145–150.

CONSEQUENCES OF INCREASED SOCIAL POWER. The Independent, August 13. Reprinted in Vol. III, pp. 153–158.

1892. ROBERT MORRIS ("Makers of America"). New York, 12mo., 172 pp.

1893. PROPOSED CLASSIFICATION OF THE SOCIAL SCIENCES. A chart printed for distribution to the classes in Social Science in Yale University. "Not published."

1894. THE ABSURD EFFORT TO MAKE THE WORLD OVER. Forum, March, Vol. XVII, pp. 92–102. Reprinted in Vol. I, pp. 195–210.

1895. THE VENEZUELA MESSAGE. Letter to the New York Times, December 18.

1896. HISTORY OF BANKING IN THE UNITED STATES. XV, 485 pp. Being Vol. I of A History of Banking in all the Leading Nations.

"PROFESSOR SUMNER ON YALE." Letter to The Yale News, January 20. Learning is more appreciated here now than thirty years ago.

THE CURRENCY CRISIS. A course of six lectures given at the house of Mr. John E. Parsons, 30 East 36th St., New York City, February 13 and 27 and March 5, 12, 19, and 26. What the lecturer said, as well as the questions and answers at the end of his lectures, was taken down in shorthand and typewritten. Mr. Herbert

514 BIBLIOGRAPHY

1896. Parsons has the transcript in bound form, and the Yale University Library also has a copy. (Sumner Estate.)

THE TREASURY AS A BANK OF ISSUE AND A SILVER WAREHOUSE. The Bond Record, March, Vol. IV, No. 2, pp. 87–89.

AN ANSWER TO MR. TIGHE'S LETTER ON YALE'S VENEZUELAN ATTITUDE. Letter to the Yale Alumni Weekly, May 20, Vol. V, No. 30, pp. 1–2.

THE FALLACY OF TERRITORIAL EXTENSION. Forum, June, Vol. XXI, pp. 416–419. Reprinted in Vol. I, pp. 285–293.

A FEW WORDS. Short address as member of the State Board of Education at the graduating exercises of the New Haven Normal School, June 18. (Sumner Estate.)

THE POLICY OF DEBASEMENT. "The Battle of the Standards." New York Journal, July 29.

THE PROPOSED DUAL ORGANIZATION OF MANKIND. Popular Science Monthly, August, Vol. XLIX, pp. 433–439. Reprinted in Vol. I, pp. 271–281.

PROSPERITY STRANGLED BY GOLD. Leslie's Weekly, August 20. Reprinted in Vol. IV, pp. 141–145.

CAUSE AND CURE OF HARD TIMES. Leslie's Weekly, September 3. Reprinted in Vol. IV, pp. 149–153.

THE FREE-COINAGE SCHEME IS IMPRACTICABLE AT EVERY POINT. Leslie's Weekly, September 10. Reprinted in Vol. IV, pp. 157–162.

DELUSION OF THE DEBTORS. Leslie's Weekly, September 17. Reprinted in Vol. IV, pp. 165–170.

THE CRIME OF 1873. Leslie's Weekly, September 24. Reprinted in Vol. IV, pp. 173–180.

THE SINGLE GOLD STANDARD. Chautauquan, October, Vol. XXIV, pp. 72–77.

BANKS OF ISSUE IN THE UNITED STATES. Forum, October, Vol. XXII, pp. 182–191.

EARTH HUNGER OR THE PHILOSOPHY OF LAND GRABBING. Printed for the first time in Vol. II, pp. 31–64.

A FREE COINAGE CATECHISM. Reprinted from The Evening Post, The Evening Post Publishing Co., New York, 16 pp.

LECTURES ON AMERICAN HISTORY, Yale University, 1896–1897. Notes taken by J. C. Schwab. MS. 13 x 21 cm. Yale University Library.

1896. ADVANCING SOCIAL AND POLITICAL ORGANIZATION IN THE UNITED STATES. 1896 or 1897. Printed for the first time in Vol. III, pp. 289–344.

1897. THE TEACHER'S UNCONSCIOUS SUCCESS. Address given at a dinner held in honor of Mr. Henry Barnard, at Jewel Hall, Hartford, January 25. Printed for the first time in Vol. II, pp. 9–13.

MONEY AND CURRENCY. A course of four lectures delivered in Boston. I. The Anxiety Lest there be not Money Enough. II. How We Resumed Specie Payments in 1879. What We Did Not Do. III. The Single Gold Standard — A Beneficent and Accomplished Fact. IV. Where we now Stand and what we have to Do. Syllabus.

SOCIOLOGY. A course of six lectures given in Albany, February 27, March 6, 13, 20, 27, and April 3. Introduction. Individuality and Sociality. Property. Industrialism and Militarism. Population. Mental Reaction on Experience. Suggested Books for a Course of Reading. Syllabus.

THE ORIGIN OF THE DOLLAR. Paper read at meeting of the British Association for the Advancement of Science at Toronto, August 19–25. (Sumner Estate.)

OUTLINE OF A PROPOSED CURRICULUM (for Yale College). 4 pages typewritten manuscript. (Sumner Estate.)

1898. THE SPANISH DOLLAR AND THE COLONIAL SHILLING. American Historical Review, Vol. III, No. 4, pp. 607–619.

SYLLABUS of six lectures given during January and February in Plainfield, N. J. I. What is a Free Man and a Free State? II. What is Democracy? III. Aggregations of Wealth and Plutocracy. IV. The Rich and the Poor. V. Woman. VI. Immigration.

LEITER HAS BEEN A HERO. Letter to The World, New York, June 15, on the Joseph Leiter deal.

THE COIN SHILLING OF MASSACHUSETTS BAY. Yale Review, November, Vol. VII, pp. 247–264, and February, 1899, Vol. VII, pp. 405–420.

1899. THE CONQUEST OF THE UNITED STATES BY SPAIN. A lecture before the Phi Beta Kappa Society of Yale University, January 16. Yale Law Journal, Vol. VIII,

1899. No. 4, pp. 168–193. Boston, D. Estes & Co., 32 pp. 23 cm. Reprinted in Vol. I, pp. 297–334.

THE POWER AND BENEFICENCE OF CAPITAL. Proceedings of the Sixth Annual Convention of The Savings Banks Association of the State of New York, held at the Rooms of the Chamber of Commerce, 32 Nassau Street, New York, May 10; pp. 77–95. J. S. Babcock, New York, printer. Reprinted in Vol. II, pp. 337–353.

1900. FIRST FRUITS OF EXPANSION. New York Evening Post, April 14, p. 13.

THE PREDICAMENT OF SOCIOLOGICAL STUDY. Printed for the first time in Vol. III, pp. 415–425. Original title of manuscript was "Sociology." Written about 1900.

PURPOSES AND CONSEQUENCES. Printed for the first time in Vol. II, pp. 67–75. Written sometime between 1900 and 1906.

RIGHTS. Printed for the first time in Vol. II, pp. 79–83. Written sometime between 1900 and 1906.

EQUALITY. Printed for the first time in Vol. II, pp. 87–89. Written sometime between 1900 and 1906.

1901. THE ANTHRACITE COAL INDUSTRY, by Peter Roberts. Introduction by W. G. Sumner. New York, London, Macmillan Co., 261 pp. Reprinted in Vol. III, pp. 387–388.

SPECIMENS OF INVESTMENT SECURITIES FOR CLASS ROOM USE. New Haven, The E. P. Judd Co., 32 pp., 27 x 35½ cm. Verbatim reprints of a large number of shares, certificates, bonds, and other evidences of ownership of debt, without independent text or comment: collected for use in college instruction.

TRUSTS. Journal of Commerce, June 24.

THE PREDOMINANT ISSUE. Burlington, Vt. Reprinted from the International Monthly, November, Vol. 2, pp. 496–509. Reprinted in Vol. I, pp. 337–352.

THE YAKUTS. Abridged from the Russian of Sieroshevski. Journal of the Anthropological Institute of Great Britain and Ireland, Vol. 31, pp. 65–110.

1902. SUICIDAL FANATICISM IN RUSSIA. The Popular Science Monthly, March, Vol. LX, pp. 442–447.

THE CONCENTRATION OF WEALTH: ITS ECONOMIC JUSTIFICATION. The Independent, April–June. Reprinted in Vol. III, pp. 81–90.

BIBLIOGRAPHY

1903. AUTOBIOGRAPHICAL SKETCH OF WILLIAM GRAHAM SUMNER. A History of the Class of 1863, Yale College, pp. 165–167. New Haven, The Tuttle, Morehouse & Taylor Co., 1905. Reprinted in Vol. II, pp. 3–5.

WAR. Printed for the first time in Vol. I, pp. 3–40.

1904. REPLY TO A SOCIALIST (THE FALLACIES OF SOCIALISM). Collier's Weekly, October 29, pp. 12–13. Reprinted in Vol. III, pp. 55–62.

1905. LYNCH-LAW, by James Elbert Cutler. Foreword by W. G. Sumner. New York, Longmans, Green, and Co., v, 287 pp. Reprinted in Vol. III, pp. 383–384.

ECONOMICS AND POLITICS. Printed for the first time in Vol. II, pp. 318–333.

THE SCIENTIFIC ATTITUDE OF MIND. Address to initiates of the Sigma Xi Society, Yale University, on March 4. Printed for the first time in Vol. II, pp. 17–28.

1906. PROTECTIONISM TWENTY YEARS AFTER. (Title given by editor.) Address at a dinner of the Committee on Tariff Reform of the Tariff Reform Club in the City of New York, June 2. Published by the Reform Club Committee on Tariff Reform, 42 Broadway, New York, N. Y. Series 1906, No. 4, 7 pp., August 15. Reprinted in Vol. IV, pp. 131–138.

1907. FOLKWAYS: A Study of the Sociological Importance of Usages, Manners, Customs, Mores, and Morals. Boston, Ginn & Co., v, 692 pp.

SOCIOLOGY AS A COLLEGE SUBJECT. American Journal of Sociology, March, Vol. 12, No. 5, pp. 597–599. Reprinted in Vol. III, pp. 407–411.

1908. DECLINE OF CONFIDENCE. Annual Financial and Commercial Review, New York Herald, January 2.

1909. WHAT IS SANE TARIFF REFORM? Annual Financial and Commercial Review, New York Herald, January 4.

THE FAMILY AND SOCIAL CHANGE. American Journal of Sociology, March, Vol. 14, No. 5, pp. 577–591. Reprinted in Vol. I, pp. 43–61.

WITCHCRAFT. Forum, May, Vol. XLI, pp. 410–423. Reprinted in Vol. I, pp. 105–126.

AUTOBIOGRAPHY and List of Books Published. Facsimile of letter and photograph in The Yale Courant, May, Vol. XLV, No. 7, on occasion of Sumner's retirement.

1909. THE STATUS OF WOMEN IN CHALDEA, EGYPT, INDIA, JUDEA, AND GREECE TO THE TIME OF CHRIST. Forum, August, Vol. XLII, pp. 113–136. Reprinted in Vol. I, pp. 65–102.

THE MORES OF THE PRESENT AND THE FUTURE. Yale Review, November, Vol. XVIII, pp. 233–245. Reprinted in Vol. I, pp. 149–164.

1910. RELIGION AND THE MORES. American Journal of Sociology, March, Vol. 15, No. 5, pp. 577–591. Reprinted in Vol. I, pp. 129–146.

COMMENT ON WILLIAM GRAHAM SUMNER. (Died April 12.) The Pioneer, Henry W. Farman. The Teacher, J. C. Schwab. The Inspirer, Irving Fisher. The Idealist, Clive Day. The Man, Albert G. Keller. The Veteran, Richard T. Ely. Yale Review, May, Vol. XIX, pp. 1–12.

MEMORIAL ADDRESSES. Delivered June 19, in Lampson Lyceum, Yale University, by Otto T. Bannard, Henry De Forest Baldwin, and Albert Galloway Keller. Printed in Vol. III, pp. 429–450.

POSTHUMOUS

1911. WAR. Yale Review (New Series), October, Vol. I, No. 1, pp. 1–27. Printed in Vol. I, pp. 3–40.

WAR AND OTHER ESSAYS. New Haven, Yale University Press, 381 pp.

1913. EARTH HUNGER OR THE PHILOSOPHY OF LAND GRABBING. Yale Review (New Series), October, Vol. III, No. 1, pp. 3–32. Printed in Vol. II, pp. 31–64.

EARTH HUNGER AND OTHER ESSAYS. New Haven, Yale University Press, 377 pp.

1914. THE CHALLENGE OF FACTS AND OTHER ESSAYS. New Haven, Yale University Press, 450 pp.

1918. THE FORGOTTEN MAN AND OTHER ESSAYS. New Haven, Yale University Press, 559 pp.

INDEX

INDEX

In the following index, *War and Other Essays* is referred to as Vol. I, *Earth Hunger and Other Essays* as Vol. II, *The Challenge of Facts and Other Essays* as Vol. III, and *The Forgotten Man and Other Essays* as Vol. IV. References in heavy type are essay titles.

521